PUBLIC RECORD OFFICE HANDBOOKS

No. 17

150

The Cabinet Office
to 1945

S. S. WILSON

LONDON
HER MAJESTY'S STATIONERY OFFICE

First published 1975

Now that the Cabinet's gone to its dinner
The Secretary stays and gets thinner and thinner
Racking his brains to record and report
What he thinks what they think they ought to have thought.

(Anon)

ISBN 0 11 440034 2

CONTENTS

(The references are to numbered paragraphs)

iii

Plates (*between pages 104 and 105*)

1. Imperial War Cabinet, 1917 (*Press Association Ltd.*)
2. Churchill's War Cabinet, 1941 (*Central Press Photos Ltd.*)
3. Sir Maurice Hankey, Secretary of the Cabinet and of the CID and Clerk to the Privy Council, 1934 (*Bassano Ltd.*)
4. General Hastings Ismay, Secretary of the CID, later Deputy Secretary (military) of the Cabinet, 1939 (*Bassano Ltd.*)
5. Sir Edward Bridges, Permanent Secretary to the Treasury, formerly Secretary of the Cabinet, 1947 (*Central Press Photos Ltd.*)
6. Sir Norman Brook, Secretary of the Cabinet and joint Secretary to the Treasury, 1957 (*Central Office of Information*)

PREFACE

The purpose of this work is to give some account of the evolution of the Cabinet Office to the end of the Churchill administration in July 1945 and in so doing to explain the surviving records of the Office contained in the various CAB classes which are now generally open to public inspection in the Public Record Office.

It can be regarded as complementary to certain of the Handbooks already published: No. 4, *List of Cabinet Papers 1880–1914*; No. 6, *List of Papers of the Committee of Imperial Defence to 1914*; No. 9, *List of Cabinet Papers 1915 and 1916*; No. 11, *The Records of the Cabinet Office to 1922*; and No. 15, *The Second World War: A Guide to Documents in the Public Record Office*.

This Handbook was prepared in 1971 by S. S. Wilson, who was Keeper of Public Records 1960–1966, and was the administrative officer in charge of the Historical Section of the Cabinet Office from 1967 to 1969; he gratefully acknowledges the assistance he received from his colleagues, and from others, now mostly retired, who were closely associated with the work of the Office before 1946.

The Public Record Office wishes to thank Mr. Nigel Nicolson, for allowing the inclusion of a passage from Harold Nicolson's *King George V, His Life and Reign*; William Heinemann, Ltd., the English publishers, and the Viking Press, Inc., who own the copyright (© 1960) throughout the United States of America and her possessions, for giving permission to reprint two extracts from Lord Ismay's *Memoirs*; Cassell and Company, Ltd., the English publishers, and Houghton Mifflin, who own the American and Canadian rights, for granting permission to include some passages from volumes I, II and IV of *The Second World War*, by W. S. Churchill; the Press Association, Ltd., the Central Press Photos, Ltd., and Bassano, Ltd., for permission to reproduce Plate 1, Plates 2 and 5 and Plates 3 and 4 respectively; and the Central Office of Information for making available the photograph of Plate 6.

PUBLIC RECORD OFFICE
October 1974

CHAPTER 1

INTRODUCTION

The Cabinet and collective responsibility

101. Over nine centuries the government of the country has developed from a feudal monarchy to one in which the government is carried on in the name of the Sovereign by an executive which has come to depend on the support of Parliament, and primarily on that of the House of Commons, whose ultimate power of control now rests on the annual approval of the Finance Bill for the raising of the national revenue, and of the departmental estimates for the manner in which that revenue is to be spent.

102. The Sovereign now selects from among the party dominant in the House of Commons a Prime Minister to head the executive, and he in turn nominates for appointment by the Sovereign the ministerial heads of the several departments, the limits of whose functions are clearly defined by statute or well-established custom. These ministers, drawn from the same or allied political parties, form a team which is united on a common national policy, but each is individually responsible to Parliament for the policies and actions of his own department, which are normally announced and defended by him without disclosure of any consultation he may have had with his colleagues.

103. The Prime Minister forms a Cabinet composed in peace-time of the ministerial heads of most departments, with the addition of a few members without onerous departmental duties—a total of about 20 members. Although the Cabinet is mentioned in the Ministers of the Crown Act 1937 and in the Parliamentary Commissioner Act 1969, it owes its existence to no statute, it has no independent legal authority and no fixed rules of its own procedure; but while it enjoys the confidence of a majority in the House of Commons, it acts as the supreme co-ordinator of national policy, its decisions are accepted without question throughout the government machine, and legal or executive form is given to those decisions by or on behalf of the appropriate minister who accepts responsibility for them to Parliament. Through discussion among its members it provides the means for reconciling the principle of ministerial with collective responsibility, under which each minister remains responsible for a particular sphere of activity and yet shares with his colleagues a collective responsibility for the government's policy as a whole—and thus ensures the coherence of the executive. Achievement of collective responsibility implies that there should be complete frankness between the members, who would not feel free to surrender their departmental and personal preferences for the object of their common policy unless they were confident that the stand they had taken and the points they had conceded would not become public knowledge and be used to their embarrassment. Accordingly a high degree of confidentiality has always attached to proceedings in Cabinet, whose members are subject to the Privy Counsellor's oath of secrecy; and the member who was unable to accept the view of a majority of his colleagues was expected to resign (*see* para. 214) and normally given permission by the Sovereign, on the advice of the Prime Minister, to make an explanation to Parliament of his reasons.

A*

104. There was some theoretical abrogation of the principle of collective responsibility in the case of the small War Cabinets of 1916–1919 and of 1939–1945, when a majority of ministers took no part in prior discussion of issues which did not affect their departments and yet were expected to acquiesce in the major decisions which were taken; but how far it was a real problem is largely an academic issue, as no case is known of resignation by a minister not in a War Cabinet through disagreement with general policy. Nevertheless in both World Wars the position was recognised as one of some constitutional difficulty. It was partly mitigated by the fact that the War Cabinets under Lloyd George and Churchill were coalitions which enjoyed the support of clear majorities in Parliament. In both World Wars ministers were summoned when questions affecting their departmental interests were to be discussed; and in the Second World War arrangements were made whereby ministers of Cabinet rank but outside the War Cabinet were kept informed of developments by the regular circulation of memoranda and conclusions, with the implication that they had opportunity to comment on them, and if necessary to object. (During September and October 1931 MacDonald as Prime Minister of the National Government restricted the size of the Cabinet to 10; but in the political circumstances at the time any question of collective responsibility was ignored or evaded.)

The Cabinet Office

105. Until 1916 Cabinets had met without an agenda and without a secretary, and ministers took executive action on their recollection or understanding of what they had decided. In December 1916 Lloyd George formed his War Cabinet of five members, and a secretarial equipment became necessary to get matters before them for their consideration, and to record and notify to those concerned the decisions they had taken. That equipment was at hand in the secretariat of the Committee of Imperial Defence which was adapted by Hankey into an organisation whose function became that of securing that the machinery whereby ministers collectively reached their policy decisions worked smoothly. To this end its main activity was the arrangement of meetings of the Cabinet and of Cabinet committees, the circulation of agenda and of memoranda, the preparation of conclusions and of minutes, the drafting of reports for committees, the taking of such follow-up action as might be appropriate, and the custody of the records.

106. In carrying out this work the Office under Hankey, Tom Jones and Howorth, and later under Bridges, Ismay and Brook, developed its own methods and traditions, which had to be harmonised with the personalities, habits and requirements of successive Prime Ministers and their colleagues, and these in turn were in part determined by the problems and the personalities in the departments. But the transient politicians and the permanent civil servants appear to have adapted themselves to each others' practices, commonsense and convenience taking precedence over formalities, and new functions were acquired or shed by the Office in response to current needs. So far as the surviving records show, no serious case arose in which friction was generated, or where the Office failed to meet the reasonable requirements of ministers.

107. As the secretarial agency for the Cabinet, the Office was conscious that advantage should not be taken of its central position and close association with ministers to influence policy or to help one point of view rather than another to prevail, as this would impair the confidence which ministers and departments should feel in the ability of the Office to distil a problem and notify for action a decision commanding the collective assent of ministers. As the secretariat of the

Committee of Imperial Defence, some latitude was taken in initiating consideration of those aspects of defence which were not directly related to the current problem of foreign policy; but in the civil field the official records show little attempt on the part of the Office to offer advice to ministers or to influence their decisions. Nevertheless, some suspicion was felt about the influence which could be exercised at the heart of government by a permanent staff which was not itself directly responsible to Parliament. Hankey's *Supreme Command* and Tom Jones' *Whitehall Diary* disclose from their private papers some of the issues where they felt their influence to have been effective, and it was partly due to the suspicion of the influence they were liable to exercise that the future of the Office was put in jeopardy in 1922 (*see* paras. 502–507). The Office did not emerge unscathed at the time and it is probable that Hankey and Tom Jones were on guard against getting involved in political issues subsequently; but Tom Jones recorded Hankey's threat in 1927 to resign on the question of belligerent rights, and in reporting this to the Prime Minister, he virtuously added 'it seemed to me a wrong conception of a civil servant's function to threaten resignation on policy' (*Whitehall Diary*, Vol. II, pp. 116, 117). Their successors in the Office (none of whom is known to have kept a running diary though some produced their memoirs*) no doubt exercised their influence unobtrusively on occasions, and depending on circumstances and personalities it is probable that similar influences at a high level from the Prime Minister's secretariat at Downing Street and from officials in the Treasury interacted with each other—but on any such issues the official records of the Office are largely silent. (In the Second World War independent advice was tendered to ministers by temporary officials in the Economic Section which had been attached to the Office largely through the circumstances of its origin—paras. 965–969.)

108. In addition to providing the secretariat for the CID in the inter-war years, the Office served the successive Cabinets shown in the following table (which refers to some of the significant points at which functions or activities changed in response to events).

December 1916–October 1922 Coalition—Lloyd George
  Imperial War Cabinet (para. 416)
  Supreme War Council (para. 417)
  Peace and other international conferences (para. 419)
October 1922–May 1923 Conservative—Bonar Law
  League of Nations and other international work transferred to the Foreign Office (paras. 502–507)
May 1923–January 1924 Conservative—Baldwin
  Chiefs of Staff Committee formed in July 1923 (para. 607)
January–November 1924 Labour—MacDonald
November 1924–June 1929 Conservative—Baldwin
  Committee of Civil Research (para. 701)
June 1929–August 1931 Labour—MacDonald
  Economic Advisory Council (para. 704)
August 1931–June 1935 National—MacDonald
  Full-time chairman of the Supply Board absorbed in April 1935 (para. 633)
June 1935–May 1937 National—Baldwin
  Provided staff for the Minister for Co-ordination of Defence in March 1936 (para. 622)

---

* For example Lord Ismay, *Memoirs* (1962); C. Hollis, *War at the Top* (1959); Sir G. Mallaby, *From My Level* (1965).

May 1937–May 1940 National—N. Chamberlain
  Hankey retired in July 1938 and succeeded by Bridges (para. 533)
  The CID disappeared on the creation of the War Cabinet in September 1939
  (para. 907)
May 1940–May 1945 Coalition—Churchill
  Provided staff for the Prime Minister as Minister of Defence (para. 920)
  Central Statistical Office and Economic Section formed in 1940 (para. 968)
  Certain co-ordinating functions passed to the Ministry of Production in 1942
  (para. 954) and to the Ministry of Reconstruction in 1943 (para. 959)
May–July 1945 Caretaker—Churchill

The Cabinet records

  The Cabinet Office records, containing as they do copies of all papers submitted
  to the Cabinet or its committees, as well as the reports of the discussions and
  decisions taken concerning them, comprise the most valuable single collection
  of modern material for historical purposes that can be obtained from official
  sources (*Report of the Committee on Departmental Records* 1954 (Cmd. 9163),
  para. 147).

109. The reader who comes to these records in the Public Record Office a generation or more after they were created, when they no longer have any immediate
sense of urgency, will recognise their high value as contemporary source material
for British political history in the period covered by two world wars, but he should
be aware of some of the qualifications which surround them.

110. They were essentially created for the purposes of current administration, and
not for the purpose of enabling historians to write history. While they contain
much of the information available to ministers collectively on the problems with
which they were faced, and a note of the decisions reached, the speed with which
events moved—and the crises which reached the Cabinet were often in their most
acute phase—could mean that on occasions the written record fell into arrears or
was not fully prepared, and that the final stages are missing. Moreover, a wide
range of matters were settled outside the Cabinet by direct discussion between
ministers, with the assistance if necessary of the Prime Minister.

111. The minutes and conclusions were deliberately prepared objectively and
impersonally, and designed to record agreement and not promote controversy;
behind many of the decisions lay tensions and influences which are not reflected
in the official records; but an account of some can be found in the letters, papers,
memoirs or biographies of the participants.

112. As most of the problems were those raised by ministers, the relevant departmental files (and possibly those of the Prime Minister and of the Treasury—in
the Public Record Office PREM and T classes respectively) would contain a great
deal more about them than will be available among the Cabinet records, where the
issues would be stated in a highly condensed form. In this connection it should be
borne in mind that on some matters the minister and his senior officials would not
have any first-hand or personal knowledge of the issues they were facing, and were
dependent on what they had been told; the historian with later and fuller access to
other sources may find that information given in all good faith to the Cabinet at
the time was in some degree inadequate or misleading.

113. The historian should also be aware that in tracing any particular topic through
the lists and indexes in the Public Record Office he is liable to find the references
he requires in different places (e.g. in the Cabinet memoranda, in the Cabinet

conclusions, in the papers of one or more committees, or among the registered files); copies of the same paper will frequently be found in several places.

114. A description of the referencing system used by the Cabinet Office and of its link with that now used in the Public Record Office is given in paras. 258–260. In the present text any particular Cabinet committee or registered file and memoranda and conclusions of the Cabinet are generally given their references in both systems. A key to the archival references used in the Public Record Office is given in para. 243 and in Annex 11.

115. As no fundamental change took place in the procedures of the Office as the secretarial agency for the Cabinet, it is convenient in Chapter 2 to outline the way in which it worked; Chapter 3 gives some of the background before 1917; Chapters 4–9 touch in greater depth on particular aspects in a roughly chronological setting; and Chapter 10 gives some account of the work of the Historical Section. To avoid overloading the text with detail, much material has been relegated to the Annexes.

THE GENERAL PROCEDURES OF THE CABINET OFFICE 1917–1945

Instructions to the Secretary

201. While there is no indication that Lloyd George's War Cabinet took any formal steps to regulate their procedure, Hankey circulated a note within the Office on 24 January 1917, entitled 'Rules of Procedure' (Annex 2—CAB 21/102), which formed the basis for the operations of the secretariat until superseded by 'Instructions to the Secretary' (CP 1—CAB 24/92), which were approved at the first meeting of the full peace-time Cabinet on 4 November 1919. These instructions were adopted in a slightly revised and amplified form at an early meeting of the Cabinet of each subsequent administration; those 'provisionally approved' by the Bonar Law Cabinet in 1922 were annexed to CC 64(22)—CAB 23/32; and those current in 1936 were codified in CP 88(36)—CAB 24/261 (Annex 3). For Chamberlain's War Cabinet they were modified by WP(G)(39)1—CAB 67/1, and later codified in 'Notes on War Cabinet Procedure' of May 1943 (Annex 4).

202. Basically these instructions or notes on procedure show little change; they contemplate that memoranda would be circulated in advance, that an agenda would be prepared, that the secretary would attend meetings for the purpose of recording the conclusions, which he would notify to those directly concerned, and that provision would be made for committees. With a Cabinet whose membership could be suddenly and radically changed by a political shift, which had no legal existence, and no fixed rules of its own procedure, it was a protection to the secretary to know that the range of his duties was defined and endorsed by the incoming members, and that he could arrange the Office accordingly. In this chapter an attempt is made to indicate generally the way in which the Office served the Cabinet and its committees.

Memoranda

203. The questions which came before the Cabinet were in the main those which raised major issues of policy, or which were liable to cause widespread public criticism or comment, or which represented an unresolved conflict of interest between departments; and were normally raised on the basis of Memoranda prepared by ministers and circulated before the meeting. It was the customary right of a minister—whether or not he was a member of the Cabinet—to circulate his views on any topic; on occasions ministers were invited to submit their views on matters of general interest (e.g. by CC 55(36)5a—CAB 23/85 of 29 July 1936 on the reform of the League of Nations); but generally a submission was on a matter of direct interest to the department of the minister, who would have carefully considered whether the subject was of sufficient importance to bring before his colleagues. 'The minister who refers too much is weak; he who refers too little is dangerous' (Ivor Jennings, *Cabinet Government* (3rd edition, 1965), p. 234). Some memoranda were prepared for information only or to report progress in some field, but most consisted of an explanation of a problem which was becoming acute, an indication of the considerations which had a bearing upon it, an outline of possible solutions and a precise recommendation on the action to be taken, for which the author sought the concurrence of his colleagues. When the memorandum had been approved by the minister, sufficient copies were sent to the Cabinet Office which circulated them to ministers in locked boxes.

204. It should not be overlooked that apart from the memoranda circulated to the Cabinet, other sources of information and advice available to ministers included the press, gossip in the lobby and communications from their party organisation, their constituents and the public; moreover they were kept in touch with developments in Commonwealth and foreign affairs by the regular distribution of copies of the more important telegrams and dispatches passing through the overseas departments.

Agenda

205. The agenda of the Cabinet was in theory settled by the Prime Minister, though in practice the secretary had discretion subject to reference to the Prime Minister on points of doubt. The first item in time of peace was generally 'Foreign Affairs', followed by other topics on which memoranda had been circulated; priority was often given to the more difficult subjects. The agenda, which became the normal means for summoning a meeting, was issued by the Office in sufficient time to allow ministers to acquaint themselves with the matters to be raised, and give them opportunity to obtain comments and advice on those matters affecting their departments. Urgent matters might be raised orally with the permission of the Prime Minister.

Meetings

206. To help ministers in planning their other engagements, each administration normally fixed a regular day and time each week for meetings of the Cabinet; but inevitably special or emergency meetings were summoned as accumulation of business required or to deal with some sudden crisis. The chair was taken by the Prime Minister unless he was unavoidably absent, when he would nominate his most senior colleague to deputise. The normal place for meetings was the Cabinet room at 10 Downing Street, although it was sometimes convenient when Parliament was in session for members to meet in the Prime Minister's room at the House of Commons; during the Second World War meetings were occasionally held in the Cabinet War Room in Storey's Gate.

207. In peace-time attendance at the Cabinet by persons other than members was unusual; the chief whip, ministers not in the Cabinet, law officers, parliamentary secretaries and chiefs of staff were sometimes present for particular items; and on occasions ambassadors or officials were summoned (e.g. the ambassador to the U.S.A. on 25 July 1922 for discussion of the American debt and the chairman and deputy chairman of the Unemployment Assistance Board at two meetings held on 29 June 1936 to discuss the draft regulations for assistance). At the two War Cabinets, ministers, chiefs of staff and others attended for discussion of matters in which they were directly concerned.

208. In peace-time the secretary was generally unaccompanied; at the two War Cabinets he was frequently accompanied by a deputy or assistant secretary to help in the drafting of the conclusions, to hand out papers, or to convey a decision to a department on which immediate action was required. Stenographers were never present, and the secretary made such notes in manuscript of the discussion and of the decisions as he found necessary on which to base the record of the proceedings;

the manuscript notes were maintained for a period while the accuracy of the record could effectively be challenged, but after a reasonable interval they were destroyed. On occasions after the business on the agenda had been disposed of, the secretary withdrew and the members of the Cabinet remained for discussion of some matter of a party political character; in such cases no record was made.

Conclusions

209. The records of the proceedings of the Cabinet have been termed 'Conclusions' since August 1919; previously they had been known as 'Minutes', and before recording the decision had often given a fairly full account of the views expressed by individual ministers. Thereafter the 'conclusions' were briefer and summarised impersonally the pros and cons of the argument; but the subsequent instructions to the secretary in November 1919 (CPI—CAB 24/92) implied a distinction between the conclusions circulated to ministers, and 'a single copy of a further note kept by the secretary in cases where the Cabinet explicitly requires it'. In practice, a fuller note was not kept, and since 1919 the conclusions now in CAB 23 and 65 form the sole official record; there is no underlying series of secret or supplementary notes (but see para. 216 for 'confidential annexes').

210. The conclusions of each Cabinet meeting now form the main records of the Cabinet Office. Each shows at the head the place, date and time of the meeting; the names of those present, distinguishing between members and others; and the names of the secretariat. The names of ministers are shown in order of precedence as determined by the Prime Minister (and notified from time to time in *Hansard*). After 1939 it became the practice to include a table of contents before the body of the conclusions. The individual conclusions at each meeting were numbered serially in the order in which the subjects were discussed. Each had a subject heading, with the previous reference (if any) below; against some of the conclusions in the 1930s there is a later insertion in manuscript 'FR' giving a reference to the conclusion at a following meeting on the same subject. The form of the conclusions was generally a brief mention of the problem (including reference to the memorandum on which it arose) followed by such summary of the discussion as might be required for guidance of those who had to take action, and ending with a concise and clear-cut decision, which put the responsibility for giving effect to it on a particular minister; if more than one minister was concerned, the primary responsibility was put on A, in consultation with B and C. It was unusual for the views of individuals expressed in discussion to be recorded although on occasions, when the issue had been troublesome, a fuller account was given, which might include the views of individuals.

211. After each meeting the secretary, often under great pressure, prepared the conclusions which were circulated in roneo form (in sealed envelopes contained in locked boxes) to the Sovereign and to those present at the meeting; at various times copies were sent to the permanent heads of the Treasury and of the Foreign Office and to the chiefs of staff; extracts would be sent to ministers not in the Cabinet on matters of concern to them. If the meeting ended before lunch the conclusions were circulated the same day; those for an afternoon or evening meeting would normally be available first thing on the following morning.

212. Until May 1917 the conclusions were approved in draft by the Prime Minister and initialled by him. Thereafter the conclusions were referred in draft to the Prime Minister only in cases where the secretary was in serious doubt; otherwise they were circulated directly they had been prepared. Suggestions for amendment were not often made; when they were of substance they were submitted to the

Prime Minister for decision. A few days after the meeting a 'record copy' was made which tidied up punctuation and grammar and incorporated any amendments which had been approved. Before 1939 the revised 'record copies' which now form CAB 23 were not circulated unless the amendments were material; after 1939 the prints which now form CAB 65 were circulated to all recipients of the original.
213. The responsibility for action on a decision of the Cabinet rested with the minister or ministers concerned, who if the matter was urgent would implement it in advance of receipt of the conclusions; on occasions the Office would telephone the substance of the decision to the department concerned with if necessary some explanation of the context in which the discussion had taken place. If difficulty was found in the implementation of a decision, the minister was expected to inform the Prime Minister for consideration whether the matter should be referred again to the Cabinet. With responsibility firmly placed on named ministers it was in theory unnecessary for the Office to institute any 'follow-up' procedure; nevertheless QACs (questions awaiting consideration) were at times maintained, and during the Second World War schedules were for a period circulated on outstanding matters. The system did not work satisfactorily; it impinged on ministerial responsibility; the urgent matter identified itself without assistance from the Office; the decisions varied from authority to dispatch a telegram forthwith to approval of long-term programmes which might take years to carry out; the schedules could not be kept up to date; and the arrangement quietly lapsed.

Dissent

214. Although differences of view were frequently expressed in Cabinet and reflected in the summary of the discussion, the decisions recorded in the conclusions were assumed to be unanimous and the alternative to acceptance was generally resignation. The conclusions contain no record of voting and the normal procedure was that discussion continued until general agreement had been reached, although on occasions the Prime Minister in summing up might virtually impose a solution. But the dissent of individual ministers, not involving their resignation, has on a few occasions been recorded; on page 10 is a facsimile of CC 42(22)4—CAB 23/30, as amended by Austen Chamberlain, on the propriety of so doing. Although on 25 November 1931 (CC 81(31)6—CAB 23/69) ministers had 'accepted the view of the Prime Minister that notes of dissent or reservation should not be recorded, as this would be contrary to the general principle of Cabinet unity', the 'Agreement to Differ' of 22 January 1932 (CC 7(32)1—CAB 23/70) was publicly announced (*see* para. 528/1932).
(Ministerial resignations which are known to have arisen from disagreement on a point of principle during 1923–1938 are mentioned in para. 528. It is not known that any member of the War Cabinet resigned on such grounds during the Second World War. But resignations for health or personal reasons, or in connection with a reconstruction of the government, may have been a cover for disagreement.)
215. Although the Cabinet has no terms of reference, certain matters have by custom been regarded as inappropriate for formal record or discussion. An example was the oral explanation by the Chancellor of the Exchequer to the Cabinet of the Budget proposals he intended to make to the House of Commons; when this was given there was insufficient time to make any substantial change in his plans and the minute normally read:
The Chancellor of the Exchequer communicated to the Cabinet particulars of the proposals in the forthcoming Budget.
In accordance with precedent, details are not recorded in the Cabinet conclusions.

Before the dissents were recorded

366

RECORD OF
DISSENT
FROM
CABINET
CONCLUSIONS.

4. ~~In connection with the preceding conclusion~~ the LORD PRIVY SEAL (Mr. Chamberlain) drew attention to the present practice of recording the dissent of individual Ministers, which appeared *to this* to be at variance with the ~~traditional view as to the unanimity of~~ *constitutional Rule that Ministers were collectively* *responsible for all* Cabinet ~~conclusions~~ *decisions*.

THE SECRETARY OF STATE FOR FOREIGN AFFAIRS (Lord Balfour) stated that ~~such unanimity~~ *the rule* was based on the importance of preserving an unbroken phalanx in the face of the public and did not ~~necessarily~~ *consider to* ~~prevent the expression or~~ *that it ~~should be infringed by the~~ was infringed by the confidential* a record of dissent. In his opinion such record could not be held in any way to weaken the doctrine of Cabinet responsibility for the conclusions reached.

THE SECRETARY OF STATE FOR THE COLONIES (Mr. Churchill) said that he had himself been able to draw some comfort when in a minority, from the fact that his dissent had been recorded in the minutes.

~~The Lord Privy Seal~~ *Sir A. Chamberlain deferred to Lord Balfour's high authority & long experience & withdrew his objection.*

Minute of 25 July 1922 as drafted by Hankey and amended in MS. by Austen Chamberlain
(*see* para. 214).

Other matters which were not usually the subject of collective business included the exercise of the prerogative of mercy, the making of appointments, honours and (since the Campbell case in 1924, CC 48(24)5—CAB 23/48) public prosecutions. Record was not normally made of purely party political aspects.

Confidential annexes

216. Conclusions of special secrecy or confidentiality which were not circulated, or circulated only to those ministers directly concerned, are for 1917–1918 (and known as A or X minutes) in CAB 23/13–17. From 1919 to 1939 there were no separate volumes of conclusions of special secrecy; there are a few references in the conclusions to a matter which was 'separately recorded' or 'recorded in the secretary's standard file'; in such cases the paper was placed in a sealed envelope which was subsequently bound into the volume of conclusions, and copies of the items now form CAB 23/90B. For the period of the Second World War matters mentioned as 'recorded in the secretary's standard file' will now be found in the separate volumes of confidential annexes to the War Cabinet conclusions in CAB 65.

217. The record copies of the conclusions for each calendar year (or where an administration changed, for the relevant part of the calendar year) were bound and retained in the secretary's private office during the lifetime of the administration; they were then deposited in the Confidential Library of the Office, whence they were transferred with the contemporary subject indexes to the Public Record Office.

218. Bound up with some of the conclusions are records of 'Conferences of Ministers'. These were frequent before 1923 (*see* para. 422), but were rare thereafter and appear to have been limited to those cases where the Prime Minister summoned an emergency meeting and some ministers could not be reached.

219. For the War Cabinet before October 1919 the record copies of the conclusions were printed on pale green paper; for 1919–1922 they were produced on poor quality white semi-absorbent duplicating paper; from 8 March to 31 October 1922, when the record was circulated only to the Sovereign and the Prime Minister (*see* para. 424), they exist on flimsy paper; from 1923 to 1927 they were duplicated on better quality white paper; from 1928 to 1939 they were typed on stout blue paper; for the War Cabinet 1939–1945 they were again printed on pale green paper.

220. In Annexes 7 and 8 the annual totals are given of the number of meetings of the Cabinet and of the memoranda to the Cabinet submitted by ministers; the figures in Annex 8 give some indication of the extent to which different ministers at different times were under pressure to consult their colleagues.

Report to the Sovereign

221. With the establishment of the Office in 1916, the practice whereby the Prime Minister sent to the Sovereign a letter reporting on proceedings in the Cabinet (*see* para. 305) was discontinued. In its place the secretary sent to the Palace a copy of the conclusions of the Cabinet, together with the minutes of certain committees, and these supplemented the information given by the Prime Minister to the King at their periodic meetings. The main point of contact between the Sovereign and the Cabinet was the Prime Minister's Office at 10 Downing Street, but from time to time informal correspondence passed between the private secretary to the King and the secretary of the Cabinet, of which perhaps the most significant is that of February 1938 (4/1/6A — CAB 21/778), when the former complained that the

King had had no forewarning of the crisis which resulted in the resignation of the Foreign Secretary (Eden). Hankey replied that he had arranged with the Prime Minister that if developments appeared to be taking an untoward turn he would endeavour to remind him of his responsibility to inform the King, and it would be for the Prime Minister to decide how this should be done. Hankey added that in a government crisis he himself was usually submerged with work, which often affected him as secretary of the Cabinet and as Clerk of the Privy Council, and if the emergency involved the services, as secretary of the CID as well.

Committees

222. In addition to recording the proceedings at more than 3000 meetings of the Cabinet from December 1916 to July 1945, the Office provided the secretariat for some 1300 committees (and sub-committees) which held an aggregate of over 16,000 meetings. Details are given in Annex 11, but the position may be summarised as follows:

	Number of committees and sub-committees (approximate)	Aggregate number of meetings (approximate)
1917–1922		
Cabinet	160	990
Committee of Imperial Defence	11	120
1923–September 1939		
Cabinet	379	1990
Committee of Imperial Defence	275	3400
Committee of Civil Research and Economic Advisory Council	70	900
September 1939–July 1945		
War Cabinet	292	5440
Chiefs of Staff	45	3050
Miscellaneous and General series	90	210

This table excludes those committees which were appointed but for some reason never met, although some memoranda may have been circulated. For 1939–1945 it also excludes meetings of the Joint Intelligence Committee (JIC) and of the Joint Planning Staff (JP); nor do the totals include meetings of the Combined Chiefs of Staff and its numerous sub-committees with whose secretariats the Office was associated.

223. Shown separately in the table in the previous paragraph are the committees and sub-committees of the CID, of the Committee of Civil Research and of the Economic Advisory Council—three bodies set up following decisions in 1904, 1925 and 1930 respectively and announced by Treasury minutes (copies in Annex 3), with the purpose of assuring the public that authoritative and continuing advice in defined fields from within and without the government service was available to the Cabinet; some account of these bodies is given in Chapters 6 and 7, but for present purposes they should be regarded as distinct from the committees which each administration found it necessary to use in order to relieve the Cabinet itself of the load of day-to-day problems with which it was faced.

224. At any given point in time, the Cabinet committee structure as it then existed was no doubt reasonably logical and convenient to ministers and officials concerned in its operation; it reflected the habits and methods of work of the Prime

Minister and his principal colleagues; it reflected the pressures and problems with which they were currently faced; and it might reflect adjustment to the traditions of the Office and the secretarial machinery it could provide. But with hindsight it would appear that not until the middle of the Second World War was there any successful attempt to create a coherent internal committee structure whereby particular types of problem were regularly referred to the same group of ministers.

225. Generalisation about Cabinet committees over a period of 30 years during which 170 ministers sat in the Cabinet is dangerous. Many ministers were no doubt glad to see matters in which they had no direct concern referred to a committee of their colleagues more closely interested, recognising that in all probability their report or their decisions would be accepted without question. A committee could also be a device for delaying or shelving a problem. But there is some unwritten evidence to suggest that there was a little reluctance to let matters pass to a committee where a minister—including a Prime Minister—might lose his influence, and consequent hesitation to hand over on any long-term basis consideration of particular aspects of policy. This may partly explain why in the inter-war years most of the Cabinet committees were appointed *ad hoc* and had a relatively short life; and why those which were regarded by an administration as in the nature of standing committees, were generally those of which the Prime Minister was chairman (*see* para. 524).

226. Most of the committees were appointed by the Prime Minister or the Cabinet either to dispose finally of some problem of relatively minor importance or, in more important matters, to focus the issues and save the time of the Cabinet by narrowing the points for decision. The terms of reference, composition and title would be carefully considered, generally on a draft by the secretary of the Cabinet, and notified to those concerned by the issue of a memorandum setting out:

(a) the authority for the appointment
(b) the terms of reference
(c) the names of the chairman and members
(d) the names of the secretary or secretaries
(e) any necessary remarks about the method of work or relations with other committees.

This memorandum would generally form the first paper in the series of documents for the committee.

227. The considerations which determined membership of any Cabinet committee would be difficult to define. Obviously those departments which were primarily concerned with the subject would be represented; personal and political factors were important; it was desirable that individual ministers should not be overburdened with committee work; and junior ministers might be given the opportunity to participate. As regards the chairman, it appears to have been the general practice that on major matters the Prime Minister himself would preside (e.g. the Foreign Policy Committee (FP(36)—CAB 27/622)). When the issue was primarily the concern of a single department, the minister for that department generally presided (e.g. the Colonial Secretary was chairman of the Migration Committee in 1928 (MC—CAB 27/380)). Where there were sharp differences of opinion, the chairman might be the Lord Chancellor or a minister not directly involved (e.g. the Home Secretary presided over the Palestine Committee in 1943 (P(M)—CAB 95/14). During the Second World War it was not unusual for junior ministers to preside over committees composed of officials, nominated by the permanent heads of the departments concerned.

228. The secretary of the committee was appointed by the secretary of the Cabinet, generally from his own staff. Where a particular department was closely connected with the work, it was often the practice to appoint as a joint or assistant secretary an official of that department who would be in a position to know where to obtain the information that would be required. It was the function of the secretary, in addition to his work in direct connection with meetings and the drafting of a report, to draw the chairman's attention to events or information affecting the committee's work and to watch the action taken to implement the conclusions.

229. The procedure at committees was generally similar to that at the Cabinet. Matters for discussion were raised by the circulation of memoranda in advance and notified in the agenda; members who wished to raise a matter orally were expected to notify the chairman and other members so that they might be fore-warned. The minutes—which were often fuller than those for the Cabinet—were circulated as soon as possible to those who had been present; copies were generally sent to other members of the Office who were thereby made aware of the field being covered and gaps or overlaps with other committees were brought to light.

230. What action was taken on the conclusions of a committee depended on the terms of reference and the decision of the chairman. A full report might be made to the Cabinet and circulated as a Cabinet memorandum either by the chairman or under a covering note by the secretary; sometimes a note of the conclusions only was circulated; on occasions the chairman would report orally to the Cabinet; on others (and more especially during the Second World War) the chairman or a member would take definitive action on his own responsibility; and not infre-quently, although a committee had been invited to report, no report was made as the matter had for a variety of reasons lost its urgency or importance or been overtaken by other circumstances and the committee unobtrusively faded out. While the decisions of a committee were normally unanimous, a member who dissented from a conclusion could ask that the matter be referred to the Cabinet for decision (e.g. in CP 360(26)—CAB 24/181 Cecil of Chelwood dissented from the recommendations of the Committee on Compulsory Arbitration (CA—CAB 27/330)).

231. Anxiety was sometimes expressed by ministers who had not been appointed to a particular committee and whose interest in the subject matter was in varying degree remote, that decisions would be taken which might embarrass their depart-ments; in such cases the committee papers were usually circulated to them and opportunity given to attend meetings if it seemed likely that their interests would be affected. In any event chairmen and secretaries were always alive to the point that collective responsibility should be preserved, and it is indeed doubtful whether legitimate complaint could have been made that decisions were taken without reasonable consultation with all those concerned within the Whitehall network.

232. Attendance at Cabinet committees by persons other than ministers or officials was unusual; but under MacDonald's administration 1929–1931, representatives of employers and of work-people and leaders of opposition parties were sometimes present (e.g. the Committee on the British Coal Industry (BCI—CAB27/395) and that on Unemployment Insurance (UI(RC)—CAB 27/452)).

233. Two series of Cabinet committees were appointed with some regularity: one, for the drafting of the King's Speech at the opening and closing of the sessions of Parliament (KS—CAB 27/250, 491, 555, 570, 593, 594, 611, 635, 647 and CAB 98/3); the other, the Emergency Business Committee (EBC—CAB 27/226, 249, 386, 463, 590), appointed at the time of a general election to handle urgent matters, and in particular to advise on the answers to be given to questionnaires from national bodies sent to ministers and government candidates.

234. It was not the usual practice to give information to Parliament or the public about the existence, terms of reference or membership of Cabinet committees. Decisions were generally announced and defended by the minister concerned as his own decision taken on his own responsibility; it was felt that the growth of any practice whereby decisions of the Cabinet or Cabinet committees were announced as such, could lead to the awkward result that some decisions would be regarded as less authoritative than others, with opportunity to argue that a decision of a particular committee should be reviewed by some other committee or by the Cabinet. Nevertheless, the existence of some committees did on occasion become known; the appointment of a standing committee on National Expenditure was announced in the Budget statement of 1925; the Defence Policy and Requirements Committee in 1936 was mentioned in Cmd. 5107; and during the Second World War Parliament was informed of the main lines of the committee organisation (e.g. *Hansard,* 4 June 1940, cols. 769–771, and *Organisation for Joint Planning* (Cmd. 6351), 1942).

235. In addition to the committees which were formally constituted, the Office at times undertook secretarial functions for less formal meetings of ministers; for example, for the conferences of ministers summoned by Lloyd George to deal with various miscellaneous matters and now recorded separately in CAB 23/35–36 or annexed to the conclusions of the Cabinet. From 1922 to 1939 ministerial meetings of this type appear generally to have been steered into the framework of the committee structure (although notes of informal meetings may be found on some of the registered files of the Office). During the Second World War and notwithstanding the growing strength of the committee system, a number of *ad hoc* meetings were held without definite terms of reference whose proceedings were recorded in the Miscellaneous or General series (CAB 78).

236. But a vast amount of government business was transacted which did not come near the Office and which is not reflected in the Cabinet records. Much was conducted personally between ministers after reference as necessary to the Prime Minister; and there was a constantly changing network of inter-departmental committees and advisory and consultative bodies of which the Office had no knowledge.

Other work

237. As executive action was taken by ministers who accepted responsibility to Parliament, it was generally inappropriate and unnecessary for the Office to enter into correspondence with outside bodies or persons about decisions of the Cabinet or Cabinet committees. But circumstances did arise where the Office found itself providing a staff for the conduct of correspondence involving directions or instructions to bodies at home or abroad on matters where responsibility could not be clearly assumed by a single departmental minister. Among these cases were:

Communications with the League of Nations 1919–1922 (para. 421).

Correspondence on behalf of the COS committee with C-in-Cs abroad and with the Combined Chiefs of Staff (paras. 938 and 979).

The various organisations connected with supply (e.g. the Supply Board (para. 611), the Anglo-French Co-ordinating Committee (para. 949), the Area Boards (para. 951), the North American Supply Committee (para. 952) and the Allied Supplies Executive (para. 955)).

Most of these cases arose from the circumstances of the Second World War; in the field of supply the anomaly whereby the Office went beyond normal secretarial functions, was largely solved by the creation of the Ministry of Production in

1942; and the Office remained responsible for the correspondence of the COS committee until the appointment of a departmental Minister of Defence in 1947. But developments of this character were closely watched and care taken not to impinge on departmental responsibilities.

The work of the Office in connection with Imperial and international conferences is outlined in paras. 801–806 and 971–972.

238. The Office acquired a corpus of knowledge and experience, particularly during the Second World War, which enabled it to offer advice informally to the Prime Minister or his staff on matters not falling clearly within the responsibility of any single department, and which included:

Drafting answers to parliamentary questions.

Conduct of ministers.

Proposals for new ministries or alteration of departmental boundaries.

Certain matters of security.

Relations of the Cabinet with the Sovereign.

Vetting manuscripts by former ministers and others which related to their Cabinet experience.

But throughout the Office has been conscious that on these and similar matters, while advice could be offered and precedents quoted, the responsibility for decision or for action rested with the Prime Minister and his ministerial colleagues. It is beyond the scope of this study to discuss those cases on which advice was tendered; what record of them exists will be found scattered among the files in CAB 21 and 104.

Security

239. The Office was acutely conscious of its responsibility to safeguard the confidentiality of ministers' deliberations, and to this end took elaborate precautions for the security of all material in its possession; the staff was carefully selected and appropriately instructed; and documents were circulated under cover, the recipients recorded and steps taken for recovery (*see* para. 252). The primary purpose was to ensure that there should be no leakage while policy was being formulated, and that when decisions had been reached, action should be taken by the ministers concerned, and any public disclosure of those decisions should be at their discretion and at the time of their choice. A secondary purpose, which has some constitutional significance, was that the confidential documents of one administration should be regarded as domestic to it, and that an incoming administration should have no right of access to them. In practice this was qualified in two ways—for continuity of administration, departmental files would generally contain sufficient information, and in a particular case the previous Prime Minister could give consent (cf. Hankey's notes attached to CC 48(24)—CAB 23/48 of 6 August 1924).

Identification of papers by symbols

240. With the great mass of agenda, memoranda, conclusions and minutes of the Cabinet, of its committees and of international conferences, flowing through the Office, some means of identification became essential, not only for the purposes of the Office itself, but for the convenience of ministers and of officials in departments who were engaged in preparing briefs or taking executive action. Before 1923 the referencing was erratic but since then documents issued from or through the Office have borne a superscription at the top, 'This document is the property of His Britannic Majesty's Government', followed by the name of the committee or body concerned, the subject and in the case of memoranda their author. In the top left-hand corner there was below any security classification a symbol followed by a serial number, and it is this reference which has been used within the Office and in departments to identify any particular document. (Readers in the Public Record Office who find a symbol reference on a departmental file should be able through the use of Annex 11 to trace the paper in the Cabinet Office series, but such symbols should not be confused with those used by departments for their own internal memoranda.) Not infrequently the same document was circulated to two or more committees or to the Cabinet, and in such cases it would bear the symbol and number in the series for each body to which it was distributed.

241. The symbol normally consisted of two parts: (a) one or more letters of the words in the title, and (b) the last two figures of the year in brackets. The same symbol was not given to more than one committee which was active at the time; where two committees were set up on the same subject, one of ministers and the other of officials, the same symbols were used, the former being distinguished by the addition of the letter 'M' and the latter by the addition of the letter 'O' (both in brackets).

242. While for the Cabinet the symbol used for memoranda was different from that used for conclusions, in the committee series the same symbol was used for all documents, distinguishing memoranda by plain serial numbers (e.g. HA(35)1, 2, 3, etc.)and minutes by ordinals (e.g. HA(35) 1st meeting, 2nd meeting, etc.). At the beginning of each calendar year the year in brackets was normally changed. Most of the CID and EAC documents—both memoranda and minutes—were numbered serially throughout, without reference to the year.

243. The symbols used for the Cabinet were:

	Conclusions	Memoranda	PRO references CAB
1916–1919	WC		23/1–17
		G	24/1–5
		or	
		GT	24/6–91
1919–1939	CC		23/18–101
		CP	24/92–288
1939–1945	WM		65/1–52
		WP	66/1–65
		WP(G)	67/1–9
		WP(R)	68/1–9
1945 (May–July)	CM		65/53 and 54
		CP	66/66 and 67

244. Thus, the fourth conclusion of the Cabinet at its 33rd meeting on 4 May 1936 dealing with X, could either be so expressed in full, or more shortly as CC 33(36)4—CAB 23/84. The relevant paper might be expressed either as a memorandum of 28 April 1936 by the Secretary of State for Y dealing with X, or more shortly as CP 259(36)—CAB 24/264.

245. At the end of each calendar year the memoranda and conclusions of the Cabinet were each bound consecutively into one or more volumes; when there was a change of administration during the year a fresh volume for each series was started. A full subject index for the memoranda and for the conclusions was prepared either annually or covering several years.

246. The papers for each committee (including its report when made) were bound together when the committee ceased to function; most volumes are prefaced with a contents sheet giving the dates of the meetings and the subjects discussed at each, together with a list of the memoranda circulated to the committee; some volumes also contain a full index.

247. After binding, the proceedings of the Cabinet, its committees, conferences, etc., were eventually placed in the Confidential Library of the Office where they were available for reference by the senior staff, and for consultation by former ministers who wished to refresh their memory of papers they would have seen while holding office (special care was taken to ensure that former ministers did not have access to papers circulated before or after they held office). The volumes were subsequently transferred to the Public Record Office for public inspection under the 30-year rule.

248. These volumes now represent the essential records of the Office, which could make no attempt to maintain a separate dossier for all the papers relating to each separate topic which reached it from departments. The files in departments are in fact the dossiers which supplement the Cabinet records; they should show in full detail what was the problem, what were the considerations bearing upon it and how it was solved. Although it was the normal practice to withhold from the departmental files the actual copies of the Cabinet memoranda and conclusions, there is generally sufficient indication on the file of the nature of the submission made and of the decision which was reached. There are, however, among the registered files of the Office now in CAB 21 and 104, some which contain material which could provide a useful commentary on particular points, but search through the file titles is necessary to relate the file to the Cabinet or committee records.

Mechanics of distribution

249. As the Office had the duty of preparing the agenda for the Cabinet and its committees and for circulating the decisions, and had to maintain an organisation for the purpose, it was accepted from the outset that economy would be achieved if it also undertook responsibility for circulating memoranda and so avoid an increase in the messenger staff of each department. The general procedure was that each department reproduced its own memoranda. A form of layout had become standard by 1923 and the department would obtain by telephone from the Cabinet Office the symbol and serial number, which would be inserted before final reproduction, generally on white paper by duplicating machine, but in the case of some important or lengthy documents by printing on pale green paper by the confidential Foreign Office press. (On occasions, for highly secret documents or where a department was overpressed or had inadequate facilities, the Office assisted by arranging reproduction itself; this became frequent during the Second World War.)

250. After reproduction the department would send sufficient copies for distribution, with a few spares, to the Office, where they were placed in a large stout envelope known as a 'skin', the title, symbol and serial number and the number of copies received being entered on the outside. After any necessary examination in the Office, who would already have determined the standard list of recipients for that series and would have noted the paper for inclusion in the agenda, the skin would be passed to the Distribution Room, where (unless already provided by the department) each copy would be given a copy number in the top right corner and the skin marked to show the individual to whom each copy was sent. The purpose of copy-numbering was to assist in tracing cases of leakage or loss, in addition to making the recipient more careful. The numbered copies were then placed in pigeon-holes, a separate one being assigned to each minister and official

on the standard distribution lists. The pigeon-holes, which were liable to accumulate papers from several different series for the same recipient, were cleared several times a day, and the contents placed in locked boxes or sealed envelopes which were taken by messengers to their destination. Pigeon-holing could be a very formidable task; at times of pressure in the Second World War papers in more than 150 series, each with its own particular distribution list, were sent for dispatch, and each had to be sorted in the right one of several hundred pigeon-holes and then boxed or enveloped in accordance with its security classification.

251. The agenda and conclusions of the Cabinet and the agenda and minutes of the committees were prepared and reproduced in the Office; the drafts from which final copies were made were preserved in the skins, and the distribution was generally made in the manner described above. To preserve secrecy the Cabinet conclusions and certain other documents were placed in sealed envelopes before being sent to the Distribution Room.

252. The skins, from which spare copies could be issued as necessary, were after a few weeks transferred by the Distribution Room to the Records Section, and as papers were returned by ministers and others when no longer needed, they were either replaced in the skins or destroyed, and taken off charge to the person to whom they had been consigned. Skins containing agenda were destroyed shortly after issue; the skins containing conclusions, minutes and memoranda, which might also contain drafts and occasionally correspondence directly relating to the papers, were destroyed after 15 or 20 years; but in all cases copies of the memoranda as circulated and of the final conclusions or minutes have been preserved.

253. Before 1939 the number of copies of papers for members of the Cabinet was generally 50, and during the Second World War rose to 75 or 80. The number of copies for committees varied.

254. At the beginning of the period the secretary of each committee had been responsible for arranging meetings, for the allocation of symbols and serial numbers for memoranda and for instructions to the Distribution Room about the circulation of papers. By the end of the period a Committee Section had emerged, staffed with a few committee clerks, each of whom served several committees, and relieved the secretaries of the labour of fixing times for meetings convenient to all members, of handling memoranda, of arranging for the circulation of papers through the Distribution Room and of their subsequent indexing. The emergence of the Committee Section was an imperceptible development over the period, but the link which it provided between the secretaries of committees and the Distribution Room was a significant contribution to the smooth working of the Office.

During the Second World War and as the pressure on the Office increased, a high degree of efficiency was reached in the preparation and circulation of conclusions, minutes and memoranda. The typing room, the Committee Section and the Distribution Room were strongly staffed and could be relied upon at any time of the day or night to circulate papers swiftly and accurately. Equally, worldwide communications by telegram were good, and the Office was kept in close touch with developments in the military situation and with any international meetings attended by the Prime Minister or others (copies of the official telegrams which passed through the Office are in CAB 105).

Registered files

255. The Office had its own internal organisation which was reflected in a registry system which was re-organised on several occasions. Over 10,000 files were opened after 1916 and had been closed at some time before the end of 1945; many of them

covered a period of several years; and there are a number of other files, opened during the period, which remained in action after 1945, whose contents will not become available to public inspection until 30 years after they ceased to be active.

256. These files covered a wide variety of matters; many dealt with minor establishment problems; some contained little or nothing beyond press cuttings, extracts from *Hansard*, copies of Foreign Office and other departmental telegrams and copies of memoranda and minutes which were available elsewhere, but had been assembled in this form for ease of reference while a topic was active; others contained ephemeral correspondence about the time, place and agenda for meetings. Examination of all files was undertaken by an experienced officer under the guidance of an Inspecting Officer of the Public Record Office; and of the total about two-thirds have been destroyed as having lost all value for administrative purposes and as being of little or no historical value. The files that survive and are contained in CAB 21 and 104 are in the main those that dealt with major matters of organisation, or which shed clear light on some of the major problems, or which had been marked as having been quoted by the official historians. But the end-products of the Office are the records of the decisions which had been reached and circulated for action; copies of these, together with the memoranda in which the considerations were set out, have been preserved.

257. Apart from its own registered files the Cabinet Office has inherited a number of collections of papers principally of the period of the Second World War; some account of these is given in para. 983.

Arrangement of Cabinet records in the Public Record Office

258. For the current work of the Office, the referencing system as it evolved was adequate for the needs of a small and compact staff; for the circulated papers it depended on the use of symbols; for internal files it depended on a complex registry organisation; both were intelligible to the staff engaged in the work at the time. If research into past decisions was necessary or if precedents were wanted, the volumes in the Confidential Library were available. The whole system made good sense while the records were in the custody of the Office, and experienced staff on hand who knew where to look for what they knew or suspected to exist.

259. This system was not suitable for retention when the records were transferred to the Public Record Office, where a standard system of reference by group, class and piece had long been in general use. Groups are related as far as possible to departments of origin, and classes correspond broadly to separate series of records, as far as these can be identified 25 years after their creation; pieces are assemblages, such as volumes or files, rather than individual documents.

260. In the Public Record Office the Cabinet records form the CAB group; within the group there are about 120 classes whose titles, with number of pieces, are given in Annex 12. Classes CAB 1–64 generally contain papers of date before September 1939, and classes CAB 65 onwards of the period of the Second World War. The main series of records of the Cabinet itself and of certain major committees constitute separate classes. CAB 27 contains the records of most of the *ad hoc* committees before 1939; for the period 1939–1945 several classes have been used for committees, each class containing papers of committees dealing with broadly similar subjects. The class lists available in the Public Record Office describe briefly the contents of each piece in the class, where the arrangement is generally chronological.

In view of the interlock between committees themselves and with the Cabinet, the reader in the Public Record Office may find it necessary to hunt through several class lists, and be prepared to find copies of the same paper in more than one place.

Staff

261. Hankey, as secretary of the CID since 1912, had used its staff as the secretariat successively for the War Council, the Dardanelles Committee and the War Committee. On the formation of the War Cabinet in December 1916 the staff was augmented at all levels to cope with the increasing tempo of work of the War Cabinet itself, of the Imperial War Cabinet, of the Supreme War Council and later of the Peace Conference and the other conferences following the First World War.

262. By 1922 the total staff numbered 120; following political pressure a drastic reduction to 40 was then made (*see* para. 507), but in the meantime the office at the assistant secretary level had been organised into a Home Affairs Branch (which became the Cabinet Office proper) and an Imperial, External Affairs and Defence Branch (which emerged as the secretariat for the Committee of Imperial Defence). Hankey was secretary of both, and the subordinate staff was common to both. From 1923 to 1930 and notwithstanding the work of the Imperial Conferences and of the Committee of Civil Research, the total staff did not exceed 50. With the appointment of the Economic Advisory Council it had by the mid-1930s increased to 70, and thereafter as war became imminent it increased rapidly towards 200. During the Second World War the number rose to 550, in addition to a number of military officers and others who were rather loosely associated with the Office for duty in London or Washington.

263. Hankey had retired in July 1938 and was succeeded by Edward Bridges as secretary of the Cabinet, and by H. L. Ismay as secretary of the CID and deputy secretary (military) of the Cabinet; R. B. Howorth became deputy secretary (civil) of the Cabinet and Clerk of the Privy Council, and on his retirement in 1942 he was succeeded as deputy secretary (civil) by Norman Brook, and the clerkship of the Privy Council became a separate appointment.

Throughout the period the ratio of subordinate to senior staff was high, and is largely explained by two factors: first, in the interests of security a good deal of clerical work was involved in recording the distribution and whereabouts of papers; and secondly, as many matters tended to reach the Office when they were at crisis point, a margin of staff had to be available to handle urgent work by day and by night, particularly in the duplication of papers and in their prompt dispatch to the recipients.

264. It is worthy of note that among the staff of the Office had been five Members of Parliament: Lieut.-Colonel L. S. Amery, Major W. G. Ormsby-Gore, Colonel Sir Mark Sykes and Lieut.-Colonel Leslie Wilson (before 1922) and Major E. Duncan Sandys during 1940. Each was a military officer seconded for service in the War Cabinet Office, and as their pay and emoluments were met from Army funds the question of an MP holding an office of profit under the Crown did not arise.

265. Annex 7 gives the number and cost of staff annually, Annex 6 lists the administrative officers who served in the office 1916–1945 and Annex 5 is a copy of the staff list in 1945. More detailed information about staff is given in later chapters.

Location of the Office

266. When the Old Palace of Whitehall was burned down in 1691 the Banqueting Hall remained, and the area around it became occupied by the town residences of a number of the nobility. Early in the nineteenth century the leases of those residences were falling in and two pieces of redevelopment occurred between 1820 and 1825. One was the building of a terrace of seven houses between the Banqueting Hall (and the adjoining Gwydyr House) and the river, on a new street known as Whitehall Gardens; the other was a terrace of eight houses (on the site of Richmond House) built at right angles to Whitehall and known as Richmond Terrace. In between these two developments was Montagu House, which was rebuilt in a chateau style in 1860. Among the residents in Whitehall Gardens had been Peel at No. 4 from 1824 to 1850, and Disraeli at No. 2 from 1875 to 1878 ('in May 1875 Cabinets were held in his house in Whitehall Gardens as he could not venture to cross the road to Downing Street'—quoted in *Survey of London*, Vol. 13 (1930), p. 209). The leases of Whitehall Gardens, Richmond Terrace and Montagu House reverted to the Crown early in the twentieth century and further redevelopment was in prospect. Gwydyr House had been acquired by the Crown in 1840, after it had been occupied for a few years by the Reform Club. Whitehall Gardens was demolished in 1939 and Montagu House in 1947, and the whole site is now occupied by the Main Building of the Ministry of Defence.

267. In 1904 No. 2 Whitehall Gardens became the Office of the newly-formed Committee of Imperial Defence; it became the Office of the War Cabinet in December 1916, and to meet the needs of the growing staff Nos. 1, 3 and 4 were quickly taken over. Nos. 1–4 Whitehall Gardens remained the Offices of the Cabinet, the Committee of Imperial Defence, the Economic Advisory Council and the Minister for Co-ordination of Defence until July 1938, when in anticipation of the demolition of Whitehall Gardens, the Office moved to a part of Richmond Terrace, and the staff of the Economic Advisory Council transferred to Gwydyr House.

268. By November 1939 the Office occupied the whole of Richmond Terrace, and in the middle of 1940 expanded into part of the New Police (Curtis Green) Building on the Embankment. Meanwhile, as part of the general preparations for war, a 'Central War Room' (later renamed the 'Cabinet War Room') had been built under the Storey's Gate side of the South Block, or 'New Public Offices' (i.e. the Edwardian building bounded by Whitehall, Great George Street, Storey's Gate and King Charles Street), to provide emergency meeting accommodation for the Cabinet and chiefs of staff committee; by the early months of the war much of the basement had been strengthened and the top two floors evacuated as a precaution against fire. The South Block, strengthened below and emptied above, was intended as the headquarters of government and in December 1940 the War Cabinet Office took possession of most of the first and second floors and shared the building with the Air Ministry, G.H.Q. Home Forces and small senior staffs of certain other departments; the postal address was Great George Street, S.W.1. Notwithstanding that some sections of the Office were outhoused—the Central Statistical Office, after many vicissitudes, in Church House (Dean's Yard) and others in Gwydyr House, Audit House (Embankment) and Norfolk House (St. James's Square)—the accommodation problem in the South Block quickly became acute; some ministers demanded offices for themselves and their secretaries, rooms had to be found for visiting ministers and for liaison officers from the Dominions and the United States, new organisations (e.g. the Production Executive) were being set up and existing staffs expanded. By the middle of 1941 the upper floors had been brought back into use, and the Lord President's sub-committee on accommodation (LP(A)—CAB 71/31–34) had to adjudicate on several occasions between different claimants. Some relief was given in 1942 when G.H.Q. Home Forces moved to Horseferry House, and although the position remained difficult the later papers on CAB 21/807 suggest that some stability was then achieved.

269. In the event relatively little use was made of the Cabinet War Room for meetings of the War Cabinet, although it was frequently used for ministerial meetings and for staff conferences in the evenings; the map room adjacent to it was kept fully operational; the Joint Planning Staff and the Joint Intelligence Committee worked continuously in the protected basement, which also provided sleeping accommodation for those required to stay in the office. The building was never damaged by enemy action and save at time of heavy air attack the main work of the Office was carried out on the second floor. In 1945 the Central Statistical Office rejoined the Office in Great George Street and the whole Office remained there until the secretariat transferred to the Old Treasury Building in Whitehall during 1964; the CSO remained in Great George Street.

270. In Whitehall Gardens, the Office had been 250 yards distant from 10 Downing Street and before 1939 most government departments lay within a radius of half a mile. This proximity was a matter of some convenience to ministers and officials, particularly when distribution of papers was made by messengers on foot or bicycle. When the Office moved to Great George Street in 1940, and when several departments were dispersed from the Whitehall neighbourhood, the centre of gravity shifted, with some inconvenience, although the distribution problem was eased by the increasing use of motor vehicles.

CHAPTER 3

THE CABINET AND COMMITTEE OF IMPERIAL DEFENCE BEFORE 1917

Eighteenth century

301. There is little in the public records about the proceedings of the Cabinet before the establishment of the Cabinet Office in 1916. Its members were Privy Counsellors, bound by the oath of secrecy; it involved no expenditure from public funds; and it had no minute book. What source material survives is mostly in the Royal Archives; there is some in private collections, and political memoirs cast light on particular episodes or controversies.

302. The Cabinet emerged by a slow and nebulous process during the eighteenth century; the nucleus appears to have consisted of a group of Crown servants, including the First Lord of the Treasury, the Lord Chancellor, the Lord President of the Council and the two Secretaries of State, who were joined on occasions by other Privy Counsellors in whom the Sovereign had particular confidence for the time being. As George I and his successor were frequently abroad, the group met in the King's absence, offered advice to him collectively—and if they were of one mind, their pressure would be considerable—and were then individually responsible for the execution of policies of which he had approved. Walpole as First Lord of the Treasury assumed a dominant role, drove out those who would not accept his leadership and established a position which under his successors became that of Prime Minister; and as a member of the House of Commons he formed the link between the executive and the legislature which has remained a cardinal feature of the British constitution. For a period that link was jeopardised by the attempt of George III to assert his personal authority and to insist that his ministers were solely and directly responsible to him, but during the nineteenth century the choice of the ministry substantially passed from the Sovereign to the House of Commons, and the Sovereign was gradually but effectively excluded from active participation in political affairs.

303. Much of the advice tendered by the Cabinet to the Sovereign in the early period was presumably conveyed orally at audiences given to ministers, but it seems that on some important matters a formal minute was sent in manuscript by one of the Secretaries of State. In the published correspondence of George III over 200 such minutes are printed (of which half are dated between 1780 and 1781).* Practice relating to these formal minutes in the first part of the nineteenth century is described in the correspondence quoted in *The Private Papers of Sir Robert Peel*, edited by C. S. Parker (1899), pp. 496–499.

304. There is some evidence that formal minutes of advice were sent on occasions thereafter (cf. Jennings, *op. cit.*, pp. 270–271); perhaps the last was that of 15 November 1910, as follows:

> The Cabinet has very carefully considered the situation created by the failure of the Conference [on House of Lords reform], in view of the declaration of

---

* Sir J. Fortescue, *Correspondence of George III* (6 vols, 1927–1928); A. Aspinall, *Later Correspondence of George III* (5 vols, 1962–1970).

policy made on their behalf by the Prime Minister in the House of Commons on the 14th of April, 1910.

The advice which they feel it their duty to tender to His Majesty is as follows:

An immediate dissolution of Parliament, as soon as the necessary parts of the Budget, the provision of Old Age Pensions to paupers, and one or two other matters have been disposed of.

The House of Lords to have the opportunity, if they desired it, at the same time (but not so as to postpone the date of the dissolution), to discuss the Government Resolutions.

His Majesty's Ministers cannot, however, take the responsibility of advising a dissolution, unless they may understand that, in the event of the policy of the Government being approved by an adequate majority in the new House of Commons, His Majesty will be ready to exercise his constitutional powers (which may involve the Prerogative of creating Peers), if needed, to secure that effect shall be given to the decision of the country.

His Majesty's Ministers are fully alive to the importance of keeping the name of the King out of the sphere of party and electoral controversy. They take upon themselves, as is their duty, the entire and exclusive responsibility for the policy which they will place before the electorate.

His Majesty will doubtless agree that it would be undesirable in the interests of the State, that any communication of the intentions of the Crown should be made public, unless and until the actual occasion should arise.

(Harold Nicolson, *King George V* (1952), p. 136)

Prime Minister's letters to Sovereign

305. Apart from formal minutes, a more detailed account of proceedings after the middle of the nineteenth century exists in the form of the private letters sent by the Prime Minister to the Sovereign after each meeting, recording the main topics discussed or decided. The originals are preserved in the Royal Archives; copies of some are printed in the *Letters of Queen Victoria* and photocopies of the 1700 letters written between 1868 and 1916 are in the Public Record Office (CAB 41). Drafts of the letters exist in various private collections, including the Gladstone papers (British Library), the Salisbury papers (Christ Church, Oxford) and the Asquith papers (Bodleian). The practice appears to have originated with Melbourne (letter of 27 December 1837) and may have been a kindly act on his part to initiate the young queen in the art and mystery of government; but the series became well established, and now forms the only continuous record which exists of the deliberations at the highest level during a period when there was rapid economic development at home, and when the British Empire was reaching its zenith. The form, style and length of the letters follow no pattern, and vary from the flowery effusions of Disraeli to the terse comments of Campbell-Bannerman. Most have some recognisable connection with the accounts of the controversies given at greater length in the memoirs or biographies of the participants. The drafting of these letters, and copying fair in manuscript, must have involved a heavy burden on a Prime Minister who, after presiding at a meeting which would often have been difficult or acrimonious, had other duties to perform, including attendance in Parliament and possibly preparing for a debate.

306. To preserve secrecy, much of the business in the Cabinet in the early days would have arisen on the basis of an oral explanation by a member, but it was inevitable that ministers would increasingly make use of written material either to give background information or to outline some proposal for which they sought

B

collective assent. Little of this material is on departmental files and what there is is rarely identifiable as having been referred to the Cabinet. What was circulated was regarded as personal to the recipient as a Privy Counsellor, and there was some expectation that it would be destroyed. Without a secretariat there was no one to make a set of papers, and such as survive are those preserved by individual ministers. There appears to have been a fairly substantial circulation during the nineteenth century; Sir Henry Taylor in his *Autobiography* (2 vols., 1885), p. 67, describes how when a clerk in the Colonial Office in 1824 he was 'working on the preparation of a paper which was immediately printed at the Foreign Office private press and laid before the Cabinet. A clerk was sent to see the type broken up and receive the printer's declaration that he had delivered all the impressions taken off and kept no copy'. PRO Handbooks Nos. 4 and 9 contain lists of 5000 printed papers circulated between 1880 and 1916, and traced in private collections; photocopies of these papers form CAB 37. The collection for these years is unlikely to be complete and no search has yet been made in private collections for papers of earlier years. (The Handbooks give some useful information about the nature of these papers.)

307. Before the days of the duplicating machine, most papers were printed on the Foreign Office press, and unless the minister had his own means of distribution, were circulated in locked red boxes by the Prime Minister's private secretary to the members of the Cabinet (but not apparently to the Sovereign). None of the papers bore symbols or copy numbers, or means of reference other than a subject title and the initials of the author.

308. In recent times, the arrangement of meetings of the Cabinet appears to have been undertaken by the Prime Minister's private secretary, who issued a summons and presumably gave the Prime Minister a rough agenda referring to the papers which he knew to have been circulated, and to other matters which he knew to be active.

309. Meetings were normally held at 10 Downing Street, but sometimes in the House of Commons; Salisbury and some of his predecessors held meetings in the Foreign Office (G. W. E. Russell, *Collections and Recollections* (1898), p. 454).

Misunderstandings

310. After discussion in Cabinet each minister took executive action in accordance with his recollection or understanding of the decision that had been reached. On the majority of problems no difficulty appears to have arisen, but in the absence of a written record confusion was possible; and on pp. 62–69 of *Diplomacy by Conference* Hankey records a number of instances where there was serious misunderstanding as to what precisely had been agreed. In a debate in the House of Lords on 19 June 1918, Curzon, speaking as a member of the War Cabinet, described the system thus:

> There was no agenda, there was no order of business. Any minister requiring to bring up a matter either of departmental or of public importance had to seek the permission of the Prime Minister to do so. No one else, broadly speaking, was warned in advance. It was difficult for any minister to secure an interstice in the discussion in which he could place his own case. No record whatever was kept of our proceedings, except the private and personal letter written by the Prime Minister to the Sovereign, the contents of which, of course, are never seen by anybody else. The Cabinet often had the very haziest notion as to what its decisions were; and I appeal not only to my experience, but to the experience of every Cabinet Minister who sits in this House, and to the records contained

in the memoirs of half-a-dozen Prime Ministers in the past, that cases frequently arose when the matter was left so much in doubt that a minister went away and acted upon what he thought was a decision which subsequently turned out to be no decision at all, or was repudiated by his colleagues. No one will deny that a system, however embedded in the traditions of the past and consecrated by constitutional custom, which was attended by these defects, was a system which was destined immediately it came into contact with the hard realities of war, to crumble into dust at once . . . and to make a long story short, I do not think anyone will deny that the old Cabinet system had irretrievably broken down, both as a war machine and as a peace machine.

There was some evidence that Curzon may have been over-stressing the weaknesses (*see* Annex 1 for comments by Bonham-Carter and Harris, and for Hankey's counter view).

311. In the Prime Minister's letters to the Sovereign (CAB 41) there are occasional indications that the Cabinet had appointed a committee to give further consideration to some problem. Among them are:

(a) on 21 October 1909 Grey, McKenna, Morley, Churchill, Runciman and Harcourt were appointed to consider a proposal that the concession of the Suez Canal Company should be extended for 40 years from 1968, and to report at the next meeting; there is no subsequent reference to any report.

(b) on 11 March 1914 Crewe, Birrell, Churchill, Seely and Simon were appointed to consider the military situation in Ulster; Asquith records that at the meeting on 17 March 1914 they made a preliminary report that additional troops should be moved from Great Britain, and the Cabinet approved.

But as before 1914 there was no provision for any secretarial equipment, no record of the proceedings or decisions remains.

312. Shortly after the Second World War Brook endeavoured to obtain the personal recollections of a few of those acquainted with Cabinet procedure before 1916. Notes by Creedy, Bonham-Carter, Harris, Hankey and Samuel are on file 4/1/56 and as they cover a number of different points, and in some respects are conflicting, full extracts are reproduced in Annex 1. The variety of the points made and their occasional conflict reflect the fact that before the First World War the Cabinet was a group of politicians whose membership was liable to sudden change, which was held together by party and personal loyalties, and which in the interests of confidentiality could meet together satisfactorily without the support of a secretariat to give some form to their proceedings.

Defence Questions

313. In the decade before the First World War, the Committee of Imperial Defence, with the Prime Minister as president, developed in parallel with the Cabinet and provided a secretarial equipment which in due course became an integral part of the Cabinet Office.

314. A principal ancestor of the CID was the Colonial Defence Committee appointed in 1878 by the Colonial Office, with representatives from the War Office and the Admiralty, to consider the defences of the more important colonial ports (CAB 7/1). It lapsed in the following year with the appointment of the Royal Commission (Carnarvon) on the defence of British possessions and commerce overseas, which reported in 1882 urging the provision of coaling stations whose defence should increasingly become the responsibility of the individual colonies (CAB 7/2–5). The Colonial Defence Committee was reconstituted in 1885 under the chairmanship of the permanent under-secretary of the Colonial Office, with representatives from the two service departments and from the Treasury. The Committee, which was mainly concerned with the defence schemes of the various colonies, continued until 1904 when it became a standing committee of the CID, and was later renamed the Oversea Defence Committee (ODC). The minutes are in CAB 7/7–15; the memoranda in CAB 8, 9, 10 and 11; and CAB 18/29–95 contain the annual returns on the naval and military resources of the colonies from 1886 to 1915.

315. A few weeks after the reconstitution of the Colonial Defence Committee in 1885, George Sydenham Clarke was appointed secretary and continued until 1892. He was closely associated with defence matters in a wider field as secretary of the Hartington Commission in 1888, and was recalled from Australia to be a member of the Esher Committee in 1903. He became secretary of the CID in 1904, retired in 1907 and played an important part in laying the foundations for closer co-operation between the services and with the Dominions.

316. A Royal Commission (under Lord Hartington—later Duke of Devonshire) was set up in 1888 to inquire into the civil and professional administration of the Admiralty and the War Office and their relations with each other and the Treasury (C.5979 of 1890); HO 73/35 and 36 contain the full evidence. It recommended *inter alia*

the formation of a naval and military council, which should probably be presided over by the Prime Minister, and consist of the parliamentary heads of the two services, and their principal professional advisers. . . . It would be essential to the usefulness of such a council and to the interests of the country, that the proceedings and decisions should be duly recorded, instances having occurred in which Cabinet decisions have been differently understood by the two departments, and have become practically a dead letter.

No action was taken on this recommendation, but a Joint Naval and Military Committee on Defence began to meet under the parliamentary secretary to the War Office to consider matters of policy affecting coastal defences of interest to both the War Office and the Admiralty (CAB 18/22). Both the Colonial Defence Committee and the Joint Naval and Military Committee were at junior level and in view of the vested interests of the two service departments were relatively ineffective.

317. Following the enforced resignation in 1895 of the Duke of Cambridge as commander-in-chief of the British Army (who had opposed innovation), a Cabinet Committee on Defence was appointed with the Lord President (Duke of Devonshire—previously Lord Hartington) as chairman. The minutes which passed between Balfour, Salisbury, Devonshire, Goschen and Lansdowne (CAB 1/2/15) suggest that there was a good deal of confusion about what its functions would be. It appears to have been intended that the professional heads of the services should be present as assessors but not as members, and that records would be kept in duplicate by the permanent secretaries of the two departments. In November 1900 Devonshire, the chairman, recorded (CAB 37/53/71):

The Committee has been nothing more than an informal committee of the Cabinet occasionally calling into council the commander-in-chief, the First Naval Lord or other professional advisers. . . . It has met rarely and generally without any definite agenda. The professional members have generally only been present during a part of the proceedings, and have rather been asked to give information on certain points, or to explain certain plans or proposals, than to take part in discussion. No minutes have been kept, and in general there have been no definite decisions to record. Either there has been a general understanding and agreement which the department concerned had afterwards to embody in a complete form, or else conflicting opinions had been expressed on which the committee had no authority to decide, and which had to be remitted for further inter-departmental discussion or Cabinet decision.

CAB 37/53/71 contains other minutes by Goschen, Lansdowne and Hicks-Beach, which generally deprecated the presence of a secretary, but would admit professional advisers to give information and advice, provided they did not take part in the discussions or decisions of the committee: 'They are not Privy Counsellors, so that free discussion before them, between ministers, is difficult; and they have not the responsibility for decision which belongs to ministers only.'

318. The country had been shocked by the disasters in the Boer War, and the Elgin Commission (of which Esher was a member) reported during 1903 (Cd. 1789–1792) drawing attention to the lack of preparations. Meanwhile, in November 1902, Brodrick and Selborne (the ministerial heads of the War Office and the Admiralty respectively) had submitted to the Cabinet a strong memorandum on 'Improvement of the intellectual equipment of the services' (CAB 37/63/152), recommending a reconstitution of the Defence Committee under the Prime Minister, with a limited number of Cabinet ministers and with the service chiefs. The first meeting of what shortly came to be called the Committee of Imperial Defence was held on 18 December 1902 with Devonshire in the chair and the Prime Minister attending; it was agreed that there should be a civilian secretary to keep minutes and records (CAB 2/1). Devonshire continued to preside until August 1903, but thereafter the Prime Minister took the chair, those present generally being the Secretaries of State for War and India, the First Lord of the Admiralty and senior officers of the service departments. At the 26th meeting on 11 December 1903, F. W. Borden (the Canadian Minister of Militia) was present (*see* facsimile on pages 30–33).

Esher Report and the CID

319. Following the reports of the Elgin Commission, the Prime Minister had appointed Esher (who had been a member of that Commission), Fisher (chief of naval staff) and G. S. Clarke (formerly secretary of the Colonial Defence Committee) to make recommendations for the reconstitution of the War Office. In their first report of 11 January 1904 (Cd. 1932) the Esher Committee explained that 'Before proceeding to discuss the reconstruction of the War Office we are impelled to urge the immediate provision of what is in actual fact the cornerstone of the needed Edifice of Reform'. They assumed that the Prime Minister would preside over the Defence Committee and recommended:

The permanent nucleus of the Defence Committee should consist of:

I. A Permanent Secretary who should be appointed for five years renewable at pleasure.

II. Under this official, two naval officers, selected by the Admiralty, two military officers chosen by the War Office, and two Indian officers, nominated by the Viceroy, with, if possible, one or more representatives of the Colonies. These officers should not be of high rank, and the duration of their appointment should be limited to two years.

The duties of the permanent nucleus of the Defence Committee would be:

A. To consider all questions of Imperial Defence from the point of view of the Navy, the Military Forces, India and the Colonies.

B. To obtain and collate information from the Admiralty, War Office, India Office and other departments of State.

4 . 12 . 1903.

(44)

10, Downing Street,
Whitehall. S.W.

Mr. Balfour with his humble duty to Your
Majesty begs respectfully to say that perhaps
the most interesting thing in principle, which
the Cabinet effected at today's sitting, related
to a new development of the Defence Committee
which, unimportant at the moment, may
have important results. Mr. Balfour
pointed out to his colleagues that the Defence
Committee was a body summoned by the Prime
Minister to aid him in regard to those large
military & naval policy
questions which lie outside the departmental

Letter from A. J. Balfour to King Edward VII (*see para.* 318).

work both of the S. of S. for War, and the First
Lord of the Admiralty. Elasticity is given by
the power which the Prime Minister for the time
being ought to possess of selecting the person to be
Summoned to each meeting. No one has a _right_
to come: though of course the advice of the
Committee would carry no weight unless it was
representative of the best military and naval opinion.
Nor a body so constituted has an extraordinary
flexibility of adaptation to varying circumstances.
It may be made, on occasion, to include representatives
of the Colonies - which is true of no other element
in our ordinary constitutional machinery. It thus
contains the potentiality of being an 'Imperial

council' dealing with Imperial questions. If indeed representation of the over-sea Empire were there _as of course_; the committee would become unmanageably large for its ordinary work. But as, at each meeting, the council is (so to speak) constituted afresh according to its business for _that meeting_, this will not happen.   2=

Balfour has been for some time on the look out for an occasion to put the theory, then explained, into practical operation: and the occasion has now presented itself. The War Minister of Canada is coming over here & recommend some modification in the constitution of the Canadian Militia. With the consent of the cabinet, and he trusts with Your Majesty's approbation, Mr. Balfour proposes to summon him (next Friday) to the Defence Committee, not as a witness, or even as an adviser, but as a <u>member</u>. He will be appointed, that is to say, for this particular purpose, and on this particular day, with all the other members of the committee on equal terms. Unfortunately it appears that this particular gentleman is of rather inferior quality:— but if the compliment to Canada remains the same, and we shall be careful what we say before him! A new precedent of great imperial significance will have thus been set.

    C. To prepare any documents required by the Prime Minister and the Defence Committee, anticipating their needs as far as possible.

    D. To furnish such advice as the Committee may ask for in regard to defence questions involving more than one Department of State.

    E. To keep adequate records for the use of the Cabinet of the day and of its successors.

320. Balfour commended most of the Esher proposals to the Cabinet (CAB 37/69/33) and substance was given to them by a Treasury minute of 4 May 1904 (Cd. 2200). The salaries and expenses of the secretary, of two assistant secretaries and of any necessary clerical assistance would be borne under a special sub-head of the Treasury vote, 'so that the House of Commons will have an opportunity of discussing the policy of H.M.G. in relation to the defence of the Empire as a whole in a manner which is not now possible seeing that debate must be strictly confined to the subject matter of the vote under consideration'. This was a significant constitutional innovation, as any normal Cabinet committee had no identifiable expenditure, and Parliament was therefore unaware of its existence, or able to discuss its policies.

321. The CID met with varying regularity until the outbreak of the First World War. The Prime Minister as the only permanent member was generally present; the service ministers and their principal advisers were always present; the Secretary of State for India, the Foreign Secretary and the Chancellor of the Exchequer usually attended; other ministers attended as the nature of the business required; and Esher and Balfour (when in opposition) were sometimes present. The Dominion Prime Ministers attended meetings in August 1909 and in May 1911, and while ministers from the Dominions were occasionally present, there was no organised or regular means of invitation.

322. The main work of the CID was conducted through committees and sub-committees generally at the official level. The principal standing bodies were:

    Colonial/Oversea Defence (ODC), CAB 7, 8, 9, 10 and 11

    Home Ports Defence (HPDC), CAB 12 and 13

    Air (AC and AP), CAB 14

    Co-ordination of Departmental Action (War Book) (K and W), CAB 15.

In addition, a number of *ad hoc* committees were appointed whose records are in CAB 16. Some of these had a ministerial chairman, and important among them was that presided over by Asquith in 1909 to inquire into certain questions of naval policy raised by Lord Charles Beresford (CAB 16/9A, 9B).

323. G. S. Clarke was secretary till 1907, and was succeeded by Sir Charles Ottley; Hankey (who had become an assistant secretary in 1908) succeeded Ottley in 1912. The two original assistant secretaries were serving officers nominated by the War Office and Admiralty respectively; a third was appointed in 1908 on the nomination of the India Office.

324. It was the practice from the outset that full minutes should be kept of the meetings of each of the subordinate bodies, and that the memoranda for consideration should be separately filed and associated with the minutes of that body. Matters to be raised in the CID itself, generally in the form of reports from the subordinate bodies, were contained in printed memoranda on pale green paper which were allocated to one of four series:

    Series A   Home Defence   CAB 3

         B   Miscellaneous   CAB 4

         C   Colonial Defence   CAB 5

         D   Indian Defence   CAB 6.

The minutes of the CID itself (CAB 2) were full and were circulated in printed form to the Sovereign and to those who had been present. It was established at the 99th meeting on 14 May 1908 that all minutes and memoranda should be returned to the secretary, apart from those held by officials who should pass them to their successors in office.

325. Thus before 1914 the secretariat of the CID had developed a technique for the orderly conduct of business in a field where more than one department was involved; sub-committees were organised, meetings were summoned, memoranda prepared and full minutes circulated, and records and indexes were kept which assisted in continuity of administration and of defence policy. The CID, which provided a forum at which professional advisers were present for consideration of those problems where the naval, military and political interests interlocked or conflicted, inevitably had some influence on the Cabinet.

326. Certain comments should be made about the CID before the First World War.

(a) In spite of its title, it was never fully 'imperial'. The Dominions were apprehensive of the commitments they might be expected to undertake, and preferred to reserve defence matters for consideration at the Imperial Conferences.

(b) Nominally it was a consultative and advisory body without administrative or executive functions. But in view of its composition some qualification is required; the Prime Minister was chairman, and when any question came before the Cabinet several of its more important members were already committed to views expressed in their capacity as members of the CID; and the full Cabinet would have the advantage of learning the views of their colleagues formed after the subject had been discussed in the presence of qualified experts.

(c) With hindsight it is surprising what little attention was devoted to the mobilisation of civilian resources to support the military and naval effort in war. Problems of manpower and munitions production were largely ignored.

(d) It is doubtful whether the CID made or could make any successful attempt to break into the vested interests of the War Office and the Admiralty, particularly on strategic planning (cf. the discussion on the action to be taken in the event of a European war at the 114th meeting on 23 August 1911, and that on the strategical position in the Mediterranean at the 117th meeting on 4 July 1912).

327. PRO Handbooks No. 6 lists chronologically the main papers of the CID to 1914.

Hankey and CID staff 1914–1916

328. With the outbreak of war, the CID as such fell into abeyance and the immediate control of the conduct of the war passed successively to the War Council (5 August 1914–14 May 1915—CAB 22/1), the Dardanelles Committee (7 June–30 October 1915—CAB 22/2) and the War Committee (3 November 1915–1 December 1916—CAB 22/3–81). Asquith as Prime Minister was chairman of each; the membership was not clearly defined, and attendance fluctuated with changes in the holders of ministerial office (a coalition was formed on 25 May 1915) and of professional appointments. Asquith was jealous of the position of the full Cabinet of 20 members, and few of the important matters discussed in the War Council or the two committees were not subsequently considered afresh in Cabinet where several of the members had little direct interest in operations.

329. Hankey and his staff of the CID were drawn in as a secretariat initially for the War Council and subsequently for the two committees. A 'G' series of memoranda was instituted (CAB 24/1 and 2) for the circulation to ministers of material directly relating to the war, and which followed the high standards of the CID in being neatly printed with an exposition of the problem and containing firm recommendations. But unlike those of the CID, the minutes were not agreed copies which had been passed round for correction; in view of the pressure of work and the need for secrecy, only a single manuscript copy of 'secretary's notes' was kept, to which were attached a miscellany of unreferenced papers which had been handed round at the meetings. The secretariat communicated the conclusions immediately after each meeting only to those responsible for taking action. In sending his memorandum of evidence to the Dardanelles Commission of Inquiry (CAB 19/29 of 6 September 1916) Hankey explained the arrangements for recording decisions.

330. CAB 22/1–3 contain the secretary's notes of meetings between August 1914 and February 1916; they are printed and all bear dates of printing after the middle of 1916. Hankey had evidently taken steps to reproduce the notes in a tidy form should their production be required by the Dardanelles Commission of Inquiry. The original manuscript notes and attachments have presumably been destroyed, but some idea of their untidy and possibly confusing state can be derived from the records of the meetings of the War Committee from February to December 1916 (a period with which the Dardanelles Commission of Inquiry was not concerned), which have not been printed and are contained in CAB 22/4–81. An innovation, however, was the circulation to the Cabinet in printed form of extracts from the conclusions of the War Committee (WC series in CAB 22/82).

331. While the immediate control of the conduct of the war had hesitatingly passed to the three successive committees mentioned above, the full Cabinet was frequently meeting. CAB 37 contains 650 printed papers for 1915, and 850 for 1916 (the numbers are unlikely to be complete) which appear to have been circulated to ministers, and dealt with a wide range of matters, including military operations, foreign policy, production, manpower and conscription, shipping, etc. Some were for information only and unlikely to have been discussed; none bore any regular means of identification and the burden on ministers in attending a Cabinet without an agenda and having those papers available which might be discussed, must have been considerable. Copies of Asquith's letters to the King describing the proceedings are in CAB 41/35–37, but there was no written record available to ministers of the decisions they had taken in an ever-widening field of governmental activity.

332. Meanwhile the CID staff was becoming useful in other directions. Apart from his fact-finding visit to the Dardanelles in July 1915, and accompanying the Prime Minister to several inter-allied conferences (IC—CAB 28), Hankey (or his staff) acted as secretary to three important Cabinet committees:

War Policy (CAB 27/2), which met with Crewe as chairman during August and September 1915, and concluded that conscription was necessary.

Co-ordination Committee on the Military and Financial Effort (CAB 27/3 and 4), which met with Asquith in the chair during January–April 1916, to consider the size and cost of the army and the numbers that could be provided without disastrous results to trade and industry.

Joint War-Air Committee (CAB 27/5) which met with Derby as chairman during February–April 1916, to co-ordinate supplies and design for the naval and military air services.

333. A list of other Cabinet committees 1914–1916 is given in Appendix C to

PRO Handbooks No. 9. CID 195-B lists eight inter-departmental committees in August 1914 which had been appointed to consider questions arising out of the war; CID 235-B shows that by March 1918 the number had risen to 165. In the original CID list the only committee composed wholly of Cabinet ministers was the Co-ordinating Committee on Trade and Supplies; it had vanished from the list of March 1915, and as none of its records have been traced, it may be assumed to have been still-born.

334. After two years of war Hankey and the CID staff had, on the basis of the CID expertise, found themselves serving ministers collectively in most of their activities other than as members of the Cabinet. The Cabinet itself was creaking and losing public confidence, and Asquith resigned on 5 December 1916.

(PRO Handbooks No. 9 lists chronologically the Cabinet papers circulated in 1915 and 1916, and the papers of the War Council, Dardanelles Committee and War Committee.)

CHAPTER 4

THE WAR CABINET 1916–1919 AND THE LLOYD GEORGE ADMINISTRATION TO OCTOBER 1922

401. The Cabinet Office records are silent on the political manoeuvres which resulted in the emergence of Lloyd George as Prime Minister on 6 December 1916, but he had no doubt taken Hankey into his confidence in framing the three-fold reorganisation he brought about—the strengthening of the Prime Minister's secretariat, the new ministries and the War Cabinet.*

402. Brief mention may first be made of the ' Garden Suburb '—the term given by *The Times* in January 1917 to the huts then being hurriedly erected in the garden of 10 Downing Street to house the expanded secretariat, of which the most prominent members were W. G. S. Adams (concerned with domestic issues, including food production and Ireland) and Philip Kerr (later Lord Lothian, concerned with imperial and inter-allied conferences). This secretariat kept Lloyd George informed of major developments and of points where he might bring pressure to bear on departmental ministers. After hostilities ceased it became increasingly influential in the field of foreign affairs, and generated much suspicion and hostility with the Foreign Office. While in the public mind it was often confused with the Cabinet Office, Hankey ensured that the functions of the two were kept separate and relations throughout were generally cordial. It is perhaps a matter for speculation whether had Hankey been of different calibre, the Prime Minister's Office would not have absorbed the Cabinet Office, and developed as a Prime Minister's department, and a presidential form of government have resulted. Most of the surviving records of the Prime Minister's secretariat are understood to be among the Lloyd George papers in the Beaverbrook Library (but a few are in PREM 1).

403. In the few days before the end of 1916 new ministries had been created for Shipping, Labour, Food and Pensions, and during 1917 for National Service, Air, Reconstruction and Information. These took over administrative responsibility for functions, which if they had been exercised at all, had lain uneasily between two or more departments, and had failed to get that degree of ministerial attention which the changing pattern of the war required.

War Cabinet

404. But the main piece of reorganisation was the creation of the War Cabinet, which undertook, subject to Parliament, the supreme direction of the war effort; originally it was composed of Lloyd George as Prime Minister, Bonar Law, Curzon, Milner and Henderson, of whom Bonar Law as Chancellor of the Exchequer (and Leader both of the House of Commons and of the Conservative party) was the only member with departmental duties. The remainder were free to devote their whole attention to the task of co-ordination and direction, and to relieve the score of departmental ministers

---

* On pp. 592–596 of Vol. II of *The Supreme Command* and on pp. 342–346 of *Hankey, Man of Secrets* (Vol. I) there are references to the Hankey, Milner and Lloyd George papers which relate to ideas on organisation current in December 1916.

from the constant necessity which rested on them under the old Cabinet system of considering those wider aspects of public policy which often had nothing to do with their departments, but for which they were collectively responsible. They are, therefore, now able to devote a far larger part of their time to those administrative duties which have become more exacting as the national activities have expanded under the pressure of war (p. 4 of War Cabinet Report for 1917, Cd. 9005).

405. Curzon, Milner and Henderson, whose fields of special interest were shipping, food and manpower respectively, had their offices initially in 2 Whitehall Gardens, and it is the recollection of some of the survivors of the period of being frequently summoned there to meet individual members of the War Cabinet who would adjudicate on the less important matters in dispute between departments, and attempt to discover any weaknesses or inefficiencies in administration. These meetings were informal, and no record of them remains in the Office, although there may be some account on departmental files.

406. The more important matters were reserved for more formal committees or for the War Cabinet itself. In view of his experience Hankey was the obvious choice as secretary and it was his endeavour (cf. p. 23 of Haldane Lecture, 1942) to introduce the methods and procedures of the CID into as wide a range of Cabinet business as possible, and to this end to assemble the memoranda giving information or outlining the points for decision, to include them in an agenda, and then to record the decisions reached and notify them promptly to those concerned. From the outset he achieved his aim so far as the recording and dissemination of decisions was concerned, but he was less successful in getting any orderly arrangement of the flood of paper which poured through the Office for the attention of the War Cabinet. Early in the war, a G series of printed papers had been introduced for the circulation of material which had a defence flavour (*see* para. 330), and the same series continued after December 1916 for the circulation of a few memoranda by War Cabinet ministers and for reports of some high-level committees. The G series (CAB 24/1–5) were well printed and their form and content were in the high tradition of the CID; but the G series had petered out by 1920, and their place been taken by the GT series, which had started in December 1916 (the addition of T to the previous symbol probably stood for 'typed').

407. Before 1914 the number of memoranda circulated to the Cabinet did not exceed 200 in a year; in 1916, including the G series, it was less than 1000; in each year between 1923 and 1938 it was rarely more than 500. But for 1917–1922 the numbers in the GT and later CP series are:

1917	3,200
1918	3,400
1919	2,100
1920	2,000
1921	1,200
1922	800

408. The vast increase was partly due to the circumstances of the war and its aftermath; but in the main it is clear that ministers and officials—particularly in the civil departments—took several years to educate and adjust themselves to the new piece of constitutional machinery which the Office was beginning to provide. It is also fair to recall that Hankey and some of his senior staff who had had experience of the CID procedures were out of the country at inter-allied, peace and other conferences for lengthy periods, and that in their absence Tom Jones and others who remained in London had no previous knowledge of the techniques and were overwhelmed with work. The papers shovelled into the War Cabinet, and now included in the GT and early CP series, are a miscellany; some sought decisions, but most conveyed more or less undigested information in the shape of statistical tables, copies of telegrams sent or received, reports of departmental or other committees, copies of letters from trade associations or the public, copies of departmental memoranda, circulars, etc. Many were of inordinate length; others bore no date; some bore no identification of the author or originating department; others gave no indication that they were for the attention of the Cabinet; and the symbol and serial number were often inserted subsequently in manuscript. It is clear that few of these memoranda were actively considered; some were syphoned off for action by individual members of the War Cabinet; but the more important found their way to the agenda.

409. It was not until the Bonar Law government took office at the end of 1922 that the generality of the memoranda for the Cabinet took on the recognisable shape and form which later prevailed, and which contributed much to the smooth working of the machine. The memoranda in the GT series and later in the CP series from 1917 to the end of 1922 are in CAB 24/6–142; most volumes contain a list of the contents.

410. While most of the papers in the GT and CP series emanated from outside the Office, the Office itself undertook between 1917 and 1922 the preparation and distribution of periodic reports about the development of political and economic affairs in the Dominions, colonies and foreign countries; these reports are in CAB 24/143–157.

411. In sharp contrast to the confusion surrounding the arrangement of the memoranda submitted to the War Cabinet is the orderliness of the minutes recording their proceedings. Meetings were held on most weekdays (sometimes two or even three in a day), generally at 10 Downing Street. In the frequent absence of the Prime Minister at conferences abroad, Bonar Law presided. In addition to the members of the War Cabinet, Balfour (Foreign Secretary) and the professional heads of the services were usually present for the whole or part of the meeting, and less frequently a member of the Prime Minister's secretariat. From June 1917 to January 1919 Smuts, who had represented South Africa at the first meetings of the Imperial War Cabinet, remained in London and attended the War Cabinet as a full member.

412. An agenda had been circulated to all ministers, with a rough time-table and a list of those expected to attend for each item, but with a right to make representations if they had been left off the list for an item in which they were concerned. The system of invitation ensured that ministers, often accompanied by their officials and experts, were present for discussion of matters which affected their departments, but it appears to have caused a good deal of mild irritation to those who were kept waiting to be summoned to the Cabinet room (cf. WC 54 (13)—CAB 23/1).

413. Hankey as secretary was present at the first meeting on 9 December 1916 and at all subsequent meetings unless he was accompanying the Prime Minister at some conference abroad, when his place was usually taken by Tom Jones. The practice developed that the other assistant secretaries would attend for discussion on those topics with which they were dealing, to take a fuller note and to hand out any relevant papers. Immediately after the meeting the minutes were prepared and sent to the members of the War Cabinet, with extracts to the ministers affected by particular decisions and for executive action by them. The records of the 635

meetings of the War Cabinet to the end of October 1919 are contained in CAB 23/1–12, the 'A' minutes which dealt with matters of special secrecy at the time are in CAB 23/13–16 and the 'X' minutes which record conversations on certain military matters are in CAB 23/17. Each volume contains a subject index.

414. The War Cabinet set up a number of committees of which the more important were:

War Policy (WP—CAB 27/6)

This committee, of which the Prime Minister was chairman and which comprised four members of the War Cabinet and the chiefs of staff, held 21 meetings from June to October 1917 and settled most major military questions during that period; after October 1917 such questions reverted to the War Cabinet or the Supreme War Council.

War Priorities (WP—CAB 15/6 and CAB 40/1–171)

Originally intended to deal with the manufacture of aircraft, this committee under Smuts came to deal with and settle questions of priority of all munitions programmes. It worked through a number of interdepartmental boards and committees, whose working papers are in CAB 40.

Eastern Committee (EC—CAB 27/24–39)

Under Curzon, it concerted the interests of the Foreign Office, India Office, War Office, Admiralty, Ministry of Shipping and Treasury in the problems of the Middle East.

Economic Defence and Development (EDDC—CAB 27/44)

Under Austen Chamberlain, it dealt with a wide range of economic matters at home and abroad.

Home Affairs (HAC—CAB 26)

This was originally set up under Cave (Home Secretary) to deal with all matters of internal policy, which did not raise large political issues. It is one of the few committees of the Cabinet which had a continuing existence to 1939, although its functions were gradually limited to the detailed examination of draft Bills and making recommendations to the Cabinet on the legislative time-table (*see also* para. 521).

Demobilisation (DC—CAB 27/41 and 42)

Under Smuts this committee was very active at the end of 1918 (*see also* papers in CAB 33).

415. In view of the novel character of a small Cabinet and to give the public some indication of the political and administrative problems involved in supporting the war effort, two reports of the War Cabinet were published, that for 1917 as Cd. 9005 and that for 1918 as Cmd. 325. Both are models of discretion, which reveal little of underlying tensions and disagreements.

Imperial War Cabinet

416. While the war was in progress, the Office had provided the secretariat for the Imperial War Cabinet, and for the British element in the Supreme War Council. The Imperial War Cabinet, under the chairmanship of Lloyd George and attended by the Prime Ministers or representatives of the Dominions and of India and by senior British ministers, met in two sessions in 1917 and 1918 (IWC—CAB 23/40–44). In addition to military problems, the deliberations covered a wide field of imperial policy, but the body was too large and the responsibilities of those present too diverse for it to justify the title of 'Cabinet' in the sense that it could settle policy and take effective decisions. It did, however, take steps to improve the channel for communication between the Prime Ministers. Parallel with the meetings of the Imperial War Cabinet were meetings of the Imperial War Conference, with representatives at a lower level, under the chairmanship of the Colonial Secretary, and dealing mainly with the economic problems of the Empire and particularly those of raw materials (CAB 32/1/1 and 2). The report of the War Cabinet for 1918 (Cmd. 325) gives an enthusiastic account of the expectations held for the permanent establishment of the Imperial Cabinet system.

417. Following the intermittent conferences between the heads of the allied governments early in the war, which had failed to secure any close or continuous working on common plans, a meeting was held at Rapallo on 7 November 1917 at which Lloyd George (Britain), Sonnino (Italy) and Painlevé (France) agreed to establish a Supreme War Council to secure such adjustment and co-ordination of national policies as would make possible the execution of a single comprehensive strategic plan of allied objectives. The three Prime Ministers met at eight full sessions during the following 12 months (with the U.S.A. holding a watching brief), and Hankey acted as the British secretary; but the main work of co-ordination in the military sphere was undertaken by the Permanent Military Representatives (including Bliss from the U.S.A.) who set up an elaborate organisation at Versailles, of which the British element, attached to the War Cabinet secretariat, was initially headed by General Sir Henry Wilson (later by Rawlinson), and whose staff included Major A. P. Wavell and Lieut.-Colonel L. S. Amery (CAB 25 and CAB 28/3–5; *see also* CAB 21/697).

418. Much of the work originally contemplated for the Supreme War Council was superseded by the appointment in April 1918 of Foch to the supreme command of the allied armies on the western front, but the Versailles organisation continued to keep watch on developments in the Balkans and on the fronts opening in Russia and Siberia. The Supreme War Council in the First World War never approached the unity of purpose of the Churchill–Roosevelt conferences in the second, but the Versailles organisation, which had contained under one roof representatives of the staffs of four powers, gave those associated with it a useful experience when many of them left to become members of their delegations to the Peace Conference.

Peace Conference

419. At the end of 1918 the question arose whether the arrangements on the British side for the forthcoming Peace Conference should be made by the Foreign Office or by the secretariat of the Cabinet Office. In the event it was decided that as a number of departments, in addition to the Foreign Office, were concerned in the treaty, as contact had to be maintained with the Dominions, and as Hankey had established contacts during the war with the home departments and with the Dominion Premiers, the responsibility should rest with the Cabinet Office, which established a branch office in Paris, organised on similar lines to that in London. In addition to organising the British delegation, Hankey himself was appointed by Clemenceau to be secretary of the Council of Four (the Prime Ministers of Britain, France and Italy and the President of the U.S.A.) by whom the major decisions were taken (the voluminous records of the Conference are in CAB 29/7–40).

Peace-time Cabinet

420. The demands of the Peace Conference kept the Prime Minister and Hankey away from London for lengthy periods during the first part of 1919. The War Cabinet in London was kept in touch with the proceedings in Paris, but other problems were growing—unrest in Ireland and in India, intervention in Russia and industrial troubles at home. Meetings of the War Cabinet were held less frequently, but the number of ministers attending for the whole meeting and not only for particular items gradually increased; what were virtually full Cabinets were meeting by the autumn, and the replacement of the small War Cabinet by a peace-time Cabinet of 20 members, which first met on 4 November 1919, was a change in name rather than in substance. Its first act was to issue instructions that 'The Secretary will attend meetings of the Cabinet to keep a record of the Cabinet proceedings' (CP 1—CAB 24/92). Henceforth at Cabinet meetings ministers were rarely accompanied by officials, and the secretary alone was present. No basic change was made in the arrangements for conducting the secretarial work, other than abandonment of the symbols WC and GT and their substitution by CC and CP for, respectively, the Cabinet conclusions and the Cabinet memoranda. Copies of the memoranda and conclusions were sent to all members of the Cabinet.

421. Two organisational changes were made:

First, by CC 8(19)8a—CAB 23/18 of 20 November 1919 the Cabinet agreed that all communications to and from the League of Nations should be distributed from the Cabinet Office; a bottleneck built up, and the arrangement lapsed in November 1922, when the Foreign Office became the channel of communication.

Secondly, by CC 1(20)2—CAB 23/20 of 6 January 1920, the Cabinet agreed that a Treasury officer should as a permanent arrangement be seconded to the Cabinet Office, and that among his duties would be to ensure that the Treasury were made aware in advance of proposals involving expenditure. F. W. Leith-Ross held the appointment for a short while in 1920, and was succeeded by Howorth. The Treasury connection was later maintained by the secondment of W. D. Wilkinson and J. H. Penson.

422. Another change was an attempt to revert to the pre-war custom that the Cabinet did not meet more often than once a week; the number of full meetings dropped from 139 in 1919 to 82 in 1920, 93 in 1921 and 63 to 19 October 1922. But two other series of ministerial meetings were held erratically under the chairmanship of the Prime Minister, which dealt with matters which might have gone to the full Cabinet. One was the Finance Committee (FC—CAB 27/71 and 72) which held 40 meetings between July 1919 and July 1922, attended by senior ministers, without any terms of reference, and which considered a wide range of matters including military commitments overseas, reparations, subsidies, departmental estimates and the system of government accounting. The other was 159 meetings held between October 1919 and September 1922, and known as 'Conferences of Ministers' whose records are in CAB 23/37-39, though copies were generally attached as appendices to the conclusions of the next meeting of the Cabinet. Most of these conferences appear to have dealt with relatively minor matters, and were attended by the ministers directly concerned; some dealt with Ireland; but perhaps the most notable were the 10 conferences held between 25 and 30 September 1922, attended by the Prime Minister, the Foreign Secretary, service ministers and chiefs of staff, to deal with the Chanak crisis. No further conferences were held after 30 September 1922, but Chanak was the main business at the full Cabinet which met at 5 p.m. on that date and on 13 further occasions in the next two weeks. Lloyd George resigned shortly after. CAB 23/35 and 36 contain the secretary's notes of various meetings held by Lloyd George with ministers and others on divers matters from 1919 to 1922.

423. Probably the most difficult problem with which the Cabinet was faced from 1919 to 1922, and that which aroused the deepest political passions, was that of

Ireland. This question constantly passed between the Cabinet and a succession of Cabinet committees in preparation for the conferences with the Irish representatives (CAB 43).

424. To meet a complaint by the Prime Minister on 5 March 1922 about leakages (the first information he had of the subjects to be discussed in Cabinet that day came, he said, from the press and not the agenda), it was agreed by CC 16(22)3—CAB 23/29 that copies of the conclusions should not be circulated, that the secretary should send such reminders as he deemed necessary to the ministers concerned, and that a file of the conclusions should be retained in his personal custody and be available for consultation by ministers or their authorised representatives. From March to October 1922 the conclusions exist in typescript only.

425. In addition to its duties for the Cabinet, the Office—following the precedent of the Peace Conference—undertook the whole or part of the secretarial arrangements for a number of the international conferences held during the Lloyd George administration (*see* Chapter 8).

Staff

426. The number had increased from less than a score employed by the CID in 1915 to 162 in mid-1919, of whom about 40 were employed in Paris. In the autumn of 1919 the Office was reorganised, under Hankey as secretary, into a Home Affairs branch, with Tom Jones as the principal assistant secretary, and four other administrative officers, including one nominated by the Treasury; and an Imperial, External Affairs and Defence branch with four administrative officers nominated by the Secretaries of State for Foreign Affairs, War and India, and by the First Lord of the Admiralty. In addition there were about 150 subordinate staff (clerks, typists and messengers) engaged in common services for both branches. The total declined to about 120 during 1922, when the Imperial, External Affairs and Defence Branch had become the staff of the CID, and the Home Affairs branch had become the Cabinet Office secretariat. Until 1920–1921, the expenses were borne on the Treasury vote; in 1920 the Treasury agreed that the Office should be placed on a permanent basis and it had its own vote in the two years 1921–1923; thereafter it reverted to the Treasury vote.

Haldane Report

427. The Haldane committee on the Machinery of Government, appointed by the Minister of Reconstruction, had reported in December 1918 (Cd. 9230); following are extracts:

6. The main functions of the Cabinet may, we think, be described as:
   (a) the final determination of the policy to be submitted to Parliament;
   (b) the supreme control of the national executive in accordance with the policy prescribed by Parliament;
   (c) the continuous co-ordination and delimitation of the activities of the several departments of state.

7. For the performance of these functions the following conditions seem to be essential or at least desirable:
   (i) the Cabinet should be small in numbers—preferably 10, or at most, 12;
   (ii) it should meet frequently;
   (iii) it should be supplied in the most convenient form with all the information and material necessary to enable it to arrive at expeditious decisions;
   (iv) it should make a point of consulting personally all the ministers whose work is likely to be affected by its decisions; and

(v) it should have a systematic method of securing that its decisions are effectively carried out by the several departments concerned.

10. ... we think there is one feature in the procedures of the War Cabinet which may well assume a permanent form, namely, the appointment of a secretary to the Cabinet charged with the duty of collecting and putting into shape its agenda, of providing the information and material necessary for its deliberations, and of drawing up records of the results for communication to the departments concerned.

12. ... in the sphere of civil government, the duty of investigation and thought, as preliminary to action, might with great advantage be more definitely recognised.

428. In the pressure of events following the end of hostilities, the Haldane report had the appearance of an academic exercise. There was an undercurrent of opinion in Parliament, in Whitehall, and outside that the conception of the War Cabinet had been wrong, and that the Office was both expensive and unconstitutional. This was partly due to the suspicion of Lloyd George felt in various political and military quarters, and partly to the confusion in wider circles between the Cabinet Office and the Prime Minister's secretariat in the 'Garden Suburb'. The unease about the Office came to a head in a debate in the House of Commons on 13 June 1922 (*Hansard*, cols. 213–278), when it centred on three points:

(a) The existence of the Office strengthened the hands of the Prime Minister, both against other ministers and against Parliament.

(b) It infringed the doctrine of secrecy and mutual confidence. Asquith said: 'Gladstone and Beaconsfield would have shuddered in their graves at the thought of an outsider being present and taking notes of what was going on. They would have considered it a breach of the fundamental practice of the constitution.'

(c) The Office was interfering with the proper work of the Foreign Office, and in particular should have nothing to do with the League of Nations affairs.

429. Austen Chamberlain defended the Office:

No one would think of going back to the old unbusinesslike system which nothing but the comparative simplicity of the matters dealt with in those days rendered possible at all . . . I have known Cabinets to break up under the impression they had settled something, and every minister going away asking his neighbour what was the decision to which they had come. The institution of a secretariat makes that impossible because the decision must be recorded, and if not clear the secretary has to ask what have I to record . . . [The reason why the League of Nations work was in the Office] was that much concerned the Dominions and the Dominions prefer to correspond with the Cabinet Office.

Lloyd George in winding up the debate said the CID had had a secretariat for many years, recording highly confidential and secret matters, and there had never been any revelations by the secretariat; the Office was a purely recording machine, acting under instructions from ministers and not influencing policy (but *see* para. 107). The motion for a reduction of the Cabinet Office vote was defeated by 205–111, but criticisms of the Office continued. Lloyd George's position was weakening and he resigned as Prime Minister on 19 October 1922.

CHAPTER 5

THE CABINET—NOVEMBER 1922–SEPTEMBER 1939

'Provisional' instructions

501. Bonar Law became Prime Minister on 23 October 1922, and on 1 November 1922 held his first Cabinet, which by CC 64(22)2—CAB 23/32 'approved *provisionally*' the Instructions to the Secretary which *inter alia* required him to 'attend meetings of the Cabinet, unless instructed to the contrary, for the purpose of recording the conclusions'. Parliament had been dissolved on 26 October 1922, and on 15 November 1922 (the day of the general election) *The Times* set out the declared policies of the political parties, and among those of the Conservative party was 'The abolition of the Cabinet Secretariat'. The result of the election was a clear majority for the Conservative party.

502. The criticism of the Office which had been voiced in the House of Commons debate on 13 June 1922 continued in various quarters. Among the documents in Box 110/1/7 of the Bonar Law papers in the Beaverbrook Library are copies of:

1. Leaflet No. 2599 of the Liberal Party (undated) which gave as the first of six examples of waste by the Coalition Government 'Mr. Lloyd George's Cabinet secretariat, which did not exist at all before the war, and is a dangerous innovation, employs 114 persons and will cost this year £32,084.'

2. An unsigned typewritten memorandum described as 'A broad outline of Conservative and Unionist policy' and dated 16 October 1922 (i.e. before Lloyd George's resignation), which contains:

Honest government . . . means purging the civil service and the whole administration of some persons and methods recently introduced. The civil service is no longer the unbiased, reliable loyal body of 30 years ago. Men of Fabian, Socialistic, Sinn Fein and even Bolshevist tendencies have been promoted deliberately to high places and numerous subordinates of disloyal tendencies have been introduced. Another evil is the swollen Cabinet secretariat interfering with the process of old departments and destroying the responsibility of ministers. The new system leads directly to revolution.

3. Bonar Law's election address issued from 10 Downing Street and dated 4 November 1922 (i.e. after the first meeting of his Cabinet on 1 November 1922) which includes:

I think it is of the utmost importance that we should return as quickly as possible, and as completely as possible, to the normal procedure which existed before the war. In pursuance of this aim I am satisfied that the time has now come when a change should be made in the machinery of the central government. Some of the work which has hitherto been done in the Cabinet secretariat is essential and must be continued, but we intend to bring that body in its present form to an end, and I am certain that the necessary work can be continued and the invaluable services of the present secretary retained in connection with the Treasury which in the past has always been the central department of government. As an illustration of the changes which we contemplate, instructions have already been given to transfer to the Foreign

Office the machinery of the League of Nations and in the same way to arrange, as regards any future international conferences, that even where it is necessary that I as Prime Minister should be present, the machinery of the conferences and the preliminary work in connection with them will be performed not by the Cabinet secretariat, but by the Foreign Office itself.

Warren Fisher's minute

503. Chapter 11 of Vol. 2 of Roskill's *Life of Hankey* contains full extracts from Hankey's private diary of the events which developed at the end of October and early in November 1922, and on pages 214–220 of Vol. 1 of *Whitehall Diary* Tom Jones records his discussions at the time on the future of the office and his own position. The registered papers of the Cabinet Office disclose little of the prevailing tensions, but CAB 63/33 is a collection of some of the papers which were kept personally by Hankey of his negotiations with Warren Fisher, the Permanent Secretary of the Treasury and Head of the Civil Service. The position was that ministers in the new government were committed, if not to the abolition of the Office, at least to its curtailment; the League of Nations work was immediately transferred to the Foreign Office; the detailed arrangements for other work, including the need for economy, were left for settlement between Fisher and Hankey, subject to approval by the Prime Minister.

504. There was a difficult meeting between the two on 25 October 1922, when Fisher argued that as the Treasury was the central department of government, it was essential that as part of Treasury control the Cabinet secretariat should become an integral part of the Treasury. Hankey demurred and retorted that it would be taken by the public as 'an attempt to camouflage the secretariat in the Treasury'; he referred to the prestige which attached to his semi-autonomous position; he agreed there would be advantage in moving the Office to the other side of White-hall (possibly to the Privy Council Office or the Scottish Office), and 'we may ultimately pool some of our clerical and messenger services with those of the Treasury'. Subsequent discussion between the two appears to have proceeded on the basis of draft submissions to the Prime Minister, which each prepared and from which the following are key extracts:

Fisher's draft (undated, probably 1 November 1922):

The Treasury, unlike Finance Ministries in other countries, is not merely the finance department but also, under the Prime Minister (First Lord) and the Cabinet, the central and co-ordinating organ of government. As such it is the natural body to provide for the secretarial needs of the Cabinet. This is the arrangement which I understand the Government to have in mind.

The present Secretary of the Cabinet, Sir Maurice Hankey, has, however, urged that during his tenure of office—which I trust may be long—the process of absorbing in the Treasury the secretarial staff may not be carried through in its entirety and that only a first step in the desired direction should be taken by providing a place in the Vote for the 'Treasury and Subordinate Departments' of the Cabinet Secretariat and Committee of Imperial Defence as a distinct and separate entity.

Obviously this suggestion does not give effect to the principle of organisation which is the natural corollary to the position of the Treasury as the central department and may serve to continue the public criticism on grounds of cost. If it were put forward as a scientific and final solution, I should have no option but to elaborate the argument against it. But in view of (i) the very distinguished services and qualities of Sir Maurice Hankey personally and (ii) the limitation of the suggested alternative to his period of office, I feel justified (subject to my observation above as to criticism of cost) in advising that the decision to transfer the functions of the Cabinet Secretariat to the Treasury should be effected in two stages—the first, for Sir Maurice's tenure of office, represented by the appearance of the Secretariat in the Estimates as a subordinate department of the Treasury, and the second, and permanent, change being the taking over by the Treasury proper of the secretarial work for the Cabinet.

Fisher also suggested in the draft that on a vacancy in the clerkship of the Privy Council Hankey should succeed to it.

Hankey's draft (2 November 1922):

In conclusion I would submit:

(1) That the Government shall decide that the Cabinet Secretariat is not to be absorbed into the Treasury;

(2) That, if it is later decided to amalgamate the Cabinet Office with the Privy Council Office, the combined office shall not be absorbed into the Treasury.

Fisher's draft (3 November 1922):

Until and unless it is decided actually to merge in the headquarters staff of the Treasury the staff required to do the secretarial work of the Cabinet, I think the Prime Minister's announcement is not inconsistent with an arrangement whereby the Cabinet Secretariat and the Committee of Imperial Defence could be shown as a unit in the Vote of the 'Treasury and Subordinate Departments'. (The Committee of Imperial Defence used always to appear in this place.) Under such an arrangement the cost of this service would be shown on the face of the Vote as a distinct item.

Hankey's draft (6 November 1922):

I wish, however, to affirm that, on grounds of principle, I am wholly opposed to absorption of the Cabinet Secretariat by the Treasury proper.

Hankey records that on the afternoon of 6 November Fisher telephoned to say that he was very anxious to avoid sending forward anything he (Hankey) could not accept; a discussion followed, some amendments were made in Fisher's submission and 'having seen the document in its final form which was entirely satisfactory to me, I told Sir Warren Fisher I did not wish to see it again until it was finally approved when he promised to send me a copy.'

505. Fisher's submission of 7 November 1922 to which Hankey had agreed, and which was initialled by Baldwin on 9 November and by Bonar Law on 15 November, was as follows:

Chancellor of the Exchequer
Prime Minister

Secretarial work for the Cabinet

In the course of the Prime Minister's Election address and of his speech at Glasgow on 26th ultimo he said in regard to the Cabinet secretariat that the Government 'intend to bring that body in its present form to an end, and I am certain that the necessary work can be continued and the invaluable services of the present Secretary retained in connection with the Treasury which in the past has always been the central department of government'; also 'I am convinced that the work can be done quite as efficiently, and far more economically, by having the Cabinet secretary, who is also the secretary of the Committee of Imperial Defence—in having him and whatever help he needs treated as part of the Treasury, which is the central department of government.'

2. The Treasury, unlike Finance Ministries in other countries, is not merely the finance department but also, under the Prime Minister (First Lord) and the Cabinet, the central and co-ordinating organ of government. As such it is the natural body to provide for the secretarial needs of the Cabinet.

3. Effect could be given to the Prime Minister's statements either by merging the staff required to do the secretarial work of the Cabinet in the headquarters staff of the Treasury or by reverting to the system in operation until March 1921 under which the Cabinet secretariat and the Committee of Imperial Defence were shown as a unit on the vote for the 'Treasury and subordinate departments'. I think the Prime Minister's announcement is not inconsistent with the latter arrangement under which the cost of this service would be shown on the face of the Vote as a distinct item.

4. I should like to suggest that, on a vacancy occurring in the post of Clerk to the Privy Council, Sir Maurice Hankey should succeed to it and thus be the officer immediately attached both to the working Privy Council and to the Ceremonial Privy Council. (The title would appear, in addition to those of Secretary of the Cabinet and Secretary of the Committee of Imperial Defence, on the Vote for the Treasury and subordinate departments, and also in its present place, but without salary, on the Privy Council Vote.) This course would have certain constitutional as well as practical and financial advantages.

5. I would further suggest that the work and staff in connection with the War History should cease to be charged to the CID and should, with all proper safeguards, be transferred elsewhere, e.g. to the British Museum or some kindred body.

6. I would ask also authority when the above vacancy occurs to find space in the Treasury buildings, if possible, for Sir Maurice and his staff, as a measure of obvious convenience.

7. One final point. Sir Maurice is much distressed by the allegations which have appeared in the Press on the conduct of his office, and asked me in the first instance to recommend to you a Committee of Enquiry. He now appreciates the difficulties involved in this request, and I understand you have in mind to dispose in Parliament of these unfair imputations.

(Intld.) N.F.W.F. 7.11.22.

(Intld.) A.B.L. 15.11.
(Intld.) S.B. 9.11.22.

506. Among the advantages of the proposal that Hankey should succeed to the vacancy in the Privy Council, Fisher no doubt had in mind that constitutionally it would solve the difficulty about attendance at the Cabinet by one who had not taken the Privy Counsellor's oath of secrecy; practically, it would avoid questions of status between the permanent secretary to the Treasury and the secretary of the Cabinet; and financially, it would reduce the Privy Council vote by £1,500—the salary paid to Fitzroy. (No progress was made on the other suggestions, i.e. to transfer the work on War Histories to the British Museum, to transfer the Cabinet secretariat to the Treasury buildings, and to make some public statement to relieve Hankey's distress about the allegations on the conduct of his office.)

507. In the upshot the following took place:
(a) The separate vote for the Cabinet Office ceased, and for 1923–1924 and subsequent years financial provision for the 'Offices of the Cabinet, Committee of Imperial Defence and the War Histories Department' was made in the vote of the 'Treasury and subordinate departments' without any reference to the possible ultimate absorption into the Treasury.

(b) By the end of March 1923, the staff had been reduced from 120 to 39 (and salaries from £31,000 to £16,000), mainly by the transfer of subordinate officers to other departments, and by the return of the assistant secretary on secondment from the Foreign Office.

(c) The League of Nations work and work in connection with international conferences was transferred to the Foreign Office.

(d) On the retirement of Fitzroy on 31 May 1923, Hankey became Clerk to the Privy Council (without separate remuneration).

(e) The 'Garden Suburb' had vanished with Lloyd George.

508. In the two years 1923 and 1924, the Cabinet Office became established as a permanent part of the central machinery of government. The 'provisional' nature of the Instructions to the Secretary of 1 November 1922 was forgotten in the events of the next few months, which included the Prime Minister's threat to his colleagues to resign over the American debt. Shortly thereafter he fell ill, and in his absence Curzon presided over the Cabinet. After Bonar Law's resignation on 20 May 1923, Baldwin's political position as his successor was weak and he was no doubt glad of the support of any piece of organisation available; and acceptance of the Salisbury report on National and Imperial Defence (Cmd. 2029) confirmed the position of the CID as an integral element in government. In January 1924 MacDonald formed his administration with a Cabinet of 20, of whom only four had previous experience of office, and were therefore more dependent on the machinery of the Office (and on officials in their departments) than their predecessors. These circumstances enabled the rump of the Office to fill the gap which its critics had intended to create, and one of the oddities of history is that Bonar Law, who was half-pledged to its abolition, was in fact responsible for its continuance.

509. But parallel with these developments at ministerial level, the civil servants in the Office and in departments had grown accustomed to each others' procedures and problems, and those responsible for advising ministers and for drafting memoranda for submission to the Cabinet were increasingly aware of the shape which those memoranda might conveniently take. From the peak circulation of over 3,000 memoranda in 1918, the number had dropped to 500 by the mid-1920s and until 1939 that number was rarely exceeded; the form had been standardised, and the content was generally limited to a concise statement of the points on which ministers sought the collective assent of their colleagues. Moreover, at both ministerial and official levels there was increasing experience of the part which committees could play in easing the pressure on the Cabinet itself.

510. By the mid-1920s any latent criticism of the existence of the Office, whether from Whitehall or outside, had largely faded, and it had assumed a shape and developed procedures which were substantially unchanged until 1939. In addition to its secretarial functions for the Cabinet and the CID and their committees, and for Imperial and certain other conferences, it undertook similar functions for the Committee of Civil Research in 1925, for the Economic Advisory Council in 1930 (*see* Chapter 7), for the Minister for Co-ordination of Defence in 1936 (*see* para. 621), and in 1937 as a purely *ad hoc* arrangement for the international committee on Non-intervention in Spain (*see* para. 712).

Five-day rule

511. From the point of view of procedure probably the most difficult problem was that of getting ministers to submit memoranda in sufficient time to enable their proposals to be fully examined in the Treasury and in other departments before they were considered in Cabinet. Matters on which ministers wanted decisions were generally contentious and urgent, and with a view to reducing the field of contention there was generally an attempt within the department to make adjustments, which delayed the submission, and made the need for the decision the more urgent. With MacDonald's approval a Treasury circular (included in Annex 3) was issued to departments in 1924 that memoranda should not be sent to the Office for circulation until their subject matter had been examined between the originating department, the Treasury, the Law Officers (when contentious Bills were involved) and any other department concerned; to give time for examination and for the preparation of dissenting memoranda if necessary, no memorandum originating proposals for Cabinet or Cabinet committee decision would be placed on the agenda until at least five days had elapsed after circulation (except when the Prime Minister specifically authorised a relaxation of the rule). The Treasury circular was reissued on several occasions, the last as TC 13/37 of 24 June 1937 in a revised and strengthened form, and the five-day rule remained current until September 1939. Nevertheless MacDonald is recorded on eight occasions (CC 51(29)3—CAB 23/62, 31(30)12—CAB 23/63, 72(30)11—CAB 23/65, 73(30)16—CAB 23/65, 15(31)4—CAB 23/66, 21(32)1—CAB 23/71, 56(32)2—CAB 23/72 and 63(33)4—CAB 23/77), as mentioning the late circulation of papers, and complaining that inability to study them properly in advance did not facilitate the transaction of Cabinet business. In fact he added to the difficulties in this respect by asking ministers to make it a regular practice before circulating memoranda, to pass them through his hands (CC 9(32)11—CAB 23/70 and 13(34)1—CAB 23/78); taken literally this would have meant an interval of about seven days, and this request together with the five-day rule itself (which could of course not apply to a memorandum commenting on one already circulated), was inevitably exercised with a good deal of discretion.

512. Among the matters on which the Prime Minister is recorded as having exhorted his colleagues were:

punctuality in attendance at the Cabinet (CC 7(24)1—CAB 23/47 and 25(24)1—CAB 23/47);

reminder that the Cabinet had first call on their time (CC 62(30)1—CAB 23/65);

the minister nearest the door of the Cabinet room should take in any messages for members (CC 24(29)1—CAB 23/61);

avoid overloading the agenda with unnecessary memoranda (CC 4(29)7—CAB 23/60 and 13(34)1—CAB 23/78);

the Chancellor of the Exchequer should be consulted on every proposal with financial implications (CC 15(31)4—CAB 23/66 and 29(31)17—CAB 23/67);

the pages of memoranda should be numbered for ease of reference (CC 73(30)16 —CAB 23/65, 26(31)4—CAB 23/67 and 89(31)3—CAB 23/69);

appeals not to make public statements or take executive action on large matters of policy without previous reference to the Cabinet, particularly where there was possibility of divergence of view or uncertainty as to government policy (CC 11(24)7—CAB 23/47 and 17(24)14—CAB 23/47);

after a government defeat in Parliament when 23 ministers were absent, ministers were invited to work as much as possible in their rooms in the House of Commons when Parliament was sitting as their presence had a good effect on the rank and file of the party (CC 28(36)1—CAB 23/83);

in addition, there are a number of references to the need for secrecy on particular matters discussed, and appeals for restraint in speeches, particularly on foreign affairs.

Press communiqué 1924

513. Before 1924 it had been the practice to issue a communiqué to the press giving a bare statement of the time and place of a meeting of the Cabinet and the names of those present. Although there is no reference in the conclusions, Mac-Donald during 1924 made arrangements to issue after each meeting a more informative communiqué about the matters that had been discussed. Hankey appears to have acquiesced, but among his first acts after the fall of the Labour government was to recommend that the practice be abandoned. He said he found it impossible to draft a communiqué which gave really useful information about what had occurred. The Privy Counsellor's oath debarred anything like a full disclosure, and the proper medium for announcing Cabinet decisions was a statement by the minister concerned, preferably in Parliament. It was often not in the public interest to mention a question which had occupied the greater part of the time at a meeting and if all mention of a subject was left out it must become obvious in due course that the communiqué was merely misleading. Baldwin quietly dropped the fuller communiqué (minute of 6 November 1924 on CAB 21/294).

Leakage of information

514. Although elaborate precautions were taken by the Office and by departments to ensure that there was no unauthorised disclosure of Cabinet deliberations, cases did arise from time to time when embarrassment was caused by leakages, and there are occasional references in the conclusions to the damage which had ensued. In at least one case (CC 13(26)3—CAB 23/52) it was clear that a temporary clerk in a department had abused the opportunities his work gave him; but in most of the other cases where it was felt that inquiry could usefully be made, it appeared that the leakage had either occurred abroad, or was the result of intelligent anticipation on the part of a lobby correspondent. Following leakages at the end of 1931, Hankey gave the Prime Minister a note of quotations on the subject of silence, which was circulated to all members of the Cabinet, and a copy sent to the King (*see* p. 53).

Custody of Cabinet papers

515. It had been the practice of the CID and of the first War Cabinet that papers should be returned when ministers ceased to hold office (WC 217(3)—CAB 23/3). Lloyd George's peace-time Cabinet decided to make no reference to the point and considered that secrecy would be 'safeguarded by the rule that no one is entitled to make use of Cabinet documents without the permission of the King' (CC 1(19)3 —CAB 23/18). By implication this resulted in ministers retaining such Cabinet documents as they wished, and in an understanding that they could have access to those circulated during their period of office (CC 47(31)1—CAB 23/67).

516. With some shadowy permission from the King, Lloyd George, Churchill and others had made considerable use of Cabinet documents in writing their own memoirs of the First World War; but in 1934 George Lansbury's son was prosecuted under the Official Secrets Acts for quoting, in a biography of his father, from papers circulated to the Cabinet in 1930 and 1931. As a result of this prosecution, and realising that there was risk of leakage of highly secret current documents relating to rearmament, the Cabinet decided by CC 11(34)5—CAB 23/78 of 21 March 1934 that:

   (a) all ministers on vacating office should return to the Office all Cabinet minutes and papers issued to them while holding office, and that members of previous

Very amusing, but will it have any effect? *E.R.I.*

Enclosure

The following is circulated by direction of the Prime Minister:-

"Men are very porous, weighty secrets oozing out of them, like quicksilver through clay jars".

(Carlyle. Frederick the Great).

"But let princes beware that the unsecreting of their affairs comes not from themselves. And as for cabinet counsels, it may be their motto "Plenus rimarum sum" (I am full of leaks): one futile person, that maketh it his glory to tell, will do more hurt than many, that know it their duty to conceal".

(Bacon's Essay. Of Counsel).

"Oftentimes I could wish that I had held my peace when I have spoken; and that I had not been in company".

(Of the Imitation of Christ.
Thomas à Kempis).

"The most part of men are given to talk much, and therefore little confidence is to be placed in them."

(Of the Imitation of Christ).

"It is necessary, moreover, not only to be silent with the tongue, but much more so in the mind".

(Polybius).

"Fourthly, in Deliberations that ought to be kept secret (whereof there be many occasions in Publique Businesse) the Counsells of many, and especially in Assemblies, are dangerous; And therefore great Assemblies are necessitated to commit such affairs to lesser numbers, and of such persons as are most versed, and in whose fidelity they have most confidence".

(Hobbes' Leviathan. Chapter XXV).

Quotations on silence sent to and with MS. comments by King George V (*see* para. 514).

Cabinets should have a right of access to those papers issued to them while they were members of the Cabinet; and

(b) ex-Cabinet ministers or their representatives should be invited to return all post-1919 Cabinet papers to the Office for safe custody. (By CC 51(35)10—CAB 23/82, the Cabinet took note of CP 218(35)—CAB 24/257 which reported the action taken on recovery; in 77 cases out of 87, the papers had been or were being recovered; in the remaining 10 cases (which included Lloyd George and Churchill) immediate recovery was not possible.)

517. Following the decision at (a) above, the Office took steps, which were generally successful, to recover papers from ministers subsequently leaving office; but the position was modified in 1945 when Churchill in WP (45)320—CAB 66/65 authorised ministers then vacating office to retain copies of Cabinet documents which they themselves had written.

Access to Cabinet papers

518. Following the decision of 21 March 1934 about custody, the question of access to them arose later in the year on an application by Lady Milner to see certain documents in order that she might reply to criticism of her late husband which had been made in a volume of Lloyd George's war memoirs which had recently been published. Realising that a precedent might be set, the Cabinet considered the application carefully and agreed (CC 35(34)5—CAB 23/80) that:

(a) access to Cabinet documents should not be given to non-official persons where the object is the production of an ordinary historical, biographical or other work; and

(b) where extracts from Cabinet or similar documents had already been published, access to them might be given to 'any person who has a good title to vindicate the memory of a deceased person and who claims that that memory has been injured by the publication in question', provided that:

(i) the documents contain nothing which would be prejudicial to the public interest;

(ii) the proofs of anything proposed to be published by the vindicator should be submitted to the Office for approval; and

(iii) the specific approval of the Prime Minister of the day, or of the Prime Minister in office when the documents were circulated, had been obtained.

To supplement this decision it was agreed within the Office that 'The King's consent must be obtained for the disclosure or publication of confidential Cabinet documents and records of Cabinet proceedings' (note of 21 January 1935 on file 28/2).

519. Lady Milner does not appear to have pursued her application for access; no other 'vindicator' sought access before 1945; and all applications by non-official persons were refused. The first application for access by an ex-Cabinet minister after the 1934 decision was by J. H. Thomas, who asked for certain Cabinet papers to be sent to his home to assist him in writing his autobiography; by CC 54(36)10—CAB 23/85, it was agreed that the papers should not be sent to his house (where there would be no facilities for safe custody) but there was no objection to him seeing them in the Office to refresh his memory; he should be asked not to refer to proceedings in Cabinet or to quote Cabinet papers, and to avoid any impression that the information in the book had been derived from secret official documents; and he should be invited to let the secretary see the proofs of what he proposed to publish. Thomas complied with these arrangements, and was able to modify his text in places to avoid direct reference to Cabinet documents or discussions; and the procedure became standard.

The 50- and the 30-year rules

520. Under the Public Records Act 1958, which established the 50-year rule, the records of the Cabinet Office created before 1910, which at that time consisted mainly of the records of the CID, became open to public inspection in the Public Record Office during 1960. In 1966 the 50-year rule was relaxed administratively, and the records became open to the end of 1922. By the Public Records Act 1967 the 30-year rule was established, and the records of 1923–1937 became open; and thereafter records were released a year at a time. In 1969 the Prime Minister announced (*Hansard*, col. 412–3 of 18 December 1969) that the principal records of the Second World War would become open in a single operation on 1 January 1972. The successive reductions in the period of closure of the Cabinet records were announced as made with the agreement of the leaders of the political parties and with the consent of the Queen and after notification to the Dominions.

Committees

521. Apart from the Committee of Imperial Defence (Chapter 6) and the Committee of Civil Research and the Economic Advisory Council (Chapter 7), the only committee of the Cabinet which had a recognisably continuing existence was the Home Affairs Committee (HAC—CAB 26), which had started to meet in July 1918 under the Home Secretary 'to consider all domestic questions which require the co-operation of more than one department, and of such importance that they would otherwise call for consideration of the Cabinet'. Initially it had dealt with matters of general administration, including aspects of demobilisation, control of aliens, agricultural and medical research, etc., but increasingly it became the forum for examination of forthcoming government legislation, and from 1922 to 1939 it generally met under the chairmanship of the Lord Chancellor, and was attended by most of the ministers dealing with civil affairs at home, by the Law Officers, the Chief Whip, Parliamentary Counsel and a number of officials from departments. The Committee met as drafts of Bills were taking their final form, made detailed adjustments to them within policies already settled and made recommendations to the Cabinet for authority for their introduction in Parliament. At one or more meetings during the year, and usually at the beginning of the parliamentary session, the Committee classified the measures then in contemplation. The categories varied from time to time, but generally included:

A. Annual or compulsory Bills.
B. Urgent or essential Bills.
C. Useful Bills.
D. Bills suitable for introduction by a private member.
E. Bills not yet ready, divided into:
    (i) those which in certain events would be essential;
    (ii) others.
F. Consolidation Bills.

It was the practice to include against each Bill an indication whether it was likely to be controversial and whether its principles had received recent Cabinet approval. The classification recommended by the committee would be considered by the Cabinet, who would make such adjustments as their policy and the state of the parliamentary time-table required. There was liable on occasions to be some confusion between departments and Parliamentary Counsel, with the former complaining that the latter were in arrears, and the latter being overpressed, with some feeling that they had had no proper instructions from departments, and were without sufficient knowledge of the priority they should attach to the various measures. To remedy the situation, a Treasury circular (E4000/01) was issued in 1935 that authority for Parliamentary Counsel to be employed would be given for those Bills which constituted the main items in the Government's legislative programme, and only for such other Bills as had received Cabinet approval in principle and for which the Chief Whip was satisfied that there was a reasonable chance that parliamentary time would be found (HA 31(35)—CAB 26/18). This resulted in some improvement in the legislative equipment by 1939, when the Home Affairs Committee was reconstituted as the Home Policy Committee (HPC— CAB 75, *see* para. 946).

522. Throughout the period 1923–1939 most of the other committees of the Cabinet were appointed *ad hoc* to deal with some immediate problem and generally with terms of reference requiring them to report to the Cabinet. Many did so, and their reports will be found both in the records of the committees and in the CP series. But there was no established means of notifying that a committee had finished its task, and in a number of cases meetings ceased and the records of the committees peter out, either because the subject had lost its interest or urgency, or because some solution had been found with which the chairman found it unnecessary to trouble the Cabinet. At a change of administration, the secretary brought to the notice of the incoming Prime Minister a list of the committees (and membership) set up by the previous administration and which could be regarded as still active; but before MacDonald's resignation in 1935, no committee had been continued from one administration to another (other than the Home Affairs Committee) and each administration formed its own committee structure to meet its own problems and methods of work. The problems, in fact, were not markedly different, and each administration set up committees on subjects such as agriculture, housing, unemployment and various aspects of foreign affairs, but the membership and terms of reference differed, no doubt with the intention that a wholly fresh approach would be made.

523. Membership of committees was generally limited to ministers, though over the period there was an increasing tendency for ministers to be accompanied to meetings by officials. An exceptional arrangement was the appointment in 1928 of the Policy Procedure Committee (PP—CAB 27/370), under the chairmanship of Anderson (then PUS at the Home Office), and composed wholly of officials, to examine and report to ministers on various aspects of the proposals then under discussion for rating and local government reform. A wholly official committee of this character did not become common until 1939, but by CC 23(33)6—CAB 23/75 of 5 April 1933, MacDonald had referred to the advantage of having official advisers present at meetings of committees of the Cabinet.

524. While outside the CID no continuing committee structure emerged, there is some evidence that certain committees were by design or practice of an administration intended as standing committees, over which the Prime Minister generally presided; these included the following:

National Expenditure (Baldwin) (NE—CAB 27/303–306)

This held 23 meetings between 1925 and 1927 following the budget statement in 1925 that the Prime Minister had appointed a standing committee to review the estimates of national expenditure with the object of making a substantial reduction in the charges on the taxpayer; it reviewed the departmental estimates before they were submitted to the Treasury.

India (CI—CAB 27/519-521)

Forty-two meetings were held between 1932 and 1935 under the chairmanship variously of MacDonald, Baldwin and Hoare to consider and settle various matters leading to the Government of India Act 1935.

General Purposes (MacDonald) (GP—CAB 27/583-584)

By CC 6(35)1—CAB 23/81 of 30 January 1935 MacDonald suggested that the leaders of the three political parties represented in the Cabinet should form a small body to discuss matters which did not belong to only one department. It would be like the CID with no executive authority, but charged with making representations on matters of policy, of which, he stated, a large number required consideration at that time. The membership would be himself in the chair, J. H. Thomas, Baldwin, N. Chamberlain, Hailsham, Simon and Runciman, with liberty to invite other members of the Cabinet concerned in particular matters. Reports from it would be considered by the Cabinet as the first item on the agenda. The Cabinet agreed to such a committee as an experiment; it met on 25 occasions before MacDonald resigned (when meetings lapsed) and was mostly concerned with the answer to Lloyd George's proposals for relieving unemployment.

Defence Policy and Requirements (MacDonald, later Baldwin and N. Chamberlain) (DPR—CAB 16/123, 136-144)

Fifty meetings were held 1935-1937, mainly on rearmament, but also concerned with the Abyssinian crisis. By its terms of reference it could report either to the Cabinet or the CID.

Defence Plans (Policy) (Baldwin, later N. Chamberlain) (DP(P)—CAB 16/181-183)

It met infrequently in 1937 to examine plans for a major war, and to provide a nucleus for a possible War Cabinet (there is some evidence that some of the members met informally during 1938 and 1939).

Foreign Policy (Baldwin, later N. Chamberlain) (FP—CAB 27/622-627)

Sixty-one meetings were held 1936-1939; it tended to assume some of the functions of the Foreign Office.

525. As international affairs deteriorated, as rearmament gathered momentum and as the Second World War approached, the lines of demarcation between the Cabinet and the CID, and between some of their respective committees, became increasingly blurred. While the CID in theory was a purely advisory body consisting of the Prime Minister and such persons as he might decide to invite, in practice half the members of the Cabinet were regular attenders at the CID, which tended on some major issues to assume functions which might now be regarded as more appropriate for the Cabinet. The confusion—which was probably not realised at the time—can be traced to the mid-1920s when the military aspects of disarmament were considered by the CID, which during the following decade became the principal forum for discussion of 'The Reduction and Limitation of Armaments'—the heading normally used in the minutes—and consequentially for examination of various aspects of foreign policy, including the negotiations on the Egyptian treaty. On major issues, the matter was referred to the Cabinet, but generally the decision had been effectively taken in the CID. As disarmament gave way to rearmament, committees proliferated, a minister was appointed for Co-ordination of Defence, and in 1937 the Prime Minister was chairman of the important committees—Defence Policy and Requirements, Defence Plans (Policy) and Foreign Policy. The following table shows the interlock of ministerial membership of these committees with the CID and with the Cabinet in the later part of 1937.

C

Cabinet		CID	Defence Policy and Requirements	Defence Plans (Policy)	Foreign Policy
Prime Minister	N. Chamberlain	x	x	x	x
Lord President	Halifax	x	x		x
Lord Chancellor	Hailsham	o			x
Lord Privy Seal	de la Warr				
Chancellor of the Exchequer	Simon	x	x	x	x
Foreign Office	Eden	x	x	x	x
Home Office	Hoare	x	x	x	x
Admiralty	Duff Cooper	x	x	x	x
Agriculture	W. S. Morrison	o			
Air	Swinton	x	x	x	x
Colonies	Ormsby-Gore	x	x		x
Co-ordination of Defence	Inskip	x	x	x	x
Dominions	M. MacDonald	x			x
Education	Stanhope				
Health	K. Wood	o			
India	Zetland	x			
Labour	Brown		x		
Scottish	Elliott	o			
Trade	Stanley	o	x		x
War	Hore-Belisha	x	x	x	

x = Member or regular attender

o = Attender at some.

Number of meetings in 1937

Cabinet	49
CID	19
DPR	12
DP(P)	4
FP	11

526. While in theory there was a distinction between the Cabinet and the CID, which was emphasised in November 1937 by the absorption of the DPR and DP(P) Committees into the CID (*see* para. 635), the distinction was becoming progressively unreal, and with the Prime Minister as chairman of the powerful committees in what were the overlapping fields of defence and foreign policy, it is perhaps not surprising that the 49 meetings of the full Cabinet in 1937 was about the lowest annual total in the inter-war years. A committee structure was developing and while there were some important changes in membership of the Cabinet during 1938, and the structure was radically altered on the outbreak of war, the secretarial organisation of the Office under Bridges' guidance kept pace with requirements and was forming a widening range of contacts with departments.

Subjects considered in Cabinet

527. It is only by search through the indexes to the Cabinet conclusions preserved in the Public Record Office that a decision on any particular subject can be traced.

The indexes are full, and the same conclusion is likely to be included under two or more subject headings; the indexes were compiled by different hands and there is some lack of consistency in the arrangement; and the entries make no distinction between those topics which were the subject of lengthy discussion and those which passed through 'on the nod'. But a rough analysis of the indexes suggests that the topics considered may very broadly be grouped as follows:

	1928–1932		1933–1937	
Overseas				
Abyssinia	—		100	
Germany	24		208	
India	213		89	
Ireland	102		32	
Spain	—		119	
Other overseas	1,031		932	
		1,370		1,480
Defence		430		700
Domestic				
Agriculture	100		31	
Coal	85		62	
Education	51		11	
Housing	31		20	
London traffic	40		9	
Unemployment	126		47	
Unemployment Insurance	99		72	
Other domestic	1,938		1,258	
		2,470		1,510
Legislation		380		440
		4,650		4,130
(Number of Cabinet meetings		345		297)

A further clue to the subjects considered can be derived from Annex 8, which shows the number of memoranda to the Cabinet originated annually by each minister.

Some political landmarks

528. Many of the topics were of a recurrent character, including imperial and foreign affairs affecting particularly Ireland, India, Palestine, Egypt, Europe and the Far East; defence; and domestic problems such as unemployment, safeguarding of industry and tariffs, agriculture, housing, pensions and reform of local government. But the following is a highly selective chronological list of a few events which resulted either in a significant change in the composition of the Cabinet, or attracted a high degree of attention by the Cabinet at a few meetings within a limited time. The list is put forward with all humility, and in full recognition that it is subject to criticism both for its inclusions and its omissions. Paras. 630–637 mention some other landmarks in the field of defence.

1922
19 October   Lloyd George resigned.
23 October   Bonar Law Prime Minister.
 1 November   First Cabinet, CC 64(22)—CAB 23/32.
15 November   General Election: 407 Conservatives and National Liberals; 54 Liberals; 142 Labour; 12 others.

1923

30 January	CC 4(23)2—CAB 23/45. 'The Cabinet heard a full account of the present position in regard to the Anglo-American debt and . . . agreed to adjourn the question to the following afternoon.'
31 January	CC 5(23)—CAB 23/45. 'The Cabinet agreed that the proposal of the United States Funding Commission should be accepted in principle.' (Robert Blake: *The Unknown Prime Minister* (1955), pp. 493–494, states that at the first meeting Bonar Law said he would resign rather than accept the terms negotiated by Baldwin.)
20 May	Bonar Law resigned on health grounds and was succeeded by Baldwin.
October–November	Imperial Conference.
6 December	General election: 258 Conservatives; 159 Liberals; 191 Labour; 7 others.
11 December	CC 58(23)—CAB 23/46. 'After careful consideration of the constitutional precedents and their bearing upon the situation which has arisen as a result of the general election, the Cabinet decided unanimously this morning that it was their constitutional duty to meet Parliament at the earliest possible moment. Parliament therefore will re-assemble as already provided for on January 8.'

1924

21 January	Baldwin government defeated in Parliament.
22 January	CC 6(24)—CAB 23/46. 'The Cabinet agreed that the Prime Minister should offer his resignation to the King at the earliest possible moment; in the event of the King deciding to send for Mr Ramsay MacDonald.' [Details follow of the timing of resignation to allow MacDonald to be sworn a member of the Privy Council before becoming Prime Minister.] MacDonald Prime Minister.
6 August	CC 48(24)5—CAB 23/48. First mention of Campbell case.
8 October	Vote of censure carried; Parliament dissolved.
29 October	General election: 419 Conservatives; 40 Liberals; 151 Labour; 5 others.
31 October	CC 57(24)2—CAB 23/48. Zinovieff letter committee appointed.
3 November	CC 58(24)1—CAB 23/48. Cabinet accepts report of Zinovieff letter committee (ZL—CAB 27/254). MacDonald resigned and succeeded by Baldwin.

1925

25 March	CC 18(25)13—CAB 23/49. Great care to be exercised in speeches on return to the gold standard.
29 April	CC 22(25)2—CAB 23/50. Chancellor of Exchequer (Churchill) outlined budget proposals, including return to the gold standard.

(The above are the only references in the Cabinet records to the return to the gold standard.)

1925

October	Locarno pact.

1926

30 April	CC 20(26)—CAB 23/52 authorised that the arrangements of the Supply and Transport organisation (ST—CAB 27/260, 261, 331–334) should be put into operation.

2–12 May	Ten meetings of the Cabinet on the General Strike.
May–November	Coal strike.
October–November	Imperial Conference.
1927	
	CC 26(27)4—CAB 23/54. A note of dissent by the Chancellor of the Exchequer (Churchill) from the decision on equal franchise for men and women was placed in a sealed envelope (now in CAB 23/90B).
May	Relations with Russia broken off.
26 July	CC 44(27)1—CAB 23/55. Cecil of Chelwood asked that it should be placed on record that he should be free to consider his position (on disarmament). He resigned shortly afterwards.
1928	
August	Kellogg pact.
1929	
30 May	General election: 260 Conservatives; 59 Liberals; 288 Labour; 8 others.
3 June	The Office was asked to summon a meeting of ministers to discuss action consequent on the result of the election; no officials were present and no minutes kept.
4 June	Baldwin government resigned.
5 June	MacDonald Prime Minister.
10 June	First Cabinet, CC 22(29)—CAB 23/61.
August–January 1930	Hague Conference.
1930	
January–April	London Naval Conference.
23 January	CP 31(30)—CAB 24/209. Mosley memorandum on unemployment policy.
8 May	CC 26(30)2—CAB 23/64 considered report of Unemployment Policy Committee (UPC—CAB 27/413).
19 May	Mosley resigned.
October–November	Imperial Conference.
November	India Round Table Conference.
Throughout	Economy declining following U.S. crash.
1931	
18 February	CC 14(31)11—CAB 23/66. Discussion on Education Bill, and voluntary schools problem.
2 March	Trevelyan (President, Board of Education) resigned.
30 July	CC 40(31)10—CAB 23/67. Cabinet committee on National Expenditure (NE—CAB 27/454) appointed to examine May report (Cmd. 3920).
20–24 August	Six meetings of the Cabinet, ending in resignation of ministers.
25 August	MacDonald formed Cabinet of 10.
20 September	CC 60(31)—CAB 23/68. Gold standard abandoned.

27 October	General election: 554 government supporters (of whom 473 Conservatives); 54 Labour; 5 others.
5 November	MacDonald formed Cabinet of 20.
25 November	CC 82(31)6—CAB 23/69. Following discussion on tariffs, 'ministers accepted the view of the Prime Minister that notes of dissent or reservation should not be recorded, as this would be contrary to the general principle of Cabinet unity'.

1932

| 22 January | CC 7(32)1—CAB 23/70. Disagreement on report of the Committee on the Balance of Trade (BT—CAB 27/467), and agreement that ministers who were in a minority might record their dissent—Snowden, Samuel, Maclean and Sinclair did so. The following communiqué was published: |

> The Cabinet has had before it the report of its committee on the Balance of Trade, and after prolonged discussion it has been found impossible to reach a unanimous conclusion on the committee's recommendations. The Cabinet, however, is deeply impressed with the paramount importance of maintaining national unity in presence of the grave problems that now confront this country and the whole world. It has accordingly determined that some modification of usual ministerial practice is required and has decided that ministers who find themselves unable to support the conclusions arrived at by the majority of their colleagues on the subject of import duties and cognate matters are to be at liberty to express their view by speech and vote. The Cabinet, being essentially united on all other matters of policy, believes that by this special provision it is best interpreting the will of the nation and the needs of the time.

February	Disarmament Conference (Geneva) opened.
February	Import Duties Act passed.
June–August	Ottawa Conference (CAB 32/101–116), and agreements for a measure of imperial preference.
28 September	CC 47(32)1—CAB 23/72. Samuel, Snowden and Sinclair resigned, as being out of sympathy with the Ottawa policy and with certain aspects of policy regarding the means test, disarmament and police pay.
21 December	CC 68(32)7—CAB 23/73. Hailsham recorded dissent from decision to grant export credits to Russia (*see also* CC 25(32)7—CAB 23/71).

1933

March	Japan withdrew from League of Nations.
June–July	London Monetary and Economic Conference.
October	Germany withdrew from Disarmament Conference and League of Nations.

1934

| June | Disarmament Conference ended in failure. |

1935

March–April	Meetings of Commonwealth Prime Ministers.
7 June	MacDonald resigned and succeeded by Baldwin.
31 July	By CC 41(35)6—CAB 23/82, in Baldwin's absence MacDonald would act, and failing him, N. Chamberlain.
October	Italy invaded Abyssinia.

14 November	General election: 432 Conservatives; 21 Liberals; 154 Labour; 9 others.
18 December	CC 56(35)2—CAB 23/82. Discussion on Hoare-Laval Pact, full record in CAB 23/90B.
	Hoare (Foreign Secretary) resigned.

1936

26 February	CC 11(36)5—CAB 23/83. Runciman and Monsell recorded dissent from the imposition of oil sanctions on Italy.
March	Germany occupied Rhineland. London Naval Treaty.
22 May	J. H. Thomas resigned.
July	Spanish civil war started.
November–December	CC 68–75(36)—CAB 23/86 relate to the abdication (records closed till 2037).

1937

May–June	Imperial Conference.
28 May	Baldwin resigned and succeeded by N. Chamberlain.
July	Anglo-German naval agreement.

1938

19 and 20 February	CC 6–8(38)—CAB 23/92. Discussion on relations with Italy.
	Eden (Foreign Secretary) resigned.
2 March	CC 10(38)6—CAB 23/92. Hailsham recorded dissent from Irish negotiations.
March	Germany incorporated Austria.
11 May	CC 23(38)6—CAB 23/93. Discussion of air programme.
16 May	Swinton (Secretary of State for Air) resigned.
Summer	Czechoslovak crisis developing.
September	Munich.
30 September	CC 47(38)—CAB 23/95. Duff Cooper resigned.

1939

March	Germany entered Czechoslovakia.
March–April	Guarantees to Poland and Roumania.
April	Italy invaded Albania.
1 September	CC 47(39)4—CAB 23/100. With a view to formation of a War Cabinet, ministers placed their resignations collectively in the Prime Minister's hands.
2 September	CC 48(39)1—CAB 23/100. Ultimatum to Germany agreed.

Staff

529. At the beginning of 1923 the staff was cut down from 120 to 39; some found other employment; of the remainder transfers were arranged to other departments, and it is understood that the only hardship suffered was the loss by some of their seniority.

530. Hankey was secretary of the Cabinet and secretary of the CID, and from June 1923 Clerk to the Privy Council (an office which took relatively little of his time), and held all three appointments till his retirement on 31 July 1938. Subject to annual leave, he attended all meetings of the Cabinet. On the CID side, there were throughout four assistant secretaries (generally of the rank of Lieut.-Colonel or the equivalent) nominated by the three service ministers and the Government of India, and seconded for a period of two or three years. On the Cabinet (civil) side, the deputy secretary until 1930 was Tom Jones (known as 'TJ' in a wide circle), concerned primarily in economic and home affairs and active in particular on Ireland and on industrial matters. His relations with Hankey appear to have been correct and formal, and he enjoyed the full confidence of Baldwin; some account of his activities is given in *Whitehall Diaries*. Tom Jones was succeeded as deputy secretary by R. B. Howorth, who had joined the Office as the Treasury watchdog in 1920. Throughout there were two or three administrative officers, seconded from the Treasury and other civil departments (*see* para. 421).

531. No increase in the total staff was involved by the creation of the Committee of Civil Research in 1925, but the staff began to expand with the appointment of the Economic Advisory Council in 1930, which was to have at least two economists as assistant secretaries (*see* para. 705). By the middle 1930s, with the appointment of a full-time chairman of the Supply Board (Arthur Robinson) and a Minister for Co-ordination of Defence (Inskip), each with a small personal staff, the number rose to 150 and had increased to 200 by the outbreak of the Second World War.

532. Until Hankey's retirement in 1938 there was immediately below him a fairly clear distinction between the administrative staffs engaged on work for the Cabinet, for the CID and for the Economic Advisory Council, but progressively to the outbreak of war the distinction was breaking down in the wide area where the strictly civil merged with the strictly military. But throughout there was no distinction at subordinate levels and the arrangements for handling, recording and distributing papers were undertaken as common services performed by a unified staff.

Hankey's successor

533. Hankey had set his imprint firmly on the Office, but there was a feeling in some quarters that he had held too many strings in his own hands, and that a certain conservatism and resistance to change had set in. In 1938 he was nominated a government director of the Suez Canal Company, and his retirement and the consequential changes were announced to the Cabinet in the following terms (CC 27(38)1—CAB 23/93):

The Prime Minister referred to an announcement that had been made on the previous day that he had nominated Sir Maurice Hankey, the Secretary to the Cabinet, for appointment as a director of the Suez Canal Company. As Sir Maurice Hankey would not be giving up his post until the 1st August next he did not raise the question for the purpose of bidding him farewell, but to inform his colleagues as to what he had arranged as to his successor. He was taking advantage of the opportunity of the change to make the new arrangements to conform to developments which had taken place during the term of the present holder of the appointment. For example, there was now a Minister for Co-ordination of Defence and a Committee of Civil Research, or, as it was at present termed, the Economic Advisory Council. Sir Maurice Hankey's successor, therefore, would be attached to the Office of the Cabinet, which included the Offices of the Minister for Co-ordination of Defence, the Committee of Imperial Defence and the Economic Advisory Council. He considered it essential that one person should be Secretary to the whole Office, thus providing a link between the Cabinet and the Committee of Imperial Defence, which could not be divided. He had therefore decided to appoint a Permanent Secretary to the Cabinet Office who would also act as Secretary to the Cabinet and who would provide a link with the Committee of Imperial Defence, of which he would be an *ex officio* member. The official he had selected was Mr E. E. Bridges, of the Treasury, a son of the late Poet Laureate, a man of exceptional ability and brilliance and possessing attractive personal qualities. Mr Bridges for some time had been the official in the Treasury connected with the Defence Programmes, and was therefore particularly well known to the Defence Departments. He himself, at the time he was Chancellor of the Exchequer, had been attracted by the outstanding quality of Mr Bridges' minutes on Defence questions, and had made it his business to get acquainted with their author. Mr Bridges had also been selected recently to sit in at the Air Ministry for purposes of consultation on the acceleration and expansion of the Air Programme.

Under the Permanent Secretary to the Cabinet Office there would be two principal officers. First was the Secretary to the Committee of Imperial Defence. Colonel H. L. Ismay, the present Deputy Secretary to the Committee of Imperial Defence, would become the Secretary to the Committee, and the work would be continued much as at present, though, as already mentioned, Mr Bridges would be an *ex officio* member of the Committee of Imperial Defence. He would not, however, be a member of the Chiefs of Staff Sub-Committee, which was a purely military committee, nor would he normally be invited to attend it, though this could be done in case of need.

The second principal officer was the Deputy Secretary to the Cabinet. Sir Rupert Howorth would continue to hold this post and would also become Clerk of the Privy Council. He himself had learned from Sir Maurice Hankey that the work of the Clerk of the Council did add to his burden, more especially for the reason that it was apt to become critical at the very time when there was pressure on the Cabinet and/or the Committee of Imperial Defence. In order to avoid the risk of over-working the Secretary to the Cabinet Office he had thought it advisable to combine the post of Clerk of the Council with that of the Deputy Secretary to the Cabinet. In addition, there would be a Principal Assistant Secretary, three Assistant Secretaries and certain Principals in the Cabinet Office.

The Prime Minister added that, after taking very careful soundings, he was satisfied that this arrangement would receive the enthusiastic support of all concerned, including the Chiefs of Staff and the present Secretary to the Cabinet.

The Chancellor of the Exchequer said that the only qualification he had to make on the above arrangements was the loss that the Treasury would suffer from the withdrawal of Mr Bridges.

534. On 1 August 1938 Bridges became permanent secretary of the Cabinet Office and secretary of the Cabinet, and the responsible official head of the whole composite office, in general charge of its various activities and personnel and *ex officio* a member of the CID. He was assisted by two deputies—Ismay, styled secretary of the CID and deputy secretary (military) of the Cabinet, and Howorth, styled Clerk of the Privy Council and deputy secretary (civil) of the Cabinet; the rest of the staff (civil and military) were available for such duties as might from time to time be allotted to them by the permanent secretary. The official but cumbrous description of the Office became 'The Offices of the Cabinet, Committee of Imperial Defence, Economic Advisory Council and Minister for Co-ordination of Defence'. An analysis of the staff before September 1939 is given in para. 974.

Hankey's contribution

535. Brief record should be made of Hankey's services as the creator of the Office and of his activities in and around the government machine. In 1908, at the age of 31 as a captain in the Royal Marines, he became an assistant secretary of the Committee of Imperial Defence, and secretary in 1912; in 1916, secretary of the

C*

War Cabinet and in 1919 of the peace-time Cabinet; in 1923, Clerk of the Privy Council—and held the three appointments until his retirement in 1938. He was secretary of a number of imperial and international conferences. During the First World War he had, before the creation of the War Cabinet, acted as secretary of the War Council, the Dardanelles Committee and the War Committee; and as such was an important witness before the Dardanelles Commission of Inquiry. By WC 497—CAB 23/8 of 5 November 1918 'The War Cabinet decided to record upon their minutes their warm appreciation of the remarkable work done by their secretary, Sir Maurice Hankey'. Those services were recognised by a monetary award of £25,000, commended by Lloyd George to Parliament in the following terms:

I have another name, the name of one who took no part in battle, but who was as essential to our success in this war as any name—I mean Sir Maurice Hankey. It is difficult for those who know to speak about Sir Maurice Hankey's services without appearing to exaggerate. His services were known only to a few, but none rendered greater service, and none, therefore, is more worthy of honour and of thanks. If any Member of this House will take the trouble to ask the leaders in any sphere of this war or of the peace about the services of Sir Maurice Hankey, they will realise what I mean. Let them ask naval leaders or military leaders, let them ask M. Clemenceau or President Wilson or Signor Orlando, and they will all bear the same testimony. He was the first to recognise before this war that if a great war came it would be a matter not merely of fighting men, but for the organisation of the whole resources of a country, and he it was who initiated, organised and inspired that war book that is one of the most remarkable productions any man could peruse. Going through it now, one can see how he foresaw things which were perhaps not visible except to very searching minds like his at the time, and which have now become part of the horrible realities of war. He served under my predecessor for a good many years, and I am permitted to read a letter Mr. Asquith wrote to him in November of last year, after the signature of the Armistice. This is Mr. Asquith's letter:

No one knows as well as I do how much we owe to you for our (ignorantly derided) pre-war preparation, nor the extent and value of your daily, and almost hourly, contribution during the first two and a half years to every measure in all spheres that was thought out and done. I know that you have continued to the end, under constant strain which cannot be measured, to render the same invaluable service. I should like you to know that in my judgment you have been in a true sense what Carnot was called, 'the organiser of victory'.

I am in accord with every word of that. He refused a highly remunerative offer in order to remain in the service of Britain. If Sir Maurice Hankey's name were left out of this list I should feel ashamed of it. There is no one who has a better right to be in it, and there is no one I recommend to the House with less hesitation. (*Hansard*, 6 August 1919.)

536. Hankey's association with Lloyd George from 1917 to 1922 was intimate; he frequently acted as the go-between with ministers and others. As there was nothing corresponding to the COS committee, which provided cohesion in the Second World War, such military co-ordination as was effected below the level of the War Cabinet was largely undertaken by Hankey; and he was the constant attender on Lloyd George at international meetings. But while as secretary of the Cabinet he had the full confidence of subsequent Prime Ministers, he does not appear to have enjoyed the same intimacy with any of them that he had with Lloyd George.

In the inter-war years he acted as secretary to numerous Cabinet committees and generally to those of which the Prime Minister was chairman. But it is noticeable that his main interest appears to have lain in questions relating to defence; as one of his contemporaries said, 'he was convinced there would be another war, and he felt it his mission to get people to do something about it'. His influence was directed to maintaining the machinery of the CID, and in general he was a big navy advocate.

537. Among the more important committees of the Cabinet or the CID with which he was directly associated were:

1920–1938	Committee on Co-ordination of Departmental Action (CAB 15)	Chairman
1920–1938	Joint Oversea and Home Defence Committee (CAB 36)	Chairman
1923–1938	Home Defence Committee (CAB 12)	Chairman
1923–1924	Salisbury Committee on National and Imperial Defence (CAB 16/46)	Secretary
1923–1938	Chiefs of Staff Committee (CAB 53)	Secretary
1932–1938	Deputy Chiefs of Staff Sub-Committee (CAB 54)	Chairman
1928–1929	Belligerent Rights Committee (CAB 16/79)	Expert assessor
1931–1935	Disarmament Conference Committee (CAB 27/505)	Secretary
1933	Private Armament Industry Committee (CAB 27/551)	Secretary
1936	Royal Commission on Private Manufacture and Trading in Arms (CAB 16/126)	Evidence given
1933–1935	Defence Requirements Committee (CAB 16/109)	Chairman
1935–1937	Defence Policy and Requirements Committee (CAB 16/136)	Secretary
1937	Defence Plans (Policy) Committee (CAB 16/181)	Secretary
1936–1938	Foreign Policy Committee (CAB 27/622)	Secretary

He left much of the committee work on civil matters to others—generally Tom Jones until 1930 and Howorth subsequently.

538. The testimony of the Cabinet to his services on his retirement was recorded as follows (CC 36(38)8—CAB 23/94):

The Prime Minister said that before he left the Meeting he wished to say a word to Sir Maurice Hankey. This was the last meeting at which he would be among them, holding the post which he had held with so much distinction for so many years. Sir Maurice's Secretaryship to the Cabinet went back to the War days, and he could fairly be called the creator of the modern Cabinet. The members of the present Cabinet were the last of a great body of statesmen who had passed through his hands, with all of whom he had been on intimate terms and who had all given him the fullest confidence. Sir Maurice had often been tempted to leave his post, and on occasions he had been sounded as to whether he would like to join a Government. He had preferred to work in comparative obscurity, and to complete the work which came from his own initiative and which he had fostered until he had brought it to perfection. Sir Maurice Hankey seemed to them all to be a part of the Cabinet room, and without him it would be a different place. He had gained the respect and affection of every one of them, and they would miss him very greatly.

In view of his long service and connection with the Cabinet, and as the first and greatest Cabinet Secretary in history, they wished to give him a personal token of their affection and esteem. They had conspired with Lady Hankey and had chosen a clock of modest dimensions which would be mounted on a stand,

and which would be inscribed with the names of the Cabinet. He hoped Sir Maurice would accept this as a token of their great regard and affection, and as a remembrance of the happy days which they had spent with him.

Sir Maurice Hankey said that he was so unused to speaking in the Cabinet Room that he hardly knew the sound of his own voice there. He found it difficult to find adequate words to thank the Prime Minister and the Cabinet. He had many memories, not only of the present Cabinet but of 7 Prime Ministers and 14 or 15 Governments. He had taken the minutes of more than 1,100 Meetings of the Cabinet proper, or over 1,700 if the War Cabinet were included.

It was true that other posts had been offered to him, but he had always felt that the greatest privilege he could have was to serve the Cabinet, and that was his unfailing thought on entering the Cabinet Room. Bacon had said that 'The greatest trust between man and man is the trust of giving counsel'. His trust had been to hear members of the Cabinet giving counsel to each other, and to record the results. That, he felt, was the highest service which he could render. He was glad that he had continued to serve the Cabinet for so long. He regarded himself as perhaps something of a robot, but robots had their feelings, their criticisms and admirations. So far as he was concerned, since the present Government had been in office, criticism had been lacking and admiration had been continuous. He would like to end on one word which the Prime Minister had used, 'affection'.

539. On the outbreak of the Second World War he entered the War Cabinet as Minister without Portfolio. Under Churchill's coalition government he ceased to be a member of the War Cabinet, but served successively as Chancellor of the Duchy of Lancaster and as Paymaster General till 1942, with a special responsibility for scientific matters; as chairman of the Scientific Advisory Committee (SAC—CAB 90/1–6) he was directly concerned in the first steps for the 'utilisation of the atomic energy of uranium'. There was some coolness between him and Churchill, which may have had its origin in the incident described on p. 280 of Vol. 1 of Roskill's *Life*.

540. After 1942 he was appointed a member of several departmental advisory committees, and at the end of the war resumed his directorship of the Suez Canal Company and other commercial interests. He died in 1963. His main works are:

Government Control in War (1945)

Diplomacy by Conference (1946), which contains much interesting material on the early history of the Cabinet and the CID

Supreme Command (1961), a full account of his activities in the First World War (the Cabinet Office discouraged publication)

Supreme Control at the Paris Peace Conference (1963), a slighter study.

541. *Hankey—Man of Secrets*, by Stephen Roskill (3 vols., 1970–1974), is a full and sympathetic record of Hankey's activities around Whitehall; it is partly based on the official records, but supplemented by his private diaries and correspondence, and forms a most useful commentary on the working of the office and on some of the political events of the time.

542. CAB 63 contains what Hankey termed the Magnum Opus papers, which consist mainly of copies of official papers he had drafted or with whose subject matter he had been actively concerned, and which he kept in his own custody; duplicates of many are to be found in other CAB classes. The collection, which was intended for reference purposes in connection with the Supreme Command and his other writings, was transferred to the Cabinet Office after his death and its arrangement was subsequently undertaken by the Public Record Office.

CHAPTER 6

THE COMMITTEE OF IMPERIAL DEFENCE
1918–1939

601. The CID as an advisory body was in abeyance during the First World War. With the end of hostilities, with growing problems at home, with the rapid run-down of the services and with uncertainty about future international groupings, little attention was initially paid at ministerial level to the future pattern of defence, and the CID did not formally meet until June 1920, when in view of the pressure on the Prime Minister, a Standing Defence Sub-Committee was set up. It met during 1921–1923 and discussed *inter alia* a new base at Singapore, the policies to be adopted at the Washington (Disarmament) Conference and the future of the Royal Air Force. The records of this Sub-Committee (SS) are in CAB 34; at the end of 1923 it was decided that their meetings should be regarded as full meetings of the CID, and accordingly the meetings were renumbered and the minutes are also in the main series (CAB 2) of the CID.

602. Meetings of the CID were held approximately monthly to 1928; for the next seven years they were held less frequently; after 1935 the number increased signi-ficantly (*see* Annex 7a). The chairman was generally Balfour (to 1923), Salisbury (1923), Haldane (1924), Curzon (1925), Baldwin (1925–1929), MacDonald (1929–1931), MacDonald or Baldwin (1931–1936); and after 1936, Inskip and later Chatfield (as Ministers for Co-ordination of Defence), with frequent attendance by Chamberlain. While in theory the Prime Minister was the only permanent member, in practice the nucleus of the membership was the three service ministers with the chiefs of staff, the secretaries of state for Foreign Affairs, Colonies, Dominions and India, a Treasury minister and the permanent heads of the Treasury and Foreign Office; as ARP developed, the Home Secretary was frequently present and other ministers and officials attended as the nature of the business required. Ministers from the Dominions attended on occasions (*see* paras. 640–646). For discussions on the Channel Tunnel, MacDonald invited Balfour, Asquith, Baldwin and Lloyd George to be present at the 186th meeting on 1 July 1924 and Lloyd George and Baldwin to the 248th meeting on 29 May 1930. Haldane was present at the 234th meeting on 25 March 1928 to discuss the report of the committee of which he had been chairman on Anti-Aircraft Research (1D/D/17—CAB 16/67). Apart from these cases there is no mention that a member of an opposition party was present at a meeting of the CID itself, although in 1930 Cecil of Chelwood was chairman of a sub-committee on the Reduction and Limitation of Arms (RA—CAB 16/99), and in 1931 the leaders of the three parties formed the com-mittee on the Disarmament Conference (DC(P)—CAB 16/102).

603. Until his retirement in 1938, Hankey as secretary was present and was generally accompanied by the assistant secretaries of the CID, and on occasions as the pressure of rearmament increased, by a civilian member of the Cabinet Office staff.

604. Following the early tradition of the CID, the minutes of all meetings to the last (374th) on 1 September 1939, were printed on pale green paper. Unlike most of the conclusions of the Cabinet, the minutes of the CID on matters of importance or controversy reflect the views of individuals, and for the discussion of certain subjects a full stenographic note was included.

605. Before the Standing Defence Sub-Committee had started to meet in 1921, the infra-structure of the CID to deal with technical aspects of defence planning had begun to re-form, and before referring to the wider aspects of policy with which the CID was dealing, and which interlocked with the Cabinet, it will be convenient to mention some of the main continuing bodies, which were subordinate to the CID, and which emerged in the inter-war years. They fall into five main groups—namely, strategy and planning, organisation for war, manpower, supply and miscellaneous.

Committees

606. *Strategy and planning.* Among the recommendations of the Salisbury Committee on National and Imperial Defence (ND—CAB 16/46 Cmd. 2029 of 1924) was that the chairman of the CID should be

assisted by the three Chiefs of Staff . . . to keep the defence situation as a whole constantly under review so as to ensure that defence preparations and plans and the expenditure thereon are co-ordinated and framed to meet policy, that full information as to the changing naval, military and air situation may always be available to the CID and that resolutions as to the requisite action thereupon may be submitted for its consideration. In addition to the functions of the Chiefs of Staff as advisers on questions of sea, land or air policy respectively, to their own Board or Council, each of the three Chiefs of Staff will have an individual and collective responsibility for advising on defence policy as a whole, the three constituting as it were a Super-Chief of a War Staff in Commission. In carrying out this function, they will meet together for discussion of questions which affect their joint responsibilities.

607. Following this recommendation the Chiefs of Staff Committee was constituted and quickly became the most influential military element in the CID; Hankey was secretary, and the records are in CAB 53. Beatty (First Sea Lord) was the first chairman, and in accord with the policy that the chairmanship should be drawn from each service in rotation (and irrespective of seniority of rank), he was succeeded in 1927 by Trenchard (CAS), in 1930 by Milne (CIGS), in 1933 by Chatfield (First Sea Lord) and in 1938 by Newell (CAS). On occasions the Prime Minister or the Minister for Co-ordination of Defence was present at meetings, but generally the chiefs met alone (with Hankey) on the basis that an agreed and combined view was more likely to be reached by speaking frankly among themselves and not having to commit themselves separately in front of ministers, including the Chancellor of the Exchequer (cf. R. Rhodes James: *Memoirs of a Conservative* (1969), p. 222).

608. The COS Committee submitted in conjunction with the Foreign Office an annual review of defence policy which was considered by the CID and by the Cabinet. Following that for 1932 the 'Ten Year Assumption' was abandoned (*see* para. 618); and following their later report (CID 1149B) the CID at the 266th meeting on 22 November 1934 instructed their sub-committees to proceed on the basis that preparations should be completed in five years from 1934 in respect of a possible conflict with Germany. The COS Committee formulated the military plans for possible intervention in the successive crises in the 1930s, and advised on their effect. Subordinate to the COS Committee was the Joint Planning Committee (JP—CAB 55) appointed in 1927; the Deputy Chiefs of Staff Committee

(DCOS—CAB 54, Hankey as chairman) in 1932; and the Joint Intelligence Committee (JIC—CAB 56) in 1936. In spite of intermittent friction between the services and the magnitude of the task of co-ordination, the COS organisation grew in strength and was the ready-made instrument as a full committee of the War Cabinet in September 1939, and as the adviser to and executant of the Minister of Defence in May 1940.

The members of the COS Committee before the Second World War were:

First Sea Lords: Beatty (to 1927), Madden (1927–1930), Field (1930–1933), Chatfield (1933–1938), Backhouse (1938–1939), Pound (1939–1943)

CIGS: Cavan (to 1926), Milne (1926–1933), Massingberd (1933–1936), Deverell (1936–1937), Gort (1937–1939), Ironside (1939–1940)

CAS: Trenchard (to 1930), J. Salmond (1930–1933), G. Salmond (1933), Ellington (1933–1937), Newall (1937–1940).

609. *Organisation for war.* This group included the pre-war committees for Oversea Defence (ODC—CAB 7–11) and for Home Defence (HDC—CAB 12 and 13), whose activities were largely co-ordinated after 1920 by the Joint Oversea and Home Defence Committee (JDC—CAB 36), of which Hankey was chairman.

In 1923–1924 committees and sub-committees were organised for:

Censorship (SCC—CAB 49)

Emergency Legislation (WEL and WL—CAB 52)

Imperial Communications (ICC—CAB 35)

Trade Questions in time of War (ATB—CAB 47)

Air Raid Precautions (ARP—CAB 46); this committee was active throughout the period, with subordinate bodies dealing with bombing tests, debris, injuries, evacuation, decontamination, compensation, etc. (reference may also be made to the Civil Defence Policy Committee (CDS(P)—CAB 16/197) set up under Anderson in 1938).

610. *Manpower.* The main committee (NS—CAB 57), originally set up in 1923 under the chairmanship of the President of the Board of Trade and later of the Minister for Co-ordination of Defence, worked through a number of sub-committees dealing with national registration, the schedule of reserved occupations, recruitment, wages, dilution, etc.

611. *Supply.* The Principal Supply Officers Committee (PSO—CAB 60) was set up in 1924 under the Master General of the Ordnance to draw up lists of munitions and war-like stores. It was reconstituted in 1927 under the chairmanship of the President of the Board of Trade, and assumed wider functions in locating capacity and considering the expansion of industry. It worked through numerous sub-committees, whose work at the official level was co-ordinated by the Supply Board, for which a full-time chairman was appointed in 1935 to press forward the rearmament programme. In 1936 the Minister for Co-ordination of Defence became chairman of the main committee. The Board of Trade supply organisation (CAB 60/64–73) was concerned with raw materials. Apart from the COS Committee, the PSO Committee was probably the most important element in the CID structure, and subject to the most pressure; but the problem of the orderly control of the organisation for supply was never fully solved.

612. The Oil Board (OB—CAB 50), appointed in 1925, kept under review the estimates for civil and military requirements, in relation to sources of production, tanker tonnage and stocks. The president was a senior minister, but the chairman was the Civil Lord of the Admiralty, to reflect the naval interest in supply.

613. The CID discussed food supplies on a number of occasions, but initially the matter rested primarily with the Board of Trade and the Ministry of Agriculture and Fisheries. In 1936 a CID committee on Food Supply in Time of War (FS—CAB 16/156–160) was set up under the Minister for Co-ordination of Defence, with a rationing sub-committee under Beveridge.

614. *Miscellaneous.* The most important of the miscellaneous standing committees within the oversight of the CID was that for the Co-ordination of Departmental Action on the Outbreak of War (K and WB—CAB 15) of which Hankey was chairman. The various enquiries by the CID and its committees, and by individual departments about the measures to be undertaken in a transition to a state of war were continuously raising points which would require co-ordination or co-operation between departments on which it was desirable to resolve responsibility in advance. This was done by means of the preparation and maintenance of 'War Books', the purpose of which was to provide, in a concise and convenient form, a record of all the measures to be taken by government through the stages of a worsening threat of war to the outbreak of war itself, in order to ensure that all departments—civil as well as military—knew precisely what was required of them for each measure at each stage; and also to be aware of what other departments were doing at precisely what stage in respect of each measure. The committee undertook the continuous revision of the Government War Book in which all departmental action, collective and individual, was recorded; and required individual departments to compile and keep constantly under revision their departmental War Books designed to explain when, how and by whom in the department the instructions to that department in the Government War Book were to be implemented.

615. Scientific research was primarily a matter for departments (including the DSIR), but mention should perhaps be made of the CID committee on Air Defence Research set up under Swinton in May 1936 and of which Churchill was a member (ADR—CAB 16/132–134) which took over some of the work of the Air Ministry committee under Tizard.

616. The foregoing embrace the principal standing committees of the CID which developed between the wars. Other committees and sub-committees were appointed *ad hoc* (the papers are in CAB 16) and there were the important committees dealing with disarmament and with rearmament which are discussed below. But those already mentioned formed the main structure for examining in depth and proposing solutions for many of the problems involved in total mobilisation for war, and particularly those which would arise in areas neglected before 1914, where the purely military interest might overlap or conflict with the civil interest. Most started at the official level, and were composed of senior military officers and civil servants from the departments concerned, with assistance from outside experts as required; some, where the problems were complex or acute, acquired a ministerial chairman. The general procedure was that the committees considered policy within their terms of reference, and after report as necessary to the CID, left the departments to work out the detail. After appointment the committees were active, but until the early 1930s a certain lethargy tended to develop, partly due to the 10-year assumption (until its abandonment in 1932) and partly due to the frequent changes in membership which occurred over the years as individuals retired or moved to other work. Nevertheless, the CID secretariat kept the committees alive; each member of the staff was secretary to several committees, and by close association with each other they were able to steer problems as they arose to the right quarter and ensure that the work of the different committees was reasonably co-ordinated. They arranged for periodic reports on progress to be made to the CID which noted them with or without comment (most of the reports will be found in the B Series—CAB 4); and at any given time the secretariat was aware of a network of committees and of individuals in departments who would have been in a position to take executive action as the occasion required. The organisation was bound together by the War Books which were kept under constant revision, and the whole was tightened up as the international situation became more threatening.

617. But while the CID itself was receiving and commenting as necessary on the reports of the subordinate bodies engaged in detailed planning in limited spheres, the main attention of ministers and their advisers at the full meetings held between 1920 and 1939 was devoted to the implications of the varying moves on the international scene, and more generally to a few major topics which in one form or another were constantly recurring; most had political overtones and the ultimate decisions were reflected in the Cabinet conclusions, though on probably no occasion (except Singapore) did the Cabinet actively dissent from a unanimous recommendation of the CID. The topics may be grouped as follows:

(a) The 10-year assumption
(b) The organisation for defence (including the Chiefs of Staff Committee)
(c) Grand strategy (including Singapore)
(d) Disarmament
(e) Rearmament
(f) Friction between the Services
(g) Relations with the Dominions.

The minutes of the meetings (CAB 2) are generally full and the underlying memoranda provide full documentation. In this study only the briefest mention can be made of a few salient points.

The 10-year assumption

618. The War Cabinet on 15 August 1919 (WC 616A—CAB 23/12) instructed that the service departments in framing their estimates should assume 'that the British Empire will not be engaged in any great war during the next 10 years, and that no expeditionary force is required for this purpose'. This assumption was generally endorsed by the CID and the Cabinet from time to time until 1928, when the formula became:

(a) That it should be assumed for the purpose of framing the estimates of the fighting services that at any given date there will be no major war for 10 years.
(b) That this assumption be revised annually by the CID before the estimates of the service departments are drawn up, that is to say, not later than the month of June, and that it shall be the duty of the secretary of the CID to remind the Prime Minister of this conclusion at the appropriate moment, and take his instructions as to placing the subject on the agenda paper for the committee.
(c) That it shall be the duty of any department in HMG in Great Britain, no less than the right of the government of any Dominion, to ask the CID to review the above conclusion at any other time if in the opinion of any of them the circumstances had so changed as to render its application to the then existing conditions doubtful (CID 236(6)—CAB 2/5 of 5 July 1928).

619. The assumption was endorsed in 1929 and 1930, but in June 1931 the Foreign Office in CID 1056-B—CAB 4/21 examined the basis underlying it and concluded:

What was at the time of giving a justifiable assumption has of late tended rather to become a speculation with hope still predominant, but with doubt shadowing the prospect.

By CID 253(1)—CAB 2/5 and CC 38(31)13—CAB 23/67 of July 1931, it was agreed that the 10-year assumption should still apply but

that the situation should again be thoroughly re-examined in the light of developments in 1932 on which the continuance or otherwise of the present policy must necessarily depend.

In their annual review of defence policy for 1932 (CID 1082B—CAB 4/21) the chiefs of staff recommended that the 10-year assumption be cancelled; this was agreed by CID 255(4)—CAB 2/5 and by CC 19(32)2—CAB 23/70 in March 1932 (priority to be given to requirements in the Far East).

Organisation for defence

620. The Geddes Committee on National Expenditure (Cmd. 1581) had recommended in 1922 'the creation of a co-ordinating authority or a ministry of defence responsible for seeing that each force plays its part and is allotted appropriate responsibility for carrying out various functions'. To examine this, and the acrimonious relationship which then existed between the Navy and the RAF, the Salisbury Committee on National and Imperial Defence (ND—CAB 16/46) was appointed; it rejected the possibility of a defence ministry at that time and instead recommended the appointment of a deputy to preside over the CID in the absence of the Prime Minister, who would be assisted by the three chiefs of staff (*see* para. 606). In spite of the Salisbury report and the creation of the Chiefs of Staff Committee, public criticism continued that the organisation for defence was inadequate and incomplete. Partially to meet the criticism the Imperial Defence College was established in 1927, and was designed to provide a body of officers with a broad outlook and aware of the changes taking place in all the services; but otherwise ministers continued to argue that the machinery of the CID was the best that could be devised, and the argument received reinforcement in 1931 from the report of the Treasury Committee on National Expenditure under Sir George May (Cmd. 3920) who were satisfied that the existing system of co-ordination through the CID 'provides in effect all the advantages of a single minister of defence without the disadvantage of entrusting supreme control to a single individual, responsible for and yet divorced from each of the three services'.

621. Nevertheless public opinion was not satisfied, and after confused discussion in the Cabinet in February 1936 (cf. CC 7(36)2—CAB 23/83 and CC 9(36)1— CAB 23/83) Inskip was in March 1936 appointed Minister for Co-ordination of Defence. His duties were defined in the Statement Relating to Defence (Cmd. 5107) as follows:

It has been decided that, while the Prime Minister will retain, as he clearly must, the chairmanship of the Committee of Imperial Defence and of the Defence Policy and Requirements Committee, a Minister will be appointed as deputy chairman of these Committees, to whom the Prime Minister will delegate the following duties:

(i) The general day-to-day supervision and control on the Prime Minister's behalf of the whole organisation and activity of the Committee of Imperial Defence; the co-ordination of executive action and of monthly progress reports to the Cabinet, or any Committee appointed by them, on the execution of the reconditioning plans; discernment of any points which either have not been taken up or are being pursued too slowly, and (in consultation with the Prime Minister or other ministers or committees as required) of appropriate measures for their rectification;

(ii) in the Prime Minister's absence, taking the chair at the Committee of Imperial Defence and the Defence Policy and Requirements Committee;

(iii) personal consultation with the Chiefs of Staff together including the right to convene under his chairmanship the Chiefs of Staff Committee whenever he or they think desirable;

(iv) the chairmanship of the Principal Supply Officers Committee.

622. The expenses of the Minister for Co-ordination of Defence were borne on the vote of the Treasury and subordinate departments, under the sub-head of 'Offices of the Cabinet, Committee of Imperial Defence, Economic Advisory Council and Minister for Co-ordination of Defence'. He was provided with office accommodation initially in 2 Whitehall Gardens and later in Richmond Terrace, and with a small personal staff. But he had at his disposal the resources of the unified Cabinet Office (whose staff began to expand) and more particularly of those who formed the secretariat of the CID. Inskip worked mainly through personal contact with ministers, service chiefs and senior civil servants, including the chairman of the Supply Board, and was active in stimulating the work of committees and in discussing the claims for finance with the Treasury. Inskip resigned in January 1939 and was succeeded by Chatfield. The surviving records of the office are in CAB 64.

623. The problems involved in rearmament and defence planning were immense; but apart from their immensity, there was always the hope that the whole exercise might prove to be a false alarm, and to that extent there was at the time an air of some unreality about them. Much progress was made for which credit is due to the two ministers, but whether because of the inherent difficulties in the circumstances of the time, or the lack of executive powers, or their own personalities, or the confidence in which the government of which they formed a part was held, in retrospect neither seems to have been able to call forth the effort from Whitehall or from the country which Churchill later claimed under the stress of war.

Grand strategy

624. At the 140th meeting of the CID on 10 June 1921 it was stated that:

So far as could be foreseen, the most likely war for some time to come would be one between those races whose interests lay in the Pacific, and the view was expressed that it was no longer possible to rely on a treaty which could be terminated at far shorter notice than the period necessary for providing adequate defences. In the case of war with Japan, Singapore, which was considered to be the keystone of imperial defence in the East, would if not adequately defended fall an easy prey to the enemy before the British fleet could arrive. Moreover the fleet would be immobile on arriving there unless the necessary fuel reserves had been provided. Opinion was unanimous therefore that from a strategical point of view it was desirable that Singapore should be developed as a naval base to the extent necessary to enable the main fleet to operate in the Pacific in time of war.

By CC 50(21)3—CAB 23/26 of 16 June 1921 general approval was given to the Singapore project. By CC 21(24)—CAB 23/47 of 17 March 1924 the Cabinet decided in the interests of their general foreign policy not to proceed. By CC 64(24)3 —CAB 23/49 of 26 November 1924 the Cabinet approved in principle that the base should proceed. By CC 20(28)12—CAB 23/57 of 4 April 1928 it was agreed that completion should be delayed. At the 244th meeting of the CID on 25 July 1929, MacDonald stated that the suspended scheme would remain in that condition. By CC 50(32)9—CAB 23/72 of 11 October 1932 work was reinstated subject to

inclusion of air in addition to gun defences, and by CC 27(33)5—CAB 23/75 of
12 April 1933 it was agreed to expedite the completion of the defences by mid-1936.
625. The many and various implications of Singapore were reflected in one form
or another at most meetings of the CID. They included the defence of the Suez
Canal, and argument about the Egyptian treaty (not completed until 1936); the
strategical importance of Palestine and Aden; the Admiralty requirement for one
year's reserve of fuel oil, which involved protection of the South Persian oil
fields; the nature of the defences to be provided at Singapore; the interests of the
Dominions; the size and composition of the fleet; and the burden on the British
taxpayer, which was constantly escalating. It was probably not until 1933 that
serious attention began to be turned to the possibility of involvement in Europe;
but Singapore remained throughout a cardinal feature in strategical thought. By
CID 261(1)—CAB 2/6 of September 1933 it was agreed that the priorities were:

    (i) defence of possessions and interests in the Far East

    (ii) European commitments

    (iii) defence of India.

Disarmament

626. Much of the time of the CID until 1934 was occupied with discussion of
'the Reduction and Limitation of Armaments'—a heading which successively
covered the draft treaty of mutual guarantee, the Geneva protocol, French security
generally, the naval conferences and the Disarmament Conference of 1931. More
than a score of CID or Cabinet committees were appointed between 1923 and 1934
to examine various aspects and their papers will generally be found under the
symbols CD, CDC, DC, DPC, RA and RLA. The most important were the Three
Party Committee on the Disarmament Conference which met under MacDonald
in 1931 (DC(P)—CAB 16/102) and included Cecil of Chelwood, A. Chamberlain,
Hoare, Inskip, Eden, Lloyd George, Samuel and Lothian; and the ministerial
committee on the Disarmament Conference in 1932 (DC(M)—CAB 27/505–511).
627. Few of these committees achieved much, either because of their own disunity
or because their proposals or those of other nations were irreconcilable. The tone
had perhaps been set by the outlook expressed in the following quotations:

    The Secretary of State for War (Derby) suggested that it would be necessary
    for the British representative to assume, though merely for purposes of dis-
    cussion, that the general principles had been accepted, and that they would
    then be able to discuss the technical details resultant on the adoption of such
    principles. He did not in any way intend to imply that the principles would
    ultimately be adopted by the government. (CID 171st meeting on 11 April
    1923—CAB 2/3.)

    The First Lord (Amery) 'was entirely in favour of the League of Nations, but
    did not consider that it was desirable to supplement or give unnecessary pre-
    cision to any of the articles of the covenant by which we were already bound'.
    (CID 173rd meeting on 29 June 1923—CAB 2/3.)

    The Lord Privy Seal (Cecil) 'was of the opinion that it would only be possible
    to guarantee peace by ultimate disarmament'. (CID 173rd meeting on 29 June
    1923—CAB 2/3.)

    The Foreign Secretary (A. Chamberlain), 'whereas we would conform to any
    agreements into which we entered on the subject of control, some other countries
    would not do so'. (CID 206th meeting on 30 November 1925—CAB 2/4.)

Similar hesitation was no doubt felt by statesmen and general staffs in other
countries.

628. Germany left the Disarmament Conference and the League of Nations in 1933, and thereafter disarmament effectively gave place to rearmament.

Rearmament

629. The paragraphs which follow set out chronologically some of the main steps from 1932 leading to rearmament and preparation for war which acquired growing momentum in the following years. The Cabinet, through the Defence Policy and Requirements Committee (DPR—CAB 16/136–144), the CID, the PSO Committee, the Supply Board and the Minister for Co-ordination of Defence, stimulated progress on approved programmes by the service departments, and regular reports from them were received. But the demands which each service was making on industry were largely uncoordinated, and the refusal to create a Ministry of Supply left industry in some doubt as to the orders it could expect and from whom. The Advisory Panel of Industrialists (IP—CAB 16/220–231), set up in December 1938, was an attempt to meet the deficiency, but it probably came too late to be fully effective, and the problem of supply remained largely unsolved until the end of the war.

630. 1932

February The Disarmament Conference opened in Geneva; proceedings lasted for two years, with deadlock between the French desire for security and the German demand for equality.

Following the Three Party Committee on the Disarmament Conference (DC(P)—CAB 16/102) which had met in 1931, a ministerial committee on the Disarmament Conference was set up in 1932 with the Prime Minister as chairman (DC(M)—CAB 27/505–511), which with several sub-committees (CAB 27/512–518) met on a number of occasions 1932–1935.

March By CID 255(4)—CAB 2/5, the 10-year assumption was abandoned; priority should be given to requirements in the Far East (CC 19(32)2—CAB 23/70).

631. 1933

March Japan withdrew from the League of Nations.

April By CID 258(2)—CAB 2/5 a committee was appointed on the Private Arms Industry (PA—CAB 27/551). (This was followed by the setting-up of a Royal Commission on the Private Manufacture of and Trading in Arms, 1935–1936, whose records are in T181; relevant papers, including Hankey's evidence, are in CAB 16/124–126.)

September By CID 261(1)—CAB 2/6 it was proposed:
(a) Expenditure on defence should be based on the following priorities:
   (i) defence of possessions and interests in the Far East;
   (ii) European commitments;
   (iii) defence of India.
(b) No expenditure should be incurred on defence to provide exclusively against attack by the United States, France or Italy.
(c) A committee to be set up of the Chiefs of Staff and the permanent heads of the Treasury and Foreign Office with Hankey as chairman, to prepare a programme for meeting the worst deficiencies (DRC—CAB 16/109–112).
These proposals were agreed by CC 62(33)5—CAB 23/77.

October   Germany withdrew from the Disarmament Conference and the League of Nations.

632. 1934

March   The report of the Defence Requirements Committee (DRC) was referred by the Cabinet (CC 19(34)2—CAB 23/79) to the ministerial committee on the Disarmament Conference (DC(M)). (It was odd to refer rearmament to a committee dealing with disarmament, but the personnel composed of the Prime Minister and senior colleagues was well equipped for the first stage.)

May   By CID 264(6)—CAB 2/6, shadow factories agreed.

June   Disarmament Conference ended in failure.

November   By CID 266(1)—CAB 2/6 the CID sub-committees were instructed to proceed on the basis that preparations should be completed in five years from 1934 in respect of a possible conflict with Germany. (It may be noted that at the 125th meeting of the COS on 4 May 1934—CAB 53/4 the CIGS had 'wondered whether it is really possible to visualise that Germany would be sufficiently strong to attack France in five years' time'.)

633. 1935

March   Statement Relating to Defence (Cmd. 4827) issued notifying intention to rearm (CC 11(35)1—CAB 23/81).

April   By CID 269(1)—CAB 2/6 Sir Arthur Robinson appointed full-time chairman of the Supply Board (CAB 60/31–33). The DC(M) Committee became the ministerial committee on Defence Requirements, and after Baldwin succeeded MacDonald on 7 June 1935 it became a CID Committee on Defence Policy and Requirements (DPR—CAB 16/136–144); the Prime Minister was chairman and Hankey secretary, and by its terms of reference it could report either to the CID or to the Cabinet or both.

Late   The Mediterannean and Abyssinian crisis was becoming acute
summer   and by CC 42(35)6—CAB 23/82 of 22 August 1935 the DPR Committee undertook the general arrangements for safeguarding the position, as well as dealing with rearmament.

October   Italy invaded Abyssinia.

November   General election.

December   Hoare-Laval pact (for discussion *see* CC 56(35)2—CAB 23/90B).

634. 1936

March   Statement Relating to Defence (Cmd. 5107) issued and Inskip appointed Minister for Co-ordination of Defence (CC 22(36)1—CAB 23/83). Germany occupied the Rhineland.

May   Air Defence Research Committee (ADR—CAB 16/132–134) appointed with Swinton as chairman and Churchill a member (CC 56(36)11—CAB 23/85 gives brief reference to the Air Ministry committee under Tizard).

July   Spanish Civil War started.

December   By CID 285(1)—CAB 2/6 the Admiralty staked a claim to remain outside the supply organisation, and if this were agreed the Air Ministry would follow.

635. 1937

January   The Defence Plans (Policy) Committee (DP(P)—CAB 16/181–183) set up with the Prime Minister as chairman and a few senior ministers, to examine plans for a major war, and to provide a nucleus for a possible War Cabinet.

June   By CID 296(1)—CAB 2/6 Italy was not to be regarded as a reliable friend.

July   Anglo-German naval agreement.

November   By CID 301(6)—CAB 2/7 it was agreed to absorb the DPR and DP(P) Committees into the CID; Hankey had explained that the three bodies were all more or less independent of each other, but all were dealing with defence questions without definite lines of demarcation. The chairmen, the expert advisers and the secretaries would be the same, but it would be a convenience to the secretariat if they could all be brought into the indexing system of the CID (*see* para. 526).

636. 1938

February   Eden (Foreign Secretary) resigned.

March   Germany incorporated Austria.

Summer   Czechoslovak crisis developing.

September   Munich.

637. 1939

January   Chatfield succeeded Inskip as Minister for Co-ordination of Defence.

March   Germany entered Czechoslovakia.

April   Creation of Ministry of Supply agreed (CC 21(39)11—CAB 23/60 of 19 April 1939).

Friction between the Services

638. While the Chiefs of Staff Committee was establishing itself as the piece of machinery which became fully effective in the Second World War, it overlay a good deal of inter-service friction in the inter-war years and in particular the endemic controversy between the Admiralty and the Air Ministry about the control of naval aviation. The RAF claimed that the air being one and indivisible should not be partitioned between the services; the Navy claimed that the sea being one and indivisible, with everything above it, it was their domain. The Army after initially claiming their own air force, became more or less neutral spectators. But the suspicion or knowledge which the public had of the lack of agreement flowing from the claim of each service for self-sufficiency, was a factor in the recurrent but largely incoherent demand for some change in the organisation for defence.

639. When the naval air controversy arose after the First World War, it was referred (along with the question of a ministry of defence) to the Salisbury Committee (ND—CAB 16/46 and 47) who in turn referred it to the Balfour Committee (ND(R)—CAB 16/48), whose report, which was accepted by the Cabinet (CC 56(23)3—CAB 23/46), was largely a vindication of the claims of the Air Ministry. Among other examples of the friction, there may be mentioned:

October 1927   (COS 58th meeting—CAB 53/2) The Admiralty claim, on the ground of seniority by rank, to the chairmanship of the COS committee.

March 1928   (CID 234(8)—CAB 2/5) Salisbury (Lord President) complained of the continual references to the Prime Minister for decision on points of difference between the Navy and Air Force.

July 1928	(CID 237(1)—CAB 2/5) Difference of opinion about AA guns for the fleet.
	(CID 239(10)—CAB 2/5) Churchill (Chancellor of the Exchequer) complained that 'the three chiefs of staff, who were jointly responsible for offering advice to the CID, should have technical secrets from one another'.
June 1932	(CID 256(1)—CAB 2/5) Difference about defences at Singapore (CD—CAB 16/105).
July 1933	(CID 260(1)—CAB 2/5) Difference about location of an airbase in Iraq.
May 1934	(CID 282(1)—CAB 2/6) Difference about vulnerability of capital ships.
December 1936	(CID 285(1)—CAB 2/6) The Admiralty staked a claim to remain outside the central supply organisation, and if so the Air Ministry would follow.
January 1937	(CID 287(4)—CAB 2/6) Difference about fleet air arm (FAA—CAB 16/151 and 152).
March 1939	(CID 349(3)—CAB 2/8) Bomb v. battleship.

Relations with the Dominions

640. Notwithstanding its title, the CID during the inter-war years never became a forum for any full discussion of the problems which would arise on the outbreak of an armed conflict affecting imperial interests as a whole. The position of the Dominions (Australia, Canada, New Zealand and South Africa, and the Irish Free State, which did not regard itself as a Dominion) remained obscure. The Oversea Defence sub-committee of the CID (ODC—CAB 7–11) was primarily concerned with the non-self-governing territories, and the presence of the Secretaries of State for the Colonies and for India on the CID itself provided the necessary link with the defence schemes for those territories. The creation of the Dominions Office in 1925, and the exchange of High Commissioners between the UK government and the governments of the self-governing Dominions, provided regular channels for communication, which supplemented the succession of Imperial Conferences, whose agenda included items relating to imperial defence.

641. But the recollection of the confusion at Gallipoli, of the status they had achieved as signatories of the 1919 Peace Treaty and as members of the League of Nations, and of their apprehensions of involvement at the time of Chanak, together with the growing demand for independence which was confirmed by the Statute of Westminster in 1931, made the Dominions suspicious of attending meetings of the CID where their presence could be taken as implying commitments on their part, however tenuous they might be.

642. The UK government made several attempts to enlist their more active co-operation. Baldwin in a speech to the Imperial Conference of 1926 (Cmd. 2769, p. 167) said:

I hope that . . . we may consider how far we can in the interest of co-ordination of defence make further use of the elastic machinery of the CID. So far as we here are concerned we shall certainly welcome your more frequent association and closer co-operation with the work of the committee on all matters affecting the Dominions or the general defence of the Empire, to whatever extent and in whatever manner you may consider appropriate.

643. At the 251st meeting of the CID on 28 November 1930 the Dominion Prime Ministers were present for a general discussion on imperial defence in the course of which Milne (CIGS and chairman of the COS Committee) made a statement (copy on 7/1/1 Part 3—CAB 21/470) in which he summed up the relative positions of Great Britain and the Dominions as follows:

The maintenance of sea communications is the first principle of imperial defence, and the major share of this responsibility still rests with HM government in Great Britain. Apart from this the chief principle is that on the one hand each of the several Dominions is responsible for its internal security and for protecting its territory and coastal trade until support arrives from outside, while HM government in Great Britain, in addition to its duty to defend its own territory, is mainly responsible for the security of the communications between the several parts of the empire, the defence of the non-self-governing colonies and protectorates and the mandated territories assigned to Great Britain and the protection of the interests of the Empire in foreign countries generally and our special position in Egypt.

The CIGS pointed out that while emphasis was laid on the responsibility of the Empire for its own local defence, no mention had been made of the possibility of collective action in the event of aggression against the Empire as a whole made by a major power. He suggested that there might be room for closer co-ordination of defence policy by the Dominions accepting responsibilities outside their own frontiers in areas in which they were directly interested.

644. In the autumn of 1934 Hankey visited Australia as the guest of the Commonwealth government for the celebrations of the centenary of Victoria; he was also invited to visit New Zealand and made the outward journey by South Africa and returned by Canada. In South Africa and Australia he had conversations with the defence ministers, explained that Britain was rearming and left the door open for co-operation by the Dominions if they wished; in Australia he advised on the local organisation for defence. CID paper 401-C gives an account of his discussion in South Africa, but no account of his other discussions appears among the records of the CID; official papers relating to the visit are in CAB 21/385 and 398 and his private papers in CAB 63/66–82. The visit appears to have given rise to a good deal of misunderstanding both at home and overseas as to why, when on what was ostensibly a private visit, he was engaged in official conversations, which if they were to be entered into at all should be at ministerial level.

645. The reaction of the Dominions to these approaches was varied, but generally inconclusive. In 1928 Australia, New Zealand and South Africa had authorised their High Commissioners in London to attend meetings of the CID, and thereafter they were invited to those meetings which were not devoted entirely to matters of domestic interest. Initially they attended with some regularity, but during the 1930s attendance became less frequent, although Australia, with its interest in Singapore, was generally represented when matters affecting the Far East were under discussion. From time to time the Dominions were represented at meetings of the sub-committees of the CID, and Menzies and Bruce attended the 170th meeting of the Chiefs of Staff committee on 31 March 1936 for a discussion on the defence of Australia.

646. It is noteworthy that the most intimate relations of the CID were with Australia. In 1924 R. G. Casey (later Minister of State in the Middle East and subsequently Governor General) was appointed as the liaison officer of the Commonwealth with the Foreign Office. He was provided with accommodation in the Cabinet Office in Whitehall Gardens, and Hankey was authorised to show him the documents of the Cabinet and CID in which Australia might be interested, although he was not to send any to Australia without consultation with Hankey

(CAB 21/469). Casey held this appointment until 1931, when Bruce became High Commissioner in London.

647. The Dominions were generally divided about the successive crises in the 1930s, and after the failure of the League of Nations on Abyssinia, it became clear at the Imperial Conference of 1937 that they wished to be free from commitments in Europe and that the UK could not count on their backing in the event of war. It appears to have been accepted that in the case of a major war each Dominion would itself decide the nature and extent of its commitment, and apart from the interest in Singapore and other bases overseas, there is little in the records of the CID to show any marked effort at co-ordination of policy (but reference should be made to the records of the Dominions Office).

648. In May 1939 a note on the Position of the Dominions in the Event of War (DP(P)54—CAB 16/183) was sent to the UK High Commissioners in the Dominions for their guidance and information, and indicating the action the Dominion governments might take on the assumption that they 'would decide to associate themselves with the action taken by the United Kingdom government'. File 10/4/8 (CAB 21/873) contains information about the actions taken by the Dominions in the early part of September 1939.

CHAPTER 7

THE COMMITTEE OF CIVIL RESEARCH AND THE ECONOMIC ADVISORY COUNCIL

Haldane Report

701. The Haldane report of 1918 on the Machinery of Government (Cd. 9230) had suggested *inter alia* that provision be made for the organised acquisition of facts and information as a preliminary to the settlement of policy. The suggestion was picked up by MacDonald in CP 366(24)—CAB 24/167, who proposed the formation of a committee analogous to the CID, which would ensure that all material facts and information at the disposal of the government service would be made available in practical form for use by the Cabinet in reaching its conclusions, and by CC 43(24)3—CAB 23/48 of 22 July 1924 agreement in principle was given. The MacDonald government took the proposal no further, but it was revived by Baldwin in CP 195(25)—CAB 24/172 and warmly endorsed by Balfour in CP 263(25)—CAB 24/173, and by CC 27(25)12—CAB 23/50 of 28 May 1925, the establishment of the Committee of Civil Research was agreed, and confirmed by Treasury minute of 13 June 1925 (Appendix IV to Annex 3) as a standing committee reporting to the Cabinet. The president would be the Prime Minister, the chairman would be a minister nominated by him, and the members, like the CID, consist of such persons as the president or chairman might invite; it would be an advisory body without administrative or executive functions, and as a normal part of its working it would refer particular inquiries to special sub-committees. Tom Jones was appointed secretary.

702. The first meeting of the committee was on 18 June 1925, and under Balfour's leadership it was active in the next six months mainly with an investigation into the iron and steel industry (CAB 58/1). It appointed a score of sub-committees (for list see under symbol CR in Annex 11) and the main committee then met infrequently to 1928 to receive reports from the sub-committees, whose membership included experts in various fields. Two of the sub-committees appointed during this period (Tsetse fly, CR(TF)—CAB 58/31–54 and Locust control, CR(L)—CAB 58/55–82) acquired a more or less independent existence and continued until 1939.

703. The main Committee of Civil Research did not meet after April 1928, but the sub-committees already appointed continued to meet. Shortly after taking office in June 1929, and partly under the stimulus of the Liberal Yellow Book, MacDonald appointed sub-committees to examine the iron and steel, cotton and fishing industries; each consisted of two ministers, with a representative of employers and workers and an accountant, and each held over 25 meetings.

Economic Advisory Council

704. CAB 58/15 contains the replies given in December 1929 to MacDonald by several industrialists and economists he had consulted (including Henry Clay, G. D. H. Cole, J. A. Hobson, J. M. Keynes and Walter Layton) on the 'Industrial

Situation' and on 'An Economic General Staff', evidently in the hope that outside the government service he might find a body of expertise which could raise the country out of the depression. The views of those consulted differed, but by CC 3(30)6—CAB 23/63 of 16 January 1930, the Cabinet agreed to set up an Economic Advisory Council to absorb the Committee of Civil Research, with the responsibility:

> To advise HMG in economic matters. To make continuous study of developments in trade and industry and in the use of national and imperial resources, of the effect of legislation and fiscal policy at home and abroad, and of all aspects of national, imperial and international economy with a bearing on the prosperity of the country.

705. The Council as a standing body reporting to the Cabinet was confirmed by Treasury minute of 27 January 1930; it was to take over and expand the functions of the Committee of Civil Research; it was not to interfere with the functions or responsibilities of ministers, and was to have no administrative or executive powers; the Prime Minister would be chairman, and the members be such ministers as he might from time to time summon, and such other persons chosen by the Prime Minister in virtue of their special knowledge or experience in industry and economics; the staff, working within the ambit of the Office, would be a secretary and assistant secretaries 'at least two of whom will be economists' (cf. Appendix IV to Annex 3).

706. Among the independent members initially summoned were E. Bevin, W. Citrine, G. D. H. Cole, J. M. Keynes, Josiah Stamp and R. H. Tawney. The secretary was Tom Jones until his retirement in August 1930, when he was succeeded by H. D. Henderson and A. F. Hemming as joint secretaries; the assistant secretaries included P. K. Debenham and, initially, H. V. Hodson and Colin Clark, and later D. H. Rickett.

Committee of Economists

707. The Council first met on 17 February 1930 and at early meetings devoted most attention to the economic outlook and the state of trade, with appreciably less reference to scientific subjects. Some of the sub-committees of the Committee of Civil Research were continued, and a number of new sub-committees were appointed (for list see under symbol EAC in Annex 11), including on 1 August 1930 a committee of Economists (EAC(E)—CAB 58/150–151).

> to review the present economic condition of Great Britain, to examine the causes which are responsible for it, and to indicate the conditions of recovery.

The members were J. M. Keynes (chairman), H. D. Henderson, A. C. Pigou, L. Robbins and Josiah Stamp, with R. F. Kahn as a joint secretary. It met 10 times before reporting on 24 October 1930 (CP 363(30)—CAB 24/216). The report was controversial; it criticised rings and monopolies and trade union restrictions; it hinted at subsidies to wages; and recommended tariffs (Robbins made a strong, and Pigou a milder, dissent).

708. The report of the Economists' committee was exhaustively considered by the Council at five meetings between November 1930 and April 1931. There were sharp differences of view between some of the members while others showed little interest in the discussions. The Council reached no decision on the recommendations, and before its next and final meeting on 15 January 1932 the Labour government had fallen and its place been taken by the National government, a majority of whose members was committed to tariffs, which were shortly imposed.

Standing committees on Scientific Research and on Economic Information

709. By mid-1931 the Council was virtually dead and most of its sub-committees withered away during the next 12 months. The Council's scientific functions and supervision of the remaining scientific committees were continued by the standing committee on Scientific Research (EAC(SR)—CAB 58/25–29), with terms of reference to advise the Economic Advisory Council as to the reports of its scientific committees and generally as to the discharge of its functions in their scientific aspects. Under Sir Daniel Hall as chairman it met periodically until 1938. Its membership included Sir Frederick Hopkins, Julian Huxley, Lord Rutherford, Sir Charles Sherrington and the secretaries of the Department of Scientific and Industrial Research and of the Medical and Agricultural Research Councils. Hemming and Rickett were the secretaries.

710. Its economic functions passed to the standing committee on Economic Information (EAC(EI)—CAB 58/17–23), with terms of reference

> to supervise the preparation of the periodic reports to the Economic Advisory Council on the economic situation and to advise as to the continuous study of economic development.

The chairman was Stamp, and the members Citrine, Cole, Keynes, A. Lewis, J. A. Salter and E. D. Simon, with Henderson (until retirement in 1934) and Hemming as joint secretaries. The Stamp committee met regularly until 1939 and made periodic surveys on the economic situation, which were circulated to the Cabinet.

711. The departments had from the outset tended to regard the Committee of Civil Research and the Economic Advisory Council with suspicion; when Baldwin and Balfour lost interest in the first, and MacDonald in the second, enthusiasm evaporated, and in the absence of departmental support none of the continuing bodies could be very effective. Those with the longest life were the tsetse fly and locust control committees, which produced large quantities of paper, and owed much to Hemming who, as an eminent lepidopterist, had a quasi-professional interest in them. The Hall Committee on Scientific Research found little to do in view of the activities of the DSIR and of the Research Councils, and of the research being conducted by the service departments. The Stamp Committee on Economic Information found the situation improving under the influence of devaluation, tariffs and rearmament, and the PSO organisation of the CID with full departmental backing was making its plans independently; nevertheless the committee continued until 1939, and provided the nucleus for the Stamp Survey (*see* para. 968).

Committee on Non-Intervention in Spain

712. With the running down of the Economic Advisory Council the staff were not fully occupied, and when late in 1936 it was necessary to provide an organisation in London for the 'International committee for the application of the agreement regarding non-intervention in Spain', Hemming was appointed secretary-general in a personal capacity and was authorised to use the resources of the Office for the secretarial work. The International committee (whose papers are in CAB 62) was wound up in 1939 and Hemming returned to the Office, where he took administrative charge of the Central Economic Information Service (*see* para. 966).

CHAPTER 8

IMPERIAL AND INTERNATIONAL CONFERENCES
1915–1939

List of conferences

801. Following were the conferences for which the Cabinet Office, either alone or in association with other departments, provided the secretariat for the United Kingdom delegation, and for which the Office maintained a full record of the proceedings.

1915–1919	A number of Anglo-French and Allied conferences (including the Supreme War Council)	CAB 28/1–9
1917 March–April	Imperial War Conference	CAB 32/1/1
1917 March–May	Imperial War Cabinet	CAB 23/40
1918 June–December	Imperial War Cabinet	CAB 23/41–44
1918 June–July	Imperial War Conference	CAB 32/1/2
1919	Peace Conference	CAB 29/1–40
1919–1922	A number of minor allied and international meetings	CAB 29/81–99
1921–1922	A number of conferences on Ireland	CAB 43/1–7
1921 June–August	Imperial Conference	CAB 32/2–6
1921 December–1922 January	Washington (Disarmament Conference)	CAB 30/1–33
1922 April	Genoa (International Economic Conference)	CAB 31/1–13
1922 December	Allied Prime Ministers in London	CAB 29/102
1923 October–November	Imperial Conference	CAB 32/7–37
1924 July–August	London Reparations Conference	CAB 29/103–106
1926 October–November	Imperial Conference	CAB 32/38–64
1928 February–July	Imperial Wireless and Cables Conference	CAB 32/65–67
1928 December–1929 May	Committee on the organisation of Imperial Communications Services	CAB 32/68
1929 August–1930 January	Hague Conference	CAB 29/107–116
1930 January–April	London Naval Conference	CAB 29/117–135
1930 October–November	Imperial Conference	CAB 32/70–100
1931 July	London Conference (Financial Co-operation)	CAB 29/136–137
1932 April	Situation in the Danube States	CAB 29/138
1932 June–July	Lausanne Conference	CAB 29/139
1932 July–August	Imperial Economic Conference, Ottawa	CAB 32/101–116

1933 February–April	Committee on Economic Consultation and Co-operation	CAB 32/117–123
1933 June–July	London Monetary and Economic Conference	CAB 29/140–145
1934 April–1935 October	London Naval Conference	CAB 29/147–158
1935 February	Anglo-French Conversations (MacDonald/Flandin)	CAB 29/146
1935 March–April	Economic Discussions with Australian Ministers	CAB 32/124
1935 April–May	Meetings of Commonwealth Prime Ministers	CAB 32/125
1935 May–July	Economic Discussions with Dominion Ministers	CAB 32/126
1937 May–June	Imperial Conference	CAB 32/127–137
1939 March–November	Anglo-French Staff Conversations	CAB 29/159–162

802. Hankey had attended most of the inter-allied conferences during the First World War, and the techniques which he had then developed, based in part on those of the CID and of the earlier Imperial Conferences, led to Clemenceau's invitation to him to act as secretary to the Council of Four by whom the major decisions were taken at the Peace Conference at Versailles. The success which he achieved there gave him an international reputation which led to his appointment in a personal capacity as secretary-general to the Hague, London Naval and Lausanne Conferences, and as secretary of the Imperial Conferences.

Responsibility for arrangement

803. The general responsibility for arrangement of the British representation at international conferences had passed to the Foreign Office at the end of 1922 (para. 507); but that for the Imperial Conferences remained with the Cabinet Office partly because the topics dealt with involved the interests of several United Kingdom departments, and partly because the Dominion Prime Ministers were a little chary of too close an association with the Colonial Office. The creation of the Dominions Office in 1925 was a recognition of their status, and thereafter the arrangements for the Imperial Conferences were made in close association between the Cabinet Office and the Dominions Office.

804. Each conference tended to have its own features and to lack any common pattern. But when the Office was involved there was generally a heavy preparatory load in co-ordinating the views of the departments concerned in order that a common UK view could be presented by ministers at the opening. There was a further load, lightened by assistance from the overseas departments concerned, in providing the secretarial services at the conference itself—arranging accommodation, hospitality and communications, copying and distributing memoranda and minutes to the participants, in briefing the press and in the drafting of the final communiqué.

805. The Cabinet conclusions contain many reflections of the proceedings at the conferences, whether in the form of the initial or revised instructions to the UK representatives, or reports of progress.

806. For the proceedings of those conferences which are not mentioned in para. 801, and of the conferences and meetings of the League of Nations, reference should be made to the records of the Foreign Office and the other overseas departments.

CHAPTER 9

THE WAR CABINET 1939–1945

Discussion on supreme control

901. In May 1928 Hankey had submitted a paper (882-B—CAB 4/17) to the CID discussing the supreme control which should be adopted if and when the necessity arose, and summarising the alternatives as:

(a) a normal peace-time system of a Cabinet advised by the CID;

(b) a Cabinet assisted by a special Cabinet committee, with powers of decision on questions within the order of ministerial competence;

(c) a Cabinet assisted by a 'War Committee' with fuller executive powers;

(d) a War Cabinet which absorbed the functions of both the Cabinet and the CID.

His argument pointed to (d), but he concluded that 'whatever preparations are made in time of peace, the question is one which in the end will have to be decided by the Prime Minister of the day'. This was followed by a paper by the chiefs of staff (883-B—CAB 4/17), putting on record their view that 'it should be a cardinal principle that the organ of supreme control should take no decision in regard to the initiation or conduct of operations without consulting the chiefs of staff [who] should attend all the meetings . . . whenever matters concerning or affecting the army, navy or air force are under discussion'. These papers were accepted by the CID (239th meeting on 13 December 1928—CAB 2/5) and subsequently endorsed (321st meeting on 5 May 1938—CAB 2/7), with the addition that 'a chief of staff attending any meetings in time of war of the organ of supreme control or other ministerial body should be definitely responsible for stating his opinion on military questions whether he is specifically invited to do so or not'. It followed from this that on the outbreak of war the Chiefs of Staff Committee would become the advisers to the supreme control on any matters affecting the military aspect of the conduct of the war, and through their respective service ministers the executants of approved military policy.

902. Little further formal action on the nature of the organ of supreme control was taken before the Munich crisis, but in the light of that experience minutes passed between Bridges, H. J. Wilson, Warren Fisher and the Prime Minister (copies on 19/10/19 Part V—CAB 104/124) in November and December 1938 in which it was agreed that the only practical course on the outbreak of hostilities with a major power would be a War Cabinet of about six members who would for the most part be free from normal departmental duties, able to meet daily and give immediate and authoritative decisions; the minutes contemplated that there would be two standing committees—one for Home Security and the other for Home Affairs. At that stage the matter could not be taken further; it was not known when, if ever, the crisis would arise; and if it did, what government would then be in office, who would be the Prime Minister, whether he would want or could secure inclusion of members of the opposition parties, and whether he could select a War Cabinet of about six individuals who would command sufficient public confidence.

The War Cabinet to May 1940

903. Chamberlain's War Cabinet was formed of himself and eight others; those with departmental duties were the Chancellor of the Exchequer (Simon), the Foreign Secretary (Halifax) and the three service ministers (Churchill, Hore Belisha and Kingsley Wood); those without departmental duties were Hoare (Lord Privy Seal), Chatfield (Minister for Co-ordination of Defence) and Hankey (Minister without Portfolio), and these three it was expected would take a special part in the co-ordination of the war effort.

Chamberlain had not included members of the Labour and Liberal Parties; he was anxious to include Churchill (who had not held office for 10 years); Churchill wanted the Admiralty, and it was therefore logical to include the other service ministers as well as the Minister for Co-ordination of Defence. This gave a larger number than originally contemplated.

The War Cabinet May 1940–May 1945

904. Churchill formed his coalition government in May 1940, with a War Cabinet of five, the Conservative element being himself, Chamberlain and Halifax, and the Labour element Attlee and Greenwood. Halifax (Foreign Secretary) was the only minister with departmental duties. By the end of 1940 the membership had increased to eight by the inclusion of Beaverbrook (Aircraft Production), Bevin (Labour and National Service) and Kingsley Wood (Treasury); Anderson had taken the place of Chamberlain (Lord President) and Eden that of Halifax. Various changes were made subsequently, by the inclusion of Lyttelton, Cripps, Casey, Morrison and Woolton, but the membership at any one time did not exceed eight before the end of the coalition in May 1945. Though the Liberal Party was not directly represented in the War Cabinet, Sinclair as its leader and Secretary of State for Air was a 'constant attender'.

Caretaker Cabinet May–July 1945

905. After the defeat of Germany, the Labour and Liberal Parties withdrew from the coalition, the members of the War Cabinet resigned and Churchill formed a 'caretaker government' with a Cabinet of 17 members, most of whom were Conservatives; several National Liberals were ministers not in the Cabinet. A general election was imminent, and as it was clear that no major decisions could be taken before the result was known, there was relatively little business before the Cabinet. The COS Committee was active in the prosecution of the war against Japan and for the Potsdam conference, but for the most part the secretariat marked time; certain of the committees met; and the symbol for the Cabinet conclusions was changed from WM to CM and for memoranda from WP to CP. The election was held on 5 July 1945, and after counting the votes of service men overseas the results were announced on 26 July 1945: 213 Conservatives; 12 Liberals; 393 Labour; 22 others. The Churchill administration resigned.

Discussion of an Imperial War Cabinet

906. The possibility of an Imperial War Cabinet had been canvassed early in the war (WP(G)(39)10—CAB 67/1 and WP(G)(40)95—CAB 67/5) but had not been proceeded with on the ground that the Prime Ministers of the Dominions would have difficulty in leaving their countries, and that they could not commit their governments without prior consultation. But elaborate arrangements were made for liaison with the Dominions through their High Commissioners in London;

D

the importance of this liaison was emphasised when Attlee as deputy Prime Minister also served as Secretary of State for the Dominions from February 1942 to September 1943. Following the outbreak of war with Japan, the Australian and New Zealand governments asked that their accredited representatives should have the right to be heard in the War Cabinet in the formulation and direction of policy; this was agreed (WM 12(42)1) on the understanding that those representatives would not have full membership, and that similar arrangements would be made with the other Dominions if they wished. The Australian representatives (generally Bruce or Evatt) became regular attenders at the Monday meetings, but a certain amount of difficulty arose about the invitations they received and the papers circulated to them (file 10/4/8/1—CAB 21/874 and CAB 104/180–181). Representatives of the government of India (WP(42)395) and visiting ministers from the Dominions were present on occasions. The Prime Ministers' Conference in 1944 (PMM—CAB 99/28) was the only occasion during the Second World War when the heads of the Dominions met formally together.

General procedure

907. The secretarial arrangements were set out in WP(G)(39)1—CAB 67/1; the CID ceased to have a separate existence; the secretary to the War Cabinet (Bridges) was assisted by a deputy secretary civil (Howorth) and by a deputy secretary military (Ismay) who was also secretary to the COS Committee; there were three agenda officers responsible to the secretary for summoning meetings and for preparing the agenda marked with the approximate time for summoning to the War Cabinet those ministers who were not members. (The title of 'agenda officers' shortly disappeared and the work was absorbed into the secretariat.) It was recognised that the five-day rule (*see* para. 511) could not be maintained, but ministers were invited not to submit questions to the War Cabinet until they had been adequately discussed with departments concerned and the point to be settled been narrowed to a definite issue. The conclusions were to be circulated to each member of the War Cabinet, to every minister holding an office which immediately prior to war was a Cabinet office, and to the Chiefs of Staff and the permanent heads of the Treasury and of the Foreign Office. The War Cabinet would meet daily at 11.30 a.m. at 10 Downing Street or in the Cabinet War Room in the New Public Offices.
908. As the war proceeded there was no basic change in the organisation of the Office as a committee machine, although the volume of work and the speed with which it was conducted significantly increased. It included the COS organisation and the staff of the Minister of Defence; but the mechanics for the distribution of memoranda, for the arrangement of meetings and for the notification of conclusions followed the general procedures which had been developed in the previous 20 years. (For Notes on War Cabinet Procedure, issued in May 1943, *see* Annex 4.)
909. In the case of memoranda for the War Cabinet, an initial change was the introduction of three series, not precisely defined, but which appear to have been:
  WP   those dealing with policy or with operations (CAB 66)
  WP(G) those dealing with more general matters, including procedures, notification of committees, etc. (CAB 67)
  WP(R) those containing regular reports and returns (CAB 68).
The distinction between the three series became progressively unreal and was abandoned during 1941–1942. Churchill reverted to his practice before and after the First World War of circulating his own memoranda in printed form on high quality white quarto paper; other memoranda were duplicated on white foolscap or printed on pale green paper.

910. War Cabinet memoranda were circulated to the members of the War Cabinet, and unless the Prime Minister gave instructions to the contrary were also circulated to ministers of Cabinet rank (who came to be known as 'ministers above the line' and comprised those at the head of departments who would normally be included in a peace-time Cabinet, together with the war-time creations of ministers of state and ministers resident abroad, cf. file 4/1/3—CAB 21/777), to the permanent heads of certain departments and to the chiefs of staff.

911. Meetings of the War Cabinet were initially held daily, generally at 11.30 a.m. (sometimes in the afternoon and evening as well). Under Churchill's administration the times became more erratic, though by 1942 some endeavour was made to secure three normal meetings a week (WM 28(42)4—CAB 65/25); those at 12 noon on Wednesdays and Thursdays would be attended by War Cabinet ministers only, except in so far as others might be invited for particular items; those at 5.30 p.m. on Mondays would include the 'constant attenders' and the chiefs of staff who would give to this 'Monday parade' a resumé of the military situation. While the 'Monday parade' was fairly constant, the time-table was no more than faintly recognisable during the following three years, and on military affairs Churchill summoned much the same individuals to meetings variously of the War Cabinet, the Defence Committee or the COS Committee (when termed a staff conference) at short notice. In Chamberlain's absence the chair was normally taken by Simon and in Churchill's absence by Attlee.

912. Under Chamberlain's administration those present at the War Cabinet in addition to the members generally included the chiefs of staff, Eden (Dominions Office), Anderson (Home Secretary), H. J. Wilson (permanent secretary to the Treasury) and a representative of the Foreign Office (normally Cadogan). Under Churchill's administration the 'constant attenders' were the three service ministers (of whom Sinclair, as Secretary of State for Air, but equally as leader of the Liberal Party, was the most regular) and the chiefs of staff; others varied from time to time and included Kingsley Wood, Beaverbrook and Cripps (after they had ceased to be members), Bracken and Cherwell, and during Eden's frequent absences abroad Law or Cadogan from the Foreign Office. On occasions ministers or high commissioners from the Dominions and India, British ambassadors and commanders-in-chief, or representatives from the USA (including Harriman, Hopkins and Marshall) were present for the whole or part of a meeting.

913. Apart from the 'constant attenders', other ministers were invited for particular items in which it appeared they would be concerned, at times which were given to them as approximate. The procedure did not always run smoothly; ministers were sometimes kept waiting, but more frequently they had not been invited to a meeting when the discussion took an unexpected turn and a decision was reached in their absence which affected them. Bridges was able to handle most of these cases with tact and no case is known to have occurred in which a minister resigned through disagreement with a decision of the War Cabinet. But the authority of the members of the War Cabinet was recognised; when Sinclair objected to a decision on the training of pilots for the RAF, and said he would find it difficult to defend this in Parliament, the Prime Minister 'said that the position as regards ministerial responsibility was necessarily different under a small War Cabinet from the position in peace-time when the Secretary of State was himself a member of the Cabinet' (confidential annex to WM 238(40)1—CAB 65/14 of 30 August 1940).

914. The business at meetings of the War Cabinet was naturally varied. When the chiefs of staff were present the proceedings generally began with a resumé of the military situation, but as the committee system developed a wide range of matters were referred initially to an appropriate committee, and those which were taken direct to the War Cabinet tended to be:

(a) major issues of foreign policy and Commonwealth affairs;
(b) questions of outstanding importance in any sphere (whether civil or military) on which it was clear that a decision could only be given at the highest level, and that preliminary consideration by a committee was unnecessary;
(c) questions of a predominantly political character (eg conscription of women, or those affecting Parliament).

915. Bridges as secretary was present at practically all meetings; Ismay as deputy secretary (military) was present at all at which military matters were under consideration; one or more assistant secretaries, civil or military, were generally present.

916. The conclusions of the War Cabinet were circulated the same day in duplicated form to those ministers who had been present, with extracts to other ministers who might be affected. After an interval of a few days to allow for receipt of amendments, which were referred as necessary to the Prime Minister for approval, they were printed and circulated to the regular recipients mentioned above. These printed conclusions, bound in volumes generally covering a period of three months, now form CAB 65. This class also includes the parallel volumes of confidential annexes, containing the 'conclusions recorded in the secretary's standard file'; these are in typed or duplicated form, and copies were sent only to those ministers directly concerned. Matters recorded in these annexes relate primarily to forthcoming military operations, and to matters of special concern to Commonwealth, allied and foreign governments; references to domestic affairs are few (but WM 140(43)—CAB 65/36 of 14 October 1943 records a full discussion on post-war claims on the Exchequer). A number of the confidential annexes—especially during the early part of the war—contain an extensive account of the discussion, including the differing views expressed by individual ministers.

917. The annual indexes to the conclusions of the War Cabinet, which are bound into the last volume for the year, detail the various topics which were considered at the 1200 meetings. Annex 8 analyses the originators of papers to the War Cabinet in the WP and WP(G) series, and Annex 9 the originators of papers to the Lord President's Committee.

Chamberlain and Churchill administrations compared

918. Under both administrations the final responsibility, subject to Parliament, rested with the War Cabinet; under both, the chiefs of staff, as the professional heads of their own services, were responsible for advice to the War Cabinet and for the execution of approved policy. But the equipment which each required, and which could be created in the circumstances of time, showed some marked differences.

919. Under the Chamberlain administration, the War Cabinet contained the three service ministers and the Minister for Co-ordination of Defence; and it appointed a Military Co-ordination Committee (MC—CAB 83).

The Chiefs of Staff, after considerable discussion of a problem, would report their conclusions, or differences, to the Ministerial Co-ordination Committee. There the whole ground would have to be gone over again, and perhaps a new set of conclusions or differences would be reached. The matter would then go to the War Cabinet, and once more the process of explanation and disputation would have to be repeated. (Ismay, *Memoirs*, p. 109.)

This system of supreme direction worked ponderously during the first eight months of war, but came near to collapse during the Norwegian campaign in April 1940.

Under the Churchill administration

The key change . . . on my taking over was of course the supervision and direction of the Chiefs of Staff Committee by a Minister of Defence with un-defined powers. As this minister was also the Prime Minister, he had all the rights inherent in that office, including very wide powers of selection and removal of all professional and political personages. . . .

[The service ministers] were not members of the War Cabinet. . . . They remained entirely responsible for their departments, but rapidly and almost imperceptibly ceased to be responsible for the formulation of strategic plans and the day-to-day conduct of operations . . . the actual war direction soon settled into a very few hands, and what had seemed so difficult before became much more simple—apart of course from Hitler. (Churchill, *The Second World War*, Vol. II, pp. 15–16.)

Henceforward the Prime Minister himself . . . exercised a personal, direct, ubiquitous and continuous supervision, not only over the formulation of military policy at every stage, but also over the general conduct of military operations. . . . All the considerations affecting any problem—political and economic, as well as military—could now be brought into focus more readily, and . . . firm decisions could be reached and translated into action far more quickly than had hitherto been the case. For the first time in their history, the Chiefs of Staff were in direct and continuous contact with the Head of the Government. . . . (Ismay, *op cit.*, p. 159.)

920. Thus from May 1940, and with the COS organisation as a basis, the Office came to contain a Ministry of Defence with undefined executive powers in the military sphere. There was no 'ministry' in the generally accepted sense of that term. The position was described by Churchill as follows:

Let me now speak of the office, or title, which I hold as Minister of Defence. About this there seem to be many misunderstandings. Perhaps the House will bear with me while I explain the method by which the war has been and will be conducted. I may say, first of all, that there is nothing which I do or have done as Minister of Defence which I could not do as Prime Minister. As Prime Minister, I am able to deal easily and smoothly with the three service depart-ments, without prejudice to the constitutional responsibilities of the Secretaries of State for War and Air and the First Lord of the Admiralty. I have not, there-fore, found the need of defining formally or precisely the relationship between the office of Minister of Defence when held by a Prime Minister and the three service departments. I have not found it necessary to define this relationship as would be necessary in the case of any Minister of Defence who was not also Prime Minister. There is, of course, no Ministry of Defence, and the three service departments remain autonomous. For the purpose of maintaining general supervision over the conduct of the war, which I do under the authority of the War Cabinet and the Defence Committee, I have at my disposal a small staff, headed by Major-General Ismay, which works under the long-established pro-cedure and machinery of the pre-war Committee of Imperial Defence and forms a part of the War Cabinet Secretariat. . . .

I do not, of course, conduct this war from day to day myself; it is conducted from day to day, and in its future outlook, by the Chiefs of Staff Committee, namely, the First Sea Lord, the Chief of the Imperial General Staff and the Chief of the Air Staff. These officers sit together every day, and often twice a day. They give executive directions and orders to the commanders-in-chief in the various theatres. They advise me, they advise the Defence Committee and the War Cabinet, on large questions of war strategy and war policy. (*Hansard*, 24 February 1942, cols. 40 and 41.)

Under the present arrangement the three Chiefs of Staff sitting almost continuously together, carry on the war from day to day, assisted not only by the machinery of the great Departments which serve them, but by the Combined General Staff, and making their decisions effective through the Navy, Army and Air Forces over which they exercise direct operational control. I supervise their activities whether as Prime Minister or Minister of Defence. I work myself under the supervision and control of the War Cabinet, to whom all important matters are referred. (*Hansard*, 2 July 1942, col. 607.)

The organisation was outlined in Cmd. 6351 of April 1942; the unity of the Office was maintained and the military members constituted the 'Office of the Minister of Defence'.

921. While Churchill as Minister of Defence with undefined powers could assume control of military affairs, no similar solution was readily available for dealing with the problems on the home front, which in many ways were more complex, and where few of the major issues, whether of manpower, production, rationing or the import programme, fell wholly within the sphere of a single department. Full mobilisation for the war effort therefore called for a high degree of co-ordination at the centre, but this could not become fully effective until departments had built up regional and local machinery which could establish contact with the homes, shops, farms and factories in the country, where most of the decisions taken at headquarters would have their final impact. In September 1939 few departments had more than embryo organisations for the purpose, and notwithstanding the Regional Commissioner organisation of the Ministry of Home Security, there was a good deal of initial frustration and confusion while the channels were being formed for passing instructions or advice downwards, and for sifting the problems being encountered locally upwards to the point of solution. The absence of enemy action in the first few months reduced the sense of urgency; in wide areas the secrecy with which various offices tended to surround themselves did not add to coherence; and it took time for departments to fit in their new recruits from industry and the universities.

922. At the level of the War Cabinet there was some reflection of the frustrations and confusions which were being encountered below. The committee structure on the civil side, outlined in WP(G)(39)17 and 93—CAB 67/1 and 2, and designed to relieve the War Cabinet of much detail, was initially built around three ministerial committees—Home Policy, Civil Defence and Priority, each with several sub-committees. Within eight weeks there were added ministerial committees on Economic Policy and on Food Policy. When the Chamberlain administration fell in May 1940, the Priority Committee had hardly met, and there was beginning to be a good deal of overlap and duplication between the Home Policy, Economic Policy and Food Committees; and the Civil Defence Committee, with little to do in the absence of air raids, was tending to concern itself with wider issues. The committees were meeting frequently, there were large attendances by ministers and there was much interlock of membership.

923. Following Churchill's minute to Bridges of 24 May 1940 that there 'are far too many committees of one kind and another which ministers have to attend and

which do not yield a sufficient result', he made his first reorganisation in June 1940 by appointing the Production Council and the Lord President's Committee. The second reorganisation was at the end of 1940 with the dissolution of the Economic Policy Committee and the Production Council, and the appointment of the Import and Production Executives and the Reconstruction Problems Committee (WP(G)(40)338—CAB 67/8). By the end of 1941 the two Executives were fading; the Ministry of Production was established in the spring of 1942 and the Ministry of Reconstruction in December 1943. But from the end of 1940, as the regional and local organisations of the civil departments were becoming stronger and as the central machinery of government was tightening up, the Lord President's Committee emerged as the principal organ of the War Cabinet in co-ordinating the social and economic aspects of the war effort on the home front.

A fuller account of the committee structure as it evolved during the war is given in later paragraphs.

Ministerial appointments overseas

924. The following special appointments were made:
Minister of State in the Middle East (July 1941)
Minister Resident at Singapore (July 1941)
Minister Resident in West Africa (June 1942)
Minister Resident for Supply, Washington (November 1942)
Minister Resident at Allied Forces HQ, NW Africa (December 1942).

Their responsibilities varied with the posts and the circumstances of their appointment, but their functions included the following:

(a) to relieve the military commanders of political responsibilities and to provide them with political guidance;

(b) to co-ordinate the activities of different British authorities and to provide a point of contact between them and representatives of allied governments.

(c) to give in case of emergency decisions on matters which would normally be referred to London.

They did not supersede the ordinary representatives of HMG in the territories concerned, but worked in close consultation with them. A small staff was attached to each, and the link with the War Cabinet was provided by a periodic letter from the secretary (*see* files 48/46/18—CAB 21/1359-1364); their reports were normally addressed to the Prime Minister (*see also* FO 660 and FO 921).

Committees—general

925. Before and during the Second World War there was a good deal of criticism of the proliferation of committees in and around the government machine (cf. Churchill's views in para. 990); the implication was that they were cumbrous and time-wasting means of avoiding responsibility. On occasions it was hoped that the remedy might lie in a change of title, and in the Cabinet Office nomenclature there have been executives, boards and councils; departmental usage has included panels, working parties and study groups. But where a number of different executive authorities are involved in the same problem and concerted action or advice is called for, no more satisfactory way of securing prompt dispatch of business has yet been found than by calling the parties together round a table in what is effectively a committee.

926. During the Second World War the Office provided the secretariat for 400 War Cabinet committees and sub-committees, which held an aggregate of over

8,000 meetings (and in addition it was associated with the secretariats of the Combined Chiefs of Staff and of the Combined Boards). A list of these committees is in Part 3 of Annex 11; each had from the Prime Minister, the War Cabinet or a parent committee defined terms of reference (which in varying degree were adhered to), but the title which had been carefully chosen, can now usually be regarded as an adequate guide to the subject intended to be covered.* The membership was generally specified in the terms of reference and constitution, but unless the committee had a short life, the names of those present at meetings tended to vary appreciably from those initially appointed either because of change of office, or the sending of substitutes, or by the attendance of those with an interest in the topic at particular meetings. Attendance was generally confined to ministers, senior military officers and civil servants who would be responsible for the execution of approved policy; but for some of the specialised scientific committees (eg Psychologists and Psychiatrists in the Services, PP—CAB 98/25–28) non-officials were appointed as advisers or assessors. As the war drew to an end some care was taken to ensure that on ministerial committees dealing with reconstruction and post-war problems there was representation not only of the departments concerned, but some adequate reflection of the outlook of the political parties which formed the coalition.

927. The success of a committee depended on a number of factors, including the difficulty of the subject itself, and the personalities of the chairman, the members and the secretary. The importance of the part which a chairman could play was emphasised by Churchill in the following extract from a directive of March 1941 (WP(G)(41)34—CAB 67/9):

> Chairmen of committees must accept responsibility for the orderly conduct of business. They must see that proper agenda papers are issued: that, save in cases of great urgency, the issues to be discussed are set out concisely in writing and circulated before the meeting. Above all, they must see that discussion is kept to the point at issue and irrelevance curtailed; that the numbers attending meetings are reduced to the minimum; and that meetings are not held unless necessary. Again, every chairman should, in advance of the meeting, digest the papers and think out the tentative line or lines on which the issues to be determined can be resolved and, if need be, take preliminary soundings.
>
> Finally, chairmen are responsible for ensuring that secretaries, under their direction, follow up items not settled at the meetings, and take steps either to get them disposed of outside the committee, or to have preliminary points discussed in order that the question may be ripe for a decision when it is again put on the agenda.

928. Each of the assistant secretaries in the Office was normally acting as secretary to several committees, and apart from his work in connection with them, became conscious through his association with his colleagues of the generality of the proceedings elsewhere.

> During most of the war civil and military staffs alike worked, slept and had their meals in the same building. They worked and lived together and shared the same thoughts far more than is usual with an office staff. . . . It was this day-to-day or hour-to-hour contact between all the members of the secretariat which prevented overlapping and gaps arising between the work of different committees; which enabled any subject to be steered towards the committee

---

* Code words were used for the following committees:
  Bolero (BC—CAB 81/48–51)—movement of U.S. troops to United Kingdom.
  Crossbow (CBC—CAB 98/36–38)—German long-range missiles.
  Overlord (OP—CAB 98/40)—invasion of France.

which could deal with it most expeditiously; and which avoided any conflicts of jurisdiction. (Bridges, quoted on p. 377 of *Grand Strategy*, Vol. VI.)

Bridges himself as head of the Office had an intangible responsibility for sensing the problems or conflicts which were arising, and for suggesting in the right quarters how they might most effectively be handled—whether left to inter-departmental solution, whether referred direct to the War Cabinet, or to an existing committee, or whether a fresh committee or sub-committee should be formed, and if so what should be its terms of reference and how it might be constituted. In parallel with this oversight, Bridges with the support of the Prime Minister exercised his influence to avoid time-wasting; among other points he urged that minutes should not be over-elaborate, and that meetings with large fixed attendances should not be summoned when many of those present would have little direct concern in the points for settlement.

929. The elaborate committee structure which evolved during the war was largely a matter of improvisation and adaptation to the unforeseen and changing circumstances as they arose—the fall of France, the threat of invasion, civil defence, the shortages of manpower and materials, the requirements for operations, plans for reconstruction, etc—but modified by the ability and availability of members of the War Cabinet to act as chairmen of those committees to deal with the more important and pressing issues. Churchill as Prime Minister and Minister of Defence was a law unto himself; he was primarily concerned in the military aspects and these were liable to be settled without much discrimination in the War Cabinet, or the Defence Committee, or a staff conference, or some *ad hoc* body, but the COS organisation gave coherence to the military decisions wherever they were taken. On the civil side Anderson and Attlee were the 'anchor men', not only as the successive chairmen of the Lord President's Committee, but as chairmen of a number of *ad hoc* committees.

930. The main division of the War Cabinet committees was into those which were primarily military and those which were predominantly civil. Of the military committees, the Military Co-ordination Committee and later the Defence Committee were standing committees at ministerial level; the COS committee was both advisory and executive, and was served by a number of sub-committees.

931. The civil committees can be divided into those whose chairman was (a) a member of the War Cabinet, (b) a junior minister (whether of Cabinet rank or a parliamentary secretary) and (c) an official; and each can be sub-divided into those which were initially intended to have a short life to deal with some immediate problem, and those intended as standing committees to keep some general situation under review—but intentions were liable to upset.

932. Whatever were the precise terms of reference to a committee of which a member of the War Cabinet was chairman, policies and decisions agreed there were normally accepted without question, and endorsement by the War Cabinet would be sought only in special circumstances. In the case of committees presided over by a junior minister it was the practice to make a report to a senior committee or to the War Cabinet on any immediate problem referred to it, and to make periodic reports when some general matter was being kept under review (eg by the Oil Control Board or the Shipping Committee). Officials frequently attended meetings of the ministerial committees, and when they did so in the absence of their own ministers were expected to keep them informed of progress and to take their instructions as necessary.

933. While many of the sub-committees of the CID had been composed wholly of officials, it had been unusual before 1939 for a Cabinet committee to consist of

D*

other than ministers, though officials were often present (*see* para. 523). But in the early days of the war several double-decker committees were appointed, one of ministers and the other of officials from the same departments, with the intention that the latter would assemble material in a digestible form and present it to ministers for their decision on the action to be taken. Double-decker committees continued for some matters, but as the war proceeded committees composed wholly of officials and with an official as chairman, were appointed to deal with specific problems, with narrow terms of reference and with defined responsibility to some ministerial body. It might have been expected that some of these problems could have been dealt with directly between officials in the departments concerned, but there is evidence that departments attached some importance to meeting on neutral ground and to having the minutes recorded by the Cabinet Office as a central and impartial secretariat (cf. Bridges' note in Appendix II to MGO 74—CAB 87/72). Many of these official committees did useful work in easing the burden on ministers and, subject to their approval, in securing co-ordination in their own spheres. But there was a tendency for some to outlive their usefulness and to continue rather as a convenient meeting place for those with common problems than for the settlement of immediate issues. On the other hand, while the war was still in progress, without finite end, and the possibility that the problem would again become acute, there was a natural hesitation to bring any piece of organisation to an end. Some suspicion of official committees was held in political circles that they might magnify or minimise the difficulties of any particular course of action, with the result that ministers were liable to be presented with cut and dried solutions; or alternatively, that in the adjustments of day-to-day administration policies were gradually built up to which ministers suddenly found themselves committed (cf. Dalton, *The Fateful Years*, p. 407).

934. Part 3 of Annex 11 lists not only the regularly constituted committees, but also a number of informal meetings in the MISC or GEN series which were held between ministers, officials and others and for which the Office has preserved a record. In addition there were of course a number of discussions between ministers at which matters of varying importance were settled and of which the Office has no record. Nor has the Office a record of the meetings which are understood to have been held with some regularity by Chamberlain and less frequently by Churchill, where junior ministers were given a general review of the war situation and some exposition of the government's policy (some brief mention is given on file 48/28—CAB 21/1344).

935. Many important decisions or recommendations were made by committees which met on only a few occasions, but notes follow on those committees which at various times during the war were commonly recognised as the senior standing committees of the War Cabinet and among whose records will be found a reflection of some of the major issues which arose (the following table shows the annual number of meetings of each).

As an introduction it may be useful to recall the two radical reorganisations which Churchill made in the committee structure: first, in May 1940, the appointment of the Defence Committee, the Lord President's Committee and the Production Council; secondly, at the end of 1940, the dissolution of the Economic Policy Committee and the Production Council, and the appointment of the Import and Production Executives, and the Reconstruction Problems Committee (para. 923). Adjustments were inevitably made subsequently, but the creation of the Ministry of Production in February 1942 and of the Ministry of Reconstruction in December 1943 involved some significant changes.

Memoranda and meetings of the War Cabinet, and meetings of the principal committees

	1939	1940 to 10 May	1940 after 10 May	1941	1942	1943	1944	1945 to 23 May	1945 23 May to 26 July	Chairman
Memoranda to War Cabinet (WP, WP(G))	314	769		411	552	526	714	401		
Meetings										
War Cabinet	123	119	193	138	174	176	176	62	17	Prime Minister
COS (incl. VCOS & O)	118	120	321	443	361	323	414	134	50	Newell–Pound–Brooke
Military Co-ordination	11	38								Chatfield–Churchill
Defence (Operations)			52	76	20	14	10			Prime Minister
Defence (Supply)			18	15	7	8	8	2		Prime Minister
Night Air Defence			4	6	4	3	3	4		Prime Minister
Battle of the Atlantic				16						Prime Minister
Anti-U-Boat					9	27	4	1		Prime Minister
Combined Chiefs of Staff					54	84	41	19		
Home Policy	22	16	37	46	38	33	40	16	1	Hoare–Attlee
Civil Defence	14	15	32	39	11	16	28	5		Anderson–Morrison
Food Policy	5	13	27	25	2					Hoare–Attlee
Economic Policy	14	12	14							Simon–Greenwood
Lord President's			29	62	77	77	59	24	2	Chamberlain–Anderson–Attlee
Production Council			13							Greenwood
N. American Supply			6	5	2					Salter–Beaverbrook–Lyttelton
Import Executive				32	3					Duncan
Production Executive				30	1					Bevin
Allied Supplies Executive				6	24	13	3	1		Beaverbrook–Lyttelton
Shipping					21	36	16	6		Harcourt–Johnston
Armistice Terms and Civil Administration						12	5			Attlee
Armistice and Post-War							23	12		Attlee
Reconstruction Problems					4	14	10			Greenwood–Jowitt
Reconstruction Priorities						31				Anderson
Reconstruction						1	80	18		Woolton
India					15	3	4	23	3	Attlee
Palestine						4	3		2	Morrison
Scientific Advisory				20	15	11	18	2		Hankey–Butler–Dale
Tube Alloys Consultative						3	7	2		Anderson

Principal military committees

936. *Chiefs of Staff Committee* (COS-minutes—CAB 79; memoranda—CAB 80). The organisation was taken over ready made from the CID. The three chiefs were the professional heads of their own services and collectively responsible for 'advising the War Cabinet on any matters affecting, or affected by the military aspect of the conduct of the war'. After early attendance at their own offices they usually met together daily at 10.30 am at the Cabinet Office (and often proceeded to the meeting of the War Cabinet later in the day). The vice-chiefs generally met in the afternoon, and the minutes of the meetings of both are numbered in the same series (CAB 79). The COS memoranda are in CAB 80. From mid-1942 to end of 1944 most of the minutes and memoranda were marked 'O' (ie operational and top secret) and given a more restricted circulation, and are now contained in separate volumes in CAB 79 and 80. Certain of the 'confidential annexes to the minutes recorded in the secretary's standard file' were noted as missing in 1949, and it must now be assumed they were accidentally destroyed; those which survive are too fragile for production, but xerox copies are in CAB 79/85–90. Most aspects of the military effort—manpower, equipment, munitions, logistics, directives to commanders, strategy, relations with allies and neutrals—are dealt with or reflected in the COS papers, to which there is a full printed subject index (CAB 79/91). A clue to the meaning of the code-words used can be found in Appendix 1 to PRO Handbooks No. 15, *The Second World War: A Guide to Documents in the Public Record Office.*

The members of the COS Committee during the Second World War were:
First Sea Lords: Pound (1939–1943); A. Cunningham (1943–1946)
CIGS: Ironside (1939–1940); Dill (1940–1941); A. Brooke (1941–1946)
CAS: Newall (1937–1940); Portal (1940–1946).

Ismay as chief staff officer to Churchill attended most meetings. Newall was chairman to October 1940; Pound to March 1942; and Brooke for the remainder of the war.

The COS appointed a number of sub-committees whose records are in CAB 81; but the principal subordinate bodies, which worked in close association in adjoining rooms adjacent to the Cabinet War Room, were:

Joint Planning Committee (later Staff) (JP—CAB 84)

This operated in three sections—strategical, executive and future operational. After 1943 formal minutes of meetings were abandoned and the memoranda sent forward to the COS represented agreed proposals.

Joint Intelligence Committee (JIC—not open to public inspection)

This, under the chairmanship of a Foreign Office representative, consisted of the directors of intelligence of the three services and a member of the Ministry of Economic Warfare, and worked in close touch with the Joint Planning Staff.

Joint Administrative Planning Staff (JAP—CAB 84/87–89)

Appointed in November 1942 to assist the Joint Planners mainly on transport matters, the staff worked on agreed memoranda, and no minutes were kept.

Much of the material produced by these bodies was circulated as COS memoranda, to be found in CAB 80.

937. Ismay as deputy secretary (military) to the War Cabinet was initially the secretary to the COS committee. In May 1940 he became chief staff officer to the Minister of Defence and an additional member of the COS committee—retaining his position as deputy secretary of the War Cabinet. Hollis succeeded him as secretary of the COS committee, and with Jacob, Price, Cornwall-Jones and a number of other military officers who served as secretaries of the various military sub-committees, constituted within the War Cabinet secretariat the 'Staff of the Office of the Minister of Defence' (Cmd. 6351).

938. In spite of criticism made from time to time in Parliament that the COS organisation was unsound, the COS Committee functioned continuously throughout the war, holding upwards of 2,000 meetings. Although the three chiefs (with Ismay) generally met alone, their meetings were sometimes attended by representatives of the Dominions, by officials of the Foreign Office or Ministry of Economic Warfare and by commanders-in-chief (including Eisenhower) when in London; the Chief of Combined Operations attended as a member when matters affecting overall strategy or combined operations were under discussion. On occasions Churchill presided (when the meetings were termed 'Staff Conferences'). Decisions of the COS Committee, after reference as necessary to the Defence Committee (Operations) or the War Cabinet, were implemented by the chiefs within their own service; though as the war proceeded instructions to commanders in the field, and communications through the British Joint Staff Mission in Washington to the Combined Chiefs of Staff, were issued direct by the COS Committee (copies of the telegrams which passed are in CAB 105).

939. *Military Co-ordination Committee* (MC—CAB 83). This was set up as a standing ministerial body at the end of October 1939 under the chairmanship of the Minister for Co-ordination of Defence (Chatfield), with the three service ministers as members and the chiefs of staff as advisers,

> to keep under constant review on behalf of the War Cabinet the main factors in the strategical situation and the progress of operations and to make recommendations from time to time to the War Cabinet as to the general conduct of the war.

Its relationship to the War Cabinet and to the COS Committee was never very clear. It considered *inter alia* the question of intervention in Finland, and the German threat to the Low Countries, and was beginning to examine the problem of supply before Chatfield resigned from the War Cabinet on 3 April 1940. Churchill as First Lord became chairman of the committee which was promptly immersed in the Norwegian operations, and though Chamberlain took the chair at several meetings during April, the major decisions were taken in the War Cabinet. On 1 May 1940 a reorganisation was proposed, under which the Prime Minister would take the chair when possible; otherwise it was to be taken by Churchill who was to have direct access to the COS Committee, and for this purpose to have a unified staff at his disposal under a senior staff liaison officer (Ismay) who would be an additional member of the COS Committee. This reorganisation was stillborn, as the Chamberlain government fell a few days later, and Churchill as Prime Minister assumed the further office of Minister of Defence.

940. *Defence Committee (Operations)* (DO—CAB 69). When Churchill became Prime Minister and Minister of Defence in May 1940 he dropped the Military Co-ordination Committee and promptly formed a corresponding group under his chairmanship composed of the service ministers and the chiefs of staff, which was announced in Parliament on 4 June 1940 as the Defence Committee. The membership shortly included Attlee, Beaverbrook and Eden, and other ministers and expert advisers attended as occasion required. It provided the opportunity for Churchill to meet with the chiefs of staff, with Eden (as Foreign Secretary) and with Attlee (as senior member of the War Cabinet) and settle strategic matters, shorn of the detail with which the COS Committee tended to be concerned, and with due regard to the implications in the field of foreign affairs. Churchill would consult the War Cabinet as necessary on the action to be taken, but he was usually able to assume acquiescence. The committee, whose meetings were generally held late in the evening, was very active during 1940 and 1941, but thereafter meetings got fewer as the COS machine was running more smoothly (with the Prime Minister attending staff conferences), as strategy was becoming formulated and as the Combined Chiefs of Staff were becoming increasingly influential.

941. *Defence Committee (Supply)* (DC(S)—CAB 70). This, with flexible membership, was summoned by Churchill to deal with particular crises in the supply of equipment to the armed forces, including guns, ammunition, tanks and aircraft; it gave much of the impetus to the bomber programme. The number of meetings declined as the Ministry of Production got into its stride.

942. Other PM military committees included:

Night Air Defence (NAD) (CAB 81/22)
Battle of the Atlantic (BA) (CAB 86/1)
Anti-U-Boat Warfare (AU) (CAB 86/2–7)
Tank Parliament (TP) (CAB 98/20)

943. *Combined Chiefs of Staff* (CGS—CAB 88). By agreement between Churchill and Roosevelt in January 1942, military co-ordination was placed in the hands of the Combined Chiefs of Staff, composed of the US Joint Chiefs of Staff and the British Chiefs of Staff. Their responsibilities were set out as follows (COS(42)112—CAB 79/20):

Under the direction of the heads of the United Nations the Combined Chiefs of Staff will collaborate in the formulation and execution of policies and plans concerning:

(a) The strategic conduct of the war.
(b) The broad programme of war requirements based on approved strategic policy.
(c) The direction of munition resources based on strategic needs and the availability of means of transportation.
(d) The requirements for overseas transportation for the fighting services of the United Nations, based on approved strategic priority.

The routine meetings of the Combined Chiefs were generally held in Washington, where the British Joint Staff Mission (responsible to the COS Committee) provided representation when the chiefs of staff were not present in person. The main lines of allied strategy were settled by Churchill and Roosevelt at conferences, with the Combined Chiefs present at some of the sessions; a list of the conferences is given in para. 971.

The papers of the Combined Chiefs of Staff Committee are in CAB 88/1–44. The principal committees of the Combined Chiefs were:

Combined Planning Staff (CPS) (CAB 88/50–56)
Combined Intelligence Committee (CIC) (CAB 88/57–60) (closed)
Munitions Assignment Board (MBW) (CAB 88/83–87)
Combined Military Transportation Committee (CMT) (CAB 88/88–95)
Combined Civil Affairs Committee (CCAC) (CAB 88/63–77)
Combined Communications Boards (CCB) (CAB 88/96–108)
Combined Administration Committee (CAdC) (CAB 88/45–48)

Officers attached to the BJSM provided the British element in the secretariat for these combined committees.

944. It is understood that the Americans have few complete sets in series of the papers circulated within the CCS organisation, but that they have a series of subject files within the Joint Chiefs of Staff organisation which include the CCS material. In this respect it seems that the files of the Joint Chiefs of Staff correspond to the subject files in the SIC series (*see* para. 983(a)). In view of their joint origin there must be some doubt whether the records of the CCS are strictly 'public records', but by UK/US agreement most of the records were made available to public inspection simultaneously in London and Washington in January 1971.

945. *Home Defence Committee* (HD—CAB 93). A Home Defence Executive had been set up by the GOC, Home Forces, in May 1940 to examine the problems connected with the possibility of invasion. Under Sir Findlater Stewart it came to handle questions of joint military and civil interest, particularly on the use of the forces to eke out civilian labour (eg civil defence, agricultural work, parcels at Christmas). In May 1941 it became the Home Defence Committee to relieve the chiefs of staff of matters which were not of strategical importance; among these were the protection of vulnerable points, requisitioning of firearms, camouflage, assault training areas, the position of US troops in the United Kingdom, and the security arrangements for Overlord (invasion of France in 1944). The minutes and memoranda are in CAB 93/1 and the working papers in CAB 112 and CAB 113.

Principal civil committees

946. *Home Policy Committee* (later, Legislation Committee) (HPC—CAB 75). This was one of the two ministerial committees which had been contemplated before the war to deal with the home front. As most of the civil departments were not represented in the War Cabinet, the terms of reference were wide and included all domestic questions other than those directly relating to civil defence; and its membership was large. In the early days of the war it was swamped with business, but its activities were shortly eroded by the Economic Policy Committee and by general uncertainty about the boundaries of its jurisdiction. It survived the reorganisation of May 1940, and was divided into two sections, one for the social services, the other for legislation. Oversight of the former passed to the Lord President's Committee in February 1942, and thereafter the Home Policy Committee—renamed the Legislation Committee—met regularly to continue the control of the legislative programme, including the massive output of Defence Regulations.

947. *Civil Defence Committee* (CDC—CAB 73). This was the second of the two ministerial committees originally contemplated to deal with the home front. It met under the chairmanship of the Home Secretary and Minister of Home Security; its membership paralleled that of the HPC, and before air attack started it was tending to stray into the sphere of that committee. It continued throughout the war and was particularly active at the time of the air raids in 1940–1941 and in 1944.

948. *Food Policy Committee* (FP(M)—CAB 74). Appointed in October 1939 as a sub-committee of the HPC, this body, with a parallel official committee under H. J. Wilson, was initially dealing with the administrative arrangements for rationing, but wider questions of subsidies and shipping resources were involved and there was a good deal of overlap with the Economic Policy Committee. The official committee lapsed in May 1940 and the ministerial committee continued until April 1942, when the Lord President became chairman, and thereafter the work of the FP committee was absorbed into the Lord President's Committee.

949. *Economic Policy Committee* (EP(M)—CAB 72/1–5). Like the ministerial committee on Food Policy this was another body rather hastily set up after the outbreak of war, originally to give ministerial cover to the Stamp Survey (P(E & F)—CAB 89/1–9, see para. 965). Its terms of reference were 'to keep under constant review the whole field of our economic war effort'; the Chancellor of the Exchequer (Simon) was the first chairman. It was paralleled by an official committee of which

Stamp was president and H. J. Wilson chairman, assisted by a group of academic economists and statisticians recruited as the Central Economic Information Service (*see* para. 966). It quickly became involved in questions of prices, subsidies, exchange control, shipping, etc, but the position was complicated by the activities and demands of the Anglo-French Co-ordinating Committee (FBC—CAB 85/8–14), a body established after the outbreak of war and which was aiming at a pooling of allied resources. Under Churchill's first reorganisation in June 1940, the ministerial committee survived under the chairmanship of Greenwood; the official committee lapsed (in view of Churchill's mistrust of H. J. Wilson and the Treasury influence) and the Stamp Survey and the associated economic staff were placed at the disposal of the ministerial committees dealing with economic and related subjects. The EP(M) committee was wound up at the second reorganisation at the end of 1940 (WP(G)(40) 338—CAB 67/8).

950. *Lord President's Committee* (LP—CAB 71). It was an important part of Churchill's first reorganisation that there should be effective co-ordination below the War Cabinet of the principal ministerial civil committees; and in Chamberlain as Lord President and former Prime Minister, he had what he hoped would be an effective co-ordinator at hand. In a minute to Bridges of 17 May 1940 (48/21 Part 4—not yet transferred to the Public Record Office) he called for

a revision of the existing system of dealing with economic problems and placing it under the Lord President. I have it in mind that trade, transport, shipping, MEW, food and agriculture would all come into a general group, over which he would exercise a large measure of executive control.

On 4 June 1940 it was announced in Parliament that Attlee (as chairman of the HP and FP committees), Greenwood (as chairman of the EP committee and Production Council), Anderson (as chairman of the CD committee) and Kingsley Wood as Chancellor of the Exchequer, would meet under the chairmanship of Chamberlain to direct and co-ordinate their work.

Thus after nine months of war, and in the turmoil of establishing a coalition government while military disasters were occurring in Norway and in France, some added coherence was given to the organisation on the home front. But the revised structure was working uneasily and was overshadowed by Dunkirk, by the fall of France, by the threat of invasion and by air raids. Chamberlain was a sick man who resigned on 3 October 1940 and died shortly after, and had never been able to activate the LP committee as originally intended. He was succeeded by Anderson and the LP committee was reconstructed as a steering committee to consist of Attlee, Bevin, Duncan, Greenwood, Morrison and Kingsley Wood, with terms of reference:

(i) To keep continuous watch on behalf of the War Cabinet over the general trend of economic development.

(ii) To concert the work of the economic committees, and to deal with any differences not requiring reference to the War Cabinet.

(iii) To deal with any residual matters and with special questions which arise from time to time.

By WP(G)(41)17—CAB 67/9 Churchill made it clear that the LP committee would deal with price policy, wages policy, financial policy, home consumption, foreign trade and export surpluses. At the end of 1940 the functions of the Central Statistical Office and of the Prime Minister's Statistical Branch had been clarified and the economists who had formed part of the Central Economic Information Service were placed at the disposal of the LP Committee; the Stamp Survey as such was discontinued (WP(G)(41)12—CAB 67/9).

1. Imperial War Cabinet, 1917

2. Churchill's War Cabinet, 1941

3. Maurice Hankey

4. Hastings Ismay

5. Edward Bridges

6. Norman Brook

From the beginning of 1941 the LP committee gradually achieved a pre-eminent position on the home front. In February 1942 it formally took on the social services section of the Home Policy Committee, and the Food Policy Committee as such became redundant when the Lord President became its chairman in the same month. The relationship of the LP committee with the Production Executive, and later with the Ministry of Production, was uneasy as in the nature of the case there could be no clear division of function; 'in general it might be said that the LP Committee concentrated its attention upon the economic consequences arising from the suction of resources into the war production zone, but did not take responsibility for the positive employment of resources in that zone' (Hancock and Gowing, *British War Economy*, p. 221). But the Lord President did take the responsibility of preparing the man-power budget for the consideration of the War Cabinet—a function which Anderson took with him when he went to the Treasury in September 1943 (MP—CAB 92/104).

The subjects dealt with by the LP committee were very varied but Annex 9 shows the number of papers submitted to it and gives some indication of the extent to which different departments were bringing their problems to the committee for solution.

The success of the LP committee was in large measure due to the personalities of Anderson and of Attlee (who succeeded as chairman in September 1943). Its status and prestige were maintained by confining its membership to a few senior ministers; and its impact was sharpened by the assistance which the chairman received from the members of the Economic Section in presenting co-ordinated and objective pictures of the economic situation as a whole and of the probable economic results of projected policies.

951. *Production Council* (PX—CAB 92/56). This was set up by Churchill in May 1940 as part of the first reorganisation, to take the place of the ministerial Priority Committee (PC—CAB 92/74 and 75) which had proved ineffective. Its terms of reference were 'to give general directions as to the organisation and the priority of production . . . and to give final decisions on priorities of all kinds'. Greenwood was chairman; it formulated the Area (later Regional) Boards; it worked mainly through sub-committees, among which was the Man-Power Requirements Committee (MPR—CAB 92/102), in which Beveridge and others (with J. H. Wilson as secretary) laid the framework for the later man-power budgets. The meetings of the full council became overloaded with officials; it could not resolve the growing friction between the supply departments and the Ministry of Labour and National Service; there was some loss of confidence in the chairman; and the Council was wound up at the end of 1940 and its place taken by the Production Executive.

952. *North American Supply Committee* (NAS—CAB 92/27–35). After the fall of France the elaborate purchasing machinery of the Anglo-French Co-ordinating Committee (FBC—CAB 85/8–14) was switched into the North American Supply Committee, formed in July 1940 with Salter as chairman, to co-ordinate the demands made on the British Purchasing Mission in the USA. For the arrangements on Lease-Lend it became a more senior committee under the chairmanship of Beaverbrook, until those functions passed to the Ministry of Production during 1942. The memoranda in the NAS series contain the minutes of the British Supply Council in North America, which met regularly in Washington under the chairmanship of the ambassador or the Minister Resident in Washington for Supply, and co-ordinated the work of the British element in the combined boards; the secretariat of the London end of the Council (known as the North American

Secretariat and later renamed the Joint American Secretariat) was provided initially by the Cabinet Office, and later jointly by the Cabinet Office and the Ministry of Production. (The working papers of the committee in London are in CAB 110 and 115.)

953. *Import Executive* (IE—CAB 92/70 and 71). This, like the Production Executive, was set up at the end of 1940 as part of Churchill's second reorganisation; Duncan was chairman. Its appointment followed difficulties about settling the import programme between the competing claims of food and raw materials, and differences between the Ministries of Shipping and Transport over the use of ports. The amalgamation of the two latter departments into the Ministry of War Transport in May 1941 solved some of the problems of the ports, and the Prime Minister's Battle of the Atlantic Committee (BA—CAB 86/1) took over many of the remaining functions. The Executive declined in importance and was abolished in May 1942, and its residual functions taken over by the Shipping Committee (SC—CAB 97/1–5).

954. *Production Executive* (PE—CAB 92/54–55). This was set up at the end of 1940 to replace the Production Council, and to deal with the allocation of available resources of raw materials, production capacity and labour, and the establishment of priorities where necessary. It was a more compact body and consisted of ministers only, under the chairmanship of Bevin; but the previous frictions continued between the supply departments themselves and with the Ministry of Labour; on munitions it tended to be surbordinate to the Defence Committee (Supply); and Parliament was critical of an arrangement whereby priorities were settled by a group of ministers who were all interested parties to the matters in dispute. Although Churchill initially stoutly upheld the system (*Hansard*, 29 July 1941, col. 1280), pressure for change continued; in the USA Donald Nelson had been appointed chairman of the War Production Board, and to give him a counterpart a Ministry of Production was created in February 1942 (after Beaverbrook had vacillated, Lyttelton became Minister). The Production Executive lapsed and its place was taken by the Minister of Production's Council, for which that ministry provided the secretariat, which also took over from the War Cabinet Office much of the work of the North American Supply Committee and of the Allied Supplies Executive, and the supervision of the Regional Boards.

The Production Council and the Production Executive had set up a number of sub-committees, most of which functioned at the official level, with secretaries provided by the departments; such of those committees as remained active were transferred to the Ministry of Production in February 1942. Among the more important of them was that on Materials (PE(M)) over which Portal presided, and with the assistance of Arnold Plant continued the allocation of raw materials among the departmental claimants. The records of these bodies are to be found in Public Record Office classes BT 28, 29, 30 and 87.

With hindsight it is clear that the problems of controlling production and supply during the war were never satisfactorily overcome; personalities and organisation were both involved. For a full account reference should be made to Postan's *British War Production* and the allied volumes in the civil series of official histories.

955. *Allied Supplies Executive* (ASE—CAB 92/1–9). Following the Moscow conference in September 1941 (BAR—CAB 99/7) this Executive was established in October 1941, under the chairmanship of Beaverbrook, to programme supplies to Russia and later to Turkey and China. Much of the work later passed to the Ministry of Production, but as several departments were concerned whose collective views had to be transmitted to some quarter abroad, a small central staff was maintained in the Cabinet Office. (The working papers of the Executive are in CAB 111.)

956. *Shipping Committee* (SC—CAB 97/1-5). This took the place of the Import Executive in May 1942. It was composed of officials, under Harcourt Johnston as chairman, to keep the shipping situation under review and in particular to make forecasts of available capacity for the import programme and for military requirements. It reported regularly to the War Cabinet and the Lord President's Committee.

957. *Reconstruction committees.* There were three main ministerial committees:
Reconstruction Problems (RP—CAB 87/1-3), February 1941–October 1943
Reconstruction Priorities (PR—CAB 87/12-13), January 1943–November 1943
Reconstruction (R—CAB 87/5-10), November 1943–May 1945.
Under the second reorganisation at the end of 1940 the Production Council and the Economic Policy Committee (over both of which Greenwood had presided) were wound up, and Greenwood became chairman of the newly-formed committee on Reconstruction Problems. He gave way to Jowitt in February 1942 and the committee continued until the end of 1943, dealing mainly with the reports of the official committee on Post-War Internal Economic Problems (IEP—CAB 87/55-57), with the Uthwatt report on Compensation and Betterment, and with the Scott report on Land Utilisation. In July 1941 it had set up the Beveridge committee on Social Insurance and Allied Services (SIC—CAB 87/76-82), whose report was published (Cmd. 6404) at the end of 1942.

(It appears that after his work on the Man-Power Requirements Committee (para. 951) Beveridge had wanted to continue with his work on the allocation of manpower; Bevin refused and Greenwood persuaded him to undertake social insurance.*)

958. The long-term implications of the Beveridge report and of other post-war claims on the Exchequer led to the appointment in January 1943 of the Reconstruction Priorities Committee, with Anderson as chairman, which met frequently during that year, and while a serious divergence of view was developing in the War Cabinet. On the one hand it was argued that the government should at that time take the major decisions as to the items which it was proposed to carry into law before the end of the war; on the other that long-term commitments could not at that time be entered into. The War Cabinet held a lengthy meeting on 14 October 1943 and the views of individual ministers are fully recorded in the confidential annex to WM 140(43)—CAB 65/40. In the upshot Churchill issued a directive on 19 October 1943 (WP(43)467—CAB 66/42); the first task was to make all necessary preprarations for the transitional period between war and settled peace, when the most important problems would be demobilisation, food, employment, the export trade and the turnover of industry to peace; decisions on these matters should be taken forthwith whether or not they involved legislation and whether or not they were controversial; consideration of longer-term problems should be postponed and would best be left until after a general election; but if it were possible to find a wide measure of agreement on matters such as education, social insurance and the rebuilding of cities, plans should be brought to a high degree of preparation during the war, to become effective early in the transitional period, which should be taken as two years from the defeat of Germany or four years from 1 January 1944, whichever was the earlier. This directive was generally endorsed by the War Cabinet on 21 October 1943 (WM 144(43)—CAB 65/36).

* Cf. Alan Bullock, *Ernest Bevin*, Vol. I (1960), p. 225; Lord Beveridge, *Power and Influence* (1953).

959. A Ministry of Reconstruction, with Woolton as Minister (with a seat in the War Cabinet) was created in November 1943, and the Reconstruction Committee set up (with Norman Brook as secretary) which held 80 meetings during 1944 and examined many aspects of post-war problems, including full employment and a national health service. (On the creation of the Ministry Norman Brook became its permanent secretary and ceased to be deputy secretary (civil) of the Cabinet Office.)

960. *Armistice Terms and Civil Administration Committee* (ACA—CAB 87/83 and 84); *Armistice and Post-War Committee* (APW—CAB 87/66–69). The first committee (ACA) was appointed in August 1943 to deal with the civil administration of occupied and liberated territories. In preparation for the Conference of Dominion Prime Ministers in May 1944 it was felt that the committee should be reconstituted to deal not only with armistice terms and their execution, but also with the general political and military questions of the post-war period. Attlee was chairman of both committees, the latter examining *inter alia* the Dumbarton Oaks proposals.

Matters affecting Commonwealth and foreign affairs were normally dealt with direct by the War Cabinet on submissions by the ministers concerned; but two important committees may be mentioned.

961. *India Committee* (I—CAB 91/1–4). Appointed under Attlee in February 1942, it held 15 meetings during that year in connection with the Cripps mission; 3 in 1943, 4 in 1944 and 23 to May 1945, mainly in connection with the constitutional position.

962. *Palestine Committee* (P(M)—CAB 95/14). This was set up in July 1943 under Morrison, to consider the long-term policy for Palestine. It held four meetings in 1943 and three in 1944. The papers contain reports on the position and reflect some sharp differences of view among ministers.

963. The following committees may be noted for their general interest.

(a) *Prevention of Oil Supplies reaching Germany* (POG—CAB 77/12, 13, 16–18). This committee, set up under Hankey in October 1939, was very active during 1940 in attempts to stop oil from Roumania and Russia reaching Germany, particularly by river transport on the Danube.

(b) *Basic English Committee* (BE—CAB 98/30 and 31). This committee, appointed in October 1943 as the result of a personal appeal by Churchill, met under Amery to consider the best means of encouraging the spread of the English language, for the diffusion of British culture and social and political ideals, for the promotion of trade and for more efficient administration and education in British dependencies. It produced an interesting report on which much of the work of the British Council was based.

(c) *Machinery of Government Committee* (MG—CAB 87/71–75). Anderson was chairman of the ministerial committee set up in November 1942 to consider what changes in the organisation and functions of the central executive were desirable to promote efficiency under post-war conditions. Its memoranda, and those of the parallel official committee, contain much useful information about the difficulties departments were encountering; there is discussion of the possibility of a system of standing committees of the Cabinet; and recognition that scientists and economists should be brought into more prominence in the government machine.

(d) *Scientific Advisory Committee* (SAC—CAB 90/1–6). The SAC was set up under the chairmanship of Hankey in October 1940 to advise the government on scientific matters, and held meetings throughout the war on a variety of subjects, which were attended by a number of persons outside government service. Among the recommendations was an investigation into psychiatric disorders, which led to the appointment of the committee on the work of Psychologists and Psychiatrists in the Services (PP—CAB 98/25–29), whose memoranda contain much information about the invaliding rates in the services, and which reported in February 1945 with recommendations for screening recruits to avoid undue wastage.

964. *Tube Alloys Consultative Council* (TA—CAB 98/47). The Defence Services Panel (SAC(DP)—CAB 90/7 and 8) was formed at the end of 1940 to deal with secret developments in the services. On 27 August 1941 they discussed 'Utilisation of Atomic Energy of Uranium'; the Maud report (CAB 90/8) was circulated on 3 September 1941, and considered at six meetings during that month, after the last of which Hankey reported to the Lord President. On 18 November 1941 the first meeting was held of the Tube Alloys Consultative Council under the chairmanship of Anderson; those present were Moore-Brabazon, Cherwell, Hankey, Appleton, Dale and Akers. Seventeen meetings were held before the end of the war, the only additions to those present being R. A. Butler, Pye and Perrin. The Council dealt with the administrative arrangements for the construction of the atom bomb; the minutes were kept within a very narrow circle, the matter was not mentioned in the War Cabinet conclusions and few were aware of the developments taking place.

Economic intelligence

965. The CID, through the Principal Supply Officers Committee, had collected much information about industrial capacity for munition production; and the Economic Advisory Council, through the Standing Committee on Economic Information (EAC(EI)—CAB 58/17–23), had acquired information about certain industries; but there had before the war been no comprehensive survey of what a war economy would involve. Following CP 146(39) of 30 June 1939, Stamp, with whom were associated H. D. Henderson and Henry Clay, was appointed (within the framework of the Cabinet Office)

> to examine the various measures to maintain the economic life of the country in time of war, which had hitherto been considered as separate problems, and to point to the gaps which still existed.

966. With the assistance of a staff of academic economists and statisticians who were recruited in the autumn of 1939 as the Central Economic Information Service, Stamp and his associates produced a quantity of memoranda (P(E & F)—CAB 89/1–9), mainly on financial matters and exchange control, which were fed to the Economic Policy Committee. The staff was expanding and was recognised in Attlee's statement to Parliament on 4 June 1940 as being at the disposal of the ministerial committees on economic and related subjects and 'to provide digests of statistics bearing on the development of the war effort, and reports on the progress achieved by departments in giving effect to decisions on economic questions reached by the ministerial committees'. (The original members of the service were Jewkes and Austin Robinson, who were later joined by Robbins, Cairncross, Chester, Meade and others; the statisticians were led by Campion, who was initially paid by the Bank of England; they were under the supervision of Hemming of the Cabinet Office, who had been secretary of the EAC.) The development of the Central Economic Information Service during 1940 gradually put the Stamp Survey as such into the shade.

967. When Churchill became First Lord of the Admiralty in September 1939 he set up within the Admiralty a statistical branch under Lindemann, later Lord Cherwell (with Harrod and MacDougal as assistants). When he became Prime

Minister he brought this branch with him as part of his personal staff; and owing to shortage of accommodation at Downing Street it was, in spite of Bridges' reluctance, housed in the Cabinet Office in Richmond Terrace. Its functions were described by Harrod (note of 14 November 1940 on 48/48 Part 1—CAB 21/1365) as

(a) being ready to answer at short notice questions by the Prime Minister relating to economic and other statistics, (b) for preparing diagrams illustrating certain selected points of interest and (c) for drawing his attention to points suggested by the statistics which might be held to require immediate action by him.

968. In the middle of 1940 the branch was causing a good deal of friction with departments by asking for facts and figures, which had often to be prepared at short notice, and which were then interpreted by Lindemann and used by the Prime Minister, often to the embarrassment or annoyance of ministers. An official in the War Office said in a minute of 27 September 1940 (48/50—CAB 21/1366):

The Prime Minister's idea seems to be that Professor Lindemann is to spy around and get information he wants without allowing departments to know what the information is to be used for. In this way the Prime Minister imagines that he will be able to penetrate the façade erected by each department to hide their misdeeds. Everything the Professor puts to the Prime Minister is kept secret from everybody else and is used for confronting people at meetings.

Similar difficulties had arisen with the Air Ministry and the Ministries of Shipping and Supply. Bridges hoped that the matter had been smoothed out by his letter of 25 October 1940 to departments inviting them to appoint liaison officers with the branch and assuring them that all figures and charts compiled by the branch from information supplied by them would be available for inspection by the liaison officer concerned. But the matter was re-opened by Churchill's minute to Bridges of 8 November 1940 (48/48 Part 1—CAB 21/1365) that:

The utmost confusion is caused when people argue on different statistical data. I wish the statistics to be concentrated in my own branch as Prime Minister and Minister of Defence from which the final authoritative working statistics will issue.

Bridges argued that while it was theoretically unsound to have two central statistical sections (one in the Prime Minister's office and the other in the Economic Section of the Cabinet Office), nevertheless each was an organic growth and in practice there was no great overlap between the two; he felt that the main problem was that certain departments had not got a proper statistical organisation, and that in default of regular returns on a well-ordered basis, they were driven to ask for special returns, which were apt to be hurriedly compiled and did not fit with the previous returns. The Prime Minister agreed that Bridges should form a committee to ensure that the statistical layout of each department was sound and coherent and that the terms on which it was based were defined and understood by all parties. Following departmental discussion during December 1940—which ran parallel with the reorganisation of the committees dealing with the home front—WP(G)(41)12—CAB 67/9 was issued on 27 January 1941, defining the revised arrangements for the central collection and presentation of statistical material and economic reports, which may be summarised as follows:

(a) *The Central Statistical Office* was established with the duty of collecting from departments a regular series of figures on a coherent and well-ordered basis covering the development of the war effort, which would be accepted and used without question in inter-departmental discussion and in documents circulated to the War Cabinet and its committees (Hemming and later Campion in charge).

(b) It was confirmed that the *Prime Minister's Statistical Branch* would continue to be responsible for analysing and presenting to the Prime Minister all statistical information he required, and to warn him of any pending shortages or discordances in the war effort (Lindemann in charge, assisted by Harrod).

(c) *The Economic Section* attached to the War Cabinet Office, and separate from the statisticians, would be at the disposal of the Lord President's Committee for the preparation of such special reports as might be required; and individual members might be detailed to provide special studies for committees, including that on post-war Reconstruction Problems (Jewkes and later Robbins in charge).

(d) *The Stamp Survey* as such would be discontinued, but at the request of the Lord President, Stamp agreed to place his services at the disposal of the Lord President's Committee (Stamp was killed in an air raid on 17 April 1941).

969. This allocation of function between the Central Statistical Office, the Economic Section and the Prime Minister's Statistical Branch continued without undue friction between them for the remainder of the war, and although the two latter tended to inject their views and advice directly to ministers at the stage of final decision, each largely overcame the suspicion with which they had initially been regarded by departments; but some apprehension of Lindemann and of his close association with Churchill continued—particularly after he was appointed Paymaster General in December 1942 and thereafter attended the War Cabinet with some regularity. The CSO continued after the war as part of the Cabinet Office organisation. The Economic Section was the subject of some anxious thought (MG—CAB 87/73–75) as to whether it was right that the advice that it could give should be at the Cabinet or at the departmental level; after the war the issue was side-stepped and it remained effectively responsible to the Lord President, until it was transferred to the Treasury in 1953.

The Central Statistical Office became responsible for the confidential circulation at regular intervals of:

Digest A Economic situation
      B Development of war effort
      C Manpower
      D Munitions, production and manpower
      E Import problems
      F Tankers and petroleum products.

Copies of these and related papers are in CAB 108.

970. The surviving papers of the Economic Section were transferred to the Treasury, but copies of their quarterly review of the economic situation are among the memoranda of the LP Committee, and copies of the briefs supplied personally to the Lord President are on the LP files (CAB 123 and 124). Those of the Prime Minister's Statistical Branch are among the Cherwell papers at Nuffield College, though copies of some of the briefs to Churchill are variously among the Prime Minister's files (CAB 120), the Churchill papers (PREM 3 and 4) and the Chartwell papers at Churchill College, Cambridge.

International meetings

971. The most important of the international meetings were the conferences between Churchill and Roosevelt, at most sessions of which the Combined Chiefs of Staff were present, and where the main lines of allied strategy were settled. These were:

Placentia Bay—Riviera, August 1941 (WP(41)202—CAB 66/18)
Washington—Arcadia, December 1941–January 1942 (CAB 99/17 and 18)
Washington—Argonaut, June 1942 (CAB 99/20)
Casablanca—Symbol, January 1943 (CAB 99/24)
Washington and North Africa—Trident, May 1943 (CAB 99/22)
Quebec—Quadrant, August 1943 (CAB 99/23)
Cairo—Sextant, November 1943 (also Chiang Kai Shek) (CAB 99/25)
Teheran—Eureka, December 1943 (also Stalin) (CAB 99/25)
Quebec—Octagon, September 1944 (CAB 99/29)
Crimea—Argonaut, January–February 1945 (also Stalin) (CAB 99/31)
Potsdam—Terminal, July–August 1945 (also Stalin) (CAB 99/38 and 39).

972. Other meetings for which the Office provided the whole or part of the secretariat included:

Supreme War Council (SWC) September 1939–June 1940 (CAB 99/3)

Minutes of 18 meetings held in London and Paris between the Prime Minister and the French President du Conseil, mainly on the co-ordination of the military effort.

Visit of Dominion Ministers (DMV) November 1939 (CAB 99/1 and 2)

Meetings with UK ministers in London, mainly on supplies.

Visit of Australian Prime Minister (VAP) March–April 1941 (CAB 99/4)

Minutes of eight meetings in London between various UK ministers and Menzies and Bruce, on Australian requirements.

Moscow Conference (BAR) September–October 1941 (CAB 99/7)

Minutes of meetings in Moscow between Beaverbrook, Harriman and Molotov about supplies to USSR.

Pacific War Council (PWC) February 1942–August 1943 (CAB 99/26)

Minutes of 14 meetings in London between Churchill and UK ministers, with representatives of the Netherlands, Australia and New Zealand, and later Canada, India, South Africa and China; the subjects considered included the defence of Java and strategic control in the Pacific. Only two meetings were held after July 1942.

Moscow meeting (Bracelet) August 1942, WP(42)373 *on* (CAB 66/28)

Minutes of meetings between Churchill, Harriman and Stalin about the second front.

Prime Ministers' Conference (PMM) May 1944 (CAB 99/28)

Minutes of 16 meetings held in London between Churchill and UK ministers, with the Prime Ministers of Canada, Australia, New Zealand, South Africa, India and Southern Rhodesia, mainly on the post-war settlement. (The Prime Ministers attended a meeting of the War Cabinet on 22 May 1944 (WM(44)67—CAB 65/46.)

Moscow meeting (Tolstoy) October 1944 (COS(44)915(o))

Minutes of meetings between Churchill, Harriman and Stalin on military matters. (Copy on A/Strategy/15.)

Athens meeting (Freehold) December 1944 (Confidential annex to WM(44)175—CAB 65/48)

Account by Churchill of his meeting with Damaskinos on the situation in Greece.

British Commonwealth Meeting (BCM) April 1945 (CAB 99/30)

Minutes of 12 meetings held in London at which Churchill presided, with representatives of Canada, Australia, New Zealand, South Africa and India.

The records of the Foreign Office, Dominions Office, Colonial Office and India Office should be consulted for other international meetings.

Staff 1939–1945

973. Bridges as secretary and Ismay as deputy secretary (military) served through-out the period and gave the Office continuing stability; of the other senior staff only Hollis and Jacob served continuously. Howorth retired as deputy secretary (civil) on 17 March 1942, and was succeeded by Norman Brook, until his appoint-ment as permanent secretary to the Ministry of Reconstruction in December 1943. Brook was succeeded in the Cabinet Office by two under-secretaries (civil), Laith-waite and Murrie (who served until September 1945 and October 1948 respec-tively). On 28 February 1945, Bridges became permanent secretary to the Treasury, and continued temporarily as secretary of the War Cabinet and permanent secretary of the War Cabinet Office; on the same date Brook returned from the Ministry of Reconstruction as additional secretary of the War Cabinet, and succeeded Bridges as secretary of the Cabinet and permanent secretary of the Cabinet Office on 1 January 1947 (when Murrie became deputy secretary).

974. During the war the staff borne on the establishment rose from about 200 to nearly 600; the following table shows the approximate numbers in the various types of activity at the beginning and at the end.

	1939 (before September)		1945	
	Administrative	*Subordinate*	*Administrative*	*Subordinate*
Civil affairs				
in London	6	22	13	47
in Washington	—	—	3	7
Military affairs				
in London	10	50	22	81
in Washington	—	—	6	8
Economic Advisory Council	3	2	—	—
Economic Section	—	—	14	5
Central Statistical Office	—	—	18	26
Historical Section	7	11	43	39
Common Services	—	95	4	240
	26	180	123	453
	206		576	

Source: For 1939, partly estimated, and includes staff for the Minister for Co-ordination of Defence, and for the Supply Board. For 1945, from file E41.

975. At both dates nearly half the total staff were those engaged in common services (i.e. in registry, typing, duplicating and messengerial work) and respon-sible for the rapid distribution of the material flowing through the Office; the numbers were probably slightly in excess of what would have been reasonable by normal standards, but the Office was manned by day and night throughout the week and crises were frequent. The nucleus of the common service staff were those who had been employed in the Office before the war. The signals staff was provided by the Air Ministry and handled the great volume of telegrams (CAB 105).

976. The administrative staff (i.e. military officers and civil servants above the rank of assistant principal) turned over fairly rapidly, and the following table shows the numbers who joined the Office during the war and who had left before the end or shortly after, either for return to their parent department or service or for employment elsewhere.

Permanent civil servants	
From Foreign Office	11
Colonial Office	6
Supply	6
Treasury	5
Labour	5
Home Office	4
Other departments	45
	— 82 (21)
Temporary civil servants	
Economists and statisticians	25
Others	31 (12)
Military historians	27
Civil historians	35
	— 118
Naval officers	18
Air officers	10
Military officers	51
	279

The numbers in brackets are those retransferred to new war-time ministries or organisations.

Source: file E168.

The secondment of over 80 permanent civil servants and a similar number of service officers was of value to the Office in keeping in touch with departments; they in turn benefited from the experience gained of the committee organisation in the War Cabinet Office. Before the war this type of secondment had been on a small scale, but it has become a regular feature of post-war recruitment.

977. The staff list at 1 January 1945 is reproduced as Annex 5, and shows the shape of the Office towards the end of the Second World War. Annex 6 contains a list of the administrative staff who served in the Cabinet Office (including the CID, but excluding the CSO, Economic Section and Historical Section) between 1916 and 1945.

In addition to those who were borne on the establishment there was a fluctuating population who were borne on some other establishment, but who were loosely connected with the Office and made use of some or all of the common services which the Office provided. During the war it had included visiting ministers and officials from the Commonwealth and allied governments and the staffs of the Production Executive and of the Lord President. At the end of the war it numbered at least 100, and included members of planning staffs, of intelligence organisations and of Combined Operations, signals officers and liaison officers from the Dominions.

978. Mention should be made of two offshoots of the Office in Washington DC. The first was the secretariat for the British Joint Staff Mission established in June 1941, which provided liaison with the American Joint Chiefs of Staff (the working papers of the BJSM are in CAB 122). The other was the British civil secretariat set up in 1943 to cater for the needs of the ambassador, the minister resident and the heads of the various missions. Its work became so dovetailed into that of the missions and of the Commonwealth organisations in Washington that it was difficult to distinguish where the secretariat ended and the other organisations began. No

separate collection of its records is known to exist, but the minutes of the British Supply Council in North America (which was the senior body) are in CAB 92/27–35. Hoyer-Millar, and later R. B. Stevens, headed this secretariat.

979. In addition to embracing the Central Statistical Office and the Economic Section, the Office in certain respects went beyond normal secretarial functions in acting on behalf of a committee in the conduct of detailed correspondence on matters for which there was no single departmental minister who could assume full responsibility in Parliament. Generally this was in the field of supply where small central staffs within the Office (and later jointly with the Ministry of Production) undertook executive functions on behalf of and by agreement with the several departments concerned, and channelled correspondence to some authority at home or abroad (*see* para. 237). But a more significant case was the correspondence on behalf of the COS committee with C-in-Cs abroad (which developed unconsciously after the Norwegian disasters in April 1940), and through the BJSM with the Combined Chiefs of Staff. Much of this correspondence was on matters for which a service minister might normally have been expected to accept responsibility to Parliament. The point never appears to have been seriously challenged, but had it been there is little doubt that Churchill as Minister of Defence with undefined powers would have dealt with it appropriately.

Bridges and Ismay.

980. On 1 August 1938 Bridges became secretary of the Cabinet and head of the Office, and Ismay became secretary of the CID and deputy secretary (military) of the Cabinet (*see* para. 534). This was in recognition of the fact that in the circumstances of the time—with rearmament and the threat of war—the arrangement whereby Hankey had held both offices was no longer suitable.

981. After a distinguished record in the First World War Bridges served in the Treasury from 1919 to 1938, and in the later part of the period had been closely concerned in the general aspects of the rearmament programme. On appointment to the Office he made no alteration in the basic procedures which had been established by Hankey, but began to give the Office a more professional appearance. The staff was expanding and he took care in its selection; he established close and intimate relations with the senior officials in departments; and shaped the Office to meet the load which would fall on it in war by emphasising the need for speed and accuracy. He enjoyed the full confidence of Chamberlain, but initially it would seem that his relations with Churchill as Prime Minister were less easy. This may have been due partly to Bridges' own austerity, partly to Churchill's mistrust of the Treasury influence and of Chamberlain's appointments, and partly to Churchill's own preoccupation with military affairs and his impatience with those matters in the civil field which were not directly related to the prosecution of the war. While Bridges was recognised as head of the Office, he left the military aspects to Ismay, and with patience and pertinacity and some frustration ensured that the civilian aspects were not overlooked, and that matters for decision were brought forward at the right point in the War Cabinet machine; in effect he became Churchill's chief civilian staff officer and the initial frigidity evaporated. He remained secretary of the Cabinet until the end of 1946, but in February 1945 had been appointed to the additional office of permanent secretary of the Treasury, a post he held until retirement in 1956. He died in 1969.

982. Ismay was an officer of the Indian army who, before his appointment as secretary of the CID and of the chiefs of staff committee, had had two periods of secondment with the CID; he was thus well acquainted with the organisation, and his free and genial temperament made him a popular figure within the Office and in the service departments. While retaining his position as deputy secretary (military) of the War Cabinet, he became chief of staff to Churchill as Minister of Defence, with whom he was on intimate terms, and as a member of the chiefs of staff committee bore the brunt of the inevitable frictions which developed from time to time between Churchill, the members of the War Cabinet, and their military advisers. He worked easily with Bridges, and the close association between the two was a significant factor in securing the firm and steady direction from the top on which the success of the war effort depended. He retired from the Office at the end of 1945 as additional secretary (military) of the Cabinet; in 1947 he acted as chief of staff to Mountbatten in connection with the transfer of power in India; from 1948 to 1951 he was chairman of the Council for the Festival of Britain; in 1951–1952 he served in Churchill's second administration as Secretary of State for Commonwealth Relations; and from 1952 to 1957 was secretary-general of the North Atlantic Treaty Organisation. He died in 1964.

Collections of papers other than the minutes and memoranda of the War Cabinet and its committees

983. The previous paragraphs have generally referred to the bound volumes of the proceedings of the War Cabinet and of its properly constituted committees where authoritative decisions were taken which formed the basis of executive action by departments. But those associated with the Office accumulated working papers containing material before or after the points were submitted for decision, and on other matters which were never formally put into the machine. Where reasonably convenient and suitable these papers were put on the registered files of the Office, and are now included in the CAB 21 series; CAB 104 contains material of continuing sensitivity. But few of these files relate directly to military operations, or to the co-ordination of activities on the home front, and the working papers on these aspects are generally to be found in other classes of which the following deserve special mention.

(a) Military
CAB 120—*Minister of Defence: Secretariat files* (also known as the PM files)

These are the working papers maintained in the Defence Secretariat of the War Cabinet by the members of the staff of Churchill in his capacity as Minister of Defence. They contain the material on military and operational matters which passed between Churchill, Ismay, and the Chiefs of Staff, together with the information collected by Ismay, Hollis, Jacob, and others for briefing him on those matters.

In the terminology of the Cabinet Office (and the official historians) this collection was known as 'the PM files'; the files maintained at 10 Downing Street were known as 'the Churchill papers' and now form PREM 3 and 4.

CAB 121—*Special (Secret) Information Centre*
By minute 9 of DO(41)42 (not yet transferred to the Public Record Office) of 17 June 1941, Churchill said he was anxious that commanders in chief should be kept fully informed of military intentions, but he was reluctant to increase the circulation of highly secret papers. Accordingly he had given instructions that a special Secret Information Centre should be organised in the office of the Minister of Defence which C-in-Cs could visit whenever they came to London. In the upshot the Defence secretariat maintained a series of subject files which accumulated day by day copies of all papers coming into or going out from the COS organisation on the particular subject, including extracts from the minutes and

papers of the top-level conferences, of the War Cabinet, Defence Committee (O & S), COS Committee, Joint Planners, Joint Intelligence Committee, Combined Chiefs of Staff and its sub-committees, minutes and telegrams by Churchill on military matters, COS telegrams, and all relevant telegrams and letters of the service departments, of the Foreign Office and other departments; drafts of letters, minutes and telegrams were not normally included. This series of subject files, which are complete from mid-1941 to the end of hostilities, constitute in effect the principal record of the Ministry of Defence. Copies of the papers should be found in other series of records, but this collection is unique in providing a consecutive account of most of the separate aspects of the military effort.

The files are divided into:

Series A. Policy and strategy, including relations with allies.
      B. United Kingdom.
      C. USA, Iceland, Central and South America.
      D. Europe and Scandinavia.
      E. Iberian peninsula and North Africa.
      F. Middle East.
      G. Far East and India.

Scattered through the files is material which is still sensitive—either on the ground of security or of personal susceptibilities. (For some account of these files *see* J. B. Astley, *The Inner Circle* (1971).)

CAB 122—*British Joint Staff Mission*

These are the working papers of the mission established in Washington in 1941 to maintain contact on behalf of the COS Committee with the American Joint Chiefs of Staff through the Combined Chiefs of Staff: copies of significant material should be found in CAB 80 and 88.

(b) *Civil*

CAB 117—*Reconstruction Secretariat files*
CAB 118—*Various Ministers: files* (previously known as Deputy Prime Minister's files)
CAB 123—*Lord President: Secretariat files*
CAB 124—*Minister of Reconstruction and Lord President: Secretariat files*

These four classes of records are included in the Cabinet group by reason of the very close association which existed during and immediately after the war between the Office and the Lord President, who was generally the chairman of the important committees dealing with matters on the home front. The holders of that office were Neville Chamberlain (May–October 1940); Anderson (October 1940–September 1943); Attlee (September 1943–May 1945); Woolton (May–July 1945); and Herbert Morrison (July 1945–March 1951). The papers of the Lord President in his capacity as chairman of the Research Councils have mostly been transferred to the Ministry of Education and Science (*see* ED/140).

CAB 118 contains some papers of Chamberlain and Anderson, but it mostly consists of the private office papers of Attlee in his capacity as leader of the Labour Party, Lord Privy Seal, Secretary of State for the Dominions and Deputy Prime Minister; they include some in his capacity as Lord President, but most of those relating to that office are in CAB 123.

CAB 123 contains the main files of the Lord President's secretariat from 1941 to May 1945, with some extending to July 1945 (the end of the Caretaker Government).

The Ministry of Reconstruction was formally in existence from November 1943 to May 1945; it had access to the papers of the earlier reconstruction committees which now form CAB 117, and built up its own collection of papers, which are now included in CAB 124. On its cessation, Woolton, who had been Minister, became Lord President but continued his concern with reconstruction, and his office combined the filing system used for reconstruction with that for his new functions. With the change of government on 26 July 1945 Herbert Morrison became Lord President, and inherited the Woolton collection of papers, with the result that CAB 124 now comprises the Ministry of Reconstruction papers 1943–1945, with those of the Lord President after May 1945. The listing of the files in CAB 124 is not chronological, and reflects the registry arrangements made at the time. (c) Several small collections of papers have been deposited in the office by ministers and others after they ceased to hold public office; depositors include:

Beaverbrook	Cripps	Ismay
Bridges	Dale	Jowitt
Cherwell	Dalton	Horace Wilson

These papers are in CAB 127.

Achievement 1939–1945

984. It is for others to record what the war effort meant in terms of human distress, or in terms of naval, military and air operations, or in terms of negotiations with the Commonwealth, allies and neutrals; but in cold statistical terms the following tables show a few of the end-results of some of the decisions taken on the responsibility of the War Cabinet, and which had some impact on every family in the country.

Redistribution of manpower (millions)

	mid-1939	mid-1943	mid-1945
Males	14·7	15·0	14·9
Females	5·1	7·3	6·7
Total working population	19·8	22·3	21·6
Armed forces and civil defence	0·6	5·1	5·2
Supplies and equipment for the forces	1·3	5·1	3·8
Manufactures for export	1·0	0·2	0·4
Manufactures for the home market	4·5	2·4	2·6
Other industries and services	11·1	9·4	9·5
Unemployed	1·3	0·1	0·1

Source: Tables in Hancock and Gowing, *British War Economy* (1949), pp. 352, 357.

	Overseas trade		Consumers' expenditure	Dwellings built
	Volume of imports	Volume of exports	(at 1938 prices	(thousands)
	(Indices 1938 = 100)		£ million)	
1938	100	100	4304	362
1939	97	94	4307	359
1940	94	72	3888	212
1941	82	56	3715	48
1942	70	36	3669	13
1943	77	29	3602	13
1944	80	31	3711	8
1945	62	46	3922	18

Sources: Tables 53, 142 and 186 of *Statistical Digest of the War* (1951).

Over the period an extra 1·5 million women were drawn into civil employment and a further 0·4 million joined the forces; the country adjusted itself to a five-fold increase in the numbers of men and women in the forces and in the munitions industries, achieved at the expense of other occupations; consumers' expenditure (in real terms) was held down; overseas trade (and particularly exports) fell heavily away; and new house building virtually disappeared. These, with other corresponding or consequential adjustments, involved an endless series of decisions on priorities and the balancing of one need against another in circumstances which were determined from time to time and in varying degree partly by the enemy, partly by the Commonwealth, allies and neutrals, but mainly by the willingness of the people to submit to the inconveniences and hardships called for by the leadership.

Churchill's impact

985. It is impossible to conclude a chapter on the War Cabinet of 1939–1945 without some reference to the impact of Churchill. He became Prime Minister and Minister of Defence on 10 May 1940 with a unique experience of Whitehall and of the government machine; he had served as President of the Board of Trade (1908–1910), Home Secretary (1910–1911), First Lord of the Admiralty (1911–1915 and 1939–1940), Chancellor of the Duchy of Lancaster (1915), Minister of Munitions (1917–1919), Secretary of State for War and Air (1919–1921), Secretary of State for the Colonies (1921–1922) and Chancellor of the Exchequer (1924–1929). As Prime Minister he had, unlike Lloyd George, no serious political challenge from Parliament.

986. It is perhaps fortunate that he has given his own frank account of what he expected; the following quotations are taken from *The Second World War*:

It was, however, understood and accepted that I should assume the general direction of the war, subject to the support of the War Cabinet and of the House of Commons. (Vol. II, p. 15)

As this Minister [of Defence] was also Prime Minister, he had all the rights inherent in that office, including very wide powers of selection and removal of all professional and political personages. (Vol. II, p. 15)

All I wanted was compliance with my wishes after reasonable discussion. (Vol. IV, p. 78)

More difficulty and toil are often incurred in overcoming opposition and adjusting diverging and conflicting views than by having the right to give decisions oneself. (Vol. IV, p. 80)

In dealing with the Labour and Liberal parties in the Coalition it was always an important basic fact that as Prime Minister and at this time Leader of the largest party I did not depend upon their votes, and I could in the ultimate issue carry on in Parliament without them. (Vol. II, p. 439)

Personally, when I was placed in charge I did not like having unharnessed ministers around me. I preferred to deal with chiefs of organisations rather than counsellors. (Vol. I, p. 373)

I reached the end of my patience, which may be deemed considerable (Vol. IV, p. 67)

987. The impact was nation-wide through his speeches on the radio and in Parliament, which gave comfort and encouragement at critical periods. But in the narrow circle of those who comprised his administration, or who were the heads of Commonwealth or allied governments, that impact was largely felt through several thousand personal minutes and telegrams; these represent an astonishing output by a man who at the same time was presiding at meetings of the War Cabinet and its more important committees, interviewing ministers and others, and when not abroad attending regularly at the House of Commons. They reflect his note of 19 July 1940 to Bridges and Ismay:

> Let it be very clearly understood that all directions emanating from me are made in writing, or should be immediately afterwards confirmed in writing, and that I do not accept any responsibility for matters relating to national defence on which I am alleged to have given decisions unless they are recorded in writing.
>
> (*Ibid.*, Vol. II, p. 17)

Of these Personal Minutes and Telegrams, some had been carefully drafted by others, but most were dictated while the subject was in his mind; a few were of commendation; occasionally they were facetious; others were giving approval to proposals or appointments; some were asking for information; but many were expressing dissatisfaction in varying degrees with some action that had or had not then been taken, and implying or demanding a remedy. The ceaseless prodding of ministers, chiefs of staff and others gave added urgency to the solution of problems which the recipients had often regarded as intractable. Some mild irritation resulted, and in some quarters a suspicion was felt that occasionally a Personal Minute may have been sent 'for the book', i.e. demanding action on some matter which was already well in hand for the purpose of having a record of his intervention and inspiration. In his volumes on the Second World War he reproduced a selection of his Personal Minutes and Telegrams, which caused some misgivings to recipients and to historians in that he did not refer to the replies he had received, which in some cases would afford a good explanation of what otherwise might appear as shortcomings. But nothing can detract from the dynamic vigour he exercised over the government machine and which found a nation-wide response. (*See Action this Day* by Sir J. W. Wheeler-Bennett and others, 1968.)

During the day Churchill worked either at 10 Downing Street (where meetings of the War Cabinet were generally held) or in the Annex in Storey's Gate where after the onset of air raids he normally spent the night, and where he was in closer touch with Ismay, the chiefs of staff, senior ministers and the Cabinet secretariat; at weekends he generally worked at Chequers. His private secretaries collected his papers in two groups known as 'Operational papers' and 'Confidential papers' respectively. The former dealt with the conduct of the war, both in the military aspects and from the standpoint of major foreign policy, and are now contained in PREM 3; the latter dealt with the work of the civil departments, and are contained in PREM 4. The distinction could not be maintained with complete consistency, but the two PREM classes should include the primary records of the Personal Minutes and Telegrams (i.e. the carbons of the outgoing and the originals of the replies).

The papers which now form PREM 3 and 4 were known within the Office and by the official historians as the 'Churchill papers', to distinguish them from the 'PM files' and from the 'Chartwell papers'.

988. On military and operational matters the originals of the Personal Minutes were sent direct to the Defence Secretariat in the War Cabinet Office where they were handled immediately by Ismay, Hollis or Jacob and referred as appropriate to the COS Committee, to an individual chief of staff or to others directly concerned; the replies would pass to Churchill through the Defence Secretariat, which inevitably accumulated a quantity of working papers known within the Office as the 'PM files' (CAB 120, *see* para. 983(a)).

The originals of the Personal Minutes on civil and non-operational matters were sent direct to the ministers concerned, and these together with the carbons of the replies to the Prime Minister should be among the records of the various departments. But in addressing a minute to a particular minister Churchill was liable to overlook the fact that other ministers might be involved, and accordingly a routine developed whereby copies of the minutes were normally sent to Bridges for opportunity to assist in the co-ordination of any action that might be required. Much of Bridges' work in this connection involved a verbal hint to a minister that he might consult a colleague or some established committee before sending a reply; but among the files in CAB 21 and 104 may be found a record of those matters on which Bridges engaged in significant correspondence.

The Prime Minister's telegrams to the heads of Commonwealth, allied or neutral governments passed through the Dominions Office or the Foreign Office, and copies should be among the records of those departments.

The result is that there is a good deal of duplication of paper on military and operational matters between PREM 3, CAB 120 (PM files) and CAB 121 (SIC files). There is some, but considerably less, duplication between PREM 4 and CAB 21 and 104.

989. The Chartwell papers in Churchill College, Cambridge, contain what Churchill regarded as his own private property; although they include some material of an official character, it seems that for the period 1940–1945 the strictly official material is mainly duplicates of what is among the public records mentioned above.

990. *Views on committees.* On 24 May 1940 Churchill had minuted Bridges (48/21 Part 4—not yet referred to the Public Record Office) that there were 'far too many committees of one kind and another which ministers have to attend, and which do not yield a sufficient result' (*see* para. 923). On 4 January 1941 he asked Bridges (48/38—CAB 21/1350) for a return of all committees of a departmental nature. The returns from 35 departments suggested that there were then some 750 committees at headquarters, and in addition over 2,500 committees of a regional or local character with which departments were concerned; it was estimated that attendance at them represented over 2 million man-hours per annum. In WP(G) (41)34—CAB 67/9 of 14 March 1941 Churchill called for a reduction in the number of committees by 25 per cent, and a reduction in the number attending those committees by 25 per cent. Later in the year Bridges reported (48/38/2—CAB 21/1353) that of the 750 headquarters committees 153 had been abolished and 93 suspended, a reduction of about one-third.

E

CHAPTER 10

THE HISTORICAL SECTION

Origin

1001. The Section owes its origin to a memorandum by Esher (CID—90B of September 1906) recommending that the responsibility for compiling the naval and military history of the nation be transferred to a department of the CID. Accordingly a section was formed which undertook the completion of the history of the war in South Africa, and then embarked on a history of the Russo-Japanese war. The text of the latter was completed by the end of 1913 (although the last volume was not published until 1920) and the CID then concluded (125th meeting on 3 March 1914) that no attempt should be made in future to compile histories of wars in which the country was not a belligerent, but that when the country was involved special arrangements should be made as the occasion arose; in the meanwhile a small permanent staff for research work should remain under the control of the secretary of the CID.

1002. Since 1914 the Section has been under the aegis of the CID and later of the Cabinet Office, although its expenditure has been shown under a separate sub-head of the vote for the Treasury and subordinate departments. Its main work has been the preparation of the 'Official Histories' of military operations in the First World War, and of the 'Histories' in the military and civil series for the Second World War (a list of the volumes published is in Annex 10). The description 'Official' was dropped in the Second World War in the attempt to avoid the mis-understanding to which the term 'Official History' was liable to give rise. The term did not imply that the work gave an official view, or that it gave a full and complete story, or that it could be expected that all its conclusions would stand in any long-term perspective. What it did imply was that authors, appointed and paid by the Office, had been invited to prepare a comprehensive, accurate and read-able account of events which had mostly been shrouded by censorship and of which the public had little knowledge at the time, in the expectation that the account would be published at an early date. To this end they were given free access to official documents and facilities for consulting those who had held official positions or possessed official information. They were expected to respect the constitutional conventions to preserve the collective responsibility of ministers and the anonymity of the civil service; and before publication they were required to submit the text to official authorities for comment, which might include a request that portions be omitted or modified in the interest of security or on other grounds of public policy, on the understanding that if agreement could not be reached publication might be withheld. But the author retained his independent judgment and respon-sibility for what was published, and each history for the Second World War is prefaced by a note: 'The author has been given free access to official documents. He and the editor are alone responsible for the statements made and the views expressed.'

1003. Any individual volume has generally been well received as a lucid and competent account of the field it covered, but in academic circles there has been some underlying mistrust of the whole concept, due to the official sponsorship and a suspicion that the results are 'the kind of history that pliant historians will write to please strong-minded bureaucrats' (p. 13 of the Webb Memorial Lecture (1950) by W. K. Hancock). Not unconnected has been the criticism directed at the costs and delays in publication (cf. questions 3679–3706 of the report of the Public Accounts Committee 1928, and the eighth report of the Estimates Committee, session 1956–1957).

1004. The difficulties of contemporary 'official' history have been fully recognised by the Office. On the one hand, the government possessed a monopoly of most of the authentic material, some of which was confidential, and some control had therefore to be exercised over its release; moreover the bulk of that material was enormous, and delay inevitably occurred while it was being assembled (a substantial part of the costs incurred by the Historical Section has been absorbed in the preparatory work of getting the material into a usable condition). On the other hand, the author who was subject to pressure to get his account completed had to deal not only with the successes, but with operations or policies which had failed, and which could imply praise or blame to persons still active in public life. The histories were liable to lack perspective, though this might well be balanced by intimacy with those who had participated. But in spite of the difficulties more than 100 volumes have been published which cover most of the military aspects of the First World War and most of the military and civil aspects of the Second World War. It is indeed doubtful whether without official sponsorship authors or publishers could have been found willing or able to contemplate the research required for a comprehensive undertaking on the scale which has been achieved. The published histories cannot tell the whole story; they should be regarded as guides and works of reference which can provide the framework for further research and to be read along with the memoirs, diaries and letters of military men, officials and politicians, and with the original material unfolding in the Public Record Office under the 30-year rule. 'The official historians of this generation have consciously submitted their work to the professional verdict of the future' (Hancock and Gowing, *British War Economy*, xii).

1005. The primary source material used by the historians is now among the records of the departments concerned, but the following are the main classes now in the Public Record Office which contain such of the supporting material used by them as has survived.

CAB 44/1–45	Drafts of some of the military histories for the First World War, as circulated for comment.
CAB 44/46–427	'Blue book' narratives of military operations in the Second World War. (The term 'blue book' was that by which these narratives were commonly known within the Historical Section; it should not be confused with the term commonly applied to official government publications.)
CAB 45/1–290	Correspondence and papers of historians, mainly for the First World War.
CAB 101	Copies of the published volumes of the histories for the Second World War, annotated with references to the confidential sources used in their compilation.
CAB 102	Historical Section papers for the Civil series of the Second World War; they mostly consist of drafts prepared by narrators and historians.
CAB 103/1–51	Progress reports and estimates of the Historical Section 1915–1946.

CAB 103/52–148   Miscellaneous correspondence and reports 1915–1950, including correspondence with official historians in the Commonwealth and foreign countries.

CAB 106/1–1200   Historical Section files (military—AL series) 1939 onwards, a heterogeneous collection acquired by the military narrators and historians of the Second World War; there is some original material, but it is mostly copies and extracts. (The copies of the captured enemy material which were used for the histories have been deposited by the Enemy Documents Branch with the Foreign Documents Section of the Imperial War Museum; the originals have been restored.)

1006. The progress of the histories and the problems encountered can be traced in the following series:

CAB 27/182 and 212   Minutes and memoranda of the Committee on the Historical Section of the CID (OHW and OH) 1922–1923.

CAB 16/52 and 53   Minutes and memoranda of the Committee on the Control of Official Histories (COH) 1923–1939.

CAB 98/7–12   Minutes and memoranda of the Committee for the Control of Official Histories (COH) 1940–1945.

CAB 98/13–16   Minutes and memoranda of the Advisory Historical Committee (COH(U)) 1941–1944.

Military histories of the First World War

1007. On the outbreak of the First World War a CID committee was formed under Admiral Slade 'to consider and advise on the question of collating material for a future history of the present war'. It met from time to time during the war, made some arrangements for the collection of war diaries and ships' logs, and in August 1915 commissioned Sir Julian Corbett (a lecturer at the Royal Naval College) to write a Naval History, and J. W. Fortescue (the librarian at Windsor Castle and author of a History of the British Army) to write a Military History. Subsequently it gave facilities to C. E. Fayle of the Garton Foundation (of which Esher was a trustee) to write an account of the effect of war on seaborne trade; in 1917 Archibald Hurd was commissioned to write on the Merchant Navy in the war; and in 1918 Sir Walter Raleigh undertook a history of the War in the Air. (The papers of the Slade committee—whose symbol was WH—have not been traced, but a full account of its proceedings can be derived from G 151—CAB 24/4 and CID 238B—CAB 4/7.)

1008. Announcements had been made in Parliament about the preparation of these histories, but events occurred during 1919 which caused doubt about their continuance. Fortescue wrote a controversial article in the *Quarterly Review* on Lord French's *1914*; the War Cabinet considered that this would impair the impartiality of any official history written by him, and as it was a breach of discipline and of good faith decided (WC 635—CAB 23/12) that his services should be dispensed with. The draft of the first intalment of Corbett's Naval History had been circulated to departments and the Secretary of State for War (Churchill) reacted by appealing to the War Cabinet:

As the period covered is that for which I was responsible as First Lord I feel bound to demur to its publication in its present isolated form. In my view the proper form of an official history is a full and fair selection of authentic documents. . . . I think the Admiralty and the War Office should prepare a series of authentic documents which were actually operative, and after editing them as far as may be necessary in the public interest, should publish them with only such comments as are required to make the account fully intelligible. It will then be for the public at large and for unofficial historians to draw their own conclusions and express them at their discretion. Let the public have the facts whatever they are. (GT 7087—CAB 24/77.)

1009. Although it was subsequently reported (CP 202—CAB 24/94) that agreement had been reached between Corbett, Churchill and the Admiralty about amendments to the Naval History, other ministers were not satisfied and by CC 12(19)—CAB 23/18, appendix V(4), of 5 December 1919 it was agreed 'after protracted discussion' that the first volume of Corbett's history should be published and the question of publishing subsequent volumes be postponed for further consideration. Correspondence on file 4/17 (CAB 103/83) shows that the decision was taken by a casting vote, and meant that ministers did not wish to be committed to continued publication of the histories if Corbett's first volume had an unfavourable reception and led to controversy and acrimony.

1010. Corbett's first volume was published in March 1920, and 'the reception was all that could be desired' (CP 1034—CAB 24/103). On this the Cabinet agreed to the publication of subsequent volumes of the Naval History (CC 20(20)4—CAB 23/37) and in the following two years gave individual approval to publication of the few volumes in other series which had then been completed. Meanwhile there were changes in authors; following Fortescue's dismissal Brigadier-General Sir James Edmonds (previously deputy engineer in chief, BEF) undertook supervision of the military histories; Raleigh died in May 1922, and H. A. Jones undertook War in the Air; Corbett died in September 1922, and Sir Henry Newbolt completed the Naval History.

1011. The debate in the House of Commons of 13 June 1922 on the future of the Cabinet Office (*see* para. 428) was immediately followed by a debate on the official histories when criticism was made of the cost, with the suggestion that the work should be completed by private enterprise. In the light of this criticism the Cabinet appointed a committee on the Official Histories of the War (OHW—CAB 27/212) under H. A. L. Fisher, which reported in 1923 that they were satisfied that the histories fulfilled a useful purpose, that their preparation should be continued, and that a permanent sub-committee of the CID should be appointed to control them. The report ignored the suggestion by Warren Fisher (*see* para. 503) that the work and staff in connection with the war histories should be transferred to the British Museum or some kindred body. In accordance with the report, a CID committee on the Control of Official Histories (COH—CAB 16/52 and 53) was constituted which met under the chairmanship of successive Presidents of the Board of Education, at yearly intervals until the Second World War, and whose proceedings record the volumes which were published and the difficulties being encountered, including: slow and unsatisfactory progress; delays in receiving comments from departments; the problem of finding authors and assistants; negotiations with publishers (not all volumes were published by HMSO); attempts to get contributions towards the cost of campaign histories from the governments of India and of the colonies; and the tendentious nature of the military histories being produced in foreign countries. The most lively meeting appears to have been on 9 March 1928 when Churchill (then Chancellor of the Exchequer) attended and took vigorous exception to certain amendments proposed by the War Office to the history of the Gallipoli campaign.

1012. Within 12 years of the end of the First World War the naval and air histories had virtually been completed, but progress on most of the campaign histories was slower; authors with established literary reputations and willing to undertake the laborious research involved could not be found, and the work was eventually entrusted to retired military officers, under the general supervision of Edmonds, who himself concentrated on operations in France and Belgium. The usual procedure was that the historian produced a first narrative which was circulated for comment and criticism to departments and to officers who had participated (COH 26 records that the draft of one volume had been sent to 799 recipients) and then amended in the light of the replies, and of other information which was constantly coming forward from allied and enemy sources—often in a foreign language—and generally of such an authoritative nature that it could not be ignored. Much careful attention was devoted to maps, but it was not always easy to synchronise their production with the printing of the text. In the upshot progress was disappointing, and the last of the military volumes for the First World War was not published until 1949.

1013. In the inter-war years the staff of the Section varied between 25 and 42; those actually engaged in writing the histories were few and rarely exceeded six in number, the majority being those employed in receiving and sorting the great mass of original material erratically dumped on the Section and making it available to the historians in a usable condition. As the histories were completed, the original material which had been gradually arranged in archival form was transferred back to the originating departments and is now mostly contained in PRO classes ADM 137, AIR 1 and 5, and WO 95 and 153. The Section gave assistance to regimental historians, and provided material to the official war historians in the Commonwealth and commented on their drafts. It was also a source of information for the Ministry of Pensions, which frequently required confirmation of actions in which claimants for pensions had been wounded, and for the Imperial War Graves Commission.

Civil publications of the Carnegie Endowment for International Peace

1014. Although the Section was not concerned in the civil aspects of the First World War, and no direct official interest was taken in recording the measures which had been adopted, some unofficial assistance at departmental level was given to the Carnegie Endowment for International Peace which had commissioned a number of studies in the belligerent countries 'to attempt to measure the economic cost of the war and the displacement which it was causing in the processes of civilisation'. Following are some of the publications in the British series, written by those who had been closely associated with the matters they discuss:

Allied Shipping Control	J. A. Salter
Prices and Wages in the U.K. 1914–1920	A. L. Bowley
Labour Supply and Regulation	Humbert Wolfe
Experiments in State Control	E. M. H. Lloyd
Taxation during the War	J. Stamp
British Food Control	W. H. Beveridge
British Coal Industry during the War	Richard Redmayne

1015. Before its dissolution in 1921 the Ministry of Munitions had arranged for its own history to be written in 12 volumes, but copies were not available in sufficient numbers to justify sale to the public. Copies of the first eight volumes, which did not contain highly secret matter, were distributed to selected libraries in the United Kingdom and the type broken up (CP 66(23)—CAB 24/158. A copy of the whole set of volumes is now in the PRO under reference MUN 5/321A.

Civil and military histories of the Second World War

1016. In 1939 the military remnant of the Historical Section of the CID was evacuated first to St. Annes-on-Sea and later to Aberystwyth, and under Edmonds continued the work on the campaign histories of the First World War. Bridges took the first steps towards a history of the Second World War by writing to all departments in September 1939 suggesting that they should keep a simple diary of all important events (CAB 103/59), but in the circumstances of the time no high priority appears to have been given to it.

1017. With the disappearance of the CID, its sub-committee on the Control of Official Histories (COH—CAB 16/52 and 53) became a committee of the War Cabinet (CAB 98/7–12) and a significant meeting was held on 29 July 1941 under the chairmanship of R. A. Butler. It was agreed that there should be a Medical History, for which Sir Arthur MacNalty would be editor-in-chief (with an editorial board which would report to the COH committee). It was recognised that the Foreign Office would prepare material for a diplomatic history (on which Llewellyn Woodward was then engaged). It was agreed that for operations, narratives should be prepared by the Air Ministry and the Admiralty for their own services, and by the Historical Section for military operations; and that W. K. Hancock (then Professor of History at Birmingham) should within the Historical Section supervise the preparation of narratives for the civil departments. No decisions could then be taken about the shape or form of any histories which might ultimately be published, but it was contemplated that there might be a few general or key volumes dealing in broad outline with the strategical situation and the interlock with diplomatic and economic action; that any military histories would be on an inter-service basis; and that any civil histories would show the organisations for war purposes established by the various departments, with some general account of their activities. It was also agreed to set up an advisory historical committee from the universities (COH(U)—CAB 98/13–16) under the chairmanship of E. A. Benians, Master of St. John's College, Cambridge (*see also* WP(G)(41)140—CAB 67/9 and WM 128(41)1—CAB 65/20).

1018. For the remainder of the war the Section was mainly concerned with the preparation of narratives giving detailed accounts of particular operations, episodes or policies, which, when the histories came to be written, would give the historian a full story which he could condense and combine with material from other sources and to which he would add his own comments; for operations the narratives were compiled by retired officers, and those for the civil departments were generally undertaken by academics from the universities. While these narratives were being prepared, the COH committee and the advisory committee were giving preliminary thought to the question of publication (*see also* WP(45)14—CAB 66/60 and WM 39(45)4—CAB 65/50). It was recognised that, particularly for the military and diplomatic histories, much further research would be required and that no early publication of any comprehensive account would be practical. The possibility of bringing out a short general history within two years of the end of the war, and covering in outline the military and civil and to a lesser extent the diplomatic history of the war period, was actively canvassed, but in spite of soundings no historian of repute could be found to undertake the task. An alternative suggestion was the publication of popular military histories pending the issue of the full official histories, and the War Office and Air Ministry made arrangements accordingly with certain well-known writers (for a list of the popular histories, which were published early in the 1950s, *see* Annex 10).

1019. *Civil histories.* Towards the end of the war it was becoming clear that several of the narrators who were out-housed for work in the civil departments were outgrowing their original function of undertaking preliminary research. They had identified the main strands of activity, they had ready access to the departmental files and papers and to those directly concerned, and were beginning to write histories from the original material they could handle on the spot. The civil histories were thus taking shape shortly after the events they described; many of the narrators and historians were anxious to return to their universities or other occupations, but were generally prepared to continue work on a part-time basis in order to complete the text. Delay inevitably ensued in checking references, in submitting the texts for departmental comment, and subsequently for printing. The first volume, published in 1949, was *British War Economy*, by W. K. Hancock and M. M. Gowing, which gave a synoptic account of the war effort on the home front. In the preface to that volume Hancock, who had been appointed editor for the civil series, outlined the scope proposed for the series and the way in which the works would be written. Most of the remaining volumes in the civil series were published by the end of the 1950s.

1020. *Military histories.* The position for the military series at the end of the war was less easy. Narratives giving a detailed day-to-day account of some operations had been compiled while the war was in progress, but most of the war diaries and other records on which those narratives could be based were held in commands overseas, and were not returned until after the end of hostilities, when they were liable to be in a state of confusion. With demobilisation, the participants in operations scattered and it was not easy to trace them for their recollections. The top level strategical material was not readily available. Nothing was known of the contents and little of the whereabouts of the captured enemy documents which would give a valuable balance to any account derived solely from British sources. In these circumstances it was premature in 1945 to consider any general scheme for a military history, but as the records were returned the narratives for operations were compiled by retired officers in the Admiralty and Air Ministry for their own services, and in the Historical Section for military operations. The series of military narratives ('blue books') had generally been completed by the mid-1950s, and are now in CAB 44/46–273 (copies of the corresponding narratives for the Commonwealth forces are in CAB 44/274–427).

1021. During the year following the end of the war, more had become known of the generality of the material available, and in October 1946, J. R. M. Butler (a fellow of Trinity College, Cambridge) was appointed chief military historian. On his suggestion a panel of senior officers was formed composed of Vice-Admiral Sir Geoffrey Blake, Lieut.-General Sir Henry Pownall, Air Chief Marshall Sir Douglas Evill and Major-General Sir Ian Jacob, to advise him on the planning and layout of the military histories. The general scheme recommended by the panel and outlined in COH (48)5 (not yet transferred to the Public Record Office) was for:

- (a) several central volumes giving a continuous comprehensive account of the conduct of the war at the highest level of policy and strategy (later known as the Grand Strategy series);
- (b) volumes dealing with major aspects and topics, considered in some cases with reference to a geographical theatre from an inter-service point of view (the Campaign series), and in others as a series of connected operations (the War at Sea and the Strategic Air Offensive);
- (c) volumes concerned less directly with operations, but devoted to some aspect

of the war or special interest or novel features (Civil Affairs and Military Government—most other aspects were ultimately dealt with in the central volumes).

On the selection of writers, the panel considered that as the requirement was for 'a broad survey from an inter-service point of view', the ideal would be a team of professional historians of recognised standing and experienced in the writing of military history, but they appreciated that such writers were rare, and such as there were would be reluctant to leave their universities; for the campaign volumes the case for military qualifications was stronger than for the other series. The COH committee gave general endorsement to these proposals, and J. R. M. Butler proceeded with the difficult task of finding qualified writers willing to work for several years in London on temporary engagements, and when found giving them guidance on the field they should cover and the detail which would be appropriate. Butler himself undertook two volumes in the Grand Strategy series.

1022. Much of the raw material was in the narratives which had been prepared in the Admiralty, the Air Ministry and the Historical Section. Within the Historical Section an Enemy Documents Branch was established (with an outpost in Washington DC) which fed in information about particular campaigns and the development of plans from the enemy's point of view. Other sources included the records of the War Cabinet, of the Combined Chiefs of Staff, of SHEAF and of SEAC, and access to participants and to official historians in the Commonwealth and the USA. For the major campaign series, the historian was generally a retired officer who led a team from the other services (some of whom had prepared the narratives) and thus was able to give the account from an inter-service standpoint. Careful attention was given to maps and photographs in the attempt to make the account intelligible.

1023. The recognised procedure was that the author, after inviting comments and criticism from individuals with special knowledge (including where relevant official historians in other countries), submitted his draft to the panel of senior officers, over which Butler presided, and after consideration of their suggestions, a further draft was circulated for official comment to the service departments and any other departments concerned. When those comments had been digested and any security requirements satisfied, the volume was sent for printing.

1024. *References.* It is the natural wish of an author to quote the source of the statements he makes, and in the drafts of the civil and military histories for the Second World War full documentation was given; but most of the references were to official files and documents which, at the time the volumes were published, were not available for public inspection. Accordingly the decision was taken that footnote references to official sources which were then closed should not be given in the published volumes. The documentation, however, has been preserved, and the volumes which are now included in CAB 101 are annotated with the references to the confidential sources used. It was the practice to mark such sources 'Used by the Official Historians', which would protect them from destruction in the process of weeding, and they should therefore become available in due course in the Public Record Office; but the student should be aware that he may encounter difficulty in tracing them—their references may have been subsequently changed in the department of origin, they may not be readily reconcilable with the archival references by which they would be identified in the Public Record Office, and in some cases, particularly where the papers were loose or unreferenced, the source may have been unintentionally misplaced or destroyed.

1025. *Staff.* The staff of the Section in the late 1940s rose to 140 and comprised

E*

historians, narrators, research assistants, cartographers, clerks, typists and messengers. There was a heavy load in referencing many thousands of war diaries, etc., in registering the movements of original material, in copying drafts and issuing them for comment, in preparing maps, and sending material for printing. At any given time there were liable to be at least a dozen volumes in different stages of preparation and requiring various degrees of checking. A small administrative section gave such assistance to regimental and unofficial historians (including Churchill) as was appropriate, and relieved the official historians and narrators of those tasks which were not directly concerned with the work they were writing.

ANNEX 1

RECOLLECTIONS OF CABINET PROCEDURE
BEFORE 1917*

Sir Herbert Creedy,† 7 August 1949

(1) . . . Before the First World War the Foreign Office used to circulate their 'sections' (prints of important telegrams to and from diplomatic posts abroad), and prints of some despatches in a special small pouch of which the Minister himself kept the key. The contents were often not shown to anyone in the Department. When Lord Kitchener became Secretary of State for War in August 1914, I was told that he never took charge of keys, and so I kept this key until the pouch system was abandoned for boxes with a less sacrosanct key, though there were still some circulations in boxes to be opened only with the old key.

(2) The War Office printed its own Cabinet Papers in the War Office Press, which was run by Messrs Harrison until HMSO took it over. These papers usually bore the number of the War Office departmental file, and were printed on green paper with the usual headings, and were always of foolscap size, except perhaps when Mr Churchill was Secretary of State. He liked white quarto.

(3) I sent back to the Cabinet Office all the earlier Cabinet papers.

(4) We found when the war came that we had to send telegrams and operational reports and, where necessary, Cabinet memoranda in separate red boxes addressed to Ministers by title and not by name, to their respective departments. For the King we had different boxes with a special key. There were two or three circulations a day and one box would not have got round in time.

(5) The Secretary of State for War usually minuted the departmental file after its subject had been discussed in Cabinet, but did not necessarily mention the fact that it was a Cabinet decision.

(6) I remember well the decision which Colonel Seely wrote on coming back from the Cabinet discussion on the Curragh incident. I was only number two then and was not with him when he wrote it, but I do recall remarking that it seemed an unexpected decision. This was in March 1914, I think.

(7) I agree with Sir Maurice Bonham Carter that more business was done between the Prime Minister and Ministers concerned without formal reference to the Cabinet, especially on interdepartmental matters affecting only a few Ministers.

(8) I remember Committees of the Cabinet being appointed to go through Army Estimates when they were between £20 million and £30 million, but do not recall Standing Committees.

(9) Generally, the volume of papers circulated to the Cabinet was very small before the war in comparison with the circulations of later years, when papers were often hektographed and were frequently of considerable length.

---

* See para. 312.

† Sir Herbert Creedy, 1878–1973, was private secretary to the Secretary of State for War 1913–1920; subsequently he was P.U.S., War Office.

Sir Maurice Bonham Carter,* 8 August 1949

(a) The Cabinet was summoned by a notice issued by the Prime Minister's chief private secretary in the following terms:

'There will be a meeting of the Cabinet at 10 Downing Street at —— o'clock on ——.'

It was circulated in the Cabinet circulation box normally to the private secretaries, but if an urgent notice had to go out after hours it would be circulated to Ministers in their houses. No agenda was issued either with the summons or thereafter. Cabinet meetings were normally held weekly when Parliament was in session.

(b) and (c) I doubt very much whether any formal agenda was stated by the Prime Minister at the beginning of the meeting. No large proportion of the business was done on the basis of memoranda, though these, of course, were freely issued by the relevant Minister, usually with the agreement of the Prime Minister, though if a memorandum was purely informative, such as frequently was the case with Foreign Office memoranda, I think the Minister concerned would issue it on his own responsibility. Memoranda were circulated like notices of the Cabinet meetings in the red circulation box to the private secretaries.

(d) It was the responsibility of the Ministers to note and carry out the decisions relating to their own departments, and requiring their own action. It has frequently been suggested, and was certainly so stated by Lord Curzon in the debate in the House of Lords on 19 June 1918, that the result of leaving the relevant Ministers to carry out the decisions of the Cabinet resulted in confusion. I am aware of one instance when this occurred, namely when a misunderstanding of a Cabinet decision led to the resignation of Seely as Secretary of State for War. If there was any doubt about a Cabinet decision the invariable practice was for the Minister concerned to consult the Prime Minister, and apart from the instance mentioned, I am not aware that any difficulty arose as to the interpretation of the Cabinet decision. Cabinet committees were from time to time appointed for specific business and not as a matter of normal routine, and there were no regular standing committees.

It will be seen from the above answers that a fundamental difference exists between procedure before the First World War and now. . . . There is, however, an important difference between the two periods, namely that before the First World War, the Cabinet consisted of men belonging to the same party, who were all of one mind on the main issues of policy, and who were in constant friendly touch in their public and private lives. Normally speaking, administrative problems were not brought to the notice of the Cabinet at all. These were decided by the Minister responsible, either alone or after a discussion with the Prime Minister, and the question of the further reference to the Cabinet would then be decided between the Prime Minister and the Minister concerned. Other Ministers were ready to accept the decisions of their colleagues, above all when backed by the authority of the Prime Minister, which was unquestioned. A great deal of foreign policy was decided by discussions between Sir Edward Grey and the Prime Minister and equally questions on defence between him and the defence Ministers. Mr Asquith held strongly to the view that Cabinet discussions should be wholly private, and that Ministers should be able to use arguments and take a line which could be varied the next day, and of which no record should be available to be brought up against them.

There appears, to an outsider at least, to have grown up a tendency amongst Ministers to cast the responsibility for even minor decisions of administration on

---

* Sir Maurice Bonham Carter, 1880–1960, was private secretary to the Prime Minister, 1910–1916.

to the shoulders of their colleagues, and to refer awkward questions more frequently to the Cabinet as a whole. In a coalition, it is of course inevitable that where members of the Government are not in fundamental agreement, doubtful questions should be referred to Cabinet discussion in order to avoid any subsequent open difference of opinion. The result is, of course, compromise and often great delay.

Sir Sidney Harris,* 13 October 1949

(i) He said that in his day, if the Home Secretary wished to circulate a memorandum to his Cabinet colleagues, it was sent over to No. 10 and circulated from there. He felt sure that the practice differed from one department to another. . . . Departments which were in the habit of sending round documents like telegrams doubtless used their own boxes for the circulation of any Cabinet papers which they wished to send round. Other departments, who had no routine machinery for circulating documents, probably asked No. 10 to arrange for the circulation of any Cabinet papers they might produce.

(ii) It was his impression that misunderstandings about Cabinet decisions were rare. In the Home Office certainly he recollected no occasion on which officials had found any difficulty in ascertaining from the Home Secretary what decision the Cabinet had reached. If the subject matter was Home Office business, the Home Secretary usually endorsed the decision on the Home Office file. And Home Office officials were rarely concerned to know of Cabinet decisions on matters which were not strictly Home Office business.

Sir Sidney Harris added that in those days, when there were fewer departments and government business was so much less complex, most Cabinet decisions were of concern only to the department which had raised the issue; and the departmental Minister, being fully aware of the point which he had raised (for he had normally to raise it orally, without the advantage of a paper written by his officials) was well able to appreciate what the Cabinet intended him to do about it. Further, most of the questions which came before the Cabinet in those days were 'political' questions, of which Ministers had as firm a grasp as had their officials. There were hardly any technical questions—like the economic questions which nowadays occupy most the Cabinet's time—which officials would handle more easily than Ministers.

(iii) Sir Sidney Harris thought that in those days the Cabinet rarely appointed formal committees; and he could not remember that there were any standing committees of the Cabinet.

He explained this by stressing the fact, which was put by Sir Maurice Bonham Carter, that informal contacts between Ministers were more common then than they are today. A Minister who was thinking of raising some question in Cabinet would often ask two or three of his colleagues to come and talk about it with him beforehand; and there were many informal meetings of this kind for preliminary exchange of views on subjects which were to come formally before the Cabinet. Ministers also knew one another as personal friends more intimately than they do today: they met a great deal at one another's houses and had many more opportunities for informal discussion of ministerial business. All this made formal Cabinet committees less necessary than they are today.

---

* Sir Sidney Harris, 1876–1962, was private secretary to the Home Secretary, 1909–1919; subsequently he was Assistant Under-Secretary, Home Office. The conversation printed here was recorded by Brook.

Lord Hankey,* 10 November 1949

General remarks

A most important factor . . . is that, during most of the period covered (1900 to December 1916) Cabinet procedure was being influenced, at first unconsciously but later and especially during the war years, consciously, by the development of the Committee of Imperial Defence. Even before 1914, the co-ordination of nearly all business over the whole field of defence had been gradually and almost imperceptibly absorbed into the CID and/or its sub-committees. After the outbreak of war the glaring contrast between the comparative efficiency of the war-time expressions of the CID, especially of the War Committee, as compared with the Cabinet, led first to a gradual transfer of business from the Cabinet to the War Committee, which accounts for the fact . . . that in 1916 between July and December there were 41 meetings of the War Committee against 18 meetings of the Cabinet.

The success of the CID War Book on the outbreak of war, and the tributes to it from all over the Empire, made a deep impression which led to the adaptation of the CID to war conditions first in the form of the War Council, next the Dardanelles Committee (a temporary setback due to the coalition Government), the War Committee and eventually the War Cabinet and Imperial War Cabinet.

At all these stages there was a good deal of passive resistance by 'old stager' Ministers and officials, who instinctively mistrusted innovations.

The circumstances that led Mr Balfour to set up the CID in 1904 throw a little light on early Cabinet procedure. There had long been a Defence Committee of the Cabinet which was established by the Marquess of Salisbury in 1895 and which was presided over first by the Duke of Devonshire, and later, after he became Prime Minister, by Mr. Balfour. But, lacking any secretariat, it was not a very 'live' body, and in 1902 the Secretary of State for War (Viscount Middleton) and the First Lord of the Admiralty (Earl of Selborne) circulated a joint memorandum to the Cabinet urging reorganisation (CID 494-B). That led to the Esher Committee on the reorganisation of the Army, on whose first report the CID with its secretariat organisation came into existence.

The growth of this new orderly machinery probably began quite early in the century to influence government departments in the form and in the methods of distribution of their memoranda; but the unforthcoming attitude of the Treasury did not conduce towards any formal extension of the CID system or its adaptation to the Cabinet.

During the years 1914–1916 Cabinet committees were not uncommon. Two or three were established at the outbreak of war. In September 1915 . . . a Cabinet Committee had been set up on War Policy, which had recommended compulsory service and was overlapping the Dardanelles Committee, but Mr Asquith scotched it by reorganising the ill-conceived Dardanelles Committee into a better balanced War Committee. Lord Crewe, the chairman of the War Policy Committee, which had no secretary, sent for me and . . . turned over to me all the papers.

The Dardanelles Committee, by the way, an emanation from the new Coalition Government, was itself in theory a Cabinet Committee, and held its first meeting without a secretary. But Asquith, Balfour, Kitchener and Lloyd George insisted on a secretary, and I was brought in and succeeded in gradually infiltrating it with

---

* Lord Hankey, 1877–1963, was secretary of the CID 1912–1938, and secretary of the Cabinet 1916–1938.

the Chiefs of Staff and all the procedure of the CID until, as already mentioned, Mr Asquith reorganised it into a War Committee.

In February 1916 a Cabinet Committee was set up on manpower . . . and I was its secretary from the first.

The above examples . . . illustrate how the CID system was influencing the Cabinet system throughout the first 16 years of the century.

So sloppy were the methods, or rather the lack of methods, under the old régime that I never had any doubt myself that in time the Cabinet would be compelled to adopt the CID system, and even before 1912 when I became secretary of the CID I used to discuss it with my colleagues. From the first Lord Haldane and later on Mr Balfour and Lloyd George favoured the idea, but Mr Asquith, who was slightly Gladstonian in his attitude, while admitting that something must be done, never quite accepted the War Cabinet system *en bloc*.

General picture (Curzon's speech in House of Lords, 19 June 1918)

This was very carefully drawn up by Lord Curzon, who discussed it very fully with me and others. It was accepted by members of the War Cabinet as accurate at the time and was based on personal experience.

Cabinet meetings and Cabinet business

'Informal discussions' were a favourite method with Mr Asquith and some of his colleagues. They were anathema to Chiefs of Staff and heads of departments, as often no one could discover what had been decided. Several important decisions of the early part of the war were taken at such meetings.

The Cabinet summons

When the War Cabinet became a peace Cabinet and I was retained as secretary, Mr Churchill begged that as many of the pre-war practices as possible should be restored, and Mr Lloyd George instructed me to do my best to comply. I succeeded in ascertaining the traditional seats of the principal members of the Cabinet which were used as the basis of the seating plan. I also obtained a specimen of the former summons.

Officials and Cabinet decisions

Ministers often gave their officials rather a garbled account of decisions and on CID questions officials often turned to me for confirmation. Sometimes I found it difficult to get the information myself. I recall one example in the early part of the 1914–1918 war when the Cabinet decided to send to Russia rifles that, as transpired later, had been promised to India, from which confusion arose when eventually the news trickled through to the departments concerned.

Circulation

I was sometimes in Sir Maurice Bonham Carter's room when he was circulating Cabinet papers. They were received, according to my recollection, sometimes from the department and sometimes from the printer, and pushed very expeditiously into the Cabinet boxes and taken away by the Downing Street messengers, sometimes to their offices and sometimes, if time was short, to their homes, in which case the messengers were allowed to take cabs. There was certainly no numbering of papers.

I think the Foreign Office circulated all their own papers, because copies of a great many were sent to me, and would arrive in Foreign Office boxes at all hours of the day and night with great efficiency.

In very secret matters a single copy of Cabinet papers would occasionally be passed round from Minister to Minister in a box, returning with the names ticked off to the Minister concerned. It must be remembered that typewriting facilities were very small, roneos almost non-existent and telephones none too good early in the century.

Even before the 1914–1918 war a few matters were kept to a small group of Ministers and not communicated to the rest of the Cabinet, e.g. the Military Staff conversation with the French in 1906. This was a great mistake as a good many staff officers and officials and others knew all about the conversations and a great deal of suspicion and friction was created in the Cabinet. The Cabinet only learned of them in 1912.

Prime Minister's consent

As the 'old system' was not a 'system' at all, but a series of endless improvisations, I doubt if these was any steady practice of obtaining the Prime Minister's consent to circulate papers. If there had been I feel sure it would have reacted into the War Committee and War Cabinet, which it did not.

The CID definitely did not undertake the circulation of Cabinet papers.

Disposal of business

As the Cabinet had no 'waiting list' for subjects requiring decision it is not surprising that early decisions were often unobtainable.

The King

King George V told me several times that until he received the Cabinet Minutes and papers (which he used to read assiduously) he had never been fully informed of what was going on.

The Cabinet letter, of course, often gave a very meagre report. A Prime Minister, after a long meeting, with important guests awaiting him at luncheon upstairs, with questions to answer in Parliament and sometimes a speech to make, often could not find time for an adequate letter, which had to be written in his own hand.

Smoking at Cabinets

The old convention was 'No smoking before lunch'. It was observed until 1924, when Mr Ramsay MacDonald renewed it at the outset of his first meeting. But Mr J. H. Thomas came in later and, knowing nothing of the rule, continued to smoke. Soon others lit their pipes, and the rule vanished for ever—to the intense discomfort of non-smokers!

Remarks

The point I wish to emphasise is that . . . there were no rules of procedure. Each Prime Minister was a law unto himself, and most of them left details to their principal private secretaries who, during the present century at any rate, do not seem to have been civil servants.

Lord Samuel,* 15 May 1950

Lord Samuel offered the following comments in conversation with Brook.

Agenda

It was customary for Ministers to seek the Prime Minister's consent to bring a matter up at Cabinet. On matters of less importance, this was arranged by a message from the Minister's private secretary to the private secretary at No. 10. On more important matters the Minister might speak personally to the Prime Minister—sometimes he would have sought the Prime Minister's advice on the problem informally and, after some preliminary discussion, the Prime Minister would say, 'better bring that up at Cabinet'.

The Prime Minister normally kept a manuscript note of the matters which were due to come up—and this formed his own informal agenda paper.

---

* Lord Samuel, 1870–1963, was a member of the Cabinet 1909–1916 and 1931–1932.

Ministers did not, however, regard themselves as under any formal obligation to warn colleagues that they were going to bring up at Cabinet a question which might concern their departmental interests.

The number of matters discussed in Cabinet was much smaller in those days than now. It was Lord Samuel's impression that nowadays departmental Ministers brought to Cabinet a large number of minor matters which in the old days they would have settled on their own.

Record of meetings

In Mr Asquith's Cabinet Lulu Harcourt made a private record of Cabinet meetings. In the early days he was seen to be scribbling furiously during Cabinet meetings, and this was a cause of resentment among some of his colleagues, who protested against having their remarks taken down in this way. As a result he subsequently made his notes less obtrusively. Lord Samuel had never heard what became of this private diary—so far as he knew, it had never been published and he presumed that it must still be among Harcourt's papers.

Cabinet committees

Lord Samuel was inclined to challenge the statement that 'some use was made of Cabinet committees as a normal method of handling particular problems'. Formal Cabinet committees were not, in his view, an important part of the Cabinet structure. What frequently happened was that, if a disagreement could not be resolved in Cabinet, the Prime Minister would ask the two or three Ministers who were in disagreement to meet informally by themselves and try to thrash things out before the next meeting of the Cabinet. This was done in a very informal way, though, on occasion, one or two 'impartial' Ministers might be asked to take a hand in reconciling the disputants. This, said Lord Samuel, was only a reflection of the much greater informality and intimacy of Cabinet proceedings in those days.

Memoranda

Lord Samuel said that the bulk of the Cabinet's business was done on the basis of written memoranda. Apart from urgent day-to-day problems, e.g. on foreign affairs, all matters of substance coming before the Cabinet were brought up on the basis of memoranda circulated in advance. Members of the Cabinet were aggrieved if they had not received this prior notice, and the opportunity which it gave of obtaining advice. In particular, drafts of Bills, or projects of Bills, were always circulated to the Cabinet.

Lord Samuel also referred to a memorandum on Palestine which he had himself circulated to the Cabinet early in 1914, when he was President of the Local Government Board. It was recognised that a Minister was free to submit to the Cabinet a memorandum on some matter of general interest which was not his departmental concern—though, even then, it was rather exceptional for a Minister to take advantage of this right. Lord Samuel made special mention of this memorandum, as it was the first occasion on which proposals for a Jewish national home had been put before United Kingdom Ministers: he has apparently referred to this in his published memoirs.

There was probably no definite rule that the Prime Minister's consent should be obtained before a memorandum was circulated. If a Minister wished to circulate a paper on some subject clearly within his own departmental jurisdiction, he would probably not think it necessary to mention the matter to the Prime Minister in advance. He would, however, send the memorandum to No. 10, for circulation from there.

All Cabinet Ministers received copies of memoranda circulated to the Cabinet.

Lord Samuel was inclined to think that all Cabinet papers were circulated from No. 10. He thought it unlikely that departments regularly circulating documents of their own used their circulation boxes for the distribution of Cabinet papers. For he clearly recollected that Foreign Office telegrams and despatches, for example, came round in a different box from Cabinet papers. The Foreign Office boxes had different keys, which were normally held by the Minister personally, whereas, apparently, the Minister's private secretary often held the Cabinet key. Lord Samuel spoke of 'Cabinet boxes' and 'Cabinet keys'. He evidently regarded the material circulated by the Foreign Office as more secret in character. He confirmed the statement that on very secret subjects a single copy of a Cabinet paper was occasionally passed on from one Minister to another in one circulating box.

Miscellaneous

Lord Samuel added two further points:

(a) . . . He thought it quite natural that the Prime Minister should discuss matters of the highest importance with a few of his most senior and trusted colleagues, in a sort of 'inner Cabinet'. When he had first held a relatively unimportant office as a comparatively young man, he had not expected to be brought into consultation on all the major matters of policy which engaged the attention of the elder statesmen in the Cabinet. One of the advantages of the greater informality of Cabinet work in those days was that, as many meetings took place on a quite informal basis, Ministers were less liable to take it amiss if they were left out of some of these consultations.

(b) When Mr Asquith formed his Coalition in 1915 Lord Samuel was one of the Liberals for whom no room could at first be found—but he was promised that he would be brought back at the first opportunity, and he did in fact come back when Sir John Simon resigned on the conscription issue. When he was given this promise that he would be brought back at the first opportunity, Lord Samuel asked whether he could continue to receive such documents as Foreign Office telegrams and despatches so that he could keep himself in touch with developments meanwhile. Mr Asquith assented to this, and from June to December 1915 Lord Samuel did in fact receive copies of most of the Foreign Office documents circulated to the Cabinet though not Cabinet papers proper.

ANNEX 2

THE WAR CABINET
RULES OF PROCEDURE JANUARY 1917*

(1) *Reference.* Questions may be referred for decision by the War Cabinet by the Prime Minister, or by members of the War Cabinet, or by any member of the Government, or by any Government department. The normal procedure for raising any question should be by a communication to the secretary, accompanied, when practicable, by a short memorandum containing a summary of the points on which a decision is required.

(2) *Consultation with departments.* Before reaching their final conclusions on any subject the War Cabinet will, as a general rule, consult the Ministers at the head of the departments concerned, who will lay before them all the evidence, written or oral, relevant and necessary to a decision.

(3) *Approval of minutes.* After each meeting the secretary will circulate copies of the draft minutes to members for their remarks. He will also circulate to Ministers summoned for particular subjects, drafts of the minutes on those subjects for their remarks. When their remarks have been received, the secretary will submit a final draft of the minutes for the approval of the Prime Minister. After the Prime Minister has initialled the minutes of the War Cabinet, the conclusions formulated therein will become operative decisions to be carried out by the responsible departments. The Prime Minister can delegate his powers in this respect in case of absence or the claims of other urgent business.

(4) *Circulation of minutes.* As soon as the Prime Minister's initials have been received, the decisions of the War Cabinet will be communicated by the secretary to the political and civil heads of the departments concerned, who will be responsible for giving effect to them.

(5) *Communication to the War Cabinet and certain departments for record.* The secretary will also communicate complete copies of the minutes of the War Cabinet for record to all members of the War Cabinet, and to the following heads of departments, as decided by the War Cabinet:

Secretary of State for Home Affairs
Secretary of State for Foreign Affairs
Secretary of State for the Colonies
Secretary of State for India
Secretary of State for War
First Lord of the Admiralty
President of the Board of Trade.

Copies of all decisions affecting the war will also be sent for record to:

First Sea Lord
Chief of the Imperial General Staff
Under Secretary of State for Foreign Affairs.

The only exception to this rule will be in the case of decisions of extreme secrecy (such as the dates of forthcoming operations, new engines of war, etc), the

---

*See para. 201

reproduction of which is not advisable; in such cases the Prime Minister may, on the advice of the War Cabinet, use his discretion to withhold either wholly, or for a time, the communication of copies of the minutes.

Under the instructions of the Prime Minister the secretary may communicate particular decisions direct to chairmen of committees, and others whom they affect.

(6) *The carrying out of the decisions of the War Cabinet.* In order to keep the War Cabinet fully informed, the head of the department responsible for action on any of the War Cabinet's decisions is requested to notify the Secretary as to the action taken or, if for any reason action is found impossible or unnecessary, to notify him accordingly. Where applicable, it would be convenient if the communication to the secretary could take the form of copies or paraphrases of the telegrams, letters or instructions actually sent.

(7) *The attendance of experts.* The First Sea Lord of the Admiralty, the Chief of the Imperial General Staff and the Permanent Under Secretary of the Foreign Office, or their representatives, will ordinarily attend at the outset of each meeting to explain respectively the latest developments of the naval, military and political situation, and will remain as long as necessary according to the nature of the business to be transacted. Other experts may be summoned as required.

(8) *The communication of information by departments.* Heads of departments are requested to communicate to the secretary, for the use of the War Cabinet, all information bearing on the higher conduct of the war, or on any other question concerning the War Cabinet, whether consisting of telegrams, despatches, memoranda, statistics, reports of committees, etc. In the case of bulky documents, attention should be drawn to passages bearing more particularly on current questions.

(9) *The circulation of information by the War Cabinet.* With the object of keeping abreast with current political and military events all ministers who are not on the regular distribution list for Foreign Office, Colonial Office, India Office, War Office, and Admiralty telegrams, the War Cabinet have arranged that the following documents should be circulated weekly to the Ministers mentioned in the Appendix:

(1) a review of the military situation by the Chief of the Imperial General Staff;

(2) a summary of Eastern political affairs to be prepared by Lieut.-Colonel Sir Mark Sykes, M.P., Assistant Secretary, War Cabinet;

(3) a summary of Western and Imperial political affairs, to be prepared by L. C. M. S. Amery, M.P., Assistant Secretary, War Cabinet.

(10) *Address.* Meetings of the War Cabinet are held at 10 Downing Street. All communications in regard to the circulation and distribution of papers should be addressed to the secretary at 2 Whitehall Gardens, S.W.

24 January 1917

264

Printed for the Cabinet. April 1936.

SECRET.

Copy No. 52

C.P. 88 (36).

CABINET.

CABINET PROCEDURE.

NOTE BY THE SECRETARY, CABINET.

BY direction of the Prime Minister I circulate herewith the following documents in regard to procedure, &c., for the information of Members of the Cabinet :—

> Appendix I.—Instructions to the Secretary of the Cabinet in regard to Cabinet Procedure.
>
> Appendix II.—Instructions as regards the procedure of Cabinet Committees and Conferences.
>
> Appendix III.—Particulars of procedure of the Committee of Imperial Defence.
>
> Appendix IV.—A Note on the Economic Advisory Council.

The last occasion on which these documents were circulated to the Cabinet was at the end of August 1931·(C.P. 205 (31)). Owing to the exhaustion of the stock of copies it has been necessary to reprint the texts, and the opportunity has been taken to bring them fully up to date.

A fuller Memorandum containing a historical account of the development of the Cabinet Secretariat and detailed particulars of its operation is available, and will be sent to any Minister who may desire to see it.

(Signed)   M. P. A. HANKEY,
Secretary, Cabinet.

2 Whitehall Gardens, S.W. 1,
April 2, 1936.

SECRET.

APPENDIX I.

CABINET PROCEDURE.

Instructions to the Secretary of the Cabinet.

THE Prime Minister will instruct the Secretary as to what subjects are to be placed on the Agenda Paper of each Meeting of the Cabinet. It is contrary to the usual practice for the Cabinet to consider other subjects. In cases, however, of very exceptional urgency such subjects may be raised with the consent of the Prime Minister, which should always be obtained prior to the Meeting. The Secretary will give Ministers as long notice as he can regarding subjects likely to be discussed, and will issue to members of the Cabinet a weekly list of subjects awaiting consideration.

2. The Secretary will attend meetings of the Cabinet, unless instructed to the contrary, for the purpose of recording the conclusions.

3. It is an instruction to the Secretary in drafting Cabinet Minutes, so far as practicable, to avoid any reference to opinions expressed by any individual and to limit the Minutes as narrowly as possible to the actual decision.

4. One copy of the draft conclusions will be sent to the King as heretofore "with Humble Duty" from the Prime Minister.

5. The conclusions of the Cabinet are to be transmitted by the Secretary to all Cabinet Ministers and, subject to the authority of the Prime Minister, the Secretary shall transmit to Ministers who are not members of the Cabinet relevant extracts of Conclusions on particular items with which such Ministers are concerned. The Lord Chancellor, however, is responsible for communicating to the Law Officers of the Crown such decisions as concern them, subject to consultation with the Cabinet at the time the decision is taken, or subsequently with the Prime Minister if he deems necessary.

6. Ministers are responsible for making such communication as they deem necessary to their respective Departments in regard to the conclusions of the Cabinet.

7. The Minutes of the Cabinet are always to be available for consultation by Cabinet Ministers, either in the Secretary's Office, or, during meetings of the Cabinet, in the Cabinet Room.

8. The Secretary is to take all possible precautions for ensuring that in the reproduction of Cabinet Conclusions the minimum staff is employed.

9. The rule is maintained under which Memoranda, Draft Bills and other constituents of the Agenda Paper of the Cabinet are sent to the Cabinet Secretariat for circulation only *after* their subject-matter has been fully examined between the Department from which they emanate, the Treasury, the Law Officers where contentious Bills are involved, and any other Departments concerned. (See attached Treasury Circulars of the 25th February, 1931, and the 28th April, 1924.) In January 1932 the Prime Minister asked that his colleagues should make it a regular practice before circulating Memoranda to the Cabinet to pass them through his hands. Since that time it has become usual for the Minister concerned, before circulating a Memorandum to the Cabinet, to consult with the Prime Minister and to send him an advance copy.

10. Subject to the above and to any instructions in regard to any particular paper he may receive from the Prime Minister or from the Minister from whom the document originates, the Secretary is to circulate to Members of the Cabinet all Memoranda and other documents prepared for the use of the Cabinet. Subject to reference in case of doubt, to the Prime Minister or the Minister from whom a document is received, the Secretary has discretion to circulate Cabinet papers to Ministers outside the Cabinet whose Departments are affected. He is also authorised to send additional copies to Ministers at their request.

11. Subject to any special instructions he may receive from the Prime Minister, the Secretary, as soon as may be after the termination of every meeting of the Cabinet, will issue a press communiqué containing the names of those present.

12. Departments will reproduce their own memoranda and forward the requisite number of copies to the Cabinet Office for circulation at least five days before the Meeting of the Cabinet at which the memoranda are to be considered, but this rule may be waived in cases of special urgency with the Prime Minister's sanction.

13. It is the duty of all Cabinet Ministers on vacating office to return forthwith to the Secretary to the Cabinet all Cabinet Conclusions and Papers issued to them while in office, and it is the duty of the Secretary to the Cabinet to recover all such Papers. The same procedure is to be followed in the case of Ministers outside the Cabinet on vacating office.

Ex-Cabinet Ministers retain the right of consulting at the Offices of the Cabinet the record copies of all Cabinet Conclusions and Papers issued to them during the time that they were members of the Cabinet.

14. The procedure as regards Cabinet Committees and Conferences is attached.

(G. 3647.) No. 8/31.

SUBMISSION OF BUSINESS TO THE CABINET.

Cabinet Decision as to Procedure.

Treasury Chambers,
Whitehall, S.W., February 25, 1931.

Sir,
I am directed by the Lords Commissioners of His Majesty's Treasury to acquaint you, for the information of
that His Majesty's Government have recently had under consideration the arrangements regarding the submission of business to the Cabinet, and in particular have had before them the Circular No. 11/24 of the 28th April, 1924, on this subject, the main provisions of which were approved by the Cabinet at their Meetings on the 10th and 21st June, 1929.

A copy of that Circular is printed hereunder, and I am to state that His Majesty's Government have reaffirmed their decision that the procedure therein indicated shall continue to be observed in its entirety.

In this connexion I am to emphasise the importance of securing that all draft Bills are fully examined by the Departments concerned before they are circulated to the Committee of Home Affairs. A Department originating legislation should, in any case, arrange for the circulation to that Committee of the draft Bill as long in advance as possible, and in every case the covering Memorandum to the Bill should, in accordance with the requirements of the Circular, contain a specific statement that the draft Bill has been examined by all Departments which are, or may be, affected by its provisions.

I am, Sir,
Your obedient Servant,
N. F. WARREN FISHER.

No. 11/24.

Copy of Treasury Circular, April 28, 1924.

Sir,
I am directed by the Lords Commissioners of His Majesty's Treasury to acquaint you, for the information of
that His Majesty's Government have had under careful consideration the question of insuring that the Cabinet—and Cabinet Committees—shall be invited to reach decisions only after the subject referred to the Cabinet has been thoroughly examined between each of the various Public Departments concerned.

This elementary rule of business is essential if the Cabinet and its Committees are to have available all the facts and points of view requisite for an enlightened decision and are to be saved the possibility of hasty or uninformed conclusions.

The observance of the rule is the more obligatory under modern conditions when the mass of Government business has so enormously increased, and as a consequence Governments can only get through it efficiently if the issues presented for decision have been carefully investigated beforehand by the Departments in collaboration.

The Cabinet feels sure that Departments are anxious to assist it in securing the observance of this rule, and has come to the conclusion that the desired object will be facilitated by the following procedure. In future all memoranda, draft Bills and other constituents of the Agenda will be sent to the Cabinet Secretariat for circulation only after their subject-matter has been fully examined between the Departments from which they emanate, the Treasury, the Law Officers where contentious Bills are involved, and any other Department concerned, and these documents will bear on the face of them a specific statement that this examination has taken place. The documents should be made as complete as possible by containing the various arguments and criticisms which might be brought against the proposals advocated. To enable the members of the Cabinet (and Cabinet Committees) to have time to consider proposals intended for Cabinet decision and in view also of the possibility that such inter-Departmental examination may result in definite differences of opinion necessitating the preparation of memoranda by the dissenting Department or Departments, no memoranda, draft Bills, &c., which originate proposals for Cabinet decision will be placed on the Agenda until an interval of at least five days has elapsed after circulation, except on any occasion when the Prime Minister expressly authorises a relaxation of the rule.

I am, Sir,
Your obedient Servant,
N. F. WARREN FISHER.

APPENDIX II.

Existing Instructions as regards the Procedure of Cabinet Committees and Conferences.

THE Secretary to the Cabinet and Secretaries of Cabinet Committees are to conform to the following instructions :—

(*a*) The Secretary will take the Chairman's instructions as to the form of record. The procedure should approximate to that of the Cabinet, but a somewhat fuller record of the proceedings is permissible in the case of Committees than in that of the Cabinet.

(*b*) The Minutes of the Committee on Home Affairs will be circulated to all Members of the Cabinet, and will not be regarded as final until approved by the Cabinet.

(*c*) The Reports of other Cabinet Committees will be circulated to the Cabinet. Conclusions in regard to matters of high policy will be reserved for approval by the Cabinet. The Chairman will be the judge of what questions should be so reserved.

(*d*) In cases where Secretaries of Cabinet Committees are not members of the Cabinet Office, they will place themselves in communication with the Secretary to the Cabinet with a view to the necessary arrangements as regards circulation and distribution of the Committee's documents.

APPENDIX III.

COMMITTEE OF IMPERIAL DEFENCE.

Origin.

1. THE Committee of Imperial Defence was formally brought into existence by a Treasury Minute dated the 4th May, 1904. The decision was taken by the Prime Minister of the day, Mr. Balfour, on the recommendation of the War Office (Reconstitution) Committee, presided over by Lord Esher. The object in view is stated in the following passage of Lord Esher's Committee report :—

> "The British Empire is pre-eminently a great Naval, Indian and Colonial Power. There are, nevertheless, no means for co-ordinating defence problems for dealing with them as a whole, for defining the proper functions of the various elements and for ensuring that, on the one hand, peace preparations are carried out upon a consistent plan, and, on the other hand. that, in times of emergency, a definite war policy based upon solid data can be formulated."

It was to supply this deficiency that the Committee of Imperial Defence was brought into existence.

Constitutional Position.

2. The essential point to bear in mind in regard to the constitutional position of the Committee of Imperial Defence is that it is consultative and advisory, but possesses no executive power. Decision on policy rests in the last resort with the Cabinet; execution with the Government's Departments.

3. In practice, the whole of the conclusions and recommendations of the Committee of Imperial Defence are not referred to the Cabinet. On any matters of higher policy the Committee's recommendations and conclusions are usually referred to the Cabinet, who then take their decision. On any matters of less important character, recommendations and conclusions are reported to the Government Departments concerned, who then take action on Ministerial responsibility.

Composition.

4. According to strict constitutional theory, the Committee of Imperial Defence consists only of the Prime Minister and such persons as he may decide to invite to the meetings. In the absence of the Prime Minister the Chair is taken by the Minister for the Co-ordination of Defence. In practice each Prime Minister, on assuming office, has decided what other persons shall be invited to the meetings. At present, invitations are regularly sent to the following :—

The Minister for Co-ordination of Defence.
The Lord President of the Council.
The Chancellor of the Exchequer.
The Secretary of State for Foreign Affairs.
The Secretary of State for War.
The Secretary of State for Dominion Affairs.
The Secretary of State for Air.
The Secretary of State for India.
The Secretary of State for the Colonies.
The First Lord of the Admiralty.
The Chiefs of Staff of the three Fighting Services.
The Permanent Secretary to the Treasury, as Head of the Civil Service.
The Permanent Under-Secretary of State for Foreign Affairs.

Other persons are invited according to the nature of the business. For example, the Chairman of any Sub-Committee whose report is being discussed is invariably invited to attend, and Ministers or High Commissioners from Dominions, Ambassadors, Governors of Colonies, Officers of the Indian Army or Officials of

B

the Government of India, are often present for the discussion of some particular subject. After the Imperial Conference, 1930, the Prime Ministers of some of the Dominions attended a meeting of the Committee, and during the Imperial Conference experts from the Dominions and India were associated with the work of several of the Sub-Committees.

5. In accordance with a Statement made by the Prime Minister on the 27th February, 1936, the Minister for the Co-ordination of Defence is entrusted with the following general duties, delegated to him by the Prime Minister :—

The general day to day supervision and control, on the Prime Minister's behalf, of the whole organisation and activity of the Committee of Imperial Defence.

The co-ordination of executive action and of monthly progress reports to the Cabinet, or any Committee appointed by them, on the execution of plans for reconditioning the Defence Services.

Discernment of any points which either have not been taken up or are being pursued too slowly, and (in consultation with the Prime Minister or other Ministers or Committees as required) of appropriate measures for their rectification.

Procedure.

6. The Committee of Imperial Defence includes so many busy men that it cannot meet very frequently, except in times of crisis. In normal times the meetings average about one month. Detailed inquiries are entrusted mainly to Sub-Committees, some of which are permanent, Standing Committees, others being appointed *ad hoc*.

Sub-Committees.

7. A diagram of the Sub-Committee organisation is attached. Broadly speaking, the work of Sub-Committees divides itself very approximately into two main groups—military and civil, though this cannot be interpreted rigidly. In the diagram, those Committees that are predominantly military are on the left-hand side of the plan, and those that are predominantly civil on the right-hand side. In the centre they tend to merge. In addition, some of the Sub-Committee have been established as permanent standing organisations, while others are merely appointed *ad hoc* and are dissolved on completing their work.

8. The strategical side of the work of the Committee of Imperial Defence is looked after mainly by the Chiefs of Staff Sub-Committee (see paragraph 11), but there is a small group of satellite Committees working in its orbit.

The Defence Policy and Requirements Committee.

9. This is a Ministerial body with the three Chiefs of Staff as Technical Advisers. Its Chairman is the Prime Minister, but, in his absence, the Chair is taken by the Minister for the Co-ordination of Defence. The rôle of the Committee is to keep the defensive situation as a whole constantly under review, so as to ensure that our defence arrangements and our foreign policy are in line It reviews and co-ordinates programmes submitted to it for meeting the general needs of the three Services and watches over their fulfilment.

Defence Requirements (Official) Committee.

10. This Committee consists of the Secretary to the Committee of Imperial Defence, the Permanent Under-Secretary for Foreign Affairs, the Permanent Secretary to the Treasury, and the three Chiefs of Staff. It is entrusted with the preparation of co-ordinated programmes, when these are called for, for remedying Service deficiencies, and reports to the Defence Policy and Requirements Committee referred to above.

The Chiefs of Staff Sub-Committee.

11. The Chief of the Naval Staff.
The Chief of the Imperial General Staff.
The Chief of the Air Staff.

The Committee is normally presided over by one of the above. The Minister for the Co-ordination has the duty of personal consultation with the Chiefs of Staff together, including the right to convene under his chairmanship the Chiefs of Staff Committee whenever he or they think desirable.

The Chiefs of Staff Sub-Committee advises the Committee of Imperial Defence on the strategical aspects of all problems of Imperial Defence affecting more than one of the Service Departments, as well as on any matters relating to Imperial Defence, on which, in their opinion, further enquiry or investigation is necessary. They submit a review of the whole defensive situation once a year to the Committee of Imperial Defence.

12. The Joint Planning Sub-Committee works under the direction of the Chiefs of Staff Sub-Committee in the preparation of strategical plans. It undertakes " long-range planning " as well as the *ad hoc* investigation of any current problems which may be referred to it by the Chiefs of Staff. It is composed of the Directors of Plans of the Service Departments and three other officers, one from each Department, specially nominated and appointed for the purpose.

Oversea Defence and Home Defence Committees.

13. These are two Sub-Committees which existed before the War and long before the Chiefs of Staff Sub-Committee came into being, and which now work within the orbit of the Chiefs of Staff Sub-Committee.

The Oversea Defence Committee is concerned with questions relating to the defence of the Dominions, Colonies, Mandated Territories, &c., referred to it by Government Departments or by the Committee of Imperial Defence.

The Home Defence Committee deals with questions connected with the defence of Great Britain, referred by Government Departments or by the Committee of Imperial Defence, and has a Sub-Committee which considers problems concerning the Air Defence of Great Britain.

14. *The Joint Defence Committee* is the name given to joint meetings between the Oversea Defence Committee and the Home Defence Committee for the consideration of questions common to the two Committees—for example, questions of principle governing local defences of ports, &c. The Secretary to the Committee of Imperial Defence usually acts as Chairman.

The Man-Power Sub-Committee.

15. *Chairman:* The Secretary of State for Air.

This Sub-Committee deals with questions of man-power in time of war.

It has five Sub-Committees studying different branches of the man-power problem.

The Principal Supply Officers Committee.

16 *Chairman:* The Minister for the Co-ordination of Defence.

This Sub-Committee and its subsidiary bodies deals with the organisation in time of peace of supplies of all kinds for war, including both raw materials and manufacture.

The Supply Board, which has a permanent Chairman and consists of representatives of the Departments concerned, as well as the Board of Trade Supply Organisation which deals primarily with the question of raw materials, besides several subordinate Sub-Committees, are included in the organisation of the Principal Supply Officers Committee.

Oil Board.

17. The co-ordination between the three Services and the civil population of Oil supplies has been taken away from the Principal Supply Officers Committee at their own request and handed over to an Oil Board.

Chairman: The First Commissioner of Works.

Imperial Communications Committee.

18. *Chairman:* The Secretary of State for the Colonies.

The Imperial Communications Committee considers questions of policy in regard to overland telegraphy, wireless telegraphy and telephony, submarine cables and visual signalling.

B 2

The Co-Ordination Committee.

19. This consists of the Civil Heads of nearly all the Departments of State, with representatives of the Staffs of the three Service Departments. The Committee is responsible for co-ordinating and allocating the responsibility for action by Government Departments on the outbreak of war. It is responsible, *inter alia*, for the War Book, a description of which has been published in the Official History. (Corbett, Naval Operations, Vol. I.)

Middle East " Ministerial " Sub-Committee.

20. This Committee, under the Chairmanship of the Secretary of State for the Colonies, has been formed to consider any questions of policy regarding the Middle East, which must necessarily affect several other Government Departments. Its composition accordingly consists of :—

> The Chancellor of the Exchequer.
> The Secretary of State for Foreign Affairs.
> The Secretary of State for War.
> The Secretary of State for Air.
> The Secretary of State for India.
> The First Lord of the Admiralty.

This Sub-Committee is assisted by a standing " Official " Middle East Committee, which consists of representatives of the above Departments. This Committee deals with all minor questions of policy and the preliminary interdepartmental investigations and discussions that may be required before presentation of a major question to the Ministerial Committee.

Defence of India Sub-Committee.

21. This Sub-Committee, under the Chairmanship of the Secretary of State for India, with the Parliamentary Under-Secretary of State as Vice-Chairman, considers all questions of the defence of India and its implication. The following Ministers are members :—

> The Chancellor of the Exchequer.
> The Secretary of State for Foreign Affairs.
> The Secretary of State for War.
> The Secretary of State for Dominion Affairs.
> The Secretary of State for Air.
> The Secretary of State for the Colonies.

The Chiefs of Staff of the three Fighting Services and the Secretary, Military Department at the India Office, are also members.

Other Sub-Committees.

22. There are other standing sub-Committees on such matters as Trade Questions in time of war; Insurance of Shipping; Air Raids Precautions (executive action for which is vested in the Home Office); Emergency Legislation; Censorship; Industrial Intelligence in Foreign Countries; Distribution of Imports in time of war; Air Defence Research; and the Official Histories. In addition, sub-committees are appointed *ad hoc* for the study of any particular questions of policy or detail.

Distribution of Papers.

23. Outside the Office of the Minister for Co-ordination and Secretariat, files of the Committee of Imperial Defence are kept permanently by the following :—

> The King.
> Admiralty : Chief of the Naval Staff and Deputy Chief.
> War Office : Chief of the Imperial General Staff and Director of Military Operations and Intelligence.
> Air Ministry : Chief and Deputy Chief of the Air Staff.
> Treasury : Permanent Secretary and Sir Richard Hopkins.
> Foreign Office : Permanent Under-Secretary of State.
> Dominions Office : Permanent Under-Secretary of State.
> Colonial Office : Permanent Under-Secretary of State.
> India Office : The Military Secretary.

Cabinet Ministers and others whose papers are sent for a particular meeting return these papers on the understanding that they can always have access to them even after they leave office.

Under arrangements carefully drawn up with the Dominions Office, certain Committee of Imperial Defence papers, including those relating to meetings at which the Dominions High Commissioners have been present, are sent to the Prime Ministers of the Dominions. Mr. Keith Officer, the Australian Liaison Officer in London, has been given access to all Committee of Imperial Defence papers, and, subject to permission in each case, is allowed to send some of these papers to the Prime Minister of the Commonwealth. Every paper issued from the Committee of Imperial Defence has a number and is charged up to the individual to whom it is sent, until its return, when it is taken off his charge. The responsibility for any particular paper can therefore be fixed at a moment's notice.

Agenda papers are issued under the authority of the Prime Minister and the Minister for Co-ordination of Defence.

·O

SECRET.

APPENDIX IV.

Composition and Functions of the Economic Advisory Council.

THE Economic Advisory Council is a standing body, reporting to the Cabinet. It was established by Mr. Ramsay MacDonald, when Prime Minister in January 1930.. As its title suggests, the Council's main function is to advise His Majesty's Government in economic matters. The Council is also charged with the duty of making continuous study of developments in trade and industry and in the use of national and imperial resources, of the effect of legislation and fiscal policy at home and abroad, and of all aspects of national, imperial and international economy with a bearing on the prosperity of the country. The Council, on its appointment, took over the functions of an earlier standing committee of the Cabinet called the Committee of Civil Research. This had been set up by Mr. Baldwin when Prime Minister in 1925 under the chairmanship of the late Earl of Balfour. The latter body was concerned mainly with long-range investigations of "scientific," as opposed to "economic" problems, *e.g.*, sleeping sickness, human and animal nutrition and cognate matters.

2. The Prime Minister is *ex officio* Chairman of the Economic Advisory Council, which consists of four other Ministers (who include the Chancellor of the Exchequer and the President of the Board of Trade) and a number of persons chosen by the Prime Minister in virtue of their special knowledge and experience in industry and economics. In annex 1 to this note is given a list of the fourteen persons who at present constitute the non-ministerial element of the Council.

3. The committees of the Council are of several kinds. In the first place, there are two main standing committees dealing respectively with the two broad divisions into which the work of the Council falls. These are the Standing Committee on Economic Information, and the Standing Committee of Scientific Research. These bodies keep a general watch on the two sides of the work of the Council, and, in addition, prepare periodical reports on points of special interest. Thus, the Standing Committee on Economic Information submits, for the consideration of the Government, a report on the economic situation every two or three months.

4. In the next class of committee are those which may be called specialist standing committees. In this class falls the Council's Committee on Locust Control, which was appointed in 1929, and their Tsetse Fly Committee, which was appointed in 1925. The former is responsible for a scheme for the systematic investigation of the locust problem, which has received international recognition at the International Locust Conferences held in Rome, Paris, and London, in 1931, 1932, and 1934. Similarly, the Tsetse Fly Committee of the Council keeps under continuous review progress in the diagnosis and treatment of human and animal trypanosomiasis, and developments in the technique of tsetse fly control.

5. Finally, there is a third class of committee, the purely *ad hoc* committee. Committees of this type are appointed to consider particular problems on which they submit a report, and then pass out of existence. Examples of this kind of committee are the Committee on the Cotton Industry, which reported in 1930. the Committee on Empire Migration, which reported in 1931, and the Committee on Cattle Diseases, which reported in 1934.

6. The members of the two main standing committees are almost exclusively drawn from the personnel of the Council itself, while those of the specialist standing committees and the *ad hoc* committees consist partly of members of the Council and partly of other persons having special knowledge or experience of the subject-matter of the inquiry. The latter are selected from a panel of persons prepared by the Council for the purpose.

[12953—4]

7. The reports and work of the Council and of its committees are confidential except in such cases as the Council may advise the Prime Minister otherwise. A number of reports, including those of the Committees named in paragraph 5 above, have been published in this way.

8. The Council, as its name indicated, is purely advisory, and any action arising out of its work is taken on the sole responsibility of His Majesty's Government, which is advised by whatever may be the appropriate Government Department. The Council has no administrative functions (other than the duty of advising the Prime Minister in regard to the appointment of government representatives at international scientific congresses held in foreign countries and the Dominions). The Secretariat of the Council work in the closest collaboration with the departments interested in the matters which form the subject of investigations either by the Council or by its committees. By such close collaboration, the Council aims at securing a concerted study of economic and scientific problems of national interest, without in any way interfering with the functions or responsibilities of Ministers or of the departments over which they preside.

9. The functions of the Council are set out in a Treasury Minute, dated the 27th January, 1930, a copy of which is attached hereto as annex 2. The functions of the (earlier) Committee of Civil Research which, as has been explained, has been absorbed by the Council, are set out in a Treasury Minute dated the 13th June, 1925, a copy of which is attached hereto as annex 3.

ANNEX 1.

ECONOMIC ADVISORY COUNCIL.

Non-Ministerial Members.

Sir John Cadman, G.C.M.G.
Mr. G. D. H. Cole.
Sir Ernest R. Debenham, Bart.
Sir Andrew Duncan.
Sir Daniel Hall, K.C.B., F.R.S.
Mr. H. D. Henderson.
Mr. J. M. Keynes, C.B.
Sir Alfred Lewis, K.B.E.
Sir William McLintock, Bart., G.B.E., C.V.O.
Mr. G. Riddle.
Lord Riverdale, K.B.E.
Sir Arthur Salter, K.C.B.
Sir Ernest Simon.
Sir Josiah Stamp, G.C.B., G.B.E.

ANNEX 2.

Copy of Treasury Minute, dated January 27, 1930, appointing an Economic Advisory Council.

The First Lord calls the attention of the Board to the decision of His Majesty's Government on the 16th January, 1930, to establish an Economic Advisory Council. This will be a standing body reporting to the Cabinet, and its purpose, position in relation to Departments, organisation and functions will be as follows :—

Purpose.

To advise His Majesty's Government in economic matters.

To make continuous study of developments in trade and industry and in the use of national and imperial resources, of the effect of legislation and fiscal policy at home and abroad, and of all aspects of national, imperial and international economy with a bearing on the prosperity of the country.

Position in relation to Departments.

The Council will be subject to the general directions of the Prime Minister, and its expenses will be borne on the Treasury Vote.

It will take over and expand the functions of the existing Committee of Civil Research.

It will keep in close touch with Departments affected by its work with a view to the concerted study of economic problems of national interest, but it will interfere in no way with the functions or responsibilities of Ministers or of the Departments over which they preside, and it will have no administrative or executive powers.

Organisation.

1. The Chairman of the Council will be the Prime Minister, and the other members will be as follows :—

(*a*) The Chancellor of the Exchequer, the Lord Privy Seal (while the present duties are attached to that office), the President of the Board of Trade and the Minister of Agriculture and Fisheries.

(*b*) Such other Ministers as the Prime Minister may from time to time summon.

(*c*) Such other persons chosen by the Prime Minister in virtue of their special knowledge and experience in industry and economics.

The Council will meet when summoned by the Chairman, and as regularly as is found possible.

2. The Chairman may appoint standing committees and also such committees for special purposes as may be required.

3. The Council will have a secretary, and assistant secretaries, at least two of whom will be economists, together with such staff as may be found necessary.

Functions.

Providing that it acts after receiving the approval of the Prime Minister, the Council may initiate inquiries into, and advise upon, any subject falling within its scope, including proposals for legislation. The Council shall consult Departments and outside authorities in regard to any work in hand or projected and shall collate such statistical or other information as may be required for the performance of its work. The Council shall also cause to be prepared a list of persons with industrial, commercial, financial and working-class experience, and persons who have made a special study of social, economic and other scientific problems who might assist the Council by serving on Committees or as advisers in matters of which they have expert knowledge, or in other ways.

Its reports and work will be confidential unless the Council advises the Prime Minister otherwise. Any action arising out of them will be taken on the sole responsibility of His Majesty's Government.

MY LORDS APPROVE.

ANNEX 3.

CIVIL RESEARCH.

Copy of Treasury Minute, dated June 13, 1925, appointing a Committee of Civil Research.

The First Lord calls the attention of the Board to the decision of His Majesty's Government on the 28th May, 1925, to establish a Committee of Civil Research. This will be a Standing Committee reporting to the Cabinet, analogous in principle to the Committee of Imperial Defence.

The President of the Committee will be the Prime Minister and the regular Chairman, in the absence of the Prime Minister, will be a Minister nominated by him for the purpose: the membership of the Committee will, as in the case of the Committee of Imperial Defence, consist of such persons as are summoned by the Prime Minister, or the Chairman on his behalf.

The Committee will, like the Committee of Imperial Defence, be an advisory body and will have no administrative or executive functions.

The Secretary of the Cabinet and of the Committee of Imperial Defence will be responsible for the Committee's secretarial arrangements which will be under the immediate supervision of Mr. T. Jones.*

The Committee will be charged with the duty of giving connected forethought from a central standpoint to the development of economic, scientific and statistical research in relation to civil policy and administration and it will define new areas in which enquiry would be valuable. Within these limits the Committee may consider such questions as are referred to it by the Cabinet, the President, the Chairman, and Government Departments.

The President (or Chairman) may also summon for consideration of particular business such outside economic, scientific and statistical experts as he may think fit.

The Committee will—on the analogy of the Committee of Imperial Defence—as a normal part of its working approve the reference of particular enquiries to special sub-committees, which may include outside specialists as well as expert officers of the Department or Departments mainly concerned. Provision will also be made for using the services of suitable Departmental Officers in the capacity of Secretary to such sub-committees as occasion requires.

MY LORDS APPROVE.

---

* NOTE.—Now Mr. F. Hemming.

ANNEX 4

Printed for the War Cabinet. May 1943.

CONFIDENTIAL.

Copy No. 73

NOTES ON WAR CABINET PROCEDURE (REVISE).

Submission of Business to the War Cabinet.

1. Memoranda for consideration by the War Cabinet should be circulated well in advance of the meeting at which they are to be considered. The pre-war rule, by which no memorandum was placed on the Agenda until at least five days after it had been circulated, was waived at the outbreak of war; but, save in cases of special urgency, it is now the normal practice to allow two clear days at least to elapse between the circulation of a memorandum and its consideration.

2. The Prime Minister asks Ministers so far as possible to adhere to the rule that questions are not submitted for consideration by the War Cabinet until the point to be settled has been narrowed to a defined issue. This will normally call for adequate prior discussion with other Departments concerned, including discussion with the Treasury of proposals which would involve expenditure or affect general financial or economic policy. This rule does not, of course, limit the right of Ministers to submit to the War Cabinet memoranda setting out their views on general issues of policy.

3. When a Minister wishes to raise a matter orally at the War Cabinet, his Private Secretary should give the earliest possible notice to the Secretary, who will seek the Prime Minister's consent.

4. The procedure outlined above applies *mutatis mutandis* to Ministerial Committees of the War Cabinet.

Absence from the War Cabinet; and Ministers' movements.

5. If a member of the War Cabinet, or a Minister who regularly attends War Cabinet meetings, is unable, for any reason, to be present at a meeting of the War Cabinet, he should notify the Secretary, who will inform the Prime Minister and will also consider whether any rearrangement of business is required.

6. The Secretary should also be informed of Ministers' week-end arrangements, in order that, if some sudden emergency arises, he may be in a position to inform the Prime Minister at once which Ministers are immediately available.

2

Attendance
at the
War Cabinet
of Ministers
not in the
War Cabinet.

7. It is of assistance to the Secretary if Private Secretaries indicate. when asking for a subject to be placed on the Agenda, which Ministers, other than members of the War Cabinet, are likely to be affected, so that arrangements may, if necessary, be made for their attendance.

8. Ministers summoned to meetings of the War Cabinet for particular items will receive an Agenda Paper on which an approximate time will be set against each item. Every endeavour is made not to keep Ministers waiting, but the time at which each item will be reached cannot be forecast exactly.

**War Cabinet
Conclusions.**

9. It is an instruction to the Secretary. in drafting War Cabinet Conclusions, to avoid. so far as practicable, reference to opinions expressed by particular Ministers. The record in respect of each item will be limited to the decision of the War Cabinet, together with such a summary of the discussion as may be necessary.

10. The Conclusions of the War Cabinet are circulated by the Secretary to (a) War Cabinet Ministers; (b) Ministers holding Offices "of Cabinet rank"; (c) the Chiefs of Staff.

11. On matters of exceptional secrecy, the Conclusions are recorded in the Secretary's Standard File, copies being sent in the form of a " Confidential Annex " only to those Ministers directly concerned.

**Action on
Conclusions.**

12. . All Ministers are themselves responsible for giving such instructions to their Departments as may be necessary to give effect to the Conclusions of the War Cabinet.

13. Ministers are also responsible for communicating to subordinate Departments or branches decisions of which they should be made aware.

14. The Lord Chancellor is responsible for communicating to the English Law Officers such decisions as concern them.

15. Where a Department has to take action upon, or is otherwise directly affected by, a particular Conclusion. the actual decisions of the War Cabinet may be copied in the Department, together with so much of the record of the discussion as is essential to a proper understanding of them, and these extracts may be passed to responsible officers in the Department, as may be necessary. The distribution within a Department of such extracts from War Cabinet Conclusions should be limited to the occasions on which it is strictly necessary for the efficient discharge of public business, and care should be taken to see that extracts are sent only to those

3

officers of the Department who need be acquainted with the actual terms of the decision. Duplicate copies of the *complete* Conclusions are not issued for this purpose by the War Cabinet Offices save in exceptional cases.

16. Where action has to be taken at once by a Department without waiting for the circulation of the full Conclusions, application may be made to the Secretary for an advance copy of the relevant Conclusion. Where an urgent matter arises unexpectedly, and a decision is reached requiring immediate action by a Department not represented at the Meeting, the Secretary will ensure that the Department concerned is notified forthwith.

Amendments to Conclusions.

17. Any suggested amendments to War Cabinet Conclusions must reach the Secretary not later than the next day but one following that on which the Meeting was held. Thereafter the Conclusions will be sent to be printed in final form.

War Cabinet Memoranda.

18. War Cabinet Memoranda should be so drafted as to bring out clearly and succinctly the issue or issues for decision. This can most easily be done by means of a summary statement setting out the recommendations for which the War Cabinet's approval is sought.

19. Subject to such special instructions in regard to any particular paper as he may receive from the Prime Minister or from the responsible Minister, the Secretary circulates memoranda and other documents prepared for their use to all War Cabinet Ministers and, in addition, either to all Ministers "of Cabinet rank" or to those Ministers whose Departments are affected.

Conclusions and Memoranda.

20. War Cabinet Conclusions and Memoranda may be shown by Ministers, at their discretion, to their Ministerial subordinates and their responsible advisers. Ministers are personally responsible for any authority given and are expected to exercise a very real discretion in this matter.

Reproduction of Memoranda.

21. War Cabinet memoranda are reproduced in the originating Departments, the required number of copies being sent to the War Cabinet Offices for circulation. *All* copies must be sent to the War Cabinet Offices, and, if the originating Department requires an additional copy or copies, application must be made to the War Cabinet Offices. If a Department so wishes, a standing arrangement may be made whereby the War Cabinet will automatically supply a fixed number of additional copies of memoranda originating in the Department.

22. In *no* circumstances, other than those provided for in paragraph 21 above, are War Cabinet memoranda to be reproduced

4

or copied in Departments. Where a Department requires an additional copy or copies of a memorandum, application must in every case be made to the War Cabinet Offices.

Return of War Cabinet Papers.

23. In normal times it is the duty of all Ministers, on vacating office, to return forthwith to the Secretary of the Cabinet all Cabinet papers issued to them while in office, and it is the duty of the Secretary of the Cabinet to ensure that this rule is complied with. For the period of the War, however, Ministers vacating office should hand over to their successors in office such War Cabinet papers as are essential for the carrying on of the business of the Department. Papers not so required should be returned to the War Cabinet Office periodically during a Minister's tenure of office, preferably at intervals of, say, three or six months.

Offices of the War Cabinet,
May, 1943.

Copy No. 52

OFFICES OF THE WAR CABINET AND MINISTER OF DEFENCE

STAFF LIST

1st JANUARY, 1945

NOTES

(1) This list only includes staff borne on the War Cabinet Office Establishment

(2) Full particulars of all War Cabinet Committees are contained in the printed list of War Cabinet Committees

Offices of the War Cabinet,
  Great George Street, S.W. 1

OFFICES OF THE WAR CABINET AND MINISTER OF DEFENCE

STAFF LIST

TABLE OF CONTENTS

3

PRINCIPAL OFFICERS

Permanent Secretary and Secretary of the War Cabinet	**Sir Edward Bridges, G.C.B., M.C.**
Private Secretaries...	W. Armstrong; M.V.O. D. F. Hubback.
Chief of Staff to the Minister of Defence and Deputy Secretary (Military) of the War Cabinet	**General Sir Hastings Ismay, K.C.B., D.S.O.**
Private Secretary	Lieut.-Cmdr. (S.) I. P. McEwan, M.V.O., R.N.V.R.
Under-Secretaries (Civil) of the War Cabinet	**Sir Gilbert Laithwaite, K.C.I.E., C.S.I.** **W. S. Murrie.**
Private Secretaries	Miss M. F. Fairlie. Miss J. G. Fyfe.
Senior Assistant Secretary (Military) of the War Cabinet	**Major-General L. C. Hollis, C.B., C.B.E., R.M.**
Private Secretary	Miss M. F. Le Sueur.

Business.	Administrative Staff.	Clerical, &c., Staff.
A. WAR CABINET.	Sir Edward Bridges, G.C.B., M.C.	C.Os. Typists.
	General Sir Hastings Ismay, K.C.B., D.S.O.	3 C.Os.
	Sir Gilbert Laithwaite, K.C.I.E., C.S.I. W. S. Murrie. L. F. Burgis, C.M.G., C.V.O.	2 C.Os. 3 Shorthand-typists.
	NOTE.—Day-to-day business of the War Cabinet is normally handled by Mr. Burgis, under the direction of Sir Edward Bridges.	**Cabinet Section.** *Staff Officer—* H. G. Woodbery. *H.C.Os.—* J. W. Mitchell, M.B.E. R. E. Crocker. 1 C.O.

[28677]

B 2

F*

4

Business.	Administrative Staff.	Clerical, &c., Staff.
B. MILITARY AFFAIRS.		
I.—*Chief of Staff to the Minister of Defence and Deputy Secretary (Military) of the War Cabinet.	General Sir Hastings Ismay, K.C.B., D.S.O.	3 C.Os.
II.—Secretariat of Defence Committee (Operations), Chiefs of Staff Committee and Sub-Committees.	Secretary. Defence Committee (Operations) and Chiefs of Staff Committee. Major-General L. C. Hollis, C.B., C.B.E., R.M.	1 C.O 1 Personal Assistant. 1 Shorthand-typist.
	Colonel C. R. Price, O.B.E., R.E. Group-Captain A. Earle.*	Lieut. and Qr. Master A. C. Beer, M.B.E. *Temporary Assistant—* Mrs. M. N. Noble, M.B.E. 1 C.O. 2 Shorthand-typists.
	Lieutenant-Colonel L. J. Carver. Major E. G. S. Elliot, R.A. (and for business concerning Joint Staff Mission, Washington, and South-East Asia Command).	*Temporary Assistant—* Miss L. J. Mainprice. 2 C.Os. (Miss I. M. Lewis in charge) 1 Clerical Assistant. 3 Shorthand-typists.
Anti-U-Boat Committee, Oil Control Board.	Captain G. H. Oswald, R.N.	*Temporary Assistant—* Miss M. B. O'Donnell.
Principal Administrative Officers Committee.	Captain (S) C. G. Neeves, R.N. ___ * Also Secretary of Night Air Defence Committee.	1 Shorthand-typist. 1 Typist.
III.—Secretariat of the Defence Committee (Supply), Joint War Production Staff and London Munitions Assignment Board.	Major-General E. I. C. Jacob, C.B., C.B.E. Lieutenant-Colonel M. R. Norman. R.A. Wing Commander W. F. Lamb, O.B.E. ___ NOTE.—Day-to-day business is handled by Major-General Jacob and Lieutenant-Colonel Norman.	*Senior Temporary Assistant—* W. D. Drysdale, M.B.E. 2 C.Os. 1 Shorthand-typist. **Defence Office.** *Staff Officer—* M. F. Pinnock, M.B.E. *H.C.Os.—* S. P. Anderson, M.B.E. C. F. Garland. *Temporary Assistant—* D. J. M. Brenton. 1 C.O. **Defence Office (Telegrams).** 6 W.A.A.F. Section Officers.* * Borne on Air Votes.
* Member of the Chiefs of Staff Committee and of the Defence Committee (Operations).		

5

Business.	Administrative Staff.	Clerical, &c., Staff.
B. MILITARY AFFAIRS (continued).		**Chiefs of Staff Section.** *Staff Officer—* M. F. Pinnock, M.B.E. *H.C.Os.—* S. E. Morris. A. Brough. 7 C.Os. 1 Clerical Assistant. 2 Temporary Clerks.
IV.—Joint Staff Secretariat (Planning, Intelligence and London Controlling Section).		*H.C.O.—* M. H. B. Green, M.B.E.
	Colonel D. C. Capel-Dunn, O.B.E., Chief Secretary.	} 1 C.O. as Personal Assistant. 1 Shorthand-typist.
	Lieutenant-Colonel H. G. C. Mallaby, O.B.E. ⎱ Operational Major M. F. Berry, R.A. ⎰ Plans.	} 1 C.O. as Personal Assistant. 1 Shorthand-typist.
	Lieutenant-Colonel A. D. Melville ⎱ Administrative Major R. Hoare, R.A. ⎰ Plans.	
	Lieutenant-Colonel E. J. King-Salter, D.S.O. ⎱ Intelligence Wing Commander A. E. Houseman, D.F.C. ⎰	1 Personal Assistant. *Temporary Assistant—* Mrs. P. A. Martin. 11 C.Os. *Superintendents of Typists—* Miss M. J. Goodwin. Miss K. H. Whitley. 8 Shorthand-typists. 11 Typists.
	Major P. O. A. Davison ⎱ Post- Major E. S. Delmar-Morgan, M.B.E. ⎰ Hostilities Planning.	1 C.O.
	Major G. Waterfield, London Controlling Section.	*H.C.O.—* E. S. Parker. 1 C.O. 2 Shorthand-typists.
V.—Graph and Diagram Section.	Lieutenant-Colonel A. M. Weber-Brown. Major K. H. Whitaker.	
VI.—Special Information Centre.	Miss P. J. M. Bright.	3 C.Os.
VII.—Joint Staff Mission Secretariat, Washington.	Brigadier A. T. Cornwall-Jones, C.B.E. Commander the Hon. R. D. Coleridge, O.B.E., R.N. Group Captain T. E. H. Birley. Major J. A. Davison. Major C. W. Garnett. Major A. H. Bishop.	*Staff Officer—* H. W. Charman. *H.C.O.—* N. H. West. 3 C.Os. 3 Shorthand-typists

8

Business.	Administrative Staff.	Clerical, &c., Staff.
C. CIVIL AFFAIRS.		
I.—Secretariat of Civil Committees and Sub-Committees.	M. T. Flett. J. McL. Buckley. Colonel C. W. G. Walker, C.M.G., D.S.O. NOTE.—Mr. W. S. Murrie superintends this Section.	**Civil Committee Section.** H.C.O.— W. Cater. 3 C.Os. 1 Temporary Clerk. 1 Shorthand-typist. NOTE.—The clerical work of one or two of the more important Civil Committees is handled by the **Cabinet Section** (see **A** above).
II.—Far East Section.	E. A. Armstrong. Sir Theodore S. Adams, C.M.G.	1 Personal Assistant.
III.—Middle East Section.	E. H. T Wiltshire.	As for **Civil Committee Section** (see **C.I.** above).
IV.—Allied Supplies Executive Secretariat.	R. C. Foy. J. D. Peek. Miss E. J. Beaven. Mrs. J. O. Daniel. Miss R. M. Whitham.	H.C.O.— A. H. Dutton. 3 C.Os. (F. W. Walton in charge). 2 Temporary Clerks. 1 Shorthand-typist.
V.—Joint American Secretariat.	A. Christelow. Mrs. M. A. Naylor. Miss A. L. T. Oppé. Miss M. D. Bryan. NOTE.—Sir Gilbert Laithwaite superintends the work of Sections II, III, IV and V.	H.C.O.— W. J. L. Solly. 3 C.Os. 1 Temporary Clerk. 6 Temporary Clerks (attached from Ministry of Production).
VI.—Economic Section.	Professor L. C. Robbins, C.B. (Director). J. E. Meade Professor S. R. Dennison } Chief D. N. Chester } Assistants. J. M. Fleming P. Chantler } Economic R. C. Tress } Assistants Grade I. Mrs. M. S. Muray } Economic Miss N. G. M. Watts } Assistants J. B. Wood } Grade II.	2 C.Os. 2 Shorthand-typists.

7

Business.	Administrative Staff.	Clerical, &c., Staff.

C. CIVIL AFFAIRS
(continued).
VII.—Central Statistical Office
(Church House).
	H. Campion, C.B.E. (Director).
	J. Stafford
	J. R. N. Stone ⎫
	R. F. Fowler ⎬ Chief
	R. H. Coase ⎭ Assistants.
	W. C. Taplin ⎭
	B. N. Davies ⎫
	E. F. Jackson ⎪
	J. Cohen ⎬ Assistants.
	C. R. Jones ⎪
	Miss J. G. Marley ⎪
	R. E. Beales ⎭
	Mrs. E. J. Donovon ⎫
	S. Dubner ⎪
	Miss M. O. Hardy ⎬ Junior
	Miss P. M. Nye ⎪ Assistants.
	L. T. Clarke ⎪
	Miss D. R. Shanahan ⎭
		Staff Officer—
		    A. C. Cooper, M.B.E.
		
		Chartists—
		    Miss J. R. J. de Meza.
		    Miss M. D. L. Wright.
		
		8 C.Os.
		2 Clerical Assistants.
		3 Temporary Clerks.
		
		Superintendent of Typists—
		    Mrs. E. F. Bloxham.
		
		2 Shorthand-typists.
		7 Typists.

VIII.—Civil Secretariat,
Washington.
	R. Stevens.
	R. Morrison.
	Major C. M. Berkeley.
		Staff Officer—
		    C. W. Pink, M.B.E.
		H.C.O.—
		    R. A. G. Clark.
		Temporary Assistant—
		    Miss A. E. Hunt.
		3 C.Os.

D. COMMON SERVICES.
I.—Establishments and
General Service Section.
	L. F. Burgis, C.M.G., C.V.O.
	    (Establishment Officer).
	1. Montgomery.
	    NOTE.—Mr. Montgomery is also
	Civil Secretary, Combined Opera-
	tions Headquarters.
		1 Shorthand-typist.
		Chief Clerk—
		    Major F. W. Rawlins, M.B.E.
		1 C.O.
		Staff Officer—
		    A. G. Banks, M.B.E.
		H.C.O.—
		    R. H. Crudass.
		3 C.Os.
		A.R.P.—
		    T. Neighbour.

II.—Security Officers.	W. M. Codrington. J. McL. Buckley.	1 Shorthand-typist.

III.—Accounts Section.		*Staff Officer—*
		    A. W. Davey.
		H.C.O.—
		    A. O. A. Dilley.
		2 C.Os.
		3 Temporary Clerks.

8

Business.	Administrative Staff.	Clerical, &c., Staff.
D. COMMON SERVICES (continued).		
IV.—Accommodation and Stationery Section.		*H.C.O.—* L. V. Walter. 2 C.Os. 2 Paper Keepers.
V.—Registry and Records Section.		*H.C.O.—* J. Sinclair. 8 C.Os.* 1 Paper Keeper.* * NOTE.—3 C.Os. and 1 Paper Keeper are at Country Headquarters.
VI.—Distribution Section.		*H.C.Os.—* W. J. Walters. A. C. Smith. 8 C.Os. 1 Clerical Assistant. 5 Temporary Clerks. 3 Established Messengers. 16 Unestablished Messengers.
VII.—Typing Section.		*Chief Superintendent—* Miss D. F. M. Brown, M.B.E. *Superintendents—* Miss C. E. Cole. Mrs. W. Butler. 16 Shorthand-typists. 18 Typists. 4 Roneo Operators.
VIII.—Messengers.		*Office Keeper—* J. W. Jackman. *Deputy Office Keeper—*S. L. Heath. 8 Established Messengers. 55 Unestablished Messengers. 4 Lamson Tube Attendants.
IX.—Telephone Room.		* *Supervisor.—* Miss L. E. E. Jones. 18 Operators.
E. HISTORICAL SECTION.		
I.—Aberystwyth Branch (Military History 1914–1918).	Brigadier-General Sir J. Edmonds, C.B., C.M.G. Captain .G. C. Wynne. Captain W. Miles. Lieutenant-Colonel R. G. Maxwell-Hyslop. Major A. F. Becke.	*Chief Clerk—* Lieutenant-Colonel G. S. Oxburgh, M.B.E. *H.C.O.—* A. W. Tarsey. *Temporary Assistant—* W. P. Wood. 1 C.O. 2 " S " Class Clerks. 1 Draughtsman. 1 Temporary Clerk. 1 Typist. 1 Paper Keeper. 2 Messengers. 2 Night Watchmen.

* Telephone staff borne on G.P.O. Vote.

9

Business.	Administrative Staff.	Clerical, &c., Staff.
E. HISTORICAL SECTION (continued). II.—London Branch, 8 Barton Street, S.W. 1 (Military History of Present War).	Colonel H. B. Latham (Head of Branch). Lieutenant-Colonel G. R. Johnston. Lieutenant-Colonel J. E. B. Barton. Lieutenant-Colonel E. E. Rich. Lieutenant-Colonel M. E. S. Laws, O.B.E., M.C. Major V. E. Nash-Williams. Major N. H. Gibbs. Major G. S. Keen. Major F. Jones. Major D. Spence. Major H. F. Joslen. Captain W. P. Spens.	*Archivist—* C. V. Owen. *Temporary Assistant—* L. C. Barber. 4 Draughtsmen. 2 Shorthand-typists. 1 Typist. 2 Paper Keepers. 2 Military Clerks. 2 Messengers.
III.—Civil Histories (Civil History of Present War).	Professor W. K. Hancock (Supervisor). Sir T. St. Quintin Hill. Professor M. M. Postan. W. M. Medlicott ⎫ R. J. Hammond ⎪ E. L. Hargreaves ⎪ R. M. Titmuss ⎪ W. H. B. Court ⎪ Sir John Shuckburgh ⎪ D. Hay ⎬ Narrators. J. Hurstfield ⎪ F. Wormald ⎪ Major C. M. Kohan ⎪ Miss C. B. A. Behrens ⎪ Miss M. E. A. Bowley ⎪ Miss E. H. Whetham ⎭ Mrs. P. F. Inman Mrs. C. R. Postan ⎫ Miss L. M. Brown ⎪ Research D. Mack Smith ⎬ Assistants. Mrs. D. M. Agnew ⎪ Miss M. D. McHattie ⎭ NOTE.—Though on the establishment of the Offices of the War Cabinet, the Principal Narrator, Narrators and Research Assistants are allocated to, and work in various Civil Departments.	*Temporary Assistant—* Miss M. Eyre.

ANNEX 6

LIST OF ADMINISTRATIVE STAFF WHO SERVED IN THE CABINET OFFICE 1916-1945

(Titles shown are those held while serving in the Office. Those engaged in the Historical Section, the Central Statistical Office and the Economic Section are excluded.)

Sir Maurice P. A. Hankey (1908–1939)
Lt Col W. Dally Jones (1914–1923)
Mr C. Longhurst (1914–1942)
Gen E. D. Swinton (1913–1917)
Lt Col L. Storr (1916–1920)
Paymaster in Chief P. J. H. L. Row, RN (1916–1918)
Mr G. M. Young (1916–1917)
Mr T. Jones (1916–1930)
Capt C. Jones (1916–1920)
Col Sir Mark Sykes (1916–1919)
Lt Col L. S. Amery (1916–1920)
Maj the Hon W. Ormsby-Gore (1917–1918)
Mr E. Beck (1917–1923)
Mr W. J. O. P. Bland (1917)
Lt Col L. Wilson (1918–1919)
Mr L. F. Burgis (1918–1949)
Maj Gen Sir G. Aston (1918–1919)
Mr P. Wicks (1918–1922)
Mr H. d'Egville (1918–1919)
Lt F. Storrs, RNVR (1918–1919)
Lt Col H. W. L. Holman (1918–1919)
Mr F. W. C. T. Jaffray (1918–1919)
Col Sir S. H. Wilson (1918–1921)
Capt Bulkeley Johnson (1918–1919)
Lt Col the Rt Hon Sir Matthew Nathan (1918–1919)
Mr J. C. Stobart (1918–1919)
Maj A. M. Caccia (1918–1922)
Capt E. G. F. Abraham (1918–1920)
Mr G. M. Evans (1919, 1941–1942)
Sir T. St. Quintin Hill (1919–1923, 1941–1942)
Mr A. J. Sylvester (1920–1921)
Cmdr R. L. Hamer, RN (1920–1921)
Sir Rupert B. Howorth (1920–1942)
Mr F. W. Leith-Ross (1920)
Sir John Chancellor (1922–1923)
The Hon C. H. Tufton (1921–1922)
Cmdr H. R. Moore, RN (1921–1924)

Maj L. A. Clemens (1922–1926)
Lt Col C. W. G. Walker (1923–1926, 1943–1947)
Wing Cmdr Sir Norman R. A. D. Leslie, Bt (1924–1929)
Cmdr the Hon C. P. Hermon-Hodge, RN (1924–1928)
Mr A. F. Hemming (1925–1941)
Gen Sir Hastings L. Ismay (1926–1930, 1936–1947)
Lt Col G. N. Macready (1926–1932)
Cmdr L. E. H. Maund, RN (1928–1931)
Wing Cmdr E. J. Hodsoll (1929–1935)
Mr H. D. Henderson (1930–1934)
Mr H. V. Hodson (1930)
Mr C. G. Clark (1930–1931)
Maj N. G. Hind (1930–1934)
Cmdr C. C. A. Allen, RN (1931–1934)
Mr W. D. Wilkinson (1930–1934, 1935–1942)
Mr P. K. Debenham (1930–1941)
Mr D. H. F. Rickett (1931–1942, 1945–1947)
Lt Col H. R. Pownall (1932–1936)
Capt A. W. Clarke, RN (1934–1937, 1939–1940)
Mr J. H. Penson (1934–1935)
Lt Col F. B. Webb (1934–1939)
Squadron Leader P. Warburton (1935–1937)
Brig V. Dykes (1935–1940, 1942)
Maj Gen Sir Leslie C. Hollis (1936–1946)
Mr H. G. Vincent (1936–1939)
Mr H. H. Sellar (1936–1939)
Capt A. D. Nicholl, RN (1937–1941)
Mr C. F. M. N. Ryan (1937–1939)
Sir Arthur Robinson (1937–1939)
Maj J. A. Davies (1937–1940)
Wing Cmdr W. Elliot (1937–1941)
Lt Col K. G. McLean (1938–1939)
Sir Edward E. Bridges (1938–1945)
Maj Gen E. I. C. Jacob (1938–1946)
Mr H. L. d'A. Hopkinson (1939–1940)
Mr G. N. Flemming (1939–1942)
Capt B. F. Adams, RN (1939–1942)
Brig A. T. Cornwall-Jones (1939–1941, 1946–1950)
Mr R. M. J. Harris (1939–1944)
Mr J. Hensley (1939)
Mr A. Bevir (1939)
Mr J. H. Peck (1939–1940)
Maj Gen H. Redman (1939–1940, 1943–1944)
Col W. Porter (1939–1940)
Lt Col H. S. Briggs (1939)
Paymaster Capt Jerram, RN (1939–1940)
Mr A. E. Watson (1939)
Maj A. N. Barnard (1939–1940)
Mr C. M. Berkeley (1939–1945)
Col S. R. Shirley (1939)
Mr J. Jewkes (1939–1941)

Mr E. P. Donaldson (1940–1944)
Capt the Hon R. D. Coleridge, RN (1940–1946)
Mr H. Somerville-Smith (1940–1942)
Brig C. R. Price (1940–1946)
Mr P. N. Loxley (1940–1941)
Mr A. E. T. Benson (1940–1943)
S. Hoare (1940)
Pay/Lt Cmdr R. Bousfield (1940–1942)
Lt Cmdr F. B. Carslake, RN (1940–1942)
Paymaster Cmdr M. K. Knott, RN (1940–1944)
Lt Col R. Le Mesurier (1940–1944)
Lt Col C. T. Edwards (1940–1941)
Maj R. White-Cooper (1940)
Col D. C. Capel-Dunn (1940–1945)
Maj A. H. Head (1940–1941)
Maj E. D. Sandys (1940)
The Hon T. H. Brand (1940–1942)
Mr W. J. Hasler (1940–1944)
Mr A. W. Willoughby (1940–1942)
Col W. G. Stirling (1940–1943)
Mr E. A. Robinson (1940–1942)
Miss P. J. M. Bright (1940–1946)
Lt Col F. S. Reid (1941)
Mr D. E. H. Peirson (1941)
Lt Col T. Haddon (1941–1942, 1945–1947)
Mr J. E. Coulson (1941–1942)
Capt J. N. O. Curle (1941–1944)
Mrs J. O. Daniel (1941–1945)
Maj R. F. G. Jayne (1941–1942)
Mr W. H. C. Frend (1941–1942)
Mr J. R. Culpin (1941–1942)
Viscount Moore (1941–1942)
Mr J. S. Daniel (1941–1942)
Sir George Chrystal (1941–1942)
Mr S. B. R. Cooke (1941)
Mr H. Stannard (1941–1942)
Mr C. V. Davidge (1941–1942)
Mrs M. A. Hamilton (1941–1942)
Sir Godfrey H. Ince (1941)
Mr E. A. Armstrong (1941–1943, 1945–1947)
Mr D. T. John (1941–1942)
Mr H. Everett (1941–1942)
Mr H. R. Fisher (1941–1943)
Capt E. G. A. Clifford, RN (1941–1943)
Gp Capt D. A. Boyle (1941)
Lt Col W. A. Hawkins (1941–1943)
Lt Col Shoosmith (1941)
Lt Col C. W. Garnett (1941–1945)
Miss E. J. Beaven (1941–1945)
Sir Norman Brook (1942–1943, 1945–1962)
Mr A. J. D. Winnifrith (1942–1944)

Mr D. B. Pitblado (1942)
Mr G. A. Fitch (1942)
Mr C. Bramwell (1942–1943)
Cmdr G. Bull, RNVR (1942–1944)
Paymaster Lt Cmdr I. P. McEwan, RNVR (1942–1945)
Wing Cmdr J. N. Jefferson (1942–1943)
Gp Capt T. E. H. Birley (1942–1945)
Maj P. O. A. Davison (1942–1945)
Lt Col M. R. Norman (1942–1945)
Maj H. S. D'A. McArthy, (1942–1943)
Lt Col L. J. Carver (1942–1945)
Maj C. F. Battiscombe (1942–1943)
Lord Strathallan (1942)
Mr E. C. S. Wade (1942–1944)
Mr E. C. R. Kahn (1942)
Mr W. M. Codrington (1942–1945)
Mr J. McL. Buckley (1942–1945)
Mrs M. A. Naylor (1942–1945)
Miss M. P. Callard (1942)
Lt Col L. T. Grove (1942)
Mr T. F. Turner (1942–1943)
Mr G. M. Smyth (1942–1944)
Maj J. C. Maude (1942)
Mr H. A. St. G. Saunders (1942–1943)
Maj T. S. D'A. Hankey (1943–1944)
Mr P. Allen (1943–1944)
Maj A. D. Powell (1943)
Miss E. A. Murdoch (1943)
Lt Col R. Chitty (1943–1944)
Mrs E. M. Chilver (1943–1944),
Miss N. G. McCleary (1943–1944)
Mrs E. P. A. Vivian (1943–1944)
Lt Col H. G. C. Mallaby (1943–1945)
Mr R. C. Foy (1943–1945)
Mr A. Ker (1943–1945)
Mr E. R. Hoyer-Millar (1943–1944)
Mr A. Johnston (1943, 1948–1951)
Miss W. M. Fox (1943–1944)
Mr R. C. Chilver (1943)
Mr A. M. Seed (1943–1944)
Mr G. B. Blaker (1943–1945)
Mr H. T. Bourdillon (1943–1944)
Mr W. Armstrong (1943–1946)
Capt G. H. Oswald, RN (1943–1945)
Gp Capt A. Earle (1943–1945)
Wing Cmdr A. E. Houseman (1943–1945)
Lt Col E. J. C. King-Salter (1943–1945)
Capt A. N. Coleridge (1943–1947)
Lt Col J. E. B. Barton (1943–1944)
Maj A. H. Bishop (1943–1946)
Maj J. A. Davison (1943–1945)

Mr G. W. Sich (1943–1944)
Maj E. S. Darlot (1944–1945)
Mrs M. P. C. Bruce-Lockhart (1944)
Miss A. D. Stevens (1944)
Mrs M. D. Montgomery (1944–1947)
Sir Gilbert Laithwaite (1944–1945)
Mr W. S. Murrie (1944–1948)
Mr E. H. T. Wiltshire (1944–1945)
Mr W. L. Gorell-Barnes (1944–1945)
Mr M. T. Flett (1944–1945)
Mr I. Montgomery (1944–1945)
Mr R. Morrison (1944–1947)
Mr R. B. Stevens (1944–1946)
Mr D. F. Hubback (1944–1948)
Wing Cmdr W. F. Lamb (1944–1947)
Paymaster Lt Cmdr K. G. Butcher, RNVR (1944–1945)
Capt C. G. Neeves, RN (1944–1946)
Lt Col A. D. Melville (1944–1945)
Maj M. F. Berry (1944–1945)
Maj E. G. S. Elliot (1944–1945)
Capt R. H. Winn (1944–1945)
Lt Col H. A. R. Powell (1944)
Lt Col Weber-Brown (1944–1945)
Maj K. H. Whitaker (1944–1946)
Mr G. G. Phillips (1944)
Maj R. Hoare (1944–1945)
Miss A. L. T. Oppé (1944–1945)
Sir T. Adams (1944–1945)
Miss R. M. Whitham (1944–1946)
Capt E. J. S. Clarke (1945–1946)
Capt A. H. Thorold, RN (1945–1946)
Mr A. Christelow (1945)
Mr F. Thistlethwaite (1945)
Maj J. K. Gardiner, RM (1945–1946)
Mr A. M. R. Topham (1945–1946)
Mr C. G. Eastwood (1945–1947)
Gp Capt D. C. Stapleton (1945–1946)
Mr J. A. Drew (1945–1948)
Gp Capt J. R. Wilson (1945–1948)
Mr W. W. McVittie (1945)
Lt Col Gleadell (1945–1946)
Mr R. F. Allen (1945–1946)
Cmdr D. J. A. Heber-Percy, RN (1945–1947)
Sir H. Creedy (1945–1946)
Maj J. A. M. Phillips (1945–1947)

NOTES TO THE TABLES IN ANNEXES 7(A) AND (B), 8 AND 9

1. These tables—in which there is some estimation—give an indication of the annual load on the Office in serving the Cabinet and its committees.

2. The number of Cabinet memoranda recorded in the tables is not directly reconcilable with the annual totals of the numbered series of CP, WP and WP(G) memoranda for the following reasons:

   (a) The tables omit the regular weekly or monthly reports to the Cabinet made by the Home Office (before 1925) and the Ministry of Labour (before 1930) and during the Second World War the resumés by the Chiefs of Staff, and the reports from the Commonwealth.

   (b) Where a paper was submitted jointly by two or more Ministers, each has for the purposes of the tables been regarded as an originator (this was significant in the case of papers submitted by the Secretary of State for Scotland, where the other originators tended to be the Home Secretary or the Minister of Agriculture and Fisheries).

   (c) Serial numbers were on occasion given to papers which for some reason were not in fact circulated.

3. Before 1939 reports of committees which were transmitted to the Cabinet were generally circulated under the name of the committee, and in these cases have been included in the tables under the heading 'Others'; after 1939 such reports tended to be circulated in the name of the chairman of the committee and in those cases have been included under the name of the Minister concerned.

4. In the case of the CID committees and the War Cabinet committees a distinction is made in the tables between those which at the first meeting had a ministerial chairman, and those which had an official (or military) chairman; the distinction is maintained, notwithstanding that at subsequent meetings the status of the chairman might change.

5. The major conferences are most of those mentioned in Chapter 8.

6. The sources for the information about the numbers and cost of staff are the Estimates and the Blue Notes.

ANNEX 7 (a)

MEETINGS OF CABINET, CID AND COMMITTEES, AND STATISTICS OF STAFF 1916-1939

	1916 (Dec)	1917	1918	1919	1920	1921	1922	1923	1924	1925	1926	1927	1928	1929	1930	1931	1932	1933	1934	1935	1936	1937	1938	1939 (to Sept)
No. of CP Memoranda	70	3200	3400	2100	2000	1200	900	424	561	522	419	308	402	366	456	349	461	323	325	251	353	327	313	199
Meetings of the Cabinet	23	285	205	139	82	93	72	59	65	61	67	64	58	55	73	93	66	70	47	56	75	49	60	49
Committees (approx)		70	144	180	210	220	160	110	160	160	140	100	90	110	150	120	110	90	110	150	120	90	110	80
Meetings of the CID					3	19	14	9	14	15	12	12	8	7	5	3	3	5	5	5	13	19	37	30
Committees: Ministerial (approx)							10	40	9	26	40	50	60	30	40	30	40	40	100	60	80	70	50	60
COS								5	9	11	12	25	13	11	11	4	6	9	21	24	30	36	39	52
Official (approx)				20	40	30	30	60	100	140	80	110	80	90	80	110	110	140	150	160	150	230	230	220
Meetings of the CCR and EAC										16	5	4	2		10	3	1							
Committees (approx)										7	30	70	30	120	150	100	90	50	40	30	30	20	20	10
Total meetings above (approx)	23	360	350	340	340	360	290	280	350	440	380	430	340	420	530	460	430	400	470	490	500	520	550	510
Major Conferences: Imperial		x	x			x		x			x				x							x		
Major Conferences: Other				x		x	x		x					x	x	x	x	x	x	x				
Staff of Cabinet Office and CID: Number				162	148	143	123	39	41	44	46	46	46	46	50	68	69	68	69	73	87	126	158	210
Cost (£000's)				46	55	40	30	15	17	17	18	18	18	19	26	25	24	25	25	27	37	43	52	65
Staff of Historical Section: Number				18	25	26	33	35	36	40	37	37	35	35	35	31	29	30	29	29	28	28	28	26
Cost (£000's)				7	11	13	12	14	16	17	16	15	15	15	14	13	12	11	11	11	10	10	10	10

MINISTERS ORIGINATING PAPERS TO THE LORD PRESIDENT'S COMMITTEE (LP Series)

	1940–45 Total	1940	1941	1942	1943	1944	1945
Post Office	4				1		3
Production	31			5	9	14	3
Reconstruction	2				1	1	
Scotland	115	3	4	26	35	28	19
Supply	37	5	7	6	10	6	3
Town and Country Planning	3				1		2
Trade	134	2	51	38	20	17	6
Transport (including Shipping and War Transport)	64	1	21	18	9	9	6
Treasury	108	7	22	29	20	25	5
Works	23	1	3	3	10	4	2
HOME	1114	30	164	269	295	230	126
Others: including Law Officers, Secretary and reports of CSO and of other Committees	121	16	30	28	23	15	9
TOTAL	1401	66	229	332	352	268	154

HISTORIES
SPONSORED THROUGH THE CABINET OFFICE

(Unless otherwise shown, all volumes were published by HMSO. A fuller description of some is given in HMSO Sectional List No. 60.)

Title	Principal author or compiler	Dates of publication
Pre-1914		
War in South Africa 1899–1902 (Hurst & Blackett) (4 vols)	F. Maurice and M. H. Grant	1906–1910
Russo-Japanese War (3 vols)	—	1910–1920
First World War		
Naval Operations (Longmans) (5 vols)	J. S. Corbett and Henry Newbolt	1920–1931
Seaborne Trade (John Murray) (3 vols)	C. E. Fayle	1920–1924
Merchant Navy (John Murray) (3 vols)	A. Hurd	1920–1929
France and Belgium (Macmillan for earlier volumes) (14 vols)	J. E. Edmonds and others	1922–1947
Principal Events 1914–1918	In diary and index form	1922
War in the Air (Oxford) (6 vols)	Walter Raleigh and H. A. Jones	1922–1935
Mesopotamia (4 vols)	F. Moberly	1923
Egypt and Palestine (2 vols)	G. MacMunn and C. Falls	1928–1930
Gallipoli (Heinemann) (2 vols)	C. F. Aspinall-Oglander	1929–1932
Togoland and Cameroons	F. Moberly	1931
Macedonia (2 vols)	C. Falls	1935–1937
Order of Battle of Divisions (6 parts)	A. F. Becke	1935–1940
Transportation on the Western Front	A. M. Henniker	1937
Blockade of the Central Empires	A. C. Bell	1937
East Africa	C. Hordern	1941
Italy	J. E. Edmonds	1949
Medical History (11 vols)	W. G. Macpherson and others	
Second World War		
POPULAR SERIES		
Arms and the Men	Ian Hay	1950
Norway, the Commandos, Dieppe	C. Buckley	1951

Title	Principal author or compiler	Dates of publication
Campaign in Italy	Eric Linklater	1951
Greece and Crete	C. Buckley	1952
North-West Europe	John North	1953
History of the Royal Air Force (3 vols)	D. Richards and H. St. G. Saunders	1953–1954
Five Ventures	C. Buckley	1954

MILITARY SERIES

Grand Strategy

August 1943–September 1944	J. Ehrman	1956
October 1944–August 1945	J. Ehrman	1956
September 1939–June 1941	J. R. M. Butler	1957
June 1941–August 1942 (2 vols)	J. M. A. Gwyer and J. R. M. Butler	1964
August 1942–August 1943	M. Howard	1971
To September 1939	N. H. Gibbs	—

Campaigns

Norway	T. K. Derry	1952
France and Flanders	L. F. Ellis	1953
Mediterranean and Middle East (6 vols)	I. S. O. Playfair and C. F. C. Molony	1954–
War at Sea (3 vols)	S. W. Roskill	1954–1961
War against Japan (5 vols)	S. W. Kirby	1957–1969
Defence of the United Kingdom	B. Collier	1957
Orders of Battle (2 vols)	H. F. Joslen	1960
Strategic Air Offensive (4 vols)	C. Webster and N. Frankland	1961
Victory in the West (2 vols)	L. F. Ellis	1962–1968

Civil Affairs and Military Government

British Military Administration in the Far East	F. S. V. Donnison	1956
Allied Military Administration of Italy	C. R. S. Harris	1957
North West Europe	F. S. V. Donnison	1961
Central Organisation and Planning	F. S. V. Donnison	1966

CIVIL SERIES

British War Economy	W. K. Hancock and M. M. Gowing	1949
Problems of Social Policy	R. M. Titmuss	1950
Coal	W. H. B. Court	1951
Food (3 vols)	R. J. Hammond	1951–1962
Statistical Digest of the War	Central Statistical Office	1951
British War Production	M. M. Postan	1952
Civil Industry and Trade	E. L. Hargreaves and M. M. Gowing	1952

Title	Principal author or compiler	Dates of publication
Economic Blockade (2 vols)	W. N. Medlicott	1952–1959
Works and Buildings	C. M. Kohan	1952
Contracts and Finance	W. Ashworth	1953
Control of Raw Materials	J. Hurstfield	1953
Studies in the Social Services	S. M. Ferguson and H. Fitzgerald	1954
Administration of War Production	J. D. Scott and R. Hughes	1955
Agriculture	K. A. H. Murray	1955
Civil Defence	T. H. O'Brien	1955
Merchant Shipping and the Demands of War	C. B. A. Behrens	1955
North American Supply	H. Duncan Hall	1955
Financial Policy	R. S. Sayers	1956
Studies of Overseas Supply	H. Duncan Hall, C. C. Wrigley and J. D. Scott	1956
Northern Ireland in the Second World War	J. W. Blake	1956
Inland Transport	C. I. Savage	1957
Labour in the Munitions Industries	P. Inman	1957
Manpower	H. M. D. Parker	1957
Factories and Plant	W. Hornby	1958
British Foreign Policy (short version)	Llewellyn Woodward	1962
Design and Development of Weapons	M. M. Postan, D. May and J. D. Scott	1964
SOE in France (sponsored by the Foreign Office)	M. R. D. Foot	1966
British Foreign Policy (full version) (5 vols)	Llewellyn Woodward	1970–
Oil	D. J. Payton-Smith	1971
Medical History (21 vols)	A. MacNalty and others	—

ANNEX 11

LIST OF COMMITTEES

NOTE ON SYMBOLS USED BY THE CABINET OFFICE

Part 1   Before 1923 (pp. 182–189)

2   1923–September 1939 (pp. 190–219)

3   September 1939–July 1945 (pp. 220–239)

Column 1   The symbol used, arranged alphabetically; an asterisk indicates a CID committee in Part 2 or a COS committee in Part 3.

2   The title of the committee or series of memoranda.

3   The chairman at the first meeting; Ministers identified by name and department (Ministers Without Portfolio marked w.p.); civil servants and military officers by department only; non-civil servants by name.

4   The months of the first and last meeting; these may differ from the dates in the PRO class lists, which relate to the first and last paper.

5   The number of meetings of the committee.

6   The PRO reference to the minutes and memoranda.

(Appendix C to PRO Handbooks No. 9 lists a number of committees which met during 1914–1916, whose papers generally bore no symbol but which were variously mentioned in the surviving records of the Cabinet.)

PART 1

		Chairman, at first meeting	Dates of first and last meetings	No. of meetings	PRO reference CAB
A	Home Defence Memoranda (CID), 1901–1939			—	3
A	Most Secret Minutes of the War Cabinet, 1917–1918			—	23/13–16
AC	Air Committee (CID)	Seely (War)	July 1912–July 1914	19	14/1
AC	Washington Conference: Committee on Limitation of Armaments, 1921–1922			—	30/9 and 10
AGC	Allocation of Guns Committee	Curzon (Ld. Pres.)	Oct–Dec 1917	4	27/10
AGW	Acceleration of Government Works Committee	Baldwin (Trade)	Oct 1921	3	27/138
AJ	Peace Conference memoranda, etc., 1920–1922				29/29–35
AP	Air Committee (CID) (*See* AC above)				
APC	Agriculture Act Committee	A. Chamberlain (LPS)	May 1921	2	27/143
APC } ARC }	Air Policy Committee } Air Raids Committee }	Smuts (w.p.)	Oct 1917	2	27/9
ASC	Committee on the Amalgamation of Services Common to the Navy, Army and Air Force	Mond (Health)	Mar–Dec 1922	9	27/171–173
B	Miscellaneous Memoranda (CID), 1901–1939			—	4
BED	British Empire Delegation: meetings during the Peace Conference			—	29/8
BED	Washington Disarmament Conference				30/1
BED	Genoa Conference				31/1
BI	Committee on the co-operation of Government Departments in the employment of ex-servicemen in the building industry	Addison (w.p.)	Apr–June 1921	2	27/141
BPC	Building Programme of Government Departments Committee	Worthington-Evans (w.p.)	May–June 1920	6	27/86
BSC	Bread Subsidy Committee	Horne (Trade)	July 1920	2	27/87
C	Colonial Defence Memoranda (CID), 1902–1939			—	5
CA	Conferences of Ambassadors, 1920–1922			—	29/42–65
CAS	Agricultural Situation Committee	Griffith-Boscawen (Ag.)	Oct 1922	2	27/175
CC	Committee on Co-ordination of Departmental Action (CID) (including CC(IS)(TA)(ABR)(NS)(TBS) and other series)	CID	Mar 1920–End 1922	Various	15/7–21
CE	Genoa Conference (Economic Commission), 1922 (including CEJ and CEL series)			—	31/9
CER	Washington Conference: Sub-Committee on Chinese Eastern Railways			—	30/23

		Chairman, at first meeting	Dates of first and last meetings	No. of meetings	PRO reference CAB
CES	Genoa Conference (Economic Commission): First Sub-Commission)			—	31/9
CF	Council of Four, 1919	Lloyd-George (P.M.)	June 1921	3	29/37–39
CFC	Future of Constantinople	Addison (Health)	Nov 1919–Dec 1920	8	27/133
CHC	Housing	Long (Adm)	Oct 1919–Nov 1920	20	27/66
CI	Ireland Committee, 1919–1920	A. Chamberlain (w.p.)	Apr–May 1918	2	27/68–70
CIC	Inter-Ally Council	Devonshire (CO)	Nov 1922	3	27/45
CIL	Irish Legislation Committee, 1922	(Memorandum only)	Aug 1921	—	27/155–158
CIP	Committee on Ireland: Sub-Committee on Belligerency				27/130
CM	Council of Foreign Ministers, 1920				29/41
CP	Cabinet Papers				24/92–140
CPO	Washington Conference: Sub-Committee on Post Offices in China, 1921				30/19
CR	Committee on the Co-ordination of Scientific Research in Government Departments (Code for sub-committees, RSC)	Balfour (Ld Pres)	Dec 1919–Feb 1921	3	27/94–97
CT	Washington Conference: Sub-Committee on Chinese Revenue, 1921				30/24
CT	Genoa Conference: Fourth Transport Commission, 1922 (including CTO, CTR and CTW series)				31/10
CU	Unemployment Committee	Worthington-Evans (w.p.)	Sept 1920–July 1922	52	27/114–129 190–192
CUI	Unemployment Insurance Committee	Addison (Health)	June 1921	1	27/137
D	Indian Defence Memoranda (CID), 1901–1939				6
DAC	Dutch Agricultural Agreement Committee	Milner (w.p.)	Nov 1917	2	27/11
DC	Demobilisation Committee	Smuts (w.p.)	Oct–Dec 1918	23	27/41 and 42
DC	Washington Conference: Drafting Sub-Committee, 1921–1922				30/21
DCF	Decontrol of Food Committee	Fisher (Ed)	Feb–Mar 1920	7	27/106
DCF	Washington Conference: Drafting Sub-Committee, 1921, 1922				30/22
DM	Demobilisation Committee	E. Geddes (Adm)	Dec 1918–Feb 1919	6	27/49
DPC	Disability Pensions Committee	Treasury	Feb 1920	2	27/162
DSP	Disposal of Surplus Government Property Committee	A. Chamberlain (w.p.)	Oct–Nov 1918	3	27/47
E	Imperial Meetings, 1921				32/2 and 6
EAC	Egyptian Administration Committee	Balfour (FO)	Sept–Oct 1917	4	27/12
EC	Eastern Committee	Curzon (Ld Pres)	Apr–Dec 1918	44	27/24–39
ECS	Washington Conference: Sub-Committee on Extra-territoriality in China, 1921			—	30/20

		Chairman, at first meeting	Dates of first and last meetings	No. of meetings	PRO reference (CAB)
E(CS)	National Expenditure Committee (Civil Services)	Horne (C of Ex)	July–Oct 1922	2	27/167
E(D)	Imperial Meetings: Drafting Committee, 1921	Churchill (CO)	Aug 1921	2	32/3
EDDC	Economic Defence and Development Committee	A. Chamberlain (w.p.)	June–Dec 1918	18	27/44
E(FS)	National Expenditure (Fighting Services)	Weir	Sept 1922–Apr 1923	63	27/169
EFT	Proposed Treaty with Emir Feisal	Churchill (CO)	Aug 1921	1	27/145
EG	Situation in Egypt Committee	Curzon (FO)	Oct 1921	1	27/134
EOC	Economic Offensive Committee	Carson (w.p.)	Oct 1917–June 1918	1	27/15 and 16
EP	Emergency Powers in War Committee (CID)	McKenna (HO)	June 1914	19	16/13
EPM	Export of Printed Matter Committee	Carson (w.p.)	Sept 1917–Jan 1918	1	27/13
E(R)	Imperial Meetings (Reparations), 1921	Horne (C of Ex)	July 1921	3	32/3
ESBC	Electricity Supply Bill Drafting Committee	A. Geddes	Apr 1919	2	27/53
E(SC)	Imperial Meetings, 1921	Churchill (CO)	July 1921	1	32/3
FC	Finance Committee	Lloyd-George (PM)	July 1919–July 1922	7	27/71 and 72
FEC	Washington Conference: Committee on Pacific and Far-Eastern Questions, 1921–1922			40	30/13–15
FL	Genoa Conference: Financial Commission, 1922 (including FLC, FLE and FSE series)			—	31/8
FSC	Permanent Armaments Advisory Commission of the League of Nations: CID Sub-Committee to Co-ordinate the views of the fighting services	Admiralty	June 1921–May 1922	5	16/40
FTJ	Genoa Conference: Transport Commission (Committee on Finance and Transport)			—	31/10
FTP	Future Transport Policy	Bonar Law (LPS)	Feb 1920	2	27/103
G	War Cabinet and Cabinet Memoranda (printed series: including papers of the War Committee, etc.), 1915–1920			—	24/1–5
GIA	Government of Ireland Act: Drafting Committee	Fisher (Ed)	Mar–June 1921	4	27/151
GIC	Government of Ireland Amendment Bill Committee	Long (CO)	Apr–June 1918	5	27/46
GR	Committee on National Expenditure (to consider the report of the Geddes Committee)	Various	1922	—	27/164–170
GRC	German Reparations Committee	Montagu (India)	Apr 1921	1	27/109
GS	War Priorities Committee: General Services files			—	40/121–146
GT	War Cabinet and Cabinet Memoranda, 1917–1922			—	24/6–90
H	Committee on Housing Policy	Griffith-Boscawen (Health)	Dec 1922–Mar 1923	6	27/208
HAC	Home Affairs Committee	Cave (Ld Chan)	Continuing July 1918–	—	26/1

		Chairman, at first meeting	Dates of first and last meetings	No. of meetings	PRO reference (CAB)
HC	Housing Committee	Horne (Trade)	June–Sept 1920	8	27/89
HD	Peace Conference: Meetings of Heads of Delegations (Five Great Powers), 1919–1920			—	29/69–77
HDP	Washington Conference: Committee on Pacific and Far-Eastern Questions			—	30/13 and 16
HDW	Washington Conference: Meetings of Heads of Delegations			2	30/11
HIC	Health Insurance Committee	Addison (Health)	Dec 1919	6	27/54
HLC	House of Lords Reform Committee	Curzon (FO)	Oct 1921–Feb 1922		27/113 and 188
HPDC	Home Ports Defence Committee Memoranda (CID)		Aug 1909–May 1922	38	12/1 and 13/1–2
HS	Committee on the Employment of ex-Servicemen on Housing Schemes	Munro (Scotland)	Jan–Feb 1921	5	27/132
IC	Minutes, etc, of Allied War Conferences, Council of Five, etc, 1915–1919			—	28/1–8
ICA ⎫ ICS ⎬	Committee on the agenda, etc, of Imperial Conference, 1921	Colonial Office	Feb 1921	3	27/112
ICC	Imperial Communications Committee (CID)			—	35/1–8
ICP	Minutes, etc, of International Conferences, 1919–1922			—	29/81–97
IDC	Indian Disorders Committee	Montagu (India)	Apr–July 1920	6	27/91–93
IF	Provisional Government of Ireland—Finance Sub-Committee	Ireland	Feb–Mar 1922	3	27/162
I(IP)	Committee on Irish Prisoners and Military Law	Birkenhead (Ld Chan)	Nov 1921	1	27/152
IMC	Indian Munitions Fraud	Montagu (India)	Aug 1921	1	27/136
I(ML)	Ireland—Committee on Military Law	Birkenhead (Ld Chan)	Aug 1921		27/155
IMR	Indian Military Requirements (CID)	A. Chamberlain (LPS)	Nov 1921–June 1922	13	16/38
IPC	Committee on Internal Protection Arrangements	Lloyd-George (PM)	Apr 1921	3	27/110
IRC	Indian Reforms Committee	(Memoranda only)	1918–1919	—	27/50
ISC	Irish Situation Committee	Lloyd-George (PM)	June 1921	2	27/107
ITC	Provisional Government of Ireland—technical departmental sub-committee	Colonial Office	Jan–Dec 1922	19	27/158
IUC	Unemployment Insurance Committee	A. Chamberlain (LPS)	Mar 1922	2	27/177
IWC	Imperial War Cabinet, 1917–1918			23	23/40–44
IWTC	Imperial Communications Committee: Imperial Wireless Telegraphy Committee	Norman	Nov 1919–May 1920		35/12
JDC	Joint Oversea and Home Defence Committee (CID), 1920–1939	Cabinet Office (Hankey)	June–Oct 1922	—	36
JSC	Provisional Government of Ireland—sub-committee to consider position of judges of the High Court	Shortt (HO)		4	27/163

	Committee	Chairman, at first meeting	Dates of first and last meetings	No. of meetings	PRO reference CAB
K	Committee on Co-ordination of Departmental Action (CID)	Foreign Office	Nov 1910–June 1914	—	15/2
L	Committee on Resources and Economic Position of London in time of war (CID)	Burns (Local Government)	Mar 1914	1	16/34
LABC	Land Acquisition Bill and Land Settlement (Facilities) Bill	Birkenhead (Ld Chan)	Mar 1919	4	27/63
LB	Protection of Houses of Parliament and Government Offices	Shortt (HO)	Nov–Dec 1920	2	27/100
LC	Liquor Control Committee	Fisher (Ed)	Apr 1921	3	27/150
LNC	League of Nations Committee	Balfour (Ld Pres)	June 1920–Apr 1921	2	27/98
LPC	Irish Land Purchase Committee	Long (Adm)	Mar–Nov 1920	3	27/85
LRC	Liquor Restrictions Committee	Fisher (Ed)	Apr–May 1919	4	27/62
LS	Land Settlement Committee	Worthington-Evans (w.p.)	Sept–Nov 1920	11	27/104 and 105
LW	Committee on the Revision of the Laws of War	Foreign Office	May–July 1922	13	16/43
M	Home Ports Defence Committee (CID)	CID (Ottley)	Aug 1909–May 1921	38	13/1
M	Oversea Defence Committee (CID), 1885–1929			—	8
M	Peace Conference Memoranda, 1919			—	29/23–27
MEC	Middle East Committee	Curzon (Ld Pres)	Jan–Feb 1918	4	27/23
MPC	Manpower Committee	Lloyd-George (PM)	Dec 1917	4	27/14
MS	Memorial Services Committee	Curzon (FO)	Oct–Nov 1920	3	27/99
MTC	Government Machinery for dealing with Trade and Commerce	Cave	May–July 1919	11	27/57
N NSC	Committee on Capital Ships in the Navy (CID)	Bonar Law (LPS)	Dec 1920–Feb 1921	11	16/37
OA	Committee on Attack on British Isles from Overseas	Asquith (PM)	Jan 1913–Feb 1914	21	16/28
OAD	Committee on the Observation of Armistice Day	Curzon (FO)	Oct 1921	1	27/142
ODC	Oversea Defence Committee			—	10
OHW	Committee on the Historical Section of the CID	Fisher (Ed)	July 1922	1	27/182
OPC	Overlapping in Propaganda	Carson (w.p.)	Oct–Nov 1917	4	27/17
OSC	Oil Companies Amalgamation Committee	Baldwin (Trade)	Mar–June 1922	10	27/180
P	Peace, 1916–1920	(Memoranda only)	1916 onwards	—	29/1–5
P	Trans-Persian Railway Committee (CID)	Grey (FO)	Jan 1913	2	16/26
PAC	Press Advisory Committee	Carson (w.p.)	Oct 1917–Jan 1918	6	27/18
PAC	Washington Conference: Committee on Programme and Procedure with respect to limitation of armaments, 1921		1921	—	30/8
PB	Peace Conference: Draft resolutions, etc, submitted to the Conference, 1919		1919	—	29/36
PC	Naval, Military and Air Force Pay Committee	Fisher (Ed)	July 1919–Feb 1920	15	27/65

	Committee	Chairman, at first meeting	Dates of first and last meetings	No. of meetings	PRO reference (CAB)
PC	Genoa Conference: Political Commission (including PCI, PCS and PCSE series)			—	31/6 and 7
PCC	Peace Celebrations	Curzon (Ld Pres)	May–July 1919	4	27/52
PGI	Provisional Government of Ireland Committee	Churchill (CO)	Dec 1921–Aug 1922	25	27/153 and 154, 161–163
PLI	Proposed Indian Legislation	Peel (India)	Aug 1922	2	27/176
PLO	Preservation of Law and Order Committee	Shortt (HO)	Mar 1922	2	27/183
POF	Post Office Finance	E. Geddes (Transport)	May 1921	1	27/147
PPC	Pre-War Pensions Committee	Worthington-Evans (w.p.)	May 1920	4	27/90
PPC	Washington Conference: Committee on Pacific and Far-Eastern Questions: Sub-Committee on Procedure, etc				30/17
R	Oversea Defence Committee (CID): Remarks (memoranda)				9
RAC	Railway Agreements Committee	A. Chamberlain (C of Ex)	Feb–Mar 1921	2	27/139
RBC	Railway Bill Committee	A. Chamberlain (C of Ex)	Mar 1921	1	27/111
RC	Research Committee	Curzon (Ld Pres)	Dec 1918–Mar 1919	6	27/64
RDC	Relief of Distress Committee	Munro (Scotland)	Oct 1921	1	27/149
RFP	Committee on the Review of the Foreign Press	Carson (w.p.)	Nov 1917	1	27/19
RGC	Committee on the Restriction of Government Contracts to firms on the King's National Roll	Shortt (HO)	Mar 1921	2	27/144
RIC	Restriction of Imports Committee	Milner (w.p.)	Nov 1917–Feb 1918	8	27/20
RR	Committee on the Relative Rank of Officers in the Navy, Army and Air Force	Baldwin (Trade)	Aug 1922	1	27/184
RSC	*See CR above*				
RTG	Rating Reform Committee	Griffith-Boscawen (Health)	Dec 1922–May 1923	3	27/207
S	Conferences of Ministers—Secretary's Notes, 1919–1922		1919–1922		23/35 and 36
SAS	Committee on the Allotment and Location of Seaplane and Aeroplane Stations (CID)	Churchill (Adm)	June–July 1914	2	16/33
SC	Railway Strike Committee	E. Geddes (Transport)	Sept–Nov 1919	12	27/60 and 61
SCT	Washington Conference: Sub-Committee on Chinese Traffic		Dec 1921		30/25
SF(B)	Conference on Ireland	Lloyd-George (PM)	Oct 1921–Oct 1922	33	43/1–7
SG	Genoa Conference: Conversations with foreign representatives, 1922				31/5

G

		Chairman, at first meeting	Dates of first and last meetings	No. of meetings	PRO reference CAB
SI	Safeguarding of Industries Act Committee	Baldwin (Trade)	July–Aug 1922	3	27/178
SIB	Committee on the Safeguards of Industries Bill	Horne (Trade)	Feb 1921	4	27/140
SIC	Irish Situation Committee	(Memoranda only)	1920	—	27/107 and 108
SNL	Washington Conference: Sub-Committee on Naval Limitation, 1921–1922			—	30/26
SO	Overseas Settlement Committee	Horne (C of Ex)	Mar 1922	1	27/174
SOP	State Opening of Parliament	Lloyd George (PM)	Dec 1921	1	27/146
SS	Standing Committee of the CID, 1921–1922	(Subsequently renumbered; see also CAB 2)		—	34/1
SS(AM)	Continental Air Menace (CID)	Admiralty	Dec 1921–Mar 1922	2	16/39
SS(AS)	Burney Airship Scheme (CID)	Amery (Adm)	July 1922	5	16/41
SS(IC)	Ireland (CID)	War Office	Apr–July 1922	10	16/42
SW	Sugar and Wheat Committee	Worthington-Evans (w.p.)	Nov 1920	4	27/88
SW	Washington Conference: Notes of Conversations between BED and foreign delegations, 1921, 1922			—	30/27
T	Ireland	Colonial Office	Feb 1922	1	27/185
TBC	Trade Boards Committee	Shortt (HO)	June 1922	1	27/181
TC	Committee on Territorial Changes	Foreign Office	Sept 1916–Feb 1917	5	16/36
TC	Supply and Transport Committee	E. Geddes (Transport)	Oct 1919–Aug 1921	46	27/73–75
TCB	Supply and Transport Committee (Bulletins), 1920, 1921	(Memoranda only)		—	27/79–81
TCP	Supply and Transport Committee: Government Publicity			6	27/83
TP	Trade Policy Committee, 1922	Lloyd-George (PM)	Aug–Sept 1920	4	27/179
TPC	Trade Policy Committee, 1919	A. Geddes (Trade)	Aug 1922	5	27/67
TSC	Supply and Transport Sub-Committee	R. Williams (Transport)	Oct 1919–May 1921	70	27/76–78
TX	Taxation Committee	A. Chamberlain (C of Ex)	Feb 1920	1	27/101
UAST	Committee on Unemployment and the State of Trade	A. Geddes	Mar 1919	9	27/58
UC	Industrial Unrest Committee	Shortt (HO)	Feb–Sept 1919	29	27/59
UIC	Unemployment Insurance Committee	Worthington-Evans	Feb–May 1921	3	27/135
V	Committee on Measures for Safeguarding Vulnerable Points at time of War	CID (Ottley)	Aug 1909–May 1910	4	16/13
VC	Genoa Conference: Verification of Credentials Commission, 1922			—	31/10

		Chairman, at first meeting	Dates of first and last meetings	No. of meetings	PRO reference CAB
VRR	Valuation and Rating Reform Committee	Addison (Health)	Apr–Dec 1921	13	27/131
WB(NE)	Committee on the Co-ordination of Departmental Action: War Book (Near East) Sub-Committee	Cabinet Office	Sept 1922	2	15/8
WC	War Cabinet Minutes, 1916–1919			—	23/1–12
WCP	Peace Conference Memoranda (War Cabinet, Paris), 1919–1920			—	29/7–22
WDC	Washington Conference, 1921–1922			—	30/5–7
WI	Imperial Communications Committee (CID): West Indies	Colonial Office	Feb 1920–Dec 1924	45	35/13
WP	Committee on the Co-ordination of Departmental Action: War Priorities Committee	Smuts (w.p.)	Sept 1917–Sept 1918	—	15/6
WP	War Policy Committee	Lloyd George (PM)	June–Nov 1917	21	27/6
WPC	War Priorities Committee	Smuts (w.p.)	1917–1918	21	40/1–171
WPE	Lochaber Water Bill and Grampian Electricity Bill	Baldwin (Trade)	Apr 1921	2	27/148
WT	Empire Wirless Telegraph Communications (CID)	Robertson (Trade)	July 1914	4	16/32
WTAC	War Trade Advisory Committee	Crewe (Ld Pres)	Sept 1915–May 1917	68	39/2–114
WT	Imperial Communications Committee (Wireless Sub-Committee)	Norman	May 1919–Aug 1922	27	35/9–11
X	X Minutes, 1918 (Conversations of a Committee on Military Matters)			—	23/17

G*

PART 2

		Chairman, at first meeting	Dates of first and last meetings	No. of meetings	PRO reference
A	*CID Home Defence Papers	(Memoranda only)	To 1939	—	CAB 3/1–8
A	Agricultural Policy Committee	Buxton (Ag)	Jan–Apr 1924	6	27/230
A	Agricultural Policy Committee	Wood (Ag)	Oct 1925–Jan 1926	3	27/293
AB	Agriculture Bill (part IV)	Zetland (India)	June 1937	1	27/631
ABC	Overseas Broadcasting	Kingsley Wood (Health)	Sept 1937–Feb 1939	7	27/641
ABE	*Bombing and anti-aircraft gunfire experiments	War Office	Apr 1937–Jan 1939	16	16/177–179
ACH	*Air Defence of Great Britain; location of Command HQ	Cabinet Office (Hankey)	Feb 1935	1	16/122
AC(O)	*Official Sub-Committee on Abyssinia	Foreign Office	July–Oct 1935	6	16/121
ACUI	Unemployment Insurance Advisory Committee	Bondfield (Labour)	July–Nov 1930	5	27/429
AD	Airship Development Committee	Thomas (CO)	Feb–May 1924	6	27/233
AD	*Allied Demands	Robinson (Supply Board)	June–Aug 1939	4	16/219
ADC	Agricultural Development Committee	Clynes (HO)	Jan–Feb 1931	4	27/444
ADGB	*Air Defence of Great Britain	Air Ministry	Oct 1934–Aug 1939	50	13/17–21
ADI	*Co-ordination of Air Defence Intelligence	Air Ministry	Jan–Apr 1929	4	16/96
ADR	Advertisements Regulations Bye-Laws Committee	Cave (Ld Chan)	June 1926	1	27/324
ADR	*Air Defence Research Committee	Cunliffe-Lister (CO)	May 1935–July 1939	21	16/132–134
ADR(F)	*Air Defence Research; Fuses Sub-Committee	DSIR	June–Dec 1937	5	16/135
AE	Air Force Expansion for Home Defence and Development of Airships	Birkenhead (India)	Nov 1925	2	27/294
AEC	Anglo-Egyptian Conversations Committee	Eden (FO)	May–July 1936	8	27/607
AER	Agricultural (Economists Report) Committee	Sanders (Ag)	Apr–July 1923	4	27/219
AET	*Egypt Sub-Committee	Baldwin (Ld Pres)	Nov 1932–Mar 1933	2	16/107
AF	This symbol was used as a prefix for the Committee papers on Anglo-French Conversations 1939. For full list see CAB 29				
AFC	Armament Firms Committee: Vickers Armstrong Fusion Scheme	(Memoranda only)	1927	—	
AFC	This symbol was used as a prefix for the Committee papers on Anglo-French Conversations, 1939. For full list see CAB 29				27/353
AFCW	This symbol was used as a prefix for the Committee papers on Anglo-French Conversations, 1939. For full list see CAB 29				

* A CID committee.

	Committee	Chairman, at first meeting	Dates of first and last meetings	No. of meetings	PRO reference CAB
AFV	Armoured Fighting Vehicles, range for	Winterton (D Lanc)	Nov 1938	2	27/649
AH	*Alexandria Harbour, development of	Foreign Office	Feb 1938	1	16/192
AI	Assyrians in Iraq	Simon (HO)	Jan–May 1937	2	27/629
AL	Acquisition of Land for public purposes	Parmoor (Ld Pres)	Nov–Dec 1929	2	27/405
AM	Afghan Medal Committee	Salisbury (LPS)	May 1929	1	27/385
AMB	Agricultural Marketing Bill Committee	Noel-Buxton (Ag)	Feb 1930	2	27/411
AP	Aden Police Force Committee	Hailsham (Ld Chan)	May 1928	1	27/372
AP	Ottawa Conference: Secretarial arrangements	(Memoranda only)	1932	—	32/106
AP	Agriculture Policy	Chamberlain (PM)	July 1937–Jan 1939	9	27/632
APC	Agricultural Policy Committee	Gilmour (Ag)	Dec 1931–Jan 1932	6	27/465
AR	Aliens Restrictions Committee	Gilmour (HO)	Apr 1933	1	27/549
ARC	*Anti-Aircraft Research Sub-Committee	Haldane	July 1925–Mar 1928	14	16/67
ARC(Sub)1	*Anti-Aircraft Research Sub-Committee No. 1	DSIR	July–Dec 1926	2	16/67
ARE	Air Raid Precautions: Expenditure	Chamberlain (PM)	Oct–Nov 1937	4	27/633
ARM	*Raw materials: accumulation of stocks	Robinson (Supply Board)	May 1936–June 1939	18	16/161 and 162
ARM(F)	*Raw materials: flax supplies sub-committee	Robinson (Supply Board)	Nov 1937–May 1938	6	16/163
ARP(AF)	*Air Raid Precautions: Administrative and Financial	Home Office	Apr 1933–Apr 1935	9	46/25
ARP(AR)	*Air Raid Precautions: Allocation of Respirators	Home Office	Mar–July 1935	2	46/30
ARP(BT)	*Air Raid Precautions: Bombing Tests	Home Office	June 1934–Jan 1935	6	46/32
ARP(C)	*Air Raid Precautions: Compensation	Treasury	Apr 1931–Oct 1935	20	46/20 and 21
ARP(CI)	*Air Raid Precautions: Communications for Intelligence	Home Office	Jan–July 1935	7	46/24
ARP(D)	*Air Raid Precautions: Decontamination	Ministry of Health	Jan–Oct 1933	7	46/24
ARP(DEB)	*Air Raid Precautions: Debris	Home Office	Feb–Mar 1934	2	46/31
ARP(E)	*Air Raid Precautions: Evacuation	Board of Trade	Mar 1931–June 1934	29	46/22
ARP(EX)	*Air Raid Precautions: Exercise	Home Office	Dec 1933–Feb 1934	2	46/29
ARP(EX)(T)	*Air Raid Precautions: Exercise (Technical)	Home Office	Jan 1934	1	46/29
ARP(MS)	*Air Raid Precautions: Merchant Shipping	Home Office	July 1933–Oct 1934	2	46/26
ARP(T)	*Air Raid Precautions: Merchant Shipping (Technical)	Home Office	July 1933–July 1935	7	46/27
ARP(O)	*Air Raid Precautions: Organisation	Home Office	Apr 1929–July 1935	58	46/7–18
ARP(P)	*Air-Raid Precautions: Policy Sub-Committee	Clynes (HO)	July 1929–Feb 1936	15	46/6
ARP(PR)	*Air Raid Precautions: Production of Respirators	Home Office	Sept 1935–Feb 1936	4	46/30
ARP(R)	*Air Raid Precautions: Respirators	Home Office	Jan 1934–May 1935	8	46/30
ARPS	*Air Raid Precautions: Services	Treasury	May–June 1937	7	16/172
ARP(TS)	*Air Raid Precautions: Personal Injuries	Board of Trade	Dec 1930	2	46/19
ARR	Agricultural Rates Relief Committee	Sanders (Ag)	Mar 1923	3	27/215

		Chairman, at first meeting	Dates of first and last meetings	No. of meetings	PRO reference
					CAB
ASM	Air Services in the Mediterranean	N. Chamberlain (C of Ex)	June–July 1936	2	27/608
AT	Arms Traffic Convention	Bridgeman (Adm)	Apr–June 1925	6	27/274
AT	United States Arbitration Treaty	MacDonald (PM)	Oct 1930	1	27/431
ATB	*Advisory Committee on Trade Questions in Time of War	FO (later a Minister)	July 1924–Nov 1938	28	47/1–6
ATB(C)	*Canton Sub-Committee	Treasury	Mar 1926	1	47/7
ATB(CL)	*Contraband Lists Sub-Committee	Admiralty	Oct 1935–June 1938	2	47/9
ATB(E)	*Requisitioning Sub-Committee	(Memoranda only)	1930	—	47/7
ATB(EP)	*Economic Pressure Sub-Committee	Elliot (Ag)	May 1933–Mar 1936	16	47/8
ATB(EPG)	*Economic Pressure on Germany Sub-Committee	Elliot (Ag)	July 1937–July 1939	15	47/12–15
ATB(J)	*Japan Sub-Committee	Foreign Office	July 1925–Nov 1926	8	47/7
ATB(L)	*Legal Sub-Committee	Foreign Office	May 1925–Jan 1928	12	47/7
ATB(MB)	*Proposals for a Ministry of Blockade Sub-Committee	Treasury	Oct 1937–Jan 1938	3	47/7 and 11
ATB(R)	*Russia Sub-Committee	Board of Trade	July–Oct 1927	2	47/10
B	*CID Miscellaneous Memoranda	(Memoranda only)	To 1939	—	4/1–30
BC	Broadcasting Committee	Simon (HO)	Apr 1936	3	27/601
BCI	British Coal Industry Committee	MacDonald (PM)	July 1929–Feb 1930	30	27/395
BD	British Dyes Committee	Haldane (Ld Chan)	Feb–July 1924	4	27/232
BDA	British War Debt to United States of America Committee	MacDonald (PM)	Feb–June 1933	11	27/548
BDG	Indian Round Table Conference. British Delegation (Government Members) Committee	MacDonald (PM)	Oct 1930–July 1931	16	27/470
BDG(F)	Indian Round Table Conference. Indian Finance Sub-Committee	Sankey (Ld Chan)	July 1931	4	27/471
BDP	British Dyes Policy Committee	Webb (Trade)	Aug 1924	1	27/248
BD(R)	This symbol was used as a prefix for the papers of the British Delegation at The Hague (Reparations) Conference, 1929. For full list see CAB 29				
BED	This symbol was used as a prefix for the papers of the British Empire Delegations at Peace Conferences, the Washington (Disarmament) Conferences and the Genoa (Economic) Conference. For full list see CAB 29–31				
BH	Baghdad–Haifa Railway and/or Pipeline Committee	Henderson (FO)	Mar–May 1930	3	27/419
BHPL	Disarmament Convention. Budgetary and HP Limitation Committee	Henderson (FO)	Oct 1930	2	27/430
BHR	Proposed Baghdad–Haifa Railway and Pipeline Committee	Baldwin (PM)	Mar 1928	1	27/367
BHR	Proposed Baghdad–Haifa Railway and Pipeline Committee	Passfield (DO)	Aug–Sept 1929	3	27/388

		Chairman, at first meeting	Dates of first and last meetings	No. of meetings	PRO reference CAB
BH(S)	Baghdad–Haifa Railway and/or Pipeline Inter-Departmental Committee	Colonial Office	May 1930	2	27/420
BMM	British Mercantile Marine Committee	Runciman (Trade)	Dec 1933–June 1934	5	27/557
BP(M)	*Building Priority (Ministerial) Committee	Morrison (D Lanc)	July 1939	3	16/205
BP(O)	*Building Priority (Official) Committee	Labour	July–Sept 1939	4	16/206
BR	*Belligerent Rights Sub-Committee	Chamberlain (FO)	Jan 1928–Mar 1929	16	16/79
BRD	Representation in the Dominions of HM Government in Great Britain Committee	Balfour (Ld Pres)	June–July 1927	3	27/347
BR(I)	*Irish Sub-Committee of Belligerent Rights Sub-Committee	Salisbury (LPS)	Mar 1929	1	16/81
BRL	*Belligerent Rights at Sea Sub-Committee	MacDonald (PM)	Nov 1929	1	16/82
BR(T)	*Technical Sub-Committee of Belligerent Rights Sub-Committee	Foreign Office	Jan 1929	8	16/80
BS	Beet Sugar Committee	N. Chamberlain (C of Ex)	July 1935	2	27/586
BT	Balance of Trade Committee	N. Chamberlain (C of Ex)	Dec 1931–Jan 1932	5	27/467
BTC	Basle Trading Company Committee	Salisbury (LPS)	Mar–May 1928	6	27/369
BTG	*Limitation of Armaments	Inskip (M Co-ord)	July 1938–Jan 1939	3	16/201
BTG(AW)	*Limitation of Armaments; Aerial Warfare Sub-Committee	Foreign Office	July 1938	3	16/202
BW	Beam Wireless Committee	Gilmour (Scotland)	Nov–Dec 1927	3	27/356
BW	*Broadcasting in Time of War Committee	Kingsley Wood (PMG)	Feb–Nov 1935	4	16/120
BWC	*Beam Wireless and Cable Services Sub-Committee	Colonies	Oct–Dec 1927	3	35/43
BWP	Policy in regard to Competition between Beam Wireless and Cable Companies Committee	Gilmour (Scotland)	Feb–Apr 1928	3	27/366
C	*CID Colonial Defence series	(Memoranda only)	To 1939	—	5
CA	Compulsory Arbitration Committee	Cave (Ld Chan)	July–Aug 1926	2	27/330
CA	Civil Aviation, Cadman Report	Inskip (M Co-ord)	Feb–Mar 1938	3	27/643
CAM	Church Assembly Measures Committee	Cave (Ld Chan)	Feb 1925	1	27/262
CAM	*Camouflage	DSIR	Oct 1936–Dec 1938	7	16/170
CAP	Agriculture Policy Committee	Sanders (Ag)	Nov 1923	2	27/227
CAP	Agriculture Policy Committee	Shaw (War)	Mar 1930	9	27/417
CAT	Future of British Commercial Air Transport	Cunliffe-Lister (Trade)	Nov–Dec 1927	6	27/354
CAT	Future of British Commercial Air Transport	Runciman (Trade)	Feb–May 1934	4	27/558
CAW	*Control of Aliens in War-time	Home Office	Jan–Aug 1939	6	16/211
CB	*Billingham Committee	Rogers (ICI)	July 1936–July 1939	12	16/168
CBR	*Construction of the proposed Baghdad–Haifa Railway, etc	Stanhope (Adm)	Mar 1926–June 1928	7	16/92

		Chairman, at first meeting	Dates of first and last meetings	No. of meetings	PRO reference CAB
CBS	Building Societies	Maugham (Ld Chan)	June 1938–Mar 1939	5	27/645
CBW	*Bacteriological Warfare	Cabinet Office (Hankey)	Nov 1936–May 1938	6	16/166 and 167
CC	Committee on China	Baldwin (PM)	Nov 1926–Nov 1927	4	27/337
CC	Committee on China	Henderson (FO)	Jan 1930	1	27/412
CC	Coronation Committee	MacDonald (Ld Pres)	Mar–May 1936	3	27/602
CCA	Cruiser Allocation Committee	N. Chamberlain (C of Ex)	Nov 1934	1	27/571
CCB	*Central Control of Business	Board of Trade	Feb–May 1939	3	16/218
CCR	Civil Constabulary Reserve Committee	Churchill (C of Ex)	May 1926	3	27/323
CCRS	Civil Constabulary Reserve Inter-Departmental Sub-Committee	War Office	May 1926	4	27/323
CC(TSM)	*Transmission of Urgent Government Messages Sub-Committee	Foreign Office	Jan 1923–Jan 1925	8	15/25
CD	Cash on Delivery Sub-Committee	Cave (Ld Chan)	July–Dec 1925	3	27/284
CD	*Coast Defence Sub-Committee	Baldwin (Ld Pres)	Feb–Apr 1932	6	16/105
CD(B)	*Air Disarmament Policy Sub-Committee of Coast Defence Sub-Committee	Baldwin (Ld Pres)	May 1932	1	16/106
CDC	Preparations for the Disarmament Conference: Committee	Simon (FO)	Dec 1931–Jan 1932	6	27/476
CDC	Co-ordination of Defence Committee	Baldwin (PM)	Feb 1936	2	27/600
CDC(SUB)	Preparations for the Disarmament Conference: Mediterranean Locarno Sub-Committee	Foreign Office	Dec 1931	1	27/476
CDM(P)	*Coast Defence Sub-Committee. Inter-Departmental Sub-Committee	Cabinet Office (Hankey)	Feb 1934–May 1935	2	16/119
CDP	Defence Programmes Co-ordination	(Memoranda only)	Aug 1939	—	27/663
CDP(O)	Co-ordination of Defence Programme (officials)	(Memoranda only)	Aug 1939	—	27/663
CDR	Censorship. Standing Inter-Departmental Committee	GPO	Mar 1927–Mar 1938	31	49/10–15
CDS(B)	*Civil Defence: Regional Boundaries Sub-Committee	Health	Jan 1939	1	16/207
CDS(P)	*Civil Defence: Policy	Anderson (LPS)	Dec 1938–July 1939	8	16/197
CDS(T)	*Civil Defence: Technical Sub-Committee	Anderson (LPS)	Nov 1938–June 1939	4	16/207
CFC	Commercial Negotiations with Foreign Countries Committee	Runciman (Trade)	Oct 1932–Feb 1933	2	27/389
CH	College of Heralds Committee	Birkenhead (India)	Nov 1927–June 1928	8	27/360
CI	Committee on India	MacDonald (PM)	Mar 1932–Feb 1935	42	27/519–521
CIU	Industrial Unrest Committee	Clynes (LPS)	Apr 1924	2	27/239
CJC	Far East Committee	MacDonald (PM)	Feb–Mar 1932	5	27/482
CLB	Royal Commission on Lotteries and Betting	Gilmour (HO)	Oct–Dec 1933	12	27/554
CLC	Control of Crown Lands Committee	Elliot (Ag)	Dec 1932–Feb 1933	4	27/499
CMA	*Co-ordination of Medical Arrangements in Time of War Committee	War Office	Nov 1936–Oct 1937	10	16/171

	Committee	Chairman, at first meeting	Dates of first and last meetings	No. of meetings	PRO reference CAB
CMB	Coal Mines: National Industrial Board	(Memorandum only)	Nov 1930	—	27/432
CMC	China (Military Details) Committee	Worthington-Evans (War)	Mar 1927	2	27/343
CMG	*Germany, Return of Colonial Mandates to, Committee	Plymouth (CO)	Mar–June 1936	12	16/145 and 146
CMI	Coal Mining Industry Committee	Runciman (Trade)	June 1935–July 1938	19	27/597 and 598
CMS	Coal Mines Situation Committee	Shaw (War)	Nov 1930	1	27/434
CMU	Conference of Ministers on Unemployment Policy	MacDonald (PM)	May–June 1930	6	27/437
CNR	Copper Production in Northern Rhodesia Committee	(Memoranda only)	1930	—	27/425
	*Censorship Organisation Sub-Committee	GPO	Feb–Oct 1934	4	48/8
CO	Coronation Oath Committee	MacDonald (LPS)	Jan 1936–Mar 1937	8	27/609
COH	*Official Histories Committee	Wood (Ed)	Jan 1924–July 1939	16	16/52 and 53
COS	*Chiefs of Staff Committee	Salisbury (Ld Pres)	July 1923–Aug 1939	317	53/1–54
COS(I)	*Seaborne Land Attack on British Isles Sub-Committee of COS	Admiralty	Mar 1930	1	53/55
CP	Cabinet Memoranda		1919–1939		24/92–288
CPC	Crown Proceedings Report Committee	Cave (Ld Chan)	Oct 1927	2	27/345
CPI	Policy in Palestine and Iraq	Passfield (CO)	Nov 1930–Jan 1931	6	27/433
CP(OB)	Coal Hydrogenation Committee	Home Office	Oct 1930	1	27/442
CP(OB)M	Coal Hydrogenation Committee (Ministerial)	Graham (Trade)	Nov 1930–July 1931	12	27/443
CQ	Title of Parliament Committee	Cave (Ld Chan)	Dec 1926	1	27/328
CR	Committee of Civil Research	Balfour (Ld Pres)	June 1925–Apr 1928	26	58/1
CR(ARO)	Agricultural Research Organisation	Warren Fisher	Nov 1929–Apr 1930	7	58/148
CR(AT)	Agricultural Training Sub-Committee	Bledisloe (Ag)	June–July 1926	11	58/102
CR(BP)	British Pharmacopoeia Sub-Committee	H. P. MacMillan	Nov 1926–Feb 1928	14	58/103–105
CR(C)	Memoranda: Series 'C'	(Memoranda only)	June 1925–Dec 1927		58/4 and 5
CR(CI)	Cotton Industry Sub-Committee	W. Graham (Trade)	Aug 1929–June 1930	25	58/132–135
CR(CT)	Channel Tunnel Sub-Committee	E. R. Peacock	Apr 1929–Feb 1930	35	58/121–126
CR(D)	Diatetics Sub-Committee	Elliot (Scotland)	June 1926–Jan 1930	8	58/109
CR(FI)	Fishing Sub-Committee	Agric & Fish	Nov 1929–Dec 1931	35	58/136–141
CR(G)	Memoranda: Series 'G'	(Memoranda only)	June 1925–Oct 1929	—	58/8
CR(GS)	Geophysical Surveying Sub-Committee	Nathan	Apr–Oct 1927	7	58/111
CR(H)	Memoranda: Series 'H'	(Memoranda only)	June 1925–Oct 1929	—	58/9 and 10
CR(I)	Irrigation Research Sub-Committee	Nathan	May 1928–Apr 1930	10	58/118–120
CR(IR)	Indian Railways Sub-Committee	Balfour (Ld Pres)	Mar 1926	1	58/100

		Chairman, at first meeting	Dates of first and last meetings	No. of meetings	PRO reference CAB
CR(I&S)	Iron and Steel Sub-Committee	Sankey (Ld Chan)	July 1929–May 1930	30	58/127–131
CR(K)	Kenya: Native Welfare	W. Graham	Dec 1926–May 1927	10	58/110
CR(L)	Committee on Locust Control	Henry Miers	May 1929–1930	4	58/55–77
CR(M)	Great Barrier Reef Sub-Committee	Heath	Sept–Oct 1927	5	58/112
CR(MC)	Mineral Content of Natural Pastures Sub-Committee	Elliot (Scotland)	July 1925–June 1931	7	58/96 and 97
CR(MT)	Mechanical Transport Sub-Committee	Fowler	Feb–June 1928	5	58/116
CR(OL)	Overseas Loans Sub-Committee	(Memoranda only)	Oct 1925	—	58/95
CR(Q)	Quinine Sub-Committee	Balfour (Ld Pres)	June 1926	1	58/101
CR(R)	Research Co-ordination Sub-Committee	Ormsby-Gore (CO)	Dec 1926–Apr 1929	28	58/106–108
CR(R)(EMB)	Research Co-ordination Empire Marketing Board Sub-Committee	Elliot (Scotland)	Feb 1927	1	58/108
CR(RE)	Rubber Research Sub-Committee	Hambling	Feb–Apr 1928	27	58/113–115
CR(RS)	Radium Sub-Committee	Rayleigh	June 1928–Mar 1929	8	58/117
CR(SB)	Severn Barrage Sub-Committee	Moore-Brabazon (Transport)	Dec 1925–Jan 1933	5	59/98 and 99
CRT	*Control of Radio Transmission	Air Ministry	Jan 1936–Aug 1939	13	16/164 and 165
CR(TF)	Tsetse Fly Committee	Ormsby-Gore (CO)	1925–1929	18	58/31–50
CS	Church Schools Committee	Percy (Ed)	June–Oct 1925	2	27/283
CS	Coal Situation Committee	Runciman (Trade)	Apr–May 1932	2	27/485
CS	Cattle Subsidy Committee	Hailsham (Ld Chan)	May 1936	2	27/605
CS	Czechoslovakian Crisis	Chamberlain (PM)	Sept–Oct 1938	17	27/646
CSA	*Situation in Akaba Sub-Committee	Colonial Office	June 1925	1	16/60
CSA	Civil Service Arbitration Committee	(Memorandum only)	Feb 1926	—	27/313
CSI	Colonial Sugar Industry Committee	Snowden (C of Ex)	Feb–Mar 1930	2	27/414
CSO	*Strength and Organisation of Cavalry Committee	Salisbury (LPS)	Dec 1927–Mar 1928	2	16/77
CSS	Parliamentary Candidature of State Servants Committee	Cave (Ld Chan)	Apr–May 1923	2	27/218
CSS	Coal Situation Committee	MacDonald (PM)	Apr–July 1931	21	27/450
CT	Cotton Trade Committee	Betterton (Labour)	Feb–Mar 1934	4	27/566
CTB	Trade Board Policy Committee	Cave (Ld Chan)	Jan 1923	2	27/209
CTU	Unemployment in the Coal Trade Committee	Salisbury (LPS)	Dec 1927	2	27/358
CU	Unemployment Committee	Griffith-Boscawen (Health)	Nov 1922–Oct 1925	37	27/190–198
CU(FA)	Unemployment Committee: Future Arrangements Sub-Committee	Griffith-Boscawen (Health)	Apr–July 1923	5	27/200

		Chairman, at first meeting	Dates of first and last meetings	No. of meetings	PRO reference
					CAB
CU(ID)	Unemployment Committee: Inter-Departmental Sub-Committee	Betterton (Labour)	Nov 1924-Feb 1925	4	27/204
CUP	Unemployment Policy Committee	MacDonald (PM)	June 1930	2	27/438
CU(SC)	Unemployment Committee: Sub-Committee on Necessitous Areas	Griffith-Boscawen (Health)	Jan 1923	2	27/199
CU(SUB)	Unemployment Committee: Ministerial Sub-Committee	Shaw (Labour)	June-Oct 1924	17	27/203
CWP	Economy, Conference of Ministers on White Paper on	Snowden (C of Ex)	Sept 1931	1	27/460
CWS	*Colonial Wireless System Sub-Committee	Colonies	Mar 1926-Feb 1927	9	35/41-42
CZ	*Czechoslovakian Crisis: Ministerial Conference on measures taken	Inskip (M Co-ord)	Sept-Oct 1938	14	16/189
D	*CID India Memoranda	(Memoranda only)	To 1939	—	6
D	Defence Programmes and their Acceleration	Inskip (M Co-ord)	Oct-Nov 1938	5	27/648
DA	Effect of Increase of Death Duties on Agricultural Interests	N. Chamberlain (C of Ex)	June 1925	1	27/282
DA	Depressed Areas: Committee on Report of Investigations into	N. Chamberlain (C of Ex)	Oct 1934-Nov 1938	15	27/577-579
DAC	Distressed Areas Committee	Baldwin (PM)	Dec 1928	1	27/381
DC	Drafting Committee on Government reply to Mr Lloyd George's proposals	N. Chamberlain (C of Ex)	July 1935	2	27/583
DC	*Review of BBC Document 'C'	M Inform	July-Aug 1939	6	16/203
DC(AL)	Operation of Dominions Legislation and Merchant Shipping Legislation Committee	Sankey (Ld Chan)	Oct-Nov 1929	2	27/399
DC(A)(SUB)	*Sub-Committee on the Disarmament Conference (Three Party Committee) Agenda Sub-Committee	Henderson (FO)	Apr 1931	1	16/103
DC(I)	Disarmament Conference 1932: Inter-Departmental Committee	Foreign Office	Mar 1932-Apr 1933	10	27/512-513
DC(M)	*Disarmament Conference 1932: Ministerial Committee	MacDonald (PM)	May 1932-June 1935	55	27/504-511
DC(M)(AF)	Disarmament Conference 1932: Allocation of Air Forces Sub-Committee	Baldwin (Ld Pres)	July 1934	6	27/514
DCM(AP)	Disarmament Conference 1932: Sub-Committee on Air Priority	Cunliffe-Lister (CO)	May 1935	4	27/518
DCM(MS)	Disarmament Conference 1932: Trading in Arms Sub-Committee	MacDonald (PM)	Nov 1934	1	27/517
DCOS	*Deputy Chiefs of Staff Sub-Committee	Cabinet Office (Hankey)	Feb 1932-Aug 1939	55	54/1-11
DCOS(IT)	*Deputy Chiefs of Staff Sub-Committee: Inter-Service Training Sub-Committee	Admiralty	Mar 1938-July 1939	8	54/12 and 13
DC(P)	*Sub-Committee on the Disarmament Conference (Three Party Committee)	MacDonald (PM)	Mar-July 1931	10	16/102
DC(S)	Disarmament Conference: Supervision Sub-Committee	Trade	Jan-May 1934	16	27/515
DC(S)(L)	Disarmament Conference: Legal Sub-Committee	Treasury	Feb-Apr 1934	6	27/516
DC(TA)	Disarmament Conference: Trading in Arms Inter-Departmental Committee	Eden (LPS)	Oct 1934-Feb 1935	5	27/517

G**

		Chairman, at first meeting	Dates of first and last meetings	No. of meetings	PRO reference
					CAB
DI	*Defence of India Sub-Committee	Birkenhead (India)	Mar 1927–Nov 1932	16	16/83–85
DI(AFR)	*Defence of India Sub-Committee: Afridi Enquiry	Benn (India)	Oct 1930	1	16/86
DI(AP)	*Defence of India Sub-Committee: Enquiry into extended use of Air Power	Benn (India)	June 1930	1	16/87
DIC	*Distribution of Imports Committee	Headlam (Transport)	Feb 1933–Mar 1937	6	16/113–116
DL	This symbol was used as a prefix to the papers of the Operation of Dominion Legislation Conference 1929. See CAB 32/69				
DM	Defence Preparedness	Chatfield (M Co-ord)	Aug–Sept 1939	4	27/662
DOP	*Defence of British Ports Oversea Sub-Committee of JDC	Cabinet Office (Hankey)	Feb. 1923–May 1924	6	36/14 and 15
DOP(A)	*Defence of British Ports Oversea (Australian Ports) Sub-Committee of JDC	Cabinet Office (Hankey)	May 1925	1	36/19
DOP(H)	*Defence of British Ports Oversea (Home) Sub-Committee of JDC	Cabinet Office (Hankey)	Sept 1924–Nov 1927	7	36/16–18
DOP(M)	*Defence of British Ports Oversea (Mediterranean) Sub-Committee of JDC	Colonial Office	June 1925–Oct 1931	4	36/21
DOP(NZ)	*Defence of British Ports Oversea (New Zealand) Sub-Committee of JDC	Colonial Office	Dec 1925	1	36/20
DOP(SA)	*Defence of British Ports Oversea (South Africa) Sub-Committee of JDC	Colonial Office	June 1927	1	36/22
DP	Defence Programmes and their Acceleration	Chatfield (M Co-ord)	Mar 1939	2	27/657
DPC	Reduction and Limitation of Armaments Sub-Committee	Henderson (FO)	Feb–July 1931	4	27/448
DP(P)	*Defence Plans (Policy)	Baldwin (PM)	Apr–July 1937	4	16/181–183
DPR	*Defence Policy and Requirements Sub-Committee	MacDonald (PM)	July 1935–Oct 1937	44	16/136–144
DPR(DR)	*Defence Policy and Requirements; Defence Requirements Enquiry Sub-Committee	Baldwin (PM)	Jan 1936	9	16/123
DR	Defence Regulations	Hoare (HO)	July 1939	1	27/661
DRC	*Defence Requirements Sub-Committee	Cabinet Office (Hankey)	Nov 1933–Nov 1935	26	16/109–112
DS	*Location of Government Staffs on Outbreak of War Committee	Treasury	Feb 1936–June 1937	12	16/154
DSC	This symbol was used as a prefix to the papers of the Four Power Conference on the Situation in the Danubian States, 1932. See CAB 29/138				
DS(P)	*Location of Government Staffs on Outbreak of War: Preparation of Plans Sub-Committee	Treasury	Feb–Nov 1937	4	16/155
DU	Inter-Departmental Committee on Unemployment	Treasury	Oct 1928–Mar 1929	6	27/378
DU	Inter-Departmental Committee on Unemployment	Thomas (LPS)	June 1929–Mar 1930	9	27/389–390
DU(P&E)	Retirements, Pensions and School-Leaving Age Sub-Committee of Unemployment Committee	Lansbury (Works)	July–Nov 1929	13	27/391

		Chairman, at first meeting	Dates of first and last meetings	No. of meetings	PRO reference
DWC	*Effect of development in Wireless Telegraphy on Censorship Sub-Committee	Admiralty	Mar–May 1926	4	CAB 49/9
DZ	*Demilitarised Zone Sub-Committee	Worthington-Evans (War)	June–Nov 1926	2	16/68
E	This symbol was used as a prefix to the papers of Imperial Conferences. For full list see CAB 32				
E	Educational Policy Committee	Baldwin (Ld Pres)	Mar 1934–Jan 1936	8	27/574
EA	Policy in East Africa	Amery (CO)	July 1927	1	27/349
EA	Policy in East Africa	Amery (DO)	Mar 1929	2	27/384
EAC	Egyptian Agreement Committee	A. Chamberlain (FO)	July–Nov 1927	2	27/351
EAC	Policy in East Africa Committee	Sankey (Ld Chan)	Jan–Apr 1930	7	27/410
EAC	Economic Advisory Council	MacDonald (PM)	Feb 1930–Jan 1932	14	58/2
EAC(A)	Memoranda: Series 'A': Questions awaiting consideration		Sept 1930–Dec 1931	—	58/3
EAC(AP)	Agricultural Policy Sub-Committee	E. D. Simon	May–July 1930	9	58/156 and 157
EAC(ARO)	Agricultural Research Sub-Committee	Warren Fisher	Nov 1929–Apr 1930	7	58/148
EAC(C)	Memoranda: Series 'C'	(Memoranda only)	Sept 1930–1939	—	58/5–7
EAC(CCS)	Slaughtering of Livestock Sub-Committee	de la Warr (Ag)	Mar 1931–July 1932	27	58/170–174
EAC(CD)	Cattle Diseases Sub-Committee	Gowland Hopkins	Oct 1932–Apr 1934	59	58/184–191
EAC(CD)(F)	Cattle Diseases Financial Sub-Committee	Burrell	Feb–Mar 1933	4	58/192
EAC(CI)	Cotton Industry Sub-Committee	W. Graham (Trade)	Aug 1929–June 1930	25	58/132–135
EAC(CLN)	Cost of Living Index (review of) Sub-Committee	A. Duncan	July–Dec 1930	5	58/147
EAC(CS)	Chinese Situation Sub-Committee	W. Graham (Trade)	Oct–Dec 1930	5	58/155
EAC(CT)	Channel Tunnel Sub-Committee	E. R. Peacock	1929–Feb 1930	35	58/121–126
EAC(CTP)	Channel Tunnel Policy Sub-Committee	Andrew Duncan	Mar 1930	2	58/144
EAC(D)	Dietetics Sub-Committee	Elliot (Scotland)	Nov 1930–June 1931	2	58/109
EAC(E)	Committee of Economists	Keynes	Sept–Oct 1930	13	58/150
EAC(EI)	Standing Committee on Economic Information	Stamp	Oct 1931–July 1939	96	58/17–23 and 30
EAC(EI)(TU)	Standing Committee on Economic Information Sub-Committee on Trend of Unemployment	H. D. Henderson	May–Dec 1935	11	58/24
EAC(EM)	Empire Migration Sub-Committee	Astor	July 1930–July 1931	20	58/163–166
EAC(EO)	Economic Outlook Sub-Committee	Keynes	Mar–May 1930	3	58/145
EAC(ESB)	Education and Supply of Biologists Sub-Committee	Chelmsford	Mar 1930–Mar 1931	21	58/159–162
EAC(ET)	Empire Trade Sub-Committee	Arthur Balfour	May–July 1930	4	58/149

		Chairman, at first meeting	Dates of first and last meetings	No. of meetings	PRO reference CAB
EAC(FFA)	Protection of the Fauna and Flora of Asia: Australia and New Zealand Sub-Committee	Onslow	July 1934–July 1939	7	58/193–196
EAC(FFC)	Application of the Convention on Fauna and Flora Sub-Committee	(Memoranda only)	1936	—	58/198
EAC(FF)(D)	Second International Conference for the Protection of the Fauna and Flora of Africa (London); Inter-Departmental Preparatory Committee on Organisation	Hemming	Apr 1938	2	58/94
EAC(FI)	Fishing Sub-Committee	Addison	1929–Dec 1931	35	58/136–141
EAC(G)	Memoranda: Series 'G'	(Memoranda only)	1930–1939	—	58/8
EAC(H)	Memoranda: Series 'H'	(Memoranda only)	1930–1934	—	58/11–13
EAC(I)	Irrigation Research Sub-Committee	Nathan	1928–1930	10	58/118–120
EAC(IC)	Committee on United Kingdom representation at International Meetings	Various	1931–1939	14	58/83–85
EAC(I&S)	Iron and Steel Sub-Committee	Sankey (Ld Chan)	1929–May 1930	30	58/127–131
EAC(IDF)	Fishing Industry Report Sub-Committee	Hemming	May–July 1932	6	58/181
EAC(ISC)	Iron and Steel Committee Report	MacDonald (PM)	June 1930	1	58/143
EAC(L)	Committee on Locust Control	Poulton	Jan 1931–Jan 1939	13	58/55–77
EAC(L)(COA)	Committee on Locust Control, Outbreak Areas Control Sub-Committee	Marshall	Jan–Oct 1938	3	58/82
EAC(L)(F)	Committee on Locust Control Finance Sub-Committee	Hemming	July 1934–Aug 1936	7	58/80
EAC(L)(K)(A)	Committee on Locust Control; Kenya, later Aircraft Experiments Sub-Committee	Hemming	Oct 1932–Mar 1934	13	58/78 and 79
EAC(L)(RLC)	Committee on Locust Control; Red Locust Control Sub-Committee	Hemming	Aug–Sept 1936	3	58/81
EAC(MC)	Mineral Content of Natural Pastures Sub-Committee	Elliot (Scotland)	1925–1931	7	58/96 and 97
EAC(MD)	Marketing and Distribution Sub-Committee	Garnsey	June 1930–Jan 1931	6	58/152 and 153
EAC(NCE)	Nutrition in the Colonial Empire Sub-Committee	de la Warr (Ag)	Nov 1936–Apr 1939	4	58/199–205
EAC(NCE)(D)	Nutrition in the Colonial Empire Drafting Sub-Committee	E. M. H. Lloyd	Dec 1937–July 1938	3	58/206–207
EAC(NCE)(R)	Nutrition in the Colonial Empire Research Sub-Committee	Mellanby	Dec 1937–Mar 1938	3	58/208
EAC(NID)	New Industrial Development Sub-Committee	J. H. Thomas (DO)	Apr 1931–May 1932	8	58/167 and 168
EAC(PFF)	Preparatory Committee for First International Conference for the Protection of the Fauna and Flora of Africa (London)	(Signed documents, etc.)	Oct–Nov 1933	—	58/86–90
EAC(PR)	Problems of Rationalisation Sub-Committee	Nathan	Sept 1931–June 1932	40	58/175–180
EAC(S)	Memoranda by the Staff	(Memoranda only)	1930–1935	—	58/14

		Chairman, at first meeting	Dates of first and last meetings	No. of meetings	PRO reference CAB
EAC(SB)	Severn Barrage Sub-Committee	Moore-Brabazon (Transport)	1932–1933	3	58/98 and 99
EAC(S1)	Financial Questions Sub-Committee	MacDonald (PM)	Sept 1931–Mar 1932	12	58/169
EAC(S1)	Limits of Economic Policy Sub-Committee	Stamp	Feb–Mar 1932	3	58/182
EAC(S2)	International Economic Policy Sub-Committee	Charles Addis	Aug 1932–Mar 1933	9	58/183
EAC(S2)(D)	International Economic Policy Drafting Sub-Committee	Basil Blackett	Sept 1932	1	58/30
EAC(SC)	Reports of the Standing Committee on Economic Information	Reports only	1932–1939	—	58/25–29
EAC(SR)	Standing Committee on Scientific Research	Daniel Hall	Apr 1932–Mar 1938	17	58/31–50
EAC(TF)	Tsetse Fly Committee	Sheils (CO)	Mar 1930–July 1938	16	58/52
EAC(TF)(CU)	Tsetse Fly Sub-Committee on closer union	Hemming	May–June 1931	2	58/53
EAC(TF)(EA)	Tsetse Fly Sub-Committee on East Africa	Hemming	July 1934–Feb 1937	8	58/51
EAC(TF)(G)	Tsetse Fly Sub-Committee on Game	Marshall	Nov 1930–Jan 1931	4	
EAC(UB)	Unemployment Benefit Sub-Committee	G. D. H. Cole	Oct–Nov 1930	4	58/154
EAC(US)	Unemployment Statistics Sub-Committee	W. McLintock	Mar–Apr 1930	2	58/146
EAC(TF)(T)	Tsetse Fly Committee: Tanganyika Sub-Committee	Hemming	Jan–Mar 1936	2	58/54
EAM	*Employment of Aliens in Munitions Works	Labour	Apr–May 1938	4	16/193
EB	Economy (Miscellaneous Provisions) Bill Committee	Hills (Treasury)	Jan 1923	4	27/211
EB	Electricity Board Committee	Hailsham (Ld Chan)	Dec 1928	1	27/379
EBC	Emergency Business Committee	Cave (Ld Chan)	Nov–Dec 1923	5	27/226
EBC	Emergency Business Committee	Haldane (Ld Chan)	Oct 1924	6	27/248
EBC	Emergency Business Committee	Hailsham (Ld Chan)	May 1929	6	27/386
EBC	Draft Economy Bill Committee	MacDonald (PM)	Sept 1931	2	27/461
EBC	Emergency Business Committee	Snowden (C of Ex)	Oct 1931	3	27/463
EBC	Emergency Business Committee	Hailsham (Ld Chan)	Nov 1935	3	27/590
EC	Supply and Transport Organisation: Emergency Committee	Henderson (HO)	Feb–Mar 1924	8	27/259
EC	Committee on Egypt	Baldwin (PM)	Nov–Dec 1924	3	27/253
EC	Committee on Egypt	Henderson (FO)	July–Aug 1929	2	27/387
EC	Exports Credits Committee	Clynes (HO)	Mar–Apr 1931	3	27/449
EC	Employment Committee	Snowden (LPS)	Feb–June 1932	3	27/479
ECC	Imperial Economic Consultation and Co-operation Inter-Departmental Committee	Treasury	Feb 1933	4	27/547
ECD	Economic Consequences of Disarmament Committee	Shaw (War)	Apr 1930–Mar 1931	10	27/416
ED	This symbol was used as a prefix to the papers of Economic Discussions with Dominions Ministers. For full list see CAB 32				
ED	Electrical Development Committee	Hogg (Att Gen)	June–Dec 1925	9	27/281

	Committee	Chairman, at first meeting	Dates of first and last meetings	No. of meetings	PRO reference
ED	Electricity Distribution Committee	Halifax (LPS)	July 1936–Jan 1937	4	CAB 27/617
EDA	This symbol was used as a prefix to the papers of Economic Discussions with Australia. For full list see CAB 32				
EDB	Electricity Distribution Bill	Stanhope (Ed)	June 1938	1	27/644
EE	This symbol was used as a prefix to the papers of Imperial Conferences. For full list see CAB 32				
EE	Future of British Empire Exhibition Committee	Snowden (C of Ex)	Aug–Oct 1924	3	27/247
EF	Equal Franchise Committee	Cave (Ld Chan)	Dec 1926–Feb 1927	3	27/336
EFU	European Federal Union: Committee on Proposal	MacDonald (PM)	July 1930	1	27/424
EGD	*Evacuation of Government Departments	Treasury	Dec 1938–Mar 1939	7	16/208
EHO	Emergency Hospital Organisation	Inskip (DO)	Apr 1939	1	27/659
EM	Empire Marketing Committee	A. Chamberlain (FO)	Feb 1926	2	27/310
EN	Economy Committee	MacDonald (PM)	Aug 1931	1	27/456
EP	Imperial Economic Policy Committee	Baldwin (PM)	Dec 1924	1	27/255
EP	Electrification Policy Committee	(Memorandum only)	1931	—	27/455
EP	Government Policy Committee	N. Chamberlain (C of Ex)	Oct 1935	2	27/591
EP(D)	Government Policy Committee (Drafting)	N. Chamberlain (C of Ex)	Oct 1935	1	27/592
EPE	Economies in Police Expenditure Committee	N. Chamberlain (C of Ex)	Apr–Oct 1932	4	27/483
ERC	*Emergency Reconstruction Committee	Elliot (Health)	Oct–Dec 1938	4	16/194
ESQ	Scope of Standing Joint Committee on Ex-Service Questions	Montague-Barlow (Labour)	July 1923	1	27/225
FAA	*Fleet Air Arm Enquiry	Inskip (M Co-ord)	July 1936–July 1938	4	16/151 and 152
FA/D/31	Saar: Question of sending British Troops	Simon (FO)	Dec 1934	2	27/573
FAO	*Armament Orders from Foreign Countries	Robinson (Supply Board)	Oct 1937–Feb 1939	4	16/187
FA/OH/25	Inter-Departmental Committee on Trading in Arms: Drafting Sub-Committee	War Office	Jan–Feb 1935	2	27/517
FB	Factories Bill Committee	Simon (HO)	Nov 1936–Apr 1937	4	27/618
FBC	Factories Bill Committee	Clynes (HO)	Oct–Nov 1929	2	27/406
FCI	*Industrial Intelligence in Foreign Countries	Dept of Overseas Trade	Mar 1930–July 1938	24	48/2–5
FCI(AT)	*Industrial Intelligence in Foreign Countries: Air Targets Sub-Committee	Dept of Overseas Trade	Dec 1936–Apr 1938	4	48/8–10

	Committee	Chairman, at first meeting	Dates of first and last meetings	No. of meetings	PRO reference CAB
FCI(SUB)	*Industrial Intelligence in Foreign Countries: Sub-Committee to examine recommendations regarding air targets	Air Ministry	Apr 1936	1	48/7
FCI(TA)	*Industrial Intelligence: Technical Aid Contracts with USSR	War Office	May–June 1932	2	48/6
FES	British Shipping in the Far East	Hoare (HO)	Sept–Nov 1937	2	27/634
FP	Foreign Policy Committee on Security	Baldwin (PM)	May 1925	2	27/275
FP	Foreign Policy Committee	Baldwin (PM)	Apr 1936–Aug 1939	61	27/622–627
FPE	*Proposed Food Prices Enquiry	Lloyd Graeme (Trade)	Nov 1924	1	27/251
FS	*Food Supply in Time of War Committee	Inskip (M Co-ord)	May 1936–Apr 1939	9	16/156–158
FS	Fighting Services Committee	MacDonald (PM)	June 1929–Jan 1931	15	27/407
FSC	Financial Situation Committee	Snowden (C of Ex)	Sept–Oct 1931	4	27/462
FS(CL)	*Food Supply Cereals for Livestock Sub-Committee	Gowers	Dec 1936–Jan 1937	7	16/160
FS(R)	*Food Supply: Rationing Sub-Committee	Beveridge	June–Oct 1936	3	16/159
G	Germany: Committee on	Baldwin (PM)	Feb 1936	1	27/599
GC	Block Grants Committee	Churchill (C of Ex)	Feb 1927	2	27/339
GP	*Geneva Protocol Sub-Committee	Cabinet Office (Hankey)	Dec 1924–Jan 1925	10	16/56
GP	General Purposes Committee	MacDonald (PM)	Feb–July 1935	25	27/583 and 584
GP(SUB)	General Purposes Committee: Lloyd George's Proposals Sub-Committee	MacDonald (PM)	Apr 1935	1	27/583
GR	German Rearmament Committee	MacDonald (PM)	Nov–Dec 1934	5	27/572
GRT	Totalisator for Greyhound Racing Tracks Committee	Gilmour (HO)	Jan 1932	2	27/498
GS	Government Employees in the General Stoppage 1926, Committee on	Alexander (Adm)	Feb 1930	2	27/415
H	This symbol was used as a prefix to the papers of the Hague Conference, 1929. For full list see CAB 29				
H	Housing Policy Committee	Griffith-Boscawen (Health)	Dec 1922–Mar 1923	6	27/208
H	Unemployment Committee: Housing Sub-Committee	Wheatley (Health)	Jan–Feb 1924	3	27/201
H	Housing Policy Committee	MacDonald (PM)	Feb 1934–June 1935	5	27/565
HAC	Home Affairs Committee	Lord Chancellor	July 1939	Annual sequence 76	26/1–24
HC	Housing Policy Committee	Hilton Young (Health)	Nov 1932	1	27/496
HDC	*Home Defence Committee	Cabinet Office (Hankey)	Feb 1923–Aug 1939	53	12/1–4 and 13/2–11
HDC(AA)	*Home Defence Committee: Air Attack Protection Sub-Committee	Home Office	Feb 1936–Jan 1939	11	13/23–25

		Chairman, at first meeting	Dates of first and last meetings	No. of meetings	PRO reference CAB
HDC(AD)	*Home Defence Committee: Air Defence Sub-Committee	War Office	Jan 1930	1	13/16
HDC(AP)	*Home Defence Committee: Active and Passive Air Defence Sub-Committee	Cabinet Office (Ismay)	July 1937–Feb 1939	8	13/26 and 27
HDC(CL)	*Home Defence Committee: Protection of Cable Landings Sub-Committee	Admiralty	Nov 1925	1	13/12
HDC(GO)	*Home Defence Committee: Protection of Government Offices Sub-Committee	Home Office	Nov–Dec 1925	2	13/13
HDC(M)	*Home Defence Committee: Memoranda	(Memoranda only)	1923–1939	—	12/5–6
HDC(O&P)	*Home Defence Committee: Protection of Oil and Petrol Stores Sub-Committee	Home Office	Dec 1925–Feb 1926	3	13/15
HDC(PGB)	*Home Defence Committee: Protection of Government Buildings Sub-Committee	Home Office	Jan–May 1938	3	13/28
HDC(P&T)	*Home Defence Committee: Protection of Ports and Telegraphs Sub-Committee	Home Office	Dec 1925	3	13/14
HDC(VP)	*Home Defence Committee: Protection of Vulnerable Points Sub-Committee	Home Office	Mar 1936–Oct 1938	7	13/22
HDS	*Home Defence Scheme	Admiralty	Feb 1938	1	16/199
HEC	Hours of Employment Bill Committee	Bondfield (Labour)	July–Dec 1929	5	27/398
HL	House of Lords Reform Committee	Cave (Ld Chan)	Aug 1925–May 1927	10	27/302
HLP	House of Lords Procedure Committee	Cave (Ld Chan)	May–June 1927	2	27/335
HM	Hunger Marchers: Committee on	Gilmour (HO)	Nov–Dec 1932	3	27/497
HWQ	Home Wheat Quota Committee	Baldwin (Ld Pres)	Jan 1932	2	27/478
IA	This symbol was used as a prefix to the papers of Imperial Conferences. For full list see CAB 32				
IA	Indian Affairs Committee	Olivier (India)	Mar–Sept 1924	15	27/229
IA	Irish Affairs Committee	A. Chamberlain (FO)	Nov–Dec 1925	13	27/295
IAC	Irish Affairs Committee	Devonshire (CO)	Mar–Nov 1923	16	27/216
IAC	Indian contribution to the Home Effective Charges of the British Army	Hailsham (Ld Chan)	Oct 1928	2	27/373
IAS	*Akhwan Situation Sub-Committee	Baldwin (PM)	June 1928	1	16/88
IB	*Employment of Tracer, Incendiary, Smoke and Explosive Bullets, Sub-Committee	Foreign Office	May–June 1927	3	16/75
IBS	*Insurance of British Shipping in Time of War	Board of Trade	July 1924–Jan 1939	13	16/57 and 58
IC	This symbol was used as a prefix to the papers of Imperial Conferences. For full list see CAB 32				
IC	Irish Claims Committee	Churchill (C of Ex)	Dec 1927	2	27/357

		Chairman, at first meeting	Dates of first and last meetings	No. of meetings	PRO reference
IC	Indian Cotton Committee	N. Chamberlain (C of Ex)	Nov 1933	3	CAB 27/556
ICC	*Imperial Communications Committee	Amery	Mar 1919–July 1939	109	35/1 and 35/15–18
ICC(SC)	*Strategic Cables Sub-Committee of ICC	Stanley (HO)	Jan 1933	3	35/45
ICC(SUB)	*External Communications Sub-Committee of ICC	Air Ministry	June 1930	1	35/14
ICD	This symbol was used as a prefix to the papers of Imperial Conferences. For full list see CAB 32				
IC(DFP)	*Imperial Conference 1936: Foreign Policy and Defence Committee	Cabinet Office (Hankey)	Oct 1936	1	16/153
ICL	Third International Conference on Locust Control	(Signed documents, etc)	1934	—	58/91
ID	Defence of India Committee	Inskip (M Co-ord)	July 1938–June 1939	6	27/653 and 654
ID/D/17	*Anti-Aircraft Research: Technical Assistants for Committee	Haldane	Dec 1927	1	16/67
ID/D/57	*ARP: Shelters Sub-Committee	Home Office	Oct 1933–June 1934	5	46/28
ID/G/149 and 189	*Royal Commission on Private Manufacture and Trading in Arms: Evidence and draft report	Cabinet Office (Hankey)	Apr 1935–Oct 1936	5	16/124–126
IE	This symbol was used as a prefix to the papers of Imperial Economic Conferences. For full list see CAB 32				
IEC	This symbol was used as a prefix to the papers of Imperial Economic Conferences. For full list see CAB 32				
IEC	Economic Consultation and Co-operation Cabinet Committee	Thomas (DO)	July–Oct 1933	2	27/553
IFC	*Industrial Intelligence in Foreign Countries, Conference on	Cabinet Office (Hankey)	Dec 1928	1	48/1
IIA	*Indianisation of the Indian Army	Balfour (Ld Pres)	Nov 1927	3	16/78
IL	Irish Loyalists Committee	Cave (Ld Chan)	July 1925	1	27/289
ILC(UK)	Third International Conference on Locust Control; United Kingdom Delegation Memoranda	(Memoranda only)	1936	—	58/92
ILP	International Labour Policy Committee	Cave (Ld Chan)	Mar–Apr 1925	3	27/272
IN	Irish Negotiations: Conferences between IFS and United Kingdom representatives	Joint	Oct 1932	4	27/494
IN	Irish Negotiations: Conferences between IFS and United Kingdom representatives	Joint	Jan–Mar 1938	8	27/642
INC	Irish Negotiations Committee	N. Chamberlain (PM)	Jan–Mar 1938	—	27/494
INC	Irish Negotiations Committee	Henderson (FO)		3	27/642
IOC	Iraq Oil Committee	A. Chamberlain (FO)	May 1930–Feb 1931	4	27/436
IP	Policy with regard to Iraq; Committee		Nov 1925	1	27/296

	Committee	Chairman, at first meeting	Dates of first and last meetings	No. of meetings	PRO reference CAB
IP	Iraq Policy Committee	A. Chamberlain (FO)	Feb–May 1926	3	27/312
IP	Continuation of the Indian Press Act Committee	Zetland (India)	July 1935	2	27/589
IP	*Advisory Panel of Industrialists	N. Chamberlain (PM)	Dec 1938–Aug 1939	61	16/220–231
IPC	*Industrial Production Sub-Committee	N. Chamberlain (C of Ex)	Feb 1936	1	16/149
IRQ	Committee on Iraq	Devonshire (CO)	Dec 1922–Mar 1923	9	27/206
ISC	Irish Situation Committee	MacDonald (PM)	Apr 1932–Apr 1938	44	27/522–528
ISC(SUB)	Irish Situation Committee: Inter-Departmental Committee	Elliot (Treasury)	July–Aug 1932	4	27/529–544
IT	*Sub-Committee on Irish Treaty: Article 6	Amery (DO)	July 1926–Nov 1927	4	16/70
IU	Indian Unrest Committee	Wedgwood Benn (India)	Apr 1930	1	27/422
IW	Committee on Report of Imperial Wireless Service	Hartshorn (PMG)	Apr–July 1924	9	27/240
IWC	This symbol was used as a prefix to the papers of the Imperial Wireless and Cable Conference, 1928. For full list see CAB 32				
JDC	*Joint Oversea and Home Defence Committee	Cabinet Office (Hankey)	Mar 1920–July 1939	68	36/1–22
JIC	*Joint Intelligence Sub-Committee	Various	July 1936–Aug 1939	34	56/1–4
JIC(A)	*Joint Intelligence Sub-Committee: Air Warfare	Various	Oct 1938–Feb 1939	6	56/6
JIC(S)	*Joint Intelligence Sub-Committee: Air Warfare in Spain	Various	June 1937–May 1938	5	56/5
JM	Jubilee Medal Committee	Gilmour (HO)	Apr 1935	1	27/585
P	*Joint Planning Committee	Various	Apr 1927–Aug 1939	270	55/1–19
JTC	Japanese Trade Competition Committee	Runciman (Trade)	Mar–June 1934	3	27/568
JU	Juvenile Unemployment Committee	N. Chamberlain (Health)	Feb 1925	2	27/267
JUC	Unemployment Committee: Juvenile Unemployment Sub-Committee	Bondfield (Labour)	Feb 1924	3	27/202
JUI	Juvenile Unemployment, Second Committee on	(Memoranda only)	1925	—	27/267
K	*Co-ordination of Departmental Action on the Outbreak of War Committee	Cabinet Office	1911–Aug 1939	29	15/1
KA	King's Anniversary (25th) Committee	Gilmour (HO)	June 1934–Jan 1935	4	27/563
KA(SUB)	King's Anniversary (25th) Committee: Inter-Departmental Committee	Home Office	June 1934	4	27/563
KS	King's Speech Committee	Baldwin (PM)	Dec 1924	2	27/250
KS	King's Speech Committee	Baldwin (PM)	Nov 1935	1	27/594
KS	King's Speech Committee	MacDonald (Ld Pres)	Oct 1936	3	27/611
KSC	King's Speech Committee	MacDonald (PM)	Oct–Dec 1932	5	27/491
KSC	King's Speech Committee	MacDonald (PM)	Nov 1933	1	27/555
KSC	King's Speech Committee	MacDonald (PM)	Nov 1934	2	27/570

		Chairman, at first meeting	Dates of first and last meetings	No. of meetings	PRO reference CAB
KSC	King's Speech Committee	Baldwin (PM)	Oct 1935	1	27/593
KSC	King's Speech Committee	N. Chamberlain (PM)	Oct 1937	2	27/635
KSC	King's Speech Committee	N. Chamberlain (PM)	Oct 1938	2	27/647
K(WB)	*War Book Sub-Committee of Co-ordination Committee	Various, later Cabinet Office	July 1926–Aug 1939	98	15/27–38
L	This symbol was used as a prefix to the papers of the Lausanne Conference, 1932. For full list see CAB 29				
L	Legislation Committee	Cave (Ld Chan)	May 1926–Mar 1927	5	27/326 and 327
LAB/G/5	Co-Partnership and Profit Sharing	Cecil of Chelwood (D Lanc)	Feb 1926	1	27/314
LC	This symbol was used as a prefix to the papers of the London Conferences, 1924 and 1931. For full list see CAB 29				
LC	*Legal Sub-Committee of Advisory Committee on Trade Questions in Time of War	Foreign Office	May 1925–Jan 1928	12	47/7
LD	Labour Discharges Committee	Alexander (Adm)	July 1929	1	27/394
LE	Leasehold Enfranchisement Committee	Cave (Ld Chan)	Mar 1926–Mar 1927	8	27/320
LF	*Composition and Organisation of Local Forces Sub-Committee of ODC	Colonial Office	Oct 1925–May 1929	16	7/16 and 17
LGD	Local Government Departments Committee	Inskip (M Co-ord)	Dec 1936–Feb 1937	2	27/614
LNA	Further Limitation of Naval Armaments Committee	Baldwin (PM)	July 1927	6	27/350
LNC	This symbol was used as a prefix to the papers of the London Naval Conferences, 1930 and 1935. For full list see CAB 29				
LNE	*League of Nations and the Near East (Turkey and Mosul Boundary Questions)	Balfour (Ld Pres)	Dec 1925	1	16/62
LP	Lane Bequest Committee	Cave (Ld Chan)	May 1926	2	27/322
LPA	Irish Free State Land Purchase Annuities Committee	(Memoranda only)	1932	—	27/500
LP(B)	Locarno Powers at Brussels: Proposed meeting of	Baldwin (PM)	July 1936	1	27/603
LP(L)	Locarno Powers: London meetings of	Baldwin (PM)	Mar–May 1936	6	27/603
LPT	London Passenger Transport Bill Committee	N. Chamberlain (C of Ex)	Nov 1931	1	27/464
LT	Luxury Tax Committee	Churchill (C of Ex)	Jan–Feb 1926	3	27/300
LT	London Traffic Committee	Morrison (Transport)	Oct–Nov 1929	3	27/401
LU	London University, King's College and the Imperial Institute Committee	Peel (Works)	Apr 1925–Mar 1926	3	27/271

		Chairman, at first meeting	Dates of first and last meetings	No. of meetings	PRO reference
LW	*Committee to consider the Report of the International Commission on the Revision of the Laws of War	Haldane (Ld Chan)	Mar 1924	1	CAB 16/55
MA	*Medical Aircraft in Time of War and Treatment of Civilians	Foreign Office	July 1936	1	16/150
MA	Milk Acts (1934 and 1937)	Simon (C of Ex)	June 1937	1	27/630
MAW	*Air Ministry: move of essential Departments to Whitehall	Hoare (HO)	Jan 1939	1	16/204
MB	Medical Branches of the Fighting Services Committee	Treasury	Oct 1925–Apr 1926	26	27/290–292
MC	Colonial Military Contributions Committee	Peel (Works)	July–Nov 1927	4	27/352
MC	Migration Committee	Amery (CO)	Nov–Dec 1928	3	27/380
MCC	*Calcium Carbide Committee	Ernest Harvey	May–Aug 1937	13	16/174 and 175
MDO	Mines Department Organisation Committee	Clynes (HO)	June 1931	1	27/453
ME	This symbol was used as a prefix to the papers of the League of Nations Monetary and Economic Conference, 1933. For full list see CAB 29				
MED	*Medical Examination of Men on Demobilisation from the Armed Forces in a future War	Pensions	Feb 1924–May 1928	5	57/10
MED(SUB)	*Medical Examination of Men on Demobilisation from the Armed Forces in a future War	Pensions	Mar 1925–Jan 1926	2	57/11
ME(M)	*Middle East: Standing Ministerial Committee on	Cunliffe Lister (CO)	Nov 1931–Jan 1935	9	51/1
ME(O)	*Middle East: Official Committee on	Foreign Office	Feb 1931–Aug 1939	69	51/2–11
MF	Position of Fleet in the Mediterranean Committee	N. Chamberlain (C of Ex)	May 1936	1	27/606
MIC	*Committee to prepare Plans for a Ministry of Information	Colville (DOT)	Oct 1935–Aug 1939	6	16/127
MIC(CC)	*Ministry of Information: Codifying Sub-Committee	Tallents	June 1937	1	16/129
MIC(DBN)	*Ministry of Information: Dissemination of British News	Hoare (HO)	June 1939	1	16/131
MIC(P)	*Ministry of Information: Propaganda in Foreign Countries Sub-Committee	Campbell-Stewart	Jan 1939	1	16/130
MIC(SUB)	*Ministry of Information Planning Sub-Committee	Treasury	Oct 1935–May 1936	7	16/128
MP	Meat Policy Committee	MacDonald (PM)	Nov 1932	1	27/495
MR	Mining Royalties Committee	Churchill (C of Ex)	July 1925	2	27/286
MRS	Protection of British Shipping in Spain	Hailsham (Ld Chan)	Apr 1937	4	27/639
MS	Committee on Ministers' Salaries	Simon (HO)	Dec 1936–Jan 1937	2	27/613
MTB	Mobilisation and Training Bill	Maugham (Ld Chan)	Apr–May 1939	3	27/660
MTB(A)	Mobilisation: Military Training Act, Auxiliary Forces Act	Morrison (D Lanc)	June 1939	4	27/660
MTC	Municipal Trading in Coal: Committee on Report of Coal Commission on	Lane-Fox (Mines)	Mar 1926	1	27/315

	Committee	Chairman, at first meeting	Dates of first and last meetings	No. of meetings	PRO reference CAB 27/223
NA	Necessitous Areas Committee	N. Chamberlain (Health)	July 1923	2	27/223
NC	This symbol was used as a prefix to the papers of the London Naval Conferences, 1930 and 1935. For full list *see* CAB 29				
ND	*National and Imperial Defence Sub-Committee	Salisbury (Ld Pres)	Mar-July 1923	19	16/46 and 47
ND(A)	*National and Imperial Defence Sub-Committee Government Airship Service Committee	Hoare (Air)	Mar-July 1923	5	16/49
ND(R)	*National and Imperial Defence Sub-Committee Relations between Navy and Air Force Sub-Committee	Balfour	Mar-July 1923	12	16/48
NE	Standing Committee on Expenditure	Baldwin (PM)	Oct 1925-Oct 1927	23	27/303-306
NE	National Expenditure: Committee on Report of Committee on	(Memoranda only)	July-Aug 1931	—	27/454
NF	Disposal of National Factories at Gretna: Committee on	(Memoranda only)	1924	—	27/243
NH	National Health Insurance Committee	Wheatley (Health)	Feb 1924	2	27/234
NHC	New Hebrides Committee	Passfield (CO)	July 1930	1	27/426
NHI	National Health Insurance Committee	Hilton-Young (Health)	Apr 1932	1	27/484
NHP	National Health Insurance and Contributing Pensions Committee	N. Chamberlain (C of Ex)	Mar 1935	1	27/582
NIC	National Insurance and Pension Schemes Committee	Clynes (HO)	Oct-Nov 1929	6	27/408
NIC	Committee on the next Imperial Conference	Thomas (DO)	Apr 1934	1	27/569
NIC(SUB)	National Insurance and Pensions Scheme Sub-Committee	Arnold (PMG)	June-Nov 1930	15	27/409
NIU	Northern Ireland Unemployment Insurance Fund Committee	Cave (Ld Chan)	May-Aug 1925	5	27/279
NMA	Marriage Allowance for Naval Officers	Wood (Health)	Oct 1937-Mar 1938	3	27/636
NP	Naval Programme Committee	Salisbury (LPS)	Mar-July 1925	9	27/273
NP	Naval Programme Committee	Birkenhead (India)	Nov 1927-Feb 1928	6	27/355
NS	Unemployment: National Schemes	Greenwood (Health)	Nov 1929	2	27/397
NS	*Manpower Sub-Committee	Lloyd-Graeme (Trade)	Feb 1923-Jan 1938	16	57/1-3
NS(AMW)	*Manpower Allocation Sub-Committee	Labour	May-June 1939	2	57/30
NS(AR)	*Manpower Sub-Committee, to consider letter from ARP Committee	Admiralty	Dec 1924	1	57/12
NS(ARP)	*Manpower: Demands made by ARP Dept Sub-Committee	Gowers	June-Dec 1937	2	57/23
NS(CM)	*Manpower: Control Sub-Committee	Gowers	Feb-Nov 1938	13	57/27
NS(D)	*Manpower: Dilution Sub-Committee	Labour	Oct 1935-Feb 1936	3	57/17
NSH	National Services Handbook	Inskip (M Co-ord)	Dec 1938-Jan 1939	2	27/650
NS(HILL)	*National Service in Future War: Sir R. Hill's Sub-Committee	Admiralty	May 1923-Apr 1924	17	57/9
NS(LAB)	*Manpower: Recruiting for Armed Forces Sub-Committee	Admiralty	July 1923-July 1939	13	57/5
NS(MC)	*Manpower: Civilian Medical Boards Sub-Committee	Admiralty	Mar 1932-Sept 1938	14	57/15 and 16

Code	Committee	Chairman, at first meeting	Dates of first and last meetings	No. of meetings	PRO reference
NS(MED)	*National Service in Future War: Questions affecting Medical Services Sub-Committee	Health	Apr 1923–July 1926	15	CAB 57/8
NS(MOB)	*Manpower: Mobilisation Scheme Sub-Committee	Admiralty	Mar 1923–Oct 1932	9	57/4
NS(N)	*Manpower: Supply of Nurses in War Sub-Committee	Health	July 1936–July 1938	7	57/19 and 20
NS(NR)	*Manpower: National Registration Sub-Committee	Reg General	Jan–Feb 1937	4	57/21
NS(P)	*Manpower: Policy Sub-Committee	Morrison (D Lanc)	Apr 1939	1	57/29
NS(PW)	*Manpower: Sub-Committee on Course of Prices	Trade	Jan 1932–July 1933	5	57/14
NS(REL)	*Manpower: Reserved Occupation Sub-Committee	Admiralty	July–Oct 1925	2	57/13
NS(RIR)	*Manpower Demands in Recruiting and Industrial Requirements	Gowers	June–July 1937	2	57/24
NS(SRO)	*Manpower: Schedule of Reserved Occupations Sub-Committee	Labour	Feb–July 1939	6	57/28
NS(SW)	*Manpower: National Service in Future War Sub-Committee	Health	Oct 1923–Mar 1924	5	57/7
NS(T)	*Manpower: Technical	Morrison (D Lanc)	Mar–July 1939	5	57/30
NS(V)	*Manpower: Preparation and Maintenance of National Register Sub-Committee	Reg General	July 1923–July 1936	12	57/6
NS(W)	*Manpower: Wages and Dilution of Labour Sub-Committee	Gowers	Jan–Nov 1937	6	57/22
NS(WL)	*Manpower: War Emergency Legislation	Gowers	Oct–Dec 1937	2	57/25
NS(WR)	*Manpower: Women's Reserve Sub-Committee	Admiralty	Oct 1935–May 1936	4	57/18
O	This symbol was used as a prefix to the papers of the Ottawa Imperial Economic Conference, 1932. For full list see CAB 32				
OAS	*Army Organisation Committee	Inskip (M Co-ord)	Feb 1938	3	16/196
OB	*Oil Board	Peel, later Ormsby-Gore (Works)	June 1925–July 1939	45	50/1–8
OB(PR)	*Oil Board: Petroleum Products Reserves Sub-Committee	Crookshank (Mines)	Feb 1936–July 1939	24	50/13–17
OBS	*Oil Board Sub-Committee	Admiralty	Oct 1924–Mar 1933	4	50/10
OB(SC)	*Oil Board Sub-Committee	Stanhope (Adm)	Nov 1925–Dec 1928	4	50/9
OB(W)	*Oil Board Welbeck Aviation Spirit Sub-Committee	Mines Dept	Jan–June 1933	4	50/12
OC	The Optional Clause Sub-Committee	MacDonald (PM)	July–Aug 1929	3	27/392
OC	Committee on Proposed Imperial Economic Conference at Ottawa	Snowden (C of Ex)	Nov 1930–July 1932	15	27/441 and 473–475
OCC	*Oil Board: oil from Coal Sub-Committee	Falmouth	Apr 1937–Jan 1938	32	50/18 and 19
OCGA	*Optional Clause and General Act	Butler (FO)	Nov 1938	3	16/214
OCS	Organisation of Communications Services Committee	Samuel	Dec 1928–May 1929	5	32/68
ODC	*Oversea Defence Committee Minutes	Colonial Office	1904–July 1939	390	7/1–15
ODC(M)	*Oversea Defence Committee Memoranda	(Memoranda only)	1904–July 1931	—	8/1–52
ODC	*Oversea Defence Committee Minutes (Note: Not Minutes of Meetings)	(Memoranda only)	1919–1939		10/1–10

	Committee	Chairman, at first meeting	Dates of first and last meetings	No. of meetings	PRO reference CAB
ODC(R)	*Oversea Defence Committee Remarks	(Memoranda only)	1887–1939	—	9/1–21
ODM	Oversea Development and Migration Committee	Thomas (LPS)	June–Aug 1929	5	27/382
OF	Removal of parts of Royal Ordnance Factories Committee	(Memoranda only)	Apr 1936	—	27/604
OHW	Historical Section of CID Committee	Fisher (Ed)	July 1922–June 1923	6	27/212
OL	Ottawa Legislation: Cabinet Committee	N. Chamberlain (C of Ex)	Oct 1932	2	27/492
OMP	Use of Official Material in Publications Committee	(Memoranda only)	1923	—	27/213
OP	Opium Policy Committee	Home Office	Dec 1924	2	27/256
OP	Opium Policy Committee	Cecil of Chelwood (D Lanc)	May 1927	1	27/344
OS	*Official Secrets Act	Hoare (HO)	Dec 1938–Jan 1939	2	16/195
P	Pre-War Pensions Committee	Wedgwood (D Lanc)	Feb 1924	1	27/231
P	Policy Committee (Rating)	Churchill (C of Ex)	Jan–Apr 1928	10	27/364
P	Political Committee	MacDonald (PM)	Jan 1934–Apr 1935	6	27/562
P	Palestine	N. Chamberlain (PM)	Oct 1938–Aug 1939	12	27/651 and 652
PA	Poplar Audit Surcharges: Committee on	N. Chamberlain (Health)	Feb–Mar 1927	2	27/340
PA	Private Armament Industry: Committee on	Runciman (Trade)	Dec 1933	3	27/551
PAC	Proposed Aerial Convention: Committee on	Simon (FO)	May 1935	1	27/587
PAL	Palestine Committee	Devonshire (CO)	July 1923	4	27/222
PAL	Palestine Committee	Cunliffe-Lister (CO)	Apr 1932	1	27/486
PAS	*Concessions and Facilities in Portuguese Atlantic Ports in connection with Aviation	Foreign Office	Aug 1928	1	16/90
PB	Parliamentary Business Committee	Cave (Ld Chan)	July 1926	1	27/325
PC	Palestine Committee	Passfield (CO)	May 1930	1	27/423
PD	*Co-ordination and Control of Civil Authorities for Passive Defence Purposes in War	Treasury	June–Sept 1938	4	16/191
PDE	*Passive Defence, Evacuation Sub-Committee	Home Office	Sept 1938	1	16/191
PE	Employment Policy Committee	Elliot (Treasury)	Dec 1931–Jan 1932	4	27/468
PEC	Public Capital Expenditure	(Memoranda only)	1938	—	27/640
PEJ	Japan: Political and Economic Relations with Committee	MacDonald (PM)	Feb–June 1936	3	27/596
PFF	This symbol was used as a prefix to the papers of Conferences on the Protection of Fauna and Flora of Africa. For full list see CAB 58				
PFS	Pay of New Entrants in Fighting Services and Marriage Allowance for Navy Committee	Gilmour (Scotland)	Mar–May 1925	9	27/301

		Chairman, at first meeting	Dates of first and last meetings	No. of meetings	PRO reference CAB
PG	*Persian Gulf Sub-Committee	A. Chamberlain (FO)	July 1928–Mar 1929	9	16/93 and 94
PGC	*ARP at Works of Government Contractors	Treasury	Nov–Dec 1938	4	16/213
PGS	*Palestine Garrison Sub-Committee	Passfield (CO)	May 1930	1	16/97
PG(SUB)	*Persian Gulf: Sub-Committee on Political Control	Treasury	May–Oct 1929	4	16/95
PI	Petroleum Policy in Iraq Committee	Curzon (Ld Pres)	Feb 1925	1	27/268
PL	Political Levies Bill Committee	Birkenhead (India)	Feb 1925	2	27/269
PLR	Poor Law Reform Committee	Wheatley (Health)	Aug 1924	1	27/246
PM	This symbol was used as a prefix to the papers of Commonwealth Prime Ministers' meetings. For full list see CAB 32				
PMC	Note on an Economic General Staff	(Memoranda only)	Dec 1929	—	58/15
PMS	Produce Markets Committee	Baldwin (Ld Pres)	Dec 1933–June 1935	19	27/560
PMS(SUB)	Pigs and Bacon Sub-Committee of Produce Markets Committee	Halifax (Ed)	Jan–June 1935	3	27/561
PO	Public Order Committee	Cave (Ld Chan)	Nov 1925–Mar 1926	4	27/287
POC	*Priority Organisation Sub-Committee	Cunliffe-Lister (Trade)	May 1927	1	16/76
PP	Police Pay Committee	Clynes (LPS)	Mar 1924	1	27/235
PP	Policy Procedure Committee	Home Office	Mar 1928	10	27/370
PP	Petrol Prices Committee	Cunliffe-Lister (Trade)	Mar 1929	1	27/383
PP	Parliamentary Procedure Committee	MacDonald (PM)	Aug 1931	1	27/457
PP	Petroleum Production Bill Committee	Runciman (Trade)	Feb 1934	1	27/564
PP	Policy in Palestine Committee	Snowden (C of Ex)	July–Aug 1930	3	27/427
PPC	Proposed Imperial Preference for Palestine Committee	Cunliffe-Lister (CO)	Oct 1932	1	27/493
PPC	Preservation of Public Order Committee	Simon (HO)	Oct 1936	5	27/610
PRA	Reduction and Limitation of Armaments Committee on Policy	Cushenden (D Lanc)	Nov 1927–Mar 1929	16	27/361–363
PRP	*Preparation of Register of Property	(Memoranda only)	May 1939	—	16/215
PS	New Entrants in Fighting Services Pay and Marriage Allowance for Navy Committee	Gilmour (Scotland)	May 1925–May 1929	16	27/307 and 308
PSO	*Principal Supply Officers Committee	War Office; after 1932 Runciman; after 1936 Inskip	May 1924–July 1939	65	60/1–17
PSO(A)	*Principal Supply Officers Committee Warlike Stores Sub-Committee	Admiralty	Dec 1924–Mar 1925	5	60/22
PSO(AP)	*Principal Supply Officers, Anticipatory Purchases of Supplies Sub-Committee	Board of Trade	Feb 1931–Oct 1935	9	60/24
PSO(BT)	*Principal Supply Officers, Board of Trade Supply Organisation	Board of Trade	Oct 1927–June 1938	31	60/64–73
PSO(E)	*Principal Supply Officers, Prohibition of Export Sub-Committee	Board of Trade	Oct 1935	3	60/27

		Chairman, at first meeting	Dates of first and last meetings	No. of meetings	PRO reference
PSO(EA)	*Principal Supply Officers, Licensing of Exports of Arms and Ammunition Sub-Committee	Board of Trade	Apr–June 1933	8	CAB 60/26
PSO(MISC)	*Principal Supply Officers, Grouping of Miscellaneous Items Sub-Committee	War Office	May 1924	2	60/22
PSO(OG)	*Principal Supply Officers, Optical Glass Sub-Committee	DSIR	Jan–July 1932	7	60/25
PSO(OP)	*Principal Supply Officers, Optical Glass Sub-Committee	Admiralty	June–Dec 1925	3	60/22
PSO(SB)	*Principal Supply Officers, Supply Board	Admiralty	Nov 1927–May 1939	65	60/29–50
PSO(SBA)	*Principal Supply Officers, Area Organisation Sub-Committee	War Office	July 1933–Dec 1935	19	60/62 and 63
PSO(SBG)	*Principal Supply Officers, Gauges Sub-Committee	War Office (Sir Alfred Herbert from second meeting)	June 1929–Feb 1939	41	60/51–55
PSO(SBT)	*Principal Supply Officers, Machine Tool Sub-Committee	Vyle	Feb 1932–Mar 1939	28	60/56–61
PSO(SC)	*Principal Supply Officers, Formation of Supply Committee	Admiralty	May 1927	1	60/23
PSO(SO)	*Principal Supply Officers, Supply Organisation in War Sub-Committee	Inskip (M Co-ord)	Jan–Nov 1937	4	60/28
PSO(SUB1)	*Principal Supply Officers, Armaments Sub-Committee	Admiralty	Oct 1924–Mar 1927	24	60/18
PSO(SUB2)	*Principal Supply Officers, Land Transport Sub-Committee	(Memoranda only)	1924–1925		60/18
PSO(SUB3)	*Principal Supply Officers, Scientific Stores Sub-Committee	Air Ministry	Oct 1924–Dec 1925	2	60/18
PSO(SUB4)	*Principal Supply Officers, Food Stuffs Sub-Committee	(Memoranda only)	1924–1925		60/19
PSO(SUB5)	*Principal Supply Officers, Medical and Veterinary Sub-Committee	War Office	Oct 1924–Dec 1925	5	60/19
PSO(SUB6)	*Principal Supply Officers, Hardwoods Sub-Committee	Works	Oct 1924–Dec 1925	7	60/20
PSO(SUB7)	*Principal Supply Officers, Metals and Hardwood Sub-Committee	War Office	Oct 1924–Dec 1925	8	60/20
PSO(SUB8)	*Principal Supply Officers, Oils, Paints and Chemicals Sub-Committee	Admiralty	Oct 1924–Oct 1925	15	60/20
PSO(SUB9)	*Principal Supply Officers, Textile Stores Sub-Committee	War Office	Oct 1924–Dec 1925	5	60/21
PSO(SUB10)	*Principal Supply Officers, Leather Stores Sub-Committee	War Office	Oct 1924–Sept 1925	7	60/21
PSO(SUB11)	*Principal Supply Officers, Engineers Construction Materials Sub-Committee	War Office	Sept–Nov 1924	2	60/21
PSO(SUB12)	*Principal Supply Officers, Engineers Construction Plant and Machinery Sub-Committee	War Office	Oct 1924–June 1925	3	60/21
PT	Physical Training Committee	N. Chamberlain (C of Ex)	Oct 1936–Jan 1937	4	27/612
PTC	*Postal and Telegraph Censorship Committee	GPO	Apr 1939	1	49/19
PVS	*Protection of Vital Services Committee	Treasury	July 1937–Mar 1938	3	16/176
PW	*Prisoners of War Committee	Foreign Office	May–July 1923	7	16/50
PW	Widows and Old-Age Pensions Committee	Churchill (C of Ex)	Apr 1925	3	27/276

		Chairman, at first meeting	Dates of first and last meeting	No. of meetings	PRO reference CAB
PWP	Pre-War Pensions Committee	Wood (Ed)	May 1923–Jan 1924	6	27/221
PWS	*Production of War-like Stores Sub-Committee	Worthington-Evans (PMG)	July–Dec 1923	3	16/51
RA	*Reduction and Limitation of Armaments Sub-Committee	Cecil of Chelwood	Jan 1930–Jan 1931	9	16/98
RA	Recruiting for the Army Committee	Stanhope (Works)	Dec 1936–Jan 1937	3	27/615
RA(BL)	*Reduction and Limitation of Armaments: Budgetary Limitation of Sub-Committee	Cecil of Chelwood	Apr–May 1930	2	16/99
RAI	*Inter-Departmental Committee on Preparations for Disarmament Conference	Foreign Office	Oct–Nov 1931	9	16/104
RA(SUB)	*Reduction and Limitation of Armaments Article 1B Disarmament Convention	Dalton (FO)	Nov–Dec 1930	2	16/100
RA(SUB)	Recruiting for the Army: Sub-Committee on Government and Local Authority	Tryon (PMG)	Dec 1936–Feb 1937	3	27/616
RA(TD)	* Reduction and Limitation of Armaments: Technical Details Sub-Committee	War Office	Feb 1931	1	16/101
RB	Russian Balances Committee	(Memoranda only)	1927	—	27/359
RB	Racecourse Betting Bill Committee	Churchill (C of Ex)	Mar–May 1928	2	27/371
RC	Russian Relations: Economic Conditions Committee	(Memoranda only)	1929	—	27/393
RC	Reparations Committee	N. Chamberlain (C of Ex)	May 1932	1	27/488
RCC	Coal Industry: Committee on Report of Royal Commission	Baldwin (PM)	Mar–Dec 1926	50	27/316–319
RCG	*Proposed Revision of the Geneva Red Cross Convention Sub-Committee	Cecil of Chelwood (D Lanc)	June 1925–June 1929	19	16/64–66
RCM	Reports of Committee on Courts Martial	Maugham (Ld Chan)	July 1939	1	27/658
RCR	Anglo-Russian Commercial Relations Committee	(Memoranda only)	Apr 1930	—	27/421
RD	Ribbon Development Committee	Cunliffe-Lister (CO)	Feb–Apr 1935	5	27/581
RH	Rural Housing and Slum Areas Committee	Salisbury (LPS)	Jan 1926	2	27/309
RLA	*Reduction and Limitation of Armaments Sub-Committee	Cecil of Chelwood (D Lanc)	Nov 1925	3	16/59 and 61
RLA	*Reduction and Limitation of Armaments Sub-Committee on Private Manufacture of Arms and Chemical Warfare (Gas Protocol)	Cecil of Chelwood (D Lanc)	Jan 1926–Nov 1928	24	16/71–74
RO	Ex-Ranker Officers Committee	Barnes	Apr 1924	7	27/238
ROC	*Overseas Defence Committee. Reprovisioning Period for Overseas Commands Sub-Committee	Admiralty	Mar 1937–Jan 1939	4	7/18
RP	Retail Prices Committee	Cunliffe-Lister (Trade)	May 1925	2	27/278

	Committee	Chairman, at first meeting	Dates of first and last meetings	No. of meetings	PRO reference CAB
RP	Retirement Pensions Committee	Alexander (Adm)	Dec 1929	3	27/402
RPM	*Civil Defence Measures taken after the Czechoslovak Crisis	Treasury	Oct–Nov 1938	3	16/190
RR	Rent Restrictions Acts and Rating Revaluation	Zetland (India)	Dec 1937–Feb 1938	3	27/637–638
RRC	Rent Restrictions Committee	Salisbury (Ld Pres)	Feb–Apr 1923	5	27/220
RS	Replacement of Fleet Units other than Capital Ships, and Singapore Sub-Committee	Clynes (LPS)	Feb–June 1924	5	27/236
RSC	Railway Situation Committee	Worthington-Evans (War)	Nov–Dec 1925	2	27/297
RTC	Indian Round Table Conference Cabinet Committee	MacDonald (PM)	Sept–Nov 1931	9	27/469
RTC(BURMA)	Indian Round Table Conference Committee	MacDonald (PM)	Nov 1931–Jan 1932	3	27/472
RTG	Rating Reform Committee	Griffith-Boscawen (Health)	Dec 1922–May 1923	3	27/207
RTS	Railway Trustee Securities Committee	Churchill (C of Ex)	Dec 1926	1	27/329
RWD	Reparations Committee and War Debts	N. Chamberlain (C of Ex)	Jan 1932	4	27/466
SA	Slaughtering of Animals Committee	Griffith-Boscawen (Health)	Feb–May 1923	2	27/214
SA	*South Africa: Co-operation in Defence with East African Colonies	Cabinet Office (Hankey)	May–June 1934	3	16/118
SAA	Sale of Arms and Ammunition Committee	Parmoor (Ld Pres)	July 1924	1	27/244
SAC	*Strategic Appreciation Committee	Chatfield (M Co-ord)	Mar–Apr 1939	6	16/209
SAF	*Supply of Arms to Foreign Countries Sub-Committee	(Memoranda only)	1926	—	16/69
SC	Situation in China Committee	Baldwin (PM)	July 1925	1	27/288
SCC	*Censorship: Standing Inter-Departmental Committee	War Office	May 1924–Nov 1938	24	49/1–7
SCC(FC)	*Censorship: Standing Inter-Departmental Film Censorship in War Committee	Admiralty	June–July 1936	3	49/17
SCC(IC)	*Censorship: Standing Inter-Departmental Inland Censorship Committee	Home Office	Feb–Mar 1931	2	49/16
SCC(TT)	*Censorship: Standing Inter-Departmental Censorship of Transit Telegrams	Admiralty	Apr–May 1936	4	49/18
SCC(WB)	*Censorship: Standing Inter-Departmental Censorship Chapter of War Book	War Office	Dec 1935	2	49/18
SCW	*Coal Supplies in War and Railway Wagon Stock	Mines Dept	Mar 1937–Mar 1939	9	16/180
SD	*Singapore Sub-Committee of COS	War Office	Feb–Mar 1928	2	16/91
SDC	Secret Documents Committee	(Memoranda only)	Apr 1926	—	27/321
SI	Safeguarding of Industries Act Committee	Churchill (C of Ex)	Jan 1925	2	27/264

	Committee	Chairman, at first meeting	Dates of first and last meetings	No. of meetings	PRO reference CAB
SI	Shipping Industry Committee	Maugham (Ld Chan)	Jan–Mar 1939	2	27/656
SIA	Safeguarding of Industries Act Committee	Salisbury (Ld Pres)	Mar 1923	1	27/217
SJC	Sutton Judgment Committee	Worthington-Evans (PMG)	June–July 1923	2	27/224
SOI	*Scientific and Optical Industry	DSIR	Apr–July 1939	5	16/216
SOI (IO)	*Scientific and Optical Industry Sub-Committee on Ideal Organisation of	DSIR	July 1939	1	16/217
SP	*Singapore: Sub-Committee	Curzon (Ld Pres)	Jan 1925–July 1928	8	16/63
SPO	*Protection for South Persian Oilfields Sub-Committee	Foreign Office	May 1924	1	16/54
SR	*Southern Rhodesia contributions to Imperial Defence Committee	Thomas (DO)	July 1934	1	16/117
SRC	Anglo-Soviet Relations Committee	MacDonald (PM)	Apr 1933	1	27/550
SRW	*Stationery Requirements for War Committee	Treasury	Dec 1937–Aug 1939	15	16/184–186
SS	Committee on the Speakers Seat	MacDonald (Ld Pres)	June–July 1935	3	27/588
SS	Situation in Spain Committee	Baldwin (PM)	Jan 1937	2	27/628
SSA	Northern Ireland Unemployment Insurance Fund Amalgamation of Social Services: Committee on	(Memoranda only)	1925	—	27/279
SS(JSC)	*The institution of a Joint Staff College Sub-Committee	Wood (Ed)	Feb–May 1923	3	16/45
ST	Supply and Transport Organisation Committee	Bridgeman (HO)	July 1923	2	27/205
ST	Supply and Transport Organisation Committee	Hoare (HO)	Dec 1924–July 1927	34	27/260 and 261, 331–334
ST	Supply and Transport Organisation Committee	Samuel (HO)	Jan–Mar 1932	8	27/477
STC	The Supreme Tribunals (Additional Judges) Committee	Cave (Ld Chan)	May 1927	1	27/342
SWA	*Allocation of Short Wavelengths Sub-Committee of ICC	Air Ministry	May–Nov 1928	5	35/40
TAC	Trade and Agriculture Committee	N. Chamberlain (C of Ex)	Apr 1936–Mar 1939	19	27/619–621
TB	Trade Boards Committee	Cave (Ld Chan)	Dec 1925	1	27/298
TC	Transference Committee	Clynes (HO)	Oct 1929	2	27/400
TCA	*Treatment of Civil Aircraft Committee	Foreign Office	July 1936–June 1938	3	16/169
TC(B)	Supply and Transport Committee: Dock Strike and Rail Strike 1924 Bulletins	(Memoranda only)	Jan–Feb 1924	—	27/257 and 258
TC(OB)	*Treatment of Coal Sub-Committee of Oil Board	Admiralty	Nov 1929–July 1930	6	50/11–17
TCS	Position of Co-operative Societies for Income Tax	N. Chamberlain (C of Ex)	Feb 1923	2	27/546
TE	Tax Evasion Revision Committee	Churchill (C of Ex)	Feb–Mar 1927	4	27/338
TEC	Trade and Unemployment Committee	MacDonald (PM)	Nov 1932–Feb 1934	10	27/502
TEC(P)	Trade and Unemployment Panel	MacDonald (PM)	Nov 1932–Feb 1934	3	27/503

	Committee	Chairman, at first meeting	Dates of first and last meetings	No. of meetings	PRO reference CAB
TLV	Track Laying Vehicles Committee	Baldwin (Ld Pres)	Jan 1934	1	27/559
TMC	Trawling in Moray Firth and Forth of Clyde Committee	(Memoranda only)	1932	—	27/481
TP	Transport Policy Committee	MacDonald (PM)	Jan–Mar 1933	2	27/545
TPC	Trade Policy Committee	Snowden (C of Ex)	Dec 1930	5	27/435
TR	Tithe Rent Committee	Salisbury (LPS)	Dec 1925	1	27/299
TR	Trade with Russia Committee	N. Chamberlain (C of Ex)	Jan–May 1932	4	27/480
TR	Tithe Rent Charge Committee	Hailsham (Ld Chan)	Dec 1935–Feb 1936	5	27/595
TRC	Tithe Rent Charge Committee	Salisbury (LPS)	Feb–Apr 1925	5	27/270
TRC	Tin Restriction Committee	Passfield (CO)	Feb 1931	2	27/447
TSC	School Teachers Superannuation Bill Committee	Cave (Ld Chan)	Feb–Mar 1925	4	27/265
TSC	Trade Survey Committee	MacDonald (PM)	Apr–July 1931	4	27/451
TS/R/16	Conferences between United Kingdom and Dominions Representatives on Meat Situation	Thomas (DO)	July 1934–Feb 1935	8	27/567
TS/T/10&12	Anglo-Persian Oil Company and Asiatic Petroleum Company Agreement	Baldwin (PM)	Feb–Nov 1928	2	27/368
TTC	Time Table Committee	Churchill (C of Ex)	Oct 1928	1	27/377
TU	Trade and Unemployment: Inter-Departmental Committee	(Memorandum only)	1928	—	27/376
TU	Trade Disputes and Trades Union Bill Committee	Sankey (Ld Chan)	Mar–Apr 1930	2	27/418
TU	Trade Unions Bill (Amendments) Committee	Henderson (FO)	Feb 1931	2	27/446
TUB	Trade Unions Bill (Amendments) Committee	Churchill (C of Ex)	May–June 1927	7	27/346
TWR	*Technical Wireless Regulations Sub-Committee of ICC	Air Ministry	Apr 1925–Jan 1927	44	35/36–39
TX	Taxation Committee	Churchill (C of Ex)	Feb 1926	1	27/311
UAR	Unemployment Assistance Board: Committee on Drafting Regulations	N. Chamberlain (C of Ex)	Nov 1934–July 1936	19	27/575 and 576
UC	Unemployment Committee	MacDonald (PM)	Sept–Nov 1932	8	27/490
U/E/4	Forestry: Conference on 10 March 1924	Adamson (Scotland)	Mar 1924	1	27/252
UGM	*Urgent Government Messages: Sub-Committee on Prefixes	Foreign Office	Jan 1931	1	15/26
UI	Unemployment Insurance Committee	Cave (Ld Chan)	Jan–Feb 1923	3	27/210
UI	Unemployment Insurance Committee	Shaw (Labour)	Mar 1924	2	27/237
UI	Unemployment Insurance Bill Committee	Baldwin (PM)	May–June 1925	3	27/280
UI	Unemployment Insurance Committee	N. Chamberlain (C of Ex)	Dec 1932–Apr 1933	7	27/501
U/I/8	Unemployment Grants	Clynes (LPS)	June–July 1924	1	27/245
UIA	Unemployment Insurance for Agriculture Committee	Gilmour (HO)	Jan–Dec 1936	4	27/580
UIB	Unemployment Insurance Bill Committee	Steel-Maitland (Labour)	June 1927	1	27/348

	Committee	Chairman, at first meeting	Dates of first and last meetings	No. of meetings	PRO reference
UIC	Unemployment Insurance Bill Committee	Bondfield (Labour)	July 1929–June 1930	6	CAB 27/396
UIC	Unemployment Insurance Policy Committee	N. Chamberlain (C of Ex)	May–Nov 1933	6	27/552
UIF	Unemployment Insurance Finance Committee	Bondfield (Labour)	Aug 1931	1	27/458
UI(RC)	Unemployment Insurance Committee	Henderson (FO)	June–July 1931	12	27/452
UK	This symbol was used as a prefix to the papers of the United Kingdom Delegation at Imperial Conferences. For full list see CAB 32				
UP	Unemployment Policy Committee	Churchill (C of Ex)	July 1928	3	27/374
UP	Unemployment Panel of Ministers	MacDonald (PM)	June 1930–May 1931	27	27/438–440
U/P/1	Juvenile Unemployment Committee	Guinness (Treasury)	Dec 1923	1	27/228
U/P/1A	Juvenile Unemployment Committee	N. Chamberlain (C of Ex)	Jan 1924	2	27/228
UPC	Unemployment Policy Committee	Snowden (C of Ex)	June–July 1924	8	27/242
UPC	Unemployment Policy Committee	Snowden (C of Ex)	Mar 1930	2	27/413
UPM	Unemployment Policy Committee: Migration Sub-Committee	Worthington-Evans (War)	July 1928	3	27/374
UPS	Unemployment Policy: Second Committee	Churchill (C of Ex)	Nov 1928	1	27/375
VCS	*Vulnerability of Capital Ships to Air Attack Committee	Inskip (M Co-ord)	Mar–Aug 1936	10	16/147
VPC	Valuation, Rating and Poor Law Reform Committee	N. Chamberlain (Health)	Dec 1924–June 1925	7	27/263
WB	*War Book: Various Editions	Various	1911–1939	—	15/1–21
WB	Waterloo Bridge Committee	Baldwin (Ld Pres)	May 1932	1	27/387
WBC	*Wire Broadcasting	Wallace (Treasury)	Jan–Feb 1939	5	16/212
WEL	*War Emergency Legislation Committee	Haldane (Ld Chan)	Jan 1925–Dec 1934	9	52/1–4
WH	Weir Houses Committee	N. Chamberlain (Health)	Feb 1925	2	27/266
WHC	Washington Hours Convention Committee	Cecil (D Lanc)	Feb–Mar 1927	2	27/341
WL	*War Emergency Legislation Committee	Lord Chancellor's Dept	July 1937–Sept 1939	16	52/5 and 6
WL(DR)	*War Legislation Defence Regulations Sub-Committee	Home Office	June 1938–Mar 1939	4	52/7
WL(O)	*War Legislation Departmental Orders	(Memoranda only)	1939	1	52/8
WM	*Wireless Messages Sub-Committee	Gilmour (Scotland)	Feb 1928	1	16/89
WMC	War Material and Warships Committee	Hartshorn (LPS)	Jan–Mar 1931	2	27/445
WOP	*War Office Production Committee	Treasury	June 1936	1	16/148
WOP	Widows, Orphans and Old Age Contributory Pensions Committee	Peel (Works)	July 1925	1	27/285
WPC	War Pensions Committee	Tryon (Pensions)	May 1925	1	27/277
WQC	Agricultural Policy: Wheat Quota and Marketing Bill Committee	Addison (Ag)	July 1930	5	27/428

		Chairman, at first meeting	Dates of first and last meetings	No. of meetings	PRO reference CAB
WRC	*War Room Communications Committee	Air Ministry	Jan–May 1939	3	16/210
WRI	War Risks Insurance Legislation Committee	Runciman (Ld Pres)	July 1939	1	27/655
WSO	Organisation of Imperial Wireless Services Committee	Robert Donald	May–Oct 1924	12	27/241
WTC	Wireless Telephony Committee	Thompson (Air)	Nov 1929–Feb 1930	7	27/403–404
WT(SUB)	*Wireless Sub-Committee of ICC	Norman	Apr 1919–June 1927	37	35/9–11
Y	*Location of Staffs	Treasury	Feb–May 1938	2	16/188
ZL	Authority of Zinoviev Letter Committee	MacDonald (PM)	Nov 1924	1	27/254
ZI	*Zinc Imports	Riverdale of Sheffield	June–Nov 1937	8	16/173

PART 3

		Chairman, at first meeting	Dates of first and last meetings	No. of meetings	PRO reference (CAB)
A	Africa Committee	Cranborne (CO)	Aug 1942–Feb 1943	4	95/10
AA(S)	*Deputy Chiefs of Staff Committee: shadow sub-committee on allocation of active air defence (1940–1944)	Air Ministry	Oct 1940–Mar 1944	29	82/29
AC	Civil Aviation	Air Ministry	July 1941–Jan 1942	16	87/85
ACA	Ministerial Committee on Armistice terms and Civil Administration	Attlee (Dep PM)	Aug 1943–Apr 1944	17	87/83 and 84
ACE	Engineering Stores Advisory Committee	Hankey (D Lanc)	May 1941–Aug 1942	41	92/113 and 114
ACE(DP)	Engineering Advisory Committee (defence services panel)	(Memoranda only)	Jan 1943	—	90/7
AC(S)	Statistics: Advisory Committee	CSO	1941	3	108/39
AD	Allied Demands Committee	Supply	Sept–Nov 1939	5	92/18 and 19
ADA	Discussions on Article VII, Mutual Aid Agreement UK/USA	Treasury	Sept 1943–Mar 1944	24	99/33
ADA(J)	Anglo-Dutch-American technical conversations	Moyne	Oct 1940–Jan 1941	5	99/8
	Anglo-Dutch-American technical conversations	(Memoranda only)	Oct 1940	—	99/8
ADGB	*Ad Hoc Committee on Air Defence Great Britain	War Office	Nov 1941	1	81/63
AD(S)	Allied Demands: Supply Sub-Committee	ECGD	Nov 1939–July 1940	13	92/20 and 21
A(E)	Africa Committee: Sub-Committee on Ethiopia	Dominions Office	Jan–June 1943	2	95/10
AEA	Allied African Economic Affairs	Economic Warfare	Nov 1942–July 1943	13	95/9
AEA	Allied African Economic Affairs	Economic Warfare	Jan–Oct 1944	4	95/17
AEA(C)	Allied African Economic Affairs: Chairman's Sub-Committee	Economic Warfare	Mar–Dec 1943	31	95/13
AEA(W)	British Missions in Washington: African Economic Affairs	Washington minutes	1944	—	92/52
AFC(PW)	Anglo-French Post-War Collaboration Inter-Departmental Committee	Hankey (w.p.)	Apr–May 1940	2	85/18
AFE	Royal Air Force Establishments	Attlee (Dep PM)	Aug 1943–Jan 1944	7	98/33
AFO	Anglo-French Allied Forces (Official) Committee	Foreign Office	July 1940–Apr 1943	33	85/19–21
AFSP	Anglo-French Supply and Purchases Committee	Supply	Oct–Dec 1939	4	85/15
AFSP(EW)	Anglo-French Economic Warfare Purchases Committee	Economic Warfare	Nov 1939	1	85/15
AG	Civil Defence: Anti-Gas Precautions Committee	Attlee (DO)	Apr 1942	1	73/23
A(IT)	Africa Committee: Sub-Committee on Inland Transport	MacMillan (CO)	Aug–Dec 1942	6	95/11
AJX	Operation 'Ajax'	Brooke (C in C Home Forces)	Oct 1941	4	98/54
AL	American liaison	Oliver Stanley	May–Dec 1941	8	99/9

		Chairman, at first meeting	Dates of first and last meetings	No. of meetings	PRO reference CAB
AO	Oil Policy: Technical Sub-Committee on Axis Oil	Harold Hartley	May 1942–Nov 1945	37	77/19–28
AP	Portuguese liaison	Joint	Mar 1941	8	99/10 and 11
AP	Anglo-Portuguese negotiations, 'INGOT' mission	Joint	June–July 1943	16	99/37
AP2	Portuguese liaison: report and proceedings	Joint	Oct–Nov 1941	9	99/12 and 13
APP	Portuguese liaison: papers	(Memoranda only)	1941–1942	—	99/14
APP	Anglo-Portuguese negotiations, 'INGOT' mission				99/37
APW	Armistice and Post-War Committee	Attlee (Dep PM)	Apr 1944–June 1945	35	87/66–69
ARD	Lord President's Committee: Air Raid Damage and Shelter Policy	N. Chamberlain (Ld Pres) (Churchill later in 1940)	Sept–Oct 1940	11	71/23 and 24
ASC	Co-ordination of Allied Supplies: Civil Supplies Sub-Committee	Shipping	Jan–Oct 1941	19	92/26
ASD(TRADE)	Discussions on Article VII, Mutual Aid Agreement UK/USA	(Memoranda only)	Feb 1944		99/35
ASE	Allied Supplies Executive	Beaverbrook (Supply)	Oct 1941–Sept 1945	48	92/1–9
ASE(C)	Allied Supplies Executive: Supplies to China Sub-Committee	Assheton (Supply)	Nov 1942–May 1945	15	92/11 and 12
ASE(ME)	Allied Supplies Executive: Middle East Sub-Committee	Grigg (War Office)	Nov 1941–May 1942	12	92/17
ASE(OA)	Allied Supplies Executive: Supplies to other Allies Sub-Committee	(Memoranda only)	1941–1945	—	92/14–16
ASE(OC)	Allied Supplies Executive: Chinese Oil Sub-Committee	Petroleum Dept	Apr–Oct 1942	5	92/13
ASE(PG)	Allied Supplies Executive: Civil Supplies in Persian Gulf Sub-Committee	Grigg (War Office)	Jan 1942	1	92/13
ASE(R)	Allied Supplies Executive: Supplies to Russia and Persian Gulf Sub-Committee	Llewellyn (Trans)	Nov–Dec 1941	3	92/13
ASE(T)	Allied Supplies Executive: Transportation Sub-Committee	Portal (Works)	May 1942–Nov 1943	4	92/10
AT	Civil Air Transport: British-United States, informal discussions	(Memoranda only)	Apr 1944	—	87/87
ATL	Civil Air Transport: British-Commonwealth conversations	Beaverbrook (LPS)	Oct 1943	3	87/86
AT(US)	Civil Air Transport: informal discussions with United States	Beaverbrook (LPS)	Apr 1944	6	87/88
AU	Anti-U-Boat Warfare Committee	Churchill (PM)	Nov 1942–Jan 1945	41	86/2–7
B	Broadcasting Committee	Woolton (Recon)	May 1944–Apr 1945	8	76/16
BA	Battle of Atlantic Committee	Churchill (PM)	Feb 1941–May 1942	20	86/1
BAC	*COS Committee: 'Bolero' accommodation	War Office	May 1942–Feb 1944	23	81/51
BAC(O)	*COS Committee: 'Bolero' accommodation	(Memoranda only)	1942	—	81/51
BAR	Moscow Conference	Molotov, Beaverbrook, Harriman	Oct 1941	11	99/7
BA(S)	Battle of Atlantic Committee: Imports into UK	(Memoranda only)	Apr 1941–Feb 1942	—	86/1
BC	Basra Committee	Amery (India)	April 1941	2	95/5

	Chairman, at first meeting	Dates of first and last meetings	No. of meetings	PRO reference
BC(L)	*COS Committee: 'Bolero' Combined Committee (London)	Findlater Stewart	May–Nov 1942	21	CAB 81/48
BCM	British Commonwealth Meeting	Cranborne (DO)	April 1945	12	99/30
BE	Basic English	Amery (India)	Oct–Nov 1943	5	98/30 and 31
BH	Conference on British-US production	Beaverbrook (Supply) Harriman	Sept 1941	2	99/6
BIE	Civil Defence: blackout restrictions in industrial establishments	Morrison (HO)	July–Aug 1943	2	73/19
BOC	Civil Defence: Blackout Committee	Privy Council Office	Aug–Sept 1940	4	73/15
BP	*COS Committee: 'Bolero' panel	(Memoranda only)	May–July 1942	—	81/52
BR	Civil Defence: Inter-Departmental Committee on Blackout Restrictions	Harcourt Johnston (DOT)	Aug 1941–Jan 1943	8	73/20
BRC	Civil Defence: Blackout Restrictions Committee	Morrison (HO)	Mar–July 1944	3	73/22
BUS	British-US staff conversations	(Memoranda only)	Jan–Apr 1941	—	99/5
BUS(J)	British-US staff conversations	Joint	Jan–Mar 1941	14	99/5
BW	*COS Committee: bacteriological warfare	Hankey (w.p.)	Feb 1940–June 1942	6	81/53
BW	*COS Committee: Biological Warfare Inter-Services Sub-Committee	Air Ministry	July 1944–Nov 1946	10	81/58
BWB	Action in event of war with Bulgaria	(Memoranda only)	Nov 1940–Feb 1941	—	107/5
BW(D)	*COS Committee: bacteriological warfare (defence)	Duff-Cooper (D Lanc)	Mar 1943–Apr 1944	3	81/57
BW(O)	*COS Committee: bacteriological warfare (operational panel)	Ernest Brown (D Lanc)	Jan 1944	1	81/56
BW(P)	*COS Committee: bacteriological warfare (Porton experiments)	Air Ministry	Sept 1940–Nov 1941	9	81/54
BW(P)	*COS Committee: bacteriological warfare (policy panel)	Ernest Brown (D Lanc)	Dec 1943–Apr 1944	3	81/55
CA	Communist activities	Anderson (Ld Pres)	Jan–Feb 1941	3	98/18
CAdC	Combined Administrative Committee	Joint	June 1943–Apr 1945	39	88/45–48
CAI	Control of Air Forces in Iraq	Air Ministry	Aug 1941	4	95/6
CAS	Co-ordination of Allied supplies	Hankey (D Lanc)	Dec 1940–Oct 1941	37	92/22–25
CAS(X)	Co-ordination of Allied supplies	(Memoranda only)	July–Oct 1941	—	92/25
CAT	Post-war civil air transport	Cranborne (LPS)	July 1943–July 1944	14	87/61 and 62
CB	Dieppe Raid	(Report only)		—	98/22
CBC	'Crossbow'	Churchill (PM)	June 1944–Mar 1945	20	98/36–38
CC	Compulsory Censorship	N.Chamberlain(LdPres)	June 1940	1	76/13
CCAC	Combined Civil Affairs Committee	Joint	July 1943–Jan 1947	57	88/63–72
CCAC(S)	Combined Civil Affairs (Supply) Sub-Committee	Joint	1943–1946	97	88/73–77
CCMA	Commonwealth Committee munitions assignment	Production	May–Nov 1942	12	99/15
CCP	Commercial policy	Anderson (C of Ex)	Aug–Nov 1944	4	87/97
CCS	'Argonaut' Conference (Malta and Crimea)	Joint	Jan–Feb 1945	—	99/31
CCS	Combined COS Committee	Joint	Jan 1942–1945	200	88/1–44

		Chairman, at first meeting	Dates of first and last meetings	No. of meetings	PRO reference CAB
CCS	Chiefs of Staff (London) Conference	Joint	July 1942	2	99/19
CCS	'Octagon' Conference (*Queen Mary* and Quebec)	Joint	Sept 1944	—	99/29
CCS	'Quadrant' Conference (Quebec)	Joint	Aug–Sept 1943	—	99/23
CCS	'Trident' Conference (Washington and North Africa)	Joint	May–June 1943	—	99/22
CCW	*COS Inter-Service Committee on Chemical Warfare	Air Ministry	Sept 1940–Oct 1945	28	81/15–18
CCW(CD)	*COS: Sub-Committee on Crop Destruction	Air Ministry	Aug 1944	1	81/19
CCW(L)	*COS: Sub-Committee on Employment of Chemical Warfare in War against Japan	Air Ministry	May–Dec 1944	4	81/19
CDA	Civil Defence: Ministerial Committee on Co-ordination of Departmental Action	Anderson (HO)	May 1940	9	73/11
CDC	Civil Defence: Ministerial Committee	Anderson (HO)	Sept 1939–May 1945	160	73/1–8
CDC(E)	Civil Defence: Sub-Committee on Civil Defence Executive	Officials (unnamed)	Sept 1940–Mar 1943	159	73/9 and 10
CDC(W)	Civil Defence: Sub-Committee on Winter Plans	Home Office	Aug 1944	4	73/12
CFR	Anglo-French: Foreign (Allied) Resistance Committee	Economic Warfare	Aug 1940–Jan 1943	152	85/22–26
CFR (Syria)	Foreign (Allied) Resistance (Syria) Committee	Economic Warfare	July–Dec 1941	8	95/7
CFR(EP)	Anglo-French: Foreign (Allied) Resistance: Sub-Committee on Economic Pressures	Foreign Office	Aug 1940–Nov 1941	80	85/27–28
CFR(MISC)	Anglo-French: Foreign (Allied) Resistance Committee	(Memoranda only)	Dec 1941–Mar 1942	—	85/26
CFR(WS)	Anglo-French: Foreign (Allied) Resistance: Sub-Committee on Welfare Security	Bessborough	Aug 1940–Feb 1941	23	85/30
CI	Organisation of the Coal Industry	Anderson (C of Ex)	Oct 1943–Feb 1944	4	87/93
CIC	Combined Intelligence Committee	Joint	May 1942–Oct 1945	30	88/57–60
CIS	Combined Intelligence Staff	Joint	Aug 1943–Feb 1944	18	88/62
CISC	Combined Intelligence Sub-Committee	Joint	Feb 1942–Aug 1943	57	88/61
CL(CCS 32nd meeting)	London Conference	Joint	July 1942	2	99/19
CLR	Civil Defence: Committee on Lighting Restrictions	Hoare (LPS)	Oct–Nov 1939	3	73/16 and 17
CM	Coal Mining Industry	Anderson (Ld Pres)	Apr–May 1942	14	87/92
CM	War Cabinet Conclusions and Confidential Annexes	Churchill (PM)	May–July 1945	17	65/53 and 54
CMB	Policy in Malaya and Borneo	Attlee (Dep PM)	Mar–Dec 1944	2	98/41
CMC	Combined Meteorological Committee	Joint	Nov 1942–Dec 1945	87	88/82
CMT	Combined Military Transportation Committee	Joint	Feb 1942–Dec 1945	96	88/88–95
COH	Control of Official Histories	Ramsbottom (Ed)	Apr 1940–June 1945	8	98/7–12
COH(U)	Control of Official Histories Advisory Committee	Butler (Ed)	Dec 1941–Jan 1944	4	98/13–16
COP	Offices or places of profit under the Crown	Greenwood (w.p.)	Nov 1941–Jan 1942	2	98/21
COS	*COS Committee: minutes	Rotates	Sept 1939–Dec 1946	1995	79/1–54

		Chairman, at first meeting	Dates of first and last meetings	No. of meetings	PRO reference CAB
COS	*COS Committee: memoranda	(Memoranda only)	Sept 1939–Dec 1946	—	80/1–55
COS	'Argonaut' Conference (Malta and Crimea)	Joint	June 1942	—	99/31
COS	'Sextant' Conference (Malta, Cairo, Teheran)	Joint	Nov 1943	—	99/25
COS	'Eureka' Conference (Teheran)	Joint	Dec 1943	—	99/25
COS	'Octagon' Conference (Queen Mary and Quebec)	Joint	Sept 1944	—	99/29
COS(41)504	'Riviera'; Discussions of Joint Chiefs of Staff	Joint	Aug 1941	—	99/18
COS(43)33(O)	'Symbol' Conference (Casablanca)	Joint	Jan 1943	—	99/24
COS(43)256(O)	'Trident' Conference (Washington and North Africa)	Joint	May–June 1943	—	99/22
COS(43)513(O)	'Quadrant' Conference (White House meetings)	Joint	Aug–Sept 1943	—	99/23
COS(AA)	*COS Sub-Committee on Active Air Defence	Air Ministry	Oct 1940–Dec 1946	64	82/13–20, 27 and 28
COS(AA)(O)	*COS Sub-Committee on Active Air Defence	Air Ministry	Apr–June 1942	3	82/21
COS(DA)	*COS Sub-Committee on Defence of Aerodromes	Air Ministry	Nov 1940–Sept 1942	15	81/20
COS(INV)	*COS Inter-Service Committee on Invasion	(Memoranda only)	Nov–Dec 1940	—	81/62
COS(O)	*COS: (operations) minutes	Rotates	Sept 1940–Dec 1944	—	79/55–85
COS(O)	*COS: (operations) memoranda	(Memoranda only)	Sept 1939–Dec 1946	—	80/56–103
COS(O)(JP)	*COS: joint planning memoranda	(Memoranda only)	Sept–Dec 1940	—	80/106
COS(Q)	'Quadrant' Conference (Quebec)	Joint	Aug–Sept 1943	—	99/23
COS(S)	*COS: secret memoranda series	(Memoranda only)	Dec 1939–May 1940	—	80/104–105
COS(T)	'Trident' Conference (Washington and North Africa)	Joint	May–June 1943	—	99/22
COS(VICTOR 2)	*'Victor' COS Committee	Admiralty	Feb 1942	6	81/61
CP	War Cabinet memoranda	(Memoranda only)	May–July 1945	—	66/66 and 67
CPA	Reconstruction: problems on central planning	Maxwell-Fyfe (Solicitor General)	June 1942	10	87/20
CPB	Cypher Policy Board	GCCS	Feb 1944–Sept 1945	5	98/44–45
CPE	Policy in regard to Ethiopia	Anderson (Ld Pres)	Oct–Nov 1941	6	95/3
CPR	Economic Policy: post-war commodity policy and relief	Economic Warfare	Mar–Oct 1942	6	72/19 and 20
CPR(FE)	Economic Policy: Far Eastern Sub-Committee	Economic Warfare	Nov 1942	1	72/19
CPS	Combined Planning Staff	Joint	June 1942–Apr 1945	125	88/50–56
CR	'Arcadia': Washington War Conference	Joint	Dec 1941–Jan 1942	—	99/17
CR(JPS)	'Arcadia': Washington War Conference	Joint	Dec 1941–Jan 1942	—	99/17
CRP	Committee on Refugee Problems	Hoare (HO)	Jan–Dec 1939	7	98/1
CRT	Radio Transmission Committee	(Memoranda only)	Sept 1939–Jan 1941	—	98/2
CS	Statistics: Anglo-American statement of munitions and war-like stores	(Memoranda only)	1942–1945	—	108/46–53
CSA	*COS: Principal Administrative Officers Sub-Committee	War Office	May 1942–Dec 1945	172	81/28–38

		Chairman, at first meeting	Dates of first and last meetings	No. of meetings	PRO reference CAB
CSA(O)	*COS: Principal Administrative Officers Sub-Committee	('Most Secret' minutes of CSA meetings)	May 1942–Aug 1945	—	81/28–38
CS(C)	Statistics: Canadian output	(Memoranda only)	1942	—	108/69
CS(EG)	Statistics: Eastern output	(Memoranda only)	1942	—	108/70
CSO(MA)	Statistics: munitions assignments	(Memoranda only)	1942–1945	—	108/71–84
CSO(RM)	Statistics: UK raw materials	(Memoranda only)	1944–1945	—	108/86–88
CS(S)	Statistics: general	(Memoranda only)	1941–1945	—	108/33–38
CS(UK)	Statistics: UK output	(Memoranda only)	1942–1945	—	108/54–68
CSO(US)	Statistics: supply to USA	CSO	1941–1942	11	108/40–42
CWC	Treatment of War Criminals	Simon (Ld Chan)	July–Nov 1942	5	98/23
DAC	*COS: Ad Hoc Sub-Committee; aerodrome defence	Findlater Stewart	May–Nov 1941	19	81/21
DBC	*COS: Sub-Committee; defence of bases	Admiralty	Feb 1943–Dec 1945	31	81/7–11
DC	Demobilisation	Jowitt (w.p.)	Aug–Nov 1943	12	87/96
DCM	Imperial Communications and Censorship Committee: issue of warnings against discussions of confidential matters in public places	Churchill (Adm)	Oct 1939	1	76/15
DCM(O)	Imperial Communications and Censorship Committee: issue of warnings against discussions of confidential matters in public places (official)	Treasury	Oct 1939	2	76/15
DCOS	*Deputy Chiefs of Staff Committee	Rotates	Sept 1939–Dec 1946	112	82/1–12
DCOS(AA)	*Deputy Chiefs: Sub-Committee on Active Air Defence	Air Ministry	Dec 1939–Oct 1940	22	82/13 and 14
DCOS(IT)	*Deputy Chiefs: Sub-Committee on Inter-Service training	Admiralty	Dec 1939–Feb 1940	2	82/22 and 23
DCOS(PF)	*Deputy Chiefs: Sub-Committee on Defence Services Police Forces	War Office	Apr 1940	1	82/25
DCOS(VP)	*Deputy Chiefs: Sub-Committee on Vulnerable Points	Home Office	Feb–Apr 1940	6	82/24
DC(S)	Defence Committee (supply)	Churchill (PM)	June 1940–Mar 1945	58	70/1–7
DI	Distribution of Industry	Bevin (Labour)	Oct 1944–Mar 1945	7	87/94
DIO	*COS:Sub-Committee on Defence Arrangements for the Indian Ocean	War Office	Jan 1942–Jan 1943	22	81/4–6
DMV	Visit of Dominion Ministers and Indian Representative	N. Chamberlain (PM)	Nov 1939	8	99/1
DMV(A)	Visit of Dominion Ministers and Indian Representative	(Memoranda only)	Nov 1939	—	99/2
DMV(C)	Visit of Dominion Ministers and Indian Representative	Eden (DO)	Nov 1939	14	99/2
DMV(G)	Visit of Dominion Ministers and Indian Representative	(Memoranda only)	Nov 1939	—	99/1
DMV(I)	Visit of Dominion Ministers and Indian Representative	Supply	Nov 1939	2	99/2
DMV(U)	Visit of Dominion Ministers and Indian Representative	Supply	Nov–Dec 1939	7	99/2

		Chairman, at first meeting	Dates of first and last meetings	No. of meetings	PRO reference CAB
DMV(Z)	Visit of Dominion Ministers and Indian Representative	Supply	Nov–Dec 1939	14	99/2
DO	Defence Committee (operations)	Churchill (PM)	May 1940–Dec 1945	190	69/1–7
DPM	Dominion Prime Ministers Meeting (preparations)	Cranborne (DO)	Feb–Apr 1944	4	99/27
DS	Committee on Dyestuffs	Hankey (w.p.)	Mar–May 1940	2	98/5
DSA	Committee on Disclosure to USA of secret information relating to supply matters	Beaverbrook (MAP)	Dec 1940–Jan 1941	3	92/117
EA	Policy in Ethiopia	Anderson (C of Ex)	July–Oct 1944	2	95/16
EC	Post-war employment	Treasury	July 1943–Jan 1944	30	87/63
EC	Working party on controls	Reconstruction	Feb–Sept 1945	6	87/89
EC(O)	Post-war employment	(Memoranda only)	Nov 1943–Jan 1944	—	87/70
EEP	External Economic Policy	Anderson (C of Ex)	Feb 1944	6	87/95
EFA	Allied African Economic Affairs	(Title changed to AEA)	Nov 1942	—	95/9
EGD	Civil Defence: Sub-Committee on Evacuation of Government Departments	Treasury	Sept 1939–Dec 1942	15	73/13
EGS	Economic Policy: economic general staff	(Memoranda only, incl reply to Mr Stettinius on Britain's Economic Organisation)	June–Dec 1940	—	72/24
EL	Lord President's Committee: emergency legislation	Lord Chancellor's Office	July 1943–Sept 1945	12	71/29 and 30
EMC	Electoral machinery	Morrison (HO)	Apr–Sept 1943	4	87/102
EP	Economic Policy Sub-Committee	Stamp and H. J. Wilson	Oct 1939–May 1940	18	72/6 and 7
EPE	Economic Policy: Eire	Attlee (DO)	Apr 1942–June 1944	9	72/25
EP(ES)(O)	Economic Policy: (official) export surpluses	Economic Warfare	Sept 1940–Nov 1941	27	72/15–17
EP(ES)(S)	Economic Policy: Export Surpluses Sugar Sub-Committee	Trade	Jan–Feb 1941	3	72/18
EP(EW)	Economic Policy: Inter-Departmental Committee on Economic Warfare	Economic Warfare	Dec 1939–Feb 1940	4	72/8 and 9
EP(M)	Economic Policy: Ministerial Committee	Simon (C of Ex)	Oct 1939–Dec 1940	40	72/1–5
EP(M)(E)	Economic Policy: Ministerial Sub-Committee on Encouragement of Exports	Stanley (Trade)	Nov 1939	1	72/10
EP(M)(ES)	Economic Policy: Ministerial Sub-Committee on Export Surpluses	Greenwood (w.p.)	Aug 1940–Nov 1941	10	72/13 and 14
EP(M)(EW)	Economic Policy: Ministerial Sub-Committee on Economic Warfare	Cross (MEW)	Nov–Dec 1939	3	72/11 and 12
EP(M)(PC)	Economic Policy: Ministerial Sub-Committee on Port Clearance	Moore Brabazon (Transport)	Dec 1940–Jan 1941	2	72/26

	Description	Chairman, at first meeting	Dates of first and last meetings	No. of meetings	PRO reference CAB
EP(M)(S)	Economic Policy: Statistical Digest	(Memoranda only)	Nov–Dec 1940	—	72/23
EP(SM)	Economic Policy: Sub-Committee on Substitute Materials	DSIR	Apr–Sept 1940	5	72/21
EP(W)(O)	Economic Policy: Official Committee on Warehousing	Trade	Nov–Dec 1940	3	72/22
ERP	Economic aspects of reconstruction problems	Greenwood (w.p.)	Oct 1941–Feb 1942	7	87/64
ESA	London Munitions Assignment Board: Engineer Stores Assignment Sub-Committee	Production	Aug 1942–Sept 1945	64	92/66–68
ES(D)	Export Surpluses Drafting Committee	(Memoranda only)	Sept–Dec 1940	—	72/27
ES(O)	Economic Policy: Sub-Committee on Export Surpluses	Economic Warfare	Mar–Apr 1942	2	72/17
ETS	Empire Telecommunications Services	Anderson (C of Ex)	July 1944–Oct 1945	10	76/7
ETS(O)	Empire Telecommunications Services: (Official) Committee	Treasury	July–Dec 1944	9	76/8
F	Fish Committee	Woolton (Ld Pres)	June 1945	2	98/42
FA	*COS: Inter-Departmental Committee on Airfields	Admiralty	Sept 1943–Aug 1944	11	81/59
FA(C)	*COS: Co-ordinating Committee on Floating Airfields	Admiralty	Dec 1943–Jan 1944	2	81/60
FBC	Anglo-French Co-ordinating Committee	Supply	Dec 1939–Apr 1940	10	85/8 and 9
FBC(I)	Anglo-French Co-ordinating Committee (British section)	Monnet (France)	Dec 1939–June 1940	10	85/10–14
FCP	Action in respect of French Colonial Possessions	War Office	June 1940	2	107/10
FWB	Action in event of war with France	Foreign Office	June 1941–Nov 1942	2	107/1
FE	Far Eastern Committee	Butler (FO)	Oct 1940–July 1945	59	96/1–5
FE(E)	Far Eastern Committee: Sub-Committee on Economic Matters	Butler (FO)	Oct 1940–May 1945	21	96/7 and 8
FE(O)	Far Eastern Committee: (official)	Foreign Office	Mar 1942	1	96/6
FE(PROP)	Far Eastern Committee: *Ad Hoc* Sub-Committee; propaganda in the Far East	Foreign Office	Feb 1941	2	96/10
FFC	Anglo-French: French Forces (Official) Committee	Foreign Office	July 1940	7	85/17
FiWB	Action in event of war with Finland	(Memoranda only)	Dec 1941	—	107/9
FOES	Future Operations (Enemy) Planning Section	(Memoranda only)	Dec 1940–Mar 1941		81/64
FP(M)	Food Policy (Ministerial) Committee	Hoare (LPS)	Nov 1939–Jan 1942	72	74/1–7
FP(O)	Food Policy (Official) Sub-Committee	Treasury	Nov 1939–May 1940	11	74/8 and 9
FP(O)(SUB)	Food Policy Food Production Sub-Committee	Agriculture	Dec 1939	1	74/10
FR	Foreign Requirements Committee	ECGD	Oct–Dec 1940	2	92/109
FRC	Control of Rents and Furnished Flats	Cranborne (LP)	May–June 1943	3	98/32
FS	Reform of the Foreign Service	Attlee (DO)	Dec 1942–Jan 1943	2	87/101
GB	Automatic Gun Board	Production	June 1941–May 1944	35	92/107–108
GEN 1	Convoys to Russia	Churchill (PM)	Jan 1943	1	78/5
GEN 2	Administration and Relief of Liberated Territories	Treasury	Apr 1943	1	78/5
GEN 3	Ceylon Constitution	Anderson (Ld Pres)	Apr 1943	1	78/5
GEN 4	Use of Shipbuilding Facilities in Northern Ireland	(Memoranda only)	Apr 1943	—	78/5

GEN	Title	Chairman, at first meeting	Dates of first and last meetings	No. of meetings	PRO reference CAB
GEN 5	Commercial Policy	Kingsley Wood (C of Ex)	Apr–July 1943	5	78/5
GEN 6	Relief and Rehabilitation	Anderson (Ld Pres)	Apr–July 1943	3	78/5
GEN 7	Allied Liaison in the Middle East	War Cabinet	Apr 1943	1	78/5
GEN 8	United Nations Conference on Food and Agriculture	Foreign Office	Mar 1943–Oct 1944	15	78/6–9
GEN 9	Economic consequences of the reunion of the French Empire	(Memoranda only)	May 1943	—	78/10
GEN 10	Select Committee on National Expenditure	Anderson (Ld Pres)	June 1943	1	78/10
GEN 11	Middle East Economic Statistics Bulletin	(Memoranda only)	June 1943–Aug 1944	—	78/10
GEN 12	Remuneration of Heads of Joint Staff Mission Washington	Anderson (Ld Pres)	June 1943	2	78/10
GEN 13	Operation 'Habbakuk'	Churchill (PM)	June 1943	1	78/11
GEN 14	Proposed formation of a Combined Petroleum Board	Lloyd (Mines)	June 1943–Feb 1944	3	78/11
GEN 15	Ad Hoc Committee on Armistice Terms	Attlee (Dep PM)	July 1943	1	78/11
GEN 16	Bulk Indents for Medical Supplies to the Middle East	Trade	July 1943	1	78/11
GEN 17	Vetting Requirements for Re-occupied Territories	Relief Dept	Aug 1943–Mar 1944	20	78/12
GEN 18	Operation 'Starkey'	Attlee (Dep PM)	Aug 1943	1	78/13
GEN 19	Anglo-American Discussions under Article VII	Various	Oct–Nov 1943	—	78/14
GEN 20	Committee on Agricultural Policy	Attlee (Dep PM)	Oct 1943	1	78/15
GEN 21	Status of Italian Prisoners of War	Anderson (C of Ex)	Oct 1943	1	78/16
GEN 22	Civil Affairs	Attlee (Dep PM)	Oct 1943	3	78/17
GEN 23	Combined Training Areas	Attlee (Dep PM)	Nov 1943	1	78/18
GEN 24	Committee on Emergency Legislation	Lord Chancellor's Dept	Nov 1943	1	78/18
GEN 25	London Airfield for Transport Services	Attlee (Dep PM)	Nov 1943–Jan 1944	2	78/18
GEN 26	Manpower	Churchill (PM)	Nov 1943	1	78/18
GEN 27	Committee on Ethiopia	Anderson (C of Ex)	Nov 1943	1	78/18
GEN 28	Emergency Arrangements for Provision of General Practitioners	Butler (Ed)	Dec 1943	1	78/18
GEN 29	United Nations Relief and Rehabilitation Administration	Various	Dec 1943	—	78/19
GEN 30	South-East Asia Command Public Relations Matters: London Committee	Air Ministry	Jan–Apr 1944	3	78/20
GEN 31	Service Pay and Allowances	Attlee (Dep PM)	Mar 1944	1	78/20
GEN 32	Proposed Colonial Declaration	Attlee (Dep PM)	Apr 1944	1	78/20
GEN 33	Committee on the Indian Food Situation	Morrison (HO)	Apr 1944	1	78/20
GEN 34	Plans for the Defeat of Japan	Churchill (PM)	Apr 1944	1	78/21
GEN 35	War Pensions	Attlee (Dep PM)	May 1944	1	78/21
GEN 36	Manpower	Attlee (Dep PM)	May 1944	1	78/21

		Chairman, at first meeting	Dates of first and last meetings	No. of meetings	PRO reference CAB
GEN 37	Informal Discussions on EITO	Foreign Office	June 1944	2	78/21
GEN 38	Special Committee on Oil	Anderson (C of Ex)	June 1944–Feb 1945	7	78/22
GEN 39	Proposed Anglo-American Supply Clearing House for NW Europe	Production	June–July 1944	2	78/23
GEN 40	German Prisoners of War	Bevin (Labour)	July 1944	1	78/23
GEN 41	Casualties in 'Overlord'	War Cabinet Office (Bridges)	Aug–Sept 1944	2	78/23
GEN 42	Publication of Statistics	War Cabinet Office (Bridges)	Aug–Sept 1944	2	78/23
GEN 43	Lend-Lease and Mutual Aid in Stage 2 Papers 68–132	(Memoranda only) (Memoranda only)	1944 To May 1945	—	78/24 78/25
GEN 44	Committee on Clauses 45 and 46 of the Town and Country Planning Bill	Attlee (Dep PM)	Oct 1944	3	78/26
GEN 45	Morale and Welfare in the Far East	Churchill (PM)	Nov 1944–Aug 1945	5	78/27
GEN 46	Local Elections	(Memoranda only)	Nov 1944	—	78/28
GEN 47	Special Civil Aviation Committee	Beaverbrook (LPS)	Nov 1944	11	78/28
GEN 48	Committee on Voting Arrangements for the Forces	Morrison (HO)	Nov 1944	1	78/28
GEN 49	Armistice and Post-War Committee	(Memoranda only)	Nov 1944	—	78/28
GEN 50	Finance of Supplies to the USSR and to Liberated Territories	Lyttelton (Produc)	Nov 1944	1	78/28
GEN 51	Housing	Churchill (PM)	Nov–Dec 1944	3	78/28
GEN 52	Breaking the German will to resist	PWE	Nov 1944–Mar 1945	3	78/29
GEN 53	Brief on European Economic Committee	War Cabinet Office	Dec 1944–Jan 1945	9	78/30
GEN 54	Ministerial Committee to Investigate a Message re Troops in Greece	Bevin (Labour)	Jan 1945	2	78/30
GEN 55	Committee to Consider the Allegations by Mr Hopkinson MP, about Regent's Park Farm Case	Attlee (Dep PM)	Jan 1945	3	78/30
GEN 56	Relief for Liberated Europe	Attlee (Dep PM)	Jan–Mar 1945	2	78/30
GEN 57	Personnel situation at Abadan	Lloyd (Mines)	Jan 1945	1	78/30
GEN 58	Food for Belgium	Attlee (Dep PM)	Feb 1945	1	78/31
GEN 59	Interdepartmental Committee on War Crimes	Lord Chancellor's Dept	Mar–July 1945	6	78/31
GEN 60	Redeployment after the defeat of Germany	Attlee (Dep PM)	Mar 1945	1	78/31
GEN 61	Commercial Policy and Related Questions	(Memoranda only)	Mar 1945	—	78/31
GEN 62	Combined Supply Review in Washington	(Memoranda only)	Mar–May 1945	—	78/32
GEN 63	Release of Miners from the Armed Forces	Bevin (Labour)	Apr 1945	1	78/33
GEN 64	Ministerial Committee on VE-Day Arrangements	Morrison (HO)	Apr 1945	1	78/33
GEN 65	Special Civil Aviation Committee	Swinton (Civil Aviation)	May–June 1945	2	78/33

		Chairman, at first meeting	Dates of first and last meetings	No. of meetings	PRO reference
					CAB
GEN 66	*Ad Hoc* Committee on Combined Supplies Review	Lyttelton (Produc)	May 1945	1	78/33
GEN 67	Ministerial Committee on Addresses of Congratulations from Parliament	Bevin (Labour)	May 1945	2	78/33
GEN 68	Far Eastern Committee	Foreign Office	May–Sept 1945	7	78/33
GEN 69	Germans in Eire	Anderson (C of Ex)	June 1945	1	78/33
GEN 70	Civil Aviation	Lyttelton (Produc)	June 1945	1	78/33
GEN 71	*Ad Hoc* Ministerial Committee on Eastern European Supplies	Lyttelton (Produc)	June 1945	1	78/33
GES	Civil Defence: Government Evacuation Scheme Sub-Committee	Florence Horsburgh (Health)	Sept 1944	3	73/21
GS	Reduction of National Government Staff	Morrison (HO)	Dec 1942–Nov 1943	13	87/98
H	Housing Committee (Ministerial)	Woolton (Recon)	Jan–Dec 1945	27	87/36 and 37
HA(I)	Lord President's Committee: Industrial Sub-Committee	Anderson (C of Ex)	July 1945	1	71/26
HC	Reconstruction: Official Committee on Housing	H. N. Hume	Oct–Dec 1944	9	87/103
HD	Home Defence Committee	Findlater Stewart	May 1941–Feb 1945	28	93/1
HD(S)E	Home Defence Security Executive	Swinton	May 1940–July 1945	109	93/2
H(O)	Housing (Official) Committee	Lord President's Office	July 1945	3	87/36 and 37
HP(BA)	Home Policy: Sub-Committee on Billeting and Office Accommodation	Works	Nov 1939	1	75/24 and 25
HPC	Home Policy: Committee	Hoare (LPS)	Jan 1940–Dec 1945	237	75/1–23
HP(CL)	Home Policy: Sub-Committee on Civil Liabilities	Caldecote (Ld Chan)	Sept 1939	2	75/26
HP(IC)	Home Policy: Sub-Committee on Publicity as to Price Rises	Macmillan (Inf)	Sept 1939	1	75/28
HP(R)	Home Policy: Sub-Committee on Rationing	Morrison (D Lanc)	Oct 1939	2	75/27
HP(SS)	Home Policy: Sub-Committee on Social Services	Caldecote (Ld Chan)	Sept–Oct 1939	2	75/29
HWB	Action in event of war with Hungary	(Memoranda only)	Feb–Dec 1941	—	107/6
I	Committee on India	Churchill (PM)	Feb 1942–June 1945	50	91/1–4
ICC	Imperial Communications and Censorship Committee	de la Warr (Ed)	Oct 1939–Jan 1946	42	76/1–5
ICC(T)	Imperial Communications and Censorship (Technical) Sub-Committee	GPO	Mar 1942–Feb 1946	14	76/6
IE	Import Executive	Duncan (Supply)	Jan 1941–Mar 1942	35	92/70 and 71
IEP	Post-war internal economic problems	War Cabinet Office	Nov 1941–Oct 1943	35	87/55–57
IEP(U)	Post-war internal economic problems: Sub-Committee on Reconstruction	Reconstruction	Oct–Dec 1942	13	87/58
IEP(UL)	Uthwatt Report on Compensation and Betterment	Health	Oct 1942–Sept 1944	146	87/59
IF	India Committee: Indian financial problems	Kingsley Wood (C of Ex)	Aug 1943–Jan 1945	9	91/5

		Chairman, at first meeting	Dates of first and last meetings	No. of meetings	PRO reference (CAB)
IFR	India Committee: Indian food grain requirements	Butler (Ed)	Feb 1944–May 1945	11	91/6
IL	Location of Industry	Greenwood (w.p.)	Jan–July 1941	3	87/91
I(P)	Persia (Iran) Committee	Anderson (Ld Pres)	Aug 1941	2	95/4
ISPS	*Joint Planning Sub-Committee	(Memoranda only)	June–Sept 1940		84/93
IWB	Action in event of war with Italy	War Cabinet Office (Bridges)	Apr–May 1940	3	107/2
JAP	*Joint Administrative Planning Staff	(Memoranda only)	Nov 1942–Dec 1945	—	84/87–91
JAP(O)	*See CSA(42)O				81/39
JMT	*COS: Joint Movement and Transportation Sub-Committee	War Office	July–Oct 1942	9	81/39
JMT(O)	*COS: Joint Movement and Transportation Sub-Committee	('Most Secret' minutes of JMT meetings)	July–Oct 1942		
JP	*Joint Planning Committee	Rotates	Sept 1939–Sept 1943 became JAP	779	84/1–86
JP(ISPS)	*Joint Planning Sub-Committee: Inter-Service Planning	(Memoranda only)	June–Sept 1940	—	84/93
JR	Reception and accommodation of refugees	Eden (FO)	Dec 1942–Oct 1945	16	95/15
JRDP	*COS: Joint Committee on Research and Development Priorities	Admiralty	May 1944–Mar 1945	11	81/47
JS	'Octagon' Conference (*Queen Mary* and Quebec) planning staff	Joint	Sept 1944	—	99/29
JS(Q)	'Quadrant' Conference (Quebec) joint planning staff	Joint	Aug–Sept 1943	5	99/23
JWB	Action in event of war with Japan	Foreign Office	Nov–Dec 1941	—	107/3
JWPS	Joint war production staff	Lyttelton (Produc)	Mar 1942–Oct 1945	39	92/39–42
JWPS(CM)	Joint war production staff: Commonwealth Supply Council (Munitions) Working Party	Production	May–Aug 1943	2	92/43
JWPS(P)	Joint war production staff planning group	Production	Apr–July 1942	7	92/44 and 45
KS	Committee on King's Speech	Simon (C of Ex)	Nov 1939–Oct 1947	As necessary	98/3
LA(W)	British Missions in Washington: Latin-American Supplies	Washington minutes	Nov 1943–Mar 1944	10	92/51
LB	Ministerial Committee on United States bases	Cranborne (DO)	Jan–Feb 1941	3	98/17
LCPRB	Combined Production and Resources (London) Committee	Lyttelton (Produc)	July 1942–Nov 1943	20	92/62–64
LD	Anglo-French Co-ordinating Committee	(Memoranda only)	Jan–June 1940		85/12
LD(AFPB)	Anglo-French Co-ordinating Committee	Purvis (in USA)	Jan–July 1940	3	85/12
LF	Land Forces	Hoare (LPS)	Sept 1939	3	92/111
LI	Imperial Communications and Censorship Committee: Leakage of information	Hankey (w.p.)	Nov 1939–May 1940	—	76/14
LL	Lease Lend	Washington minutes	July 1941–July 1945		92/72–73
LM	Minister of Production's Mission to Washington	(Memoranda only)	Dec 1942		92/115
LMAB	London Munitions Assignment Board	Lyttelton (Produc)	Apr 1942–Oct 1945	18	92/57–59

		Chairman, at first meeting	Dates of first and last meetings	No. of meetings	PRO reference CAB
LMAB(B)	London Munitions Assignment Board: British working group	Lyttelton (Produc)	Mar 1942–Oct 1945	18	92/60 and 61
LP	Lord President's Committee	N. Chamberlain (Ld Pres) (Anderson from Oct 1940, Attlee, from Sept 1943)	June 1940–Dec 1945	351	71/1–22
LP(A)	Lord President's Committee: Sub-Committee on Accommodation	Anderson (Ld Pres)	Aug 1941–Sept 1945	9	71/31–34
LP(B)	Lord President's Committee: Sub-Committee on Supply of Books	Peake (HO)	May–Aug 1942	8	71/28
LPC	London Political Warfare Co-ordinating Committee	Foreign Office	Oct 1943–Apr 1944	12	98/34
LP(ST)	Lord President's Committee: service travel	(Memoranda only)	Nov 1943–Jan 1944	—	71/25
MB	Ministerial Committee on United States Bases	Greenwood (w.p.)	Feb 1941	5	98/17
MBW	Munitions Assignment Board	Joint	Feb 1942–Aug 1945	176	88/83–87
MC	Ministerial Committee on Military Co-ordination	Chatfield (M Co-ord)	Nov 1939–May 1940	50	83/1–5
ME(M)	Ministerial Committee on Military Policy in Middle East	Eden (WO)	July 1940–July 1941	13	95/2
ME(O)	Official Committee; questions concerning Middle East	Colonial Office	Sept 1939–July 1943	25	95/1
MESC(W)	Middle East Supplies (Washington) Committee	Washington minutes	Nov–Dec 1942	—	92/50
MG	Machinery of Government (Ministerial) Committee	Anderson (Ld Pres)	Nov 1942–Nov 1945	47	87/73–75
MGO	Machinery of Government (Official) Committee	Treasury	Nov 1942–May 1945	83	87/71 and 72
MGP	Machinery of Government: Sub-Committee on Parliamentary procedure	Maxwell-Fyfe (Solicitor Gen)	Jan–Dec 1944	21	87/100
MISC 1	Committee for the Co-ordination of Allied Supplies	Hankey (w.p.)	Aug–Sept 1941	2	78/1
MISC 1	The Dominions	Beaverbrook (Supply)	Jan 1942	1	78/3
MISC 2	Release of Mine Workers from the Army	LPS	Aug 1941	1	78/1
MISC 3	International Wheat Advisory Committee, Washington	(Memorandum only)	1941	—	78/1
MISC 4	Railway and Port Development in the Middle East and Persia	Churchill (PM)	Sept 1941	1	78/1
MISC 5	Spitzbergen	War Cabinet Office (Bridges)	Sept–Nov 1941	4	78/1
MISC 7	Engineering Advisory Committee	Falmouth	Sept–Nov 1941	3	78/1
MISC 8	Manpower demands on the Dominions	Assheton (Treasury)	Sept 1941	1	78/1
MISC 9	Collective Military Counter Action to meet an Attack	War Cabinet Office	Sept 1941	1	78/1
MISC 10	Method of conducting discussions with the American Delegation	Beaverbrook (Supply)	Sept 1941	1	78/1
MISC 11	Health Conditions on the Continent of Europe	Air Ministry	Sept 1941	1	78/1
MISC 13	Loan of Military Personnel for Non-Military Work of National Importance	(Memorandum only)	Oct 1941	—	78/2
MISC 14	Resettlement	(Memorandum only)	Oct 1941	—	78/2
MISC 16	Smoke Protection	Beaverbrook (Supply)	Oct 1941	1	78/2
MISC 17	Manpower	Anderson (Ld Pres)	Oct 1941	1	78/2

		Chairman, at first meeting	Dates of first and last meetings	No. of meetings	PRO reference CAB
MISC 18	Availability and requirements of Armoured Formations	Churchill (PM)	Nov 1941	1	78/2
MISC 19	Air Service to the Middle East	Moyne (CO)	Nov 1941	1	78/2
MISC 19	Air Services to the Middle East	Cranborne (CO)	Mar 1942	1	78/3
MISC 20	Policy in regard to Ethiopia	Anderson (Ld Pres)	Nov 1941	3	78/2
MISC 21	Engineering Advisory Committee: Sub-Committee on Underground Chambers	Hankey (PMG)	Dec 1941	1	78/2
MISC 21	Engineering Advisory Committee: Sub-Committee on Underground Chambers	(Memoranda only)	Jan 1942	—	78/3
MISC 23	Allied Co-ordination	(Memoranda only)	Dec 1941	—	78/2
MISC 24	Evacuation of British Subjects from Japan and Japanese Occupied Territory	Foreign Office	Feb 1942	1	78/3
MISC 25	Functions of the Minister of State in the Middle East	Treasury	Mar 1942	2	78/3
MISC 26	Nitrate requirements of Egypt	Anderson (Ld Pres)	Apr 1942	1	78/3
MISC 28	Conversations on Chemical Warfare with the Russian Delegation	(Memoranda only)	Apr–May 1942	—	78/3
MISC 29	Civil Administration in Occupied Areas	War Cabinet Office (Bridges)	June 1942	1	78/3
MISC 30	Inter-Service Committee on Anti-Aircraft Requirements	War Office	July 1942	4	78/3
MISC 31	Evacuation of Refugees from the Middle East	Attlee (DO)	July 1942	2	78/4
MISC 32	'Bolero' Movement and the Shipping Situation	Churchill (PM)	July–Aug 1942	2	78/4
MISC 33	Naval Construction	(Memorandum only)	Aug 1942	—	78/4
MISC 34	Public Statements by Serving Officers	War Cabinet Office (Bridges)	Sept 1942	1	78/4
MISC 35	The Aircraft Programme	Lyttelton (Produc)	Oct 1942	2	78/4
MISC 36	Manpower requirements of the Armed Forces for the period 1 July 1942 to 31 December 1943	Anderson (Ld Pres)	Nov 1942	1	78/4
MISC 37	Army Organisation	Churchill (PM)	Dec 1942	1	78/4
MISC 38	Portuguese East Africa	Churchill (PM)	Dec 1942	1	78/4
MOC	Ministerial Oil Committee	Leathers (MWT)	Mar–May 1944	7	77/15
MOI	Combined Chiefs of Staff: Memoranda for information		Apr 1942–Dec 1944	—	88/78–81
MOS	Military Overseas Supply Requirements Committee	Lyttelton (Produc)	June 1943	1	92/53
MOS(W)	Military Overseas Supply Requirements and Working Committee	War Cabinet Office	June 1943	1	92/53
MP	Committee on Manpower	Anderson (C of Ex)	Nov 1943–Nov 1945	25	92/104
MPR	Manpower Requirements Committee	Labour	Aug 1940–Jan 1941	9	92/102
MPR(S)	Manpower Requirements: Service Requirements Sub-Committee	Labour	Oct–Dec 1940	4	92/102

		Chairman, at first meeting	Dates of first and last meetings	No. of meetings	PRO reference CAB
MPI	Ministerial Committee: Priority of Import Programmes	(Memoranda only)	Dec 1939	—	92/78
MPS	*COS: 'Bolero'; provision of medical services	War Office	June–Nov 1942	12	81/49
MPS(O)	*COS: 'Bolero'; provision of medical services	(Memoranda only)	June 1942	—	81/49
MR	Anglo-French Liaison Committee	Admiralty	Sept 1939–June 1940	165	85/1–5
MR(J)	Anglo-French Liaison Committee	(Memoranda only)	Sept 1939–June 1940	—	85/6 and 7
MR(J)(S)	Anglo-French Military Committee	(Memoranda only)	Apr–June 1940	—	85/16
MRP	Military representatives of Associated Pacific Powers	Joint	May 1942–June 1943	9	88/49
MR(P)	Anglo-French Military Committee	War Office	April 1940	1	85/16
MR(S)	Anglo-French Military Committee	(Memoranda only)	Feb–Mar 1940	—	85/16
MSC	Conferences with Minister of State, Middle East	(Memoranda only)	Sept 1941–July 1943	—	95/8
MTC	*COS: 'Bolero'; movement and transportation	War Transport	May–Dec 1942	17	81/50
MTC(O)	*COS: 'Bolero'; movement and transportation	(Memoranda only)	July 1943	—	81/50
NAD	*Committee on Night Air Defence	Churchill (PM)	Oct 1940–Mar 1944	20	81/22
NAS	North American Supply Committee	Salter (Shipping)	July 1940–Sept 1942*	13	92/27–35
NAS(MISC)	North American Supply Committee: Miscellaneous Sub-Committee	(Memoranda only)	1943	—	92/36
NAS(S)	North American Supply Committee: Scientific Sub-Committee	Air Ministry	Oct 1942–Aug 1945	9	92/37
NAS(STATS)	North American Supply Committee: Statistics from British Supply Council	(Memoranda only)	1941–1943	—	92/36
NAS(X)	North American Supply Committee	(Memoranda only)	1941–1946	—	92/38
NFC	Statistics: Non-food consumption levels in UK, USA and Canada	CSO	1944	2	108/85
NS(MPP)	Manpower Committee	Assheton (Labour)	Aug 1940–June 1942	20	92/103
NS(SRO)	Ministerial Priority Committee: reserved occupations	Labour	Sept 1939–1944	Many	92/80–101
NS(T)	Ministerial Priority Committee: manpower priority	W. S. Morrison (D Lanc)	Sept 1939–Mar 1940	7	92/79
OC(B)	Oil Control Board	Lloyd (Mines)	Nov 1939–July 1945	52	77/1–9
OCB(S)	Oil Control Board: Sub-Committee on Supplies	Hudson (Adm)	Jan–Feb 1940	2	77/10 and 11
ODC	Overseas Defence Committee	Dominions Office	Sept 1939–Mar 1942	18	94/1–4
ODC(CI)	Civil Defence: Sub-Committee on Camouflage of Important Places	Admiralty	Mar 1940	1	73/18
OM	Overseas Mail Committee	Moyne (CO)	Feb 1941–Dec 1944	15	76/17 and 18

*Continues to 1946 with Minister of British Supply Council in North America

	Committee	Chairman, at first meeting	Dates of first and last meetings	No. of meetings	PRO reference CAB
OMP	Committee on Overseas Manpower	Assheton (Labour)	Jan–May 1942	3	92/105 and 106
OM(SC)	Overseas Mail Sub-Committee	GPO	May 1943–Sept 1945	34	76/19–21
OP	'Overlord' preparations	Churchill (PM)	Feb–Apr 1944	8	98/40
OP(IT)	'Overlord' preparations: Sub-Committee on Inland Transport (use of Service vehicles)	Attlee (Dep PM)	Mar 1944	2	98/40
OP(SM)	'Overlord' preparations: Sub-Committee on Security	Lyttelton (Produc)	Feb–Mar 1944	4	98/40
OP(ST)	'Overlord' preparations: Sub-Committee on Service Leave and Travel	(Memoranda only)	Mar 1944	—	98/40
OR	Oil Rehabilitation Committee	Trade	Sept 1943–Aug 1944	6	77/14
P	Press Censorship	Anderson (Ld Pres)	Mar 1942	2	76/12
PC	Ministerial Committee on Priority	Chatfield (M Co-ord)	Apr 1940	1	92/74 and 75
PC(F)	Ministerial Committee on Priority: Sub-Committee: Flax	Llewellin (Supply)	Nov 1939	1	92/76 and 77
PDC	*COS: Sub-Committee: Port Defence	War Office	Nov 1939–Jan 1943	40	81/1–3
PDC(O)	*COS: Sub-Committee: Port Defence	War Office	Dec 1941	1	81/2
PE	Production Executive	Bevin (Labour)	Jan 1941–Jan 1942	31	92/54 and 55
P(E&F)	Survey of Economic and Financial Plans	Stamp	July 1939–Mar 1941	189	89/1–9
P(E&F)(S)	Survey of Economic and Financial Plans Sub-Committee	(Memoranda only)		—	89/9
PFC	Polish Forces	Foreign Office	Jan–Nov 1940	10	92/110
PHP	*COS: Post Hostilities Planning Sub-Committee	Foreign Office	Aug 1943–May 1944	64	81/40–43
PHP(O)	*COS: Post-Hostilities Planning Sub-Committee	Foreign Office	Oct 1943	1	81/44–46
P(M)	Palestine	Morrison (HO)	Aug 1943–Oct 1945	11	95/14
PMM	Prime Minister's Conference (London)	Churchill (PM)	May 1944	16	99/28
PO	Official Committee on Control of Key Prices	Treasury	Feb 1941	—	98/53
POG	Oil Policy: Lord Hankey's Committee on preventing oil from reaching Germany	Hankey (w.p.)	Oct 1939–Dec 1941	30	77/12 and 13
POG(D)	Oil Policy: River Transport Inter-Departmental Committee	Admiralty	Jan–Mar 1940	10	77/17
POG(L)	Oil Policy: German oil position	Lloyd (Mines)	Jan 1940–Nov 1941	10	77/18
POG(S)	Oil Policy: prevention of oil from reaching Germany	Hankey (w.p.)	Oct 1939–Jan 1940	3	77/16
PP	Expert Committee on Work of Psychologists and Psychiatrists in the Services	Health	Sept 1942–Dec 1944	32	98/25–27

		Chairman, at first meeting	Dates of first and last meetings	No. of meetings	PRO reference
PP(LC)	Expert Committee on work of Psychologists and Psychiatrists in the Services	Air Ministry	Jan–Feb 1943	2	CAB 98/28
PPM	Psychologists and Psychiatrists in the Services	Anderson (Ld Pres) Walters (Univ of Reading)	July 1943–Mar 1944	2	98/29
PP(SC)	Expert Committee on Work of Psychologists and Psychiatrists in the Services: Informal Liaison Committee		Oct 1942–Nov 1944	35	98/28
PR	Reconstruction Priorities	Anderson (Ld Pres)	Jan–Nov 1943	31	87/12 and 13
PRB	Public Relations Branches	Kingsley Wood (C of Ex)	Aug 1943–May 1944	4	98/35
PS	Post-War Settlement	Attlee (Dep PM)	Aug 1943	4	87/65
PT	Planning and Timing of Investments	Treasury	Dec 1941–July 1942	2	87/99
PURCO	Anglo-French Committee: telegrams Monet/Purvis	(Telegrams only)		—	85/13 and 14
PWB	Action in event of war with Portugal	Foreign Office	Jan 1942	1	107/7
PWC	Pacific War Council	Churchill (PM)	Feb 1942–Aug 1943	14	99/26
PWS	Post-War Credit	Kingsley Wood (C of Ex)	Nov–Dec 1941	3	98/19
PWSC	Post-War Scientific Collaboration	DSIR	Nov 1944	1	98/56
PX	Production Council	Greenwood (w.p.)	May–Dec 1940	13	92/56
R	Reconstruction Committee	Woolton (Recon)	Dec 1943–May 1945	99	87/5–10
RA	Rocket Committee	Morrison (HO)	Aug–Sept 1944	4	98/39
RAP	*Joint Planning Committee: 'Round up' (invasion of France) administration planning staff	War Office	May–Dec 1942	14	84/92
RAP(O)	*Joint Planning Committee: 'Round up' (invasion of France) administration planning staff	('Most Secret' minutes of RAP)	May–Dec 1942	—	84/92
RAW	*COS inter-service responsibility for amphibious warfare	Air Ministry	May–June 1944	6	81/27
RB	Reconstruction: control of post-war building	Portal (Works)	Dec 1943–Feb 1944	16	87/11
R(BL)	Reconstruction: war-time contravention of building laws	Treasury	June–Nov 1944	6	87/35
R(C)	Reconstruction: official sub-committee on the rehabilitation of South-East towns	Reconstruction	Apr–Sept 1944	7	87/16
RC	Reconstruction: relief policy	Foreign Office	Apr 1944–Sept 1945	12	87/22–34
RDF	*Radio Direction Finding Policy	Air Ministry (later Tizard)	July 1941–Feb 1942	18	81/12
RF	Committee on Recruitment for the Armed Forces	Kingsley Wood (LPS)	Apr 1940	1	92/116
RG	Reconstruction: civil liabilities and resettlement grants	Reconstruction	Sept 1944–Jan 1945	7	87/16
R(H)	Reconstruction: housing	Woolton (Recon)	Sept–Nov 1944	11	87/35
R(I)	Reconstruction: industrial problems	Woolton (Recon)	May 1944–June 1945	16	87/14 and 15
R(IE)	Reconstruction: export questions	Woolton (Recon)	Sept 1944–May 1945	6	87/14 and 15

	Committee	Chairman, at first meeting	Dates of first and last meetings	No. of meetings	PRO reference (CAB)
R(IO)	Reconstruction: (official) industrial problems	Reconstruction	Mar 1944–May 1945	32	87/17 and 18
RJ	Reconstruction: joint advisory council	Jowitt (PMG)	Dec 1942–Jan 1945	8	87/19
RP	Reconstruction Problems Committee	Greenwood (w.p.)	Mar 1941–Oct 1943	28	87/1–3
RP(A)	Reconstruction: Sub-Committee on Civil Aviation	Jowitt (w.p.)	Jan–June 1943	5	87/104
RPC	*COS: radio policy		Feb–Aug 1942	19	81/13
RP(E)	Reconstruction: Sub-Committee on Electricity Industry	Jowitt (w.p.)	Nov 1942–Mar 1943	3	87/105 and 106
RP(ES)	Future of Electricity Industry	Lloyd (Fuel and Power)	Apr–Sept 1943	14	87/4
RRC	Home Policy: rent, rates and mortgages	Caldecote (Ld Chan)	Apr 1940	2	75/37
R(SI)	Reconstruction: social insurance	Anderson (C of Ex)	Jan–Feb 1944	5	87/11
RTC	Reconstruction: town and country	Anderson (Ld Pres)	Dec 1940–Jan 1941	4	87/21
R(W)	Reconstruction: workmen's compensation	Anderson (C of Ex)	Apr 1944	2	87/11
RWB	Action in event of war with Roumania	(Memoranda only)	Feb–Dec 1941	—	107/8
S	Security arrangements in Government departments	War Cabinet Office	Feb 1942–Apr 1945	11	98/48–51
SAA	Anglo-American Committee on Standardisation of Arms	(Memoranda only)	Aug 1940	—	99/16
	Defence Committee: allocation of small arms ammunition	Air Ministry	Nov 1940–Dec 1945	63	70/8–13
SAC	Scientific Advisory Committee	Hankey (D Lanc)	Oct 1940–July 1946	82	90/1–6
SAC(DP)	Scientific Advisory Committee: defence services panel	Hankey (D Lanc) (including Maud report)	Oct 1940–Nov 1942	19	90/7 and 8
SAC(SB)	Scientific Advisory Committee: supervisory body for record of scientific research and development during the war	Dale	June–Dec 1944	5	90/9
SA(J)	Anglo-American Committee on Standardisation of Arms	Air Ministry	Aug 1940	3	99/16
SC	Shipping Committee	Harcourt Johnson (DOT)	May 1942–Mar 1945	79	97/1–5
SC(A)	Shipping Committee: Adjustment Board (availability of cargoes (operational))	Washington minutes	Nov 1942–Mar 1945	—	97/6
SC(AC)	Shipping Committee: availability of cargoes	War Cabinet Office	July–Nov 1943	9	97/6
SCC	Standing Inter-Departmental Committee on Censorship	Censorship	Oct 1939–Oct 1945	29	76/9–11
SCC(OS)	Standing Inter-Departmental Committee on Censorship: examination of mails at overseas stations	Information	Feb 1940	2	76/22
SC(M)	Suez Canal Committee	Attlee (Ld Pres)	Oct 1944–Mar 1945	6	95/18
SC(O)	Shipping (Operational) Committee	(Memoranda only)	Dec 1942–Apr 1945	—	97/6
SD	Scandinavian Delegation Sub-Committee		Mar 1940	1	98/4
SE(CP)	Control at Ports Committee	Hoare (HO)	Mar 1941–July 1945	47	93/5

		Chairman, at first meeting	Dates of first and last meetings	No. of meetings	PRO reference CAB
SE(LOC)	Security Executive Liaison Officers' Conference		July 1940–July 1945	289	93/4
SEP/14	Shipping problems		1940		97/8
SFC	Food Policy: Scientific Sub-Committee	Bragg	June 1940–Feb 1943	41	74/11 and 12
SIC	Security Intelligence Centre		June–Sept 1940	14	93/5
SLA	Social Insurance and Allied Services	Beveridge	July 1941–Oct 1942	44	87/76–82
	Ministerial Committee on Supply Questions in Liberated and Conquered areas	Lyttelton (Produc)	Jan 1944–Jan 1945	5	87/38
SLAO	Ministerial Committee on Supply Questions in Liberated and Conquered areas (official)	Production	Dec 1943–June 1945	11	87/39–50
SLAO(ER)	Ministerial Committee on Supply Questions in Liberated and Conquered areas (official)	(Memoranda only)	Mar 1944–Mar 1945	—	87/51 and 52
SLAO(ESS)	Ministerial Committee on Supply Questions in Liberated and Conquered areas; Eastern European Surpluses Sub-Committee	Brand	Apr–May 1945	4	87/53
SME	Middle East Supply Committee	Crookshank (Treasury)	Apr 1942–May 1945	32	92/46–48
SME(A)	Middle East Supply Committee	Washington minutes	Dec 1942	—	92/46 and 49
SME(W)	Middle East Supply Committee (Washington)	Washington minutes	1944	—	92/50
SMO	*COS: Sub-Committee on Smoke	DSIR	May–June 1940	3	81/14
SOI	Committee on Scientific and Optical Instruments	(Memoranda only)	Sept 1939	1	98/52
SP	Civil Defence: Sub-Committee on Signposts	Findlater Stewart	Dec 1940	9	73/14
SPA	Service Pay and Allowances	Assheton (Treasury)	Jan 1943–May 1945	9	98/24
SPC	London Munitions Assignment Board: Inter-Service Shipping Committee	War Office	Apr 1942–Feb 1943	10	92/69
SS	Shipping Committee: shipping situation	Leathers (MWT)	Feb 1942	4	97/7
SWC	Supreme War Council	N. Chamberlain (PM)	Sept 1939–June 1940	16	99/3
SWB	Co-ordination of Departmental Action in event of war with Spain	(Memoranda only)	June 1940–Sept 1941	—	107/4
TA	Tube Alloys Consultative Council	Anderson (Ld Pres)	Nov 1941–June 1945	18	98/47
TP	Tank Parliament	Churchill (PM)	May–June 1941	4	98/20
TSA	London Munitions Assignment Board: Transportation Stores Assignment Sub-Committee	Production	Aug 1944–Aug 1945	13	92/65
TWC	*COS: Joint Technical Warfare Sub-Committee	Admiralty	Nov 1943–Dec 1945	40	81/23–26
USB	United States: bases	Foreign Office	Sept–Dec 1940	9	98/6
USE	Post-war economic problems of Anglo-American co-operation	Office of Min without Portfolio	Aug 1941–1942	7	87/60
USP	United States: British planning	War Office	Apr 1942	5	98/46
US(MR)	Statistics: US munitions record	(Memoranda only)	1942–1943	—	108/45

		Chairman, at first meeting	Dates of first and last meetings	No. of meetings	PRO reference
US(S)	Statistics: War effort of US	(Memoranda only)	1941–1942	—	CAB 108/43 and 44
VAP	Visit of Australian Prime Minister	Cross (Shipping)	Mar–April 1941	8	99/4
WA	Committee on War Aims	Attlee (LPS)	Oct–Dec 1940	5	87/90
WA(RM)	Resident Minister in West Africa	(Memoranda only)	July–Dec 1943	—	95/12
WFI	White Fish Industry	Woolton (Recon)	May 1945	2	98/43
WL	Home Policy: war legislation	Lord Chancellor's Office	Sept–Nov 1939	7	75/30–32
WL(CL)	Home Policy: civil liabilities	Lord Chancellor's Office	Oct 1939–Mar 1941	60	75/33–36
WP	War Cabinet memoranda	(Memoranda only)	Sept 1939–May 1945	—	66/1–65
WP	'Argonaut' Conference: report of political proceedings		Mar 1945		99/31
WP(G)	War Cabinet memoranda	(Memoranda only)	Sept 1939–May 1941	—	67/1–9
WP(R)	War Cabinet memoranda	(Memoranda only)	Sept 1939–1942	—	68/1–9
WM	War Cabinet conclusions and confidential annexes	N. Chamberlain (later Churchill) (PM)	Sept 1939–May 1945	1161	65/1–52
WS	Women's services	Assheton (Treasury)	Apr–June 1943	6	92/112
WW	'Arcadia' Conference (Washington)	Joint	Dec 1941–Jan 1942	—	99/17
WW(JPC)	'Arcadia' Conference (Washington): planning staff	Joint	Dec 1941–Jan 1942	—	99/17
WWPG	Committee on Widows' War Pensions and Gratuities	Anderson (C of Ex)	Jan 1944	1	98/55

LIST OF CABINET OFFICE CLASSES

(List of the classes in the Public Record Office into which the Cabinet records are arranged; the class lists in the Public Record Office identify the individual items. Classes 1–64 generally contain records created before September 1939 and classes 65 onwards those from September 1939–July 1945.)

CAB	Description	No. of pieces (ie. vols or files)
1	Miscellaneous Records	42
	CID:	
2	Minutes	9
	Memoranda:	
3	Home Defence	8
4	Miscellaneous	30
5	Colonial Defence	9
6	Defence of India	6
	Colonial/Oversea Defence Committee:	
7	Minutes, etc	18
8	Memoranda	56
9	Remarks	21
10	Minutes by the Committee	10
11	Defence Schemes, etc	216
	Home Ports Defence Committee:	
12	Minutes	6
13	Memoranda and Sub-Committee Papers	29
14	Air Committee: Minutes, Memoranda, etc	1
15	Committee on the Co-ordination of Departmental Action	39
16	*Ad Hoc* Sub-Committees of Enquiry: Proceedings and Memoranda	231
17	Correspondence and Miscellaneous Papers	199
18	Miscellaneous Volumes	99
19	War Cabinet: Dardanelles and Mesopotamia Special Commissions	33
20	Historical Section: German Army Documents: Schlieffen Papers	4
21	Cabinet Registered Files	1614
22	War Council, Dardanelles Committee and War Committee	82
23	Cabinet Minutes to 1939	101
24	Cabinet Memoranda to 1939	288
25	Supreme War Council, 1917–1919	127
26	Home Affairs Committee	24
27	Committees: General Series to 1939	663
28	Allied (War) Conferences	9

CAB	Description	No. of pieces (i.e. vols or files)
29	International Conferences to 1939	162
30	Washington (Disarmament) Conference	33
31	Genoa (International Economic) Conference	13
32	Imperial Conferences to 1939	137
33	Post-War Priority and Demobilisation Committees, 1918–1919	26
	CID:	
34	Standing Sub-Committee	1
35	Imperial Communications Committee	45
36	Joint Oversea and Home Ports Defence Committee	23
37	Photographic Copies of Cabinet Papers	162
38	CID: Photographic Copies of Minutes and Memoranda	28
39	War Trade Advisory Committee	114
40	War Priorities Committee	171
41	Photographic copies of Cabinet Letters in the Royal Archives	40
42	Photographic Copies of Papers of the War Council, Dardanelles Committee and War Committee	26
43	Conferences on Ireland	7
	Historical Section:	
	Official War Histories:	
44	Narratives (Military)	428
45	Correspondence and Papers	291
	CID:	
46	Air Raids Precautions Committees	32
47	Advisory Committee on Trade Questions in time of War	15
48	Industrial Intelligence in Foreign Countries	10
49	Inter-Departmental Standing Committee on Censorship	20
50	The Oil Board	19
51	Middle East Questions	11
52	War Legislation Committees	8
53	Chiefs of Staff Committee	55
54	Deputy Chiefs of Staff Committee	13
55	Joint Planning Committee	19
56	Joint Intelligence Committee	6
57	Man Power Committee	30
58	Economic Advisory Council: Minutes and Memoranda	208
60	CID: Principal Supply Officers' Committee	73
61	Irish Boundary Commission, 1924–1925	168
62	International Committee for the Application of the Agreement Regarding Non-Intervention in Spain	89
63	Private Collections: Hankey Papers	191
64	Minister for the Co-ordination of Defence: Registered Files	36
	War Cabinet:	
65	Minutes	55
	Memoranda:	
66	(WP) and (CP) Series	67

CAB	Description	No. of pieces (i.e. vols or files)
109	London Munitions Assignment Board: Secretary's Files	130
110	Joint American Secretariat: Secretary's Files	250
111	Allied Supplies Executive: Files	399
112	Vulnerable Points Adviser: Files	27
113	Home Defence Executive: Secretary's Files	45
114	Home Defence (Security) Executive: Secretary's Files	54
115	Central Office for North American Supplies	756
116	Departmental Security Officer: Files	50
117	Reconstruction Secretariat: Files	272
118	Various Ministers: Files	91
119	Joint Planning Staff: Files	221
120	Minister of Defence: Secretariat Files	
121	Special Secret Information Centre: Files	785
122	British Joint Staff Mission: Washington Office Files	1601
123	Lord President of the Council: Secretariat Files	297
124	Minister of Reconstruction and Lord President of the Council: Secretariat Files	1110
125	Radio Board	
126	Atomic Energy Files	459
127	Private Collections: Ministers and Officials	

INDEX

(References are to numbered paragraphs. Offices noted under personal names which were held later than 1945 will not necessarily be found in the text.)

Printed in England for Her Majesty's Stationery Office, by The Campfield Press, St. Albans

(16950) Dd 504271 K 16 6/75